ESSAYS

IN

ANGLO-SAXON LAW.

———oo§o§oo———

THE LAWBOOK EXCHANGE, LTD.
Clark, New Jersey

ISBN 978-1-58477-435-8

Lawbook Exchange edition 2005, 2017

The quality of this reprint is equivalent to the quality of the original work.

THE LAWBOOK EXCHANGE, LTD.

33 Terminal Avenue
Clark, New Jersey 07066-1321

*Please see our website for a selection of our other publications
and fine facsimile reprints of classic works of legal history:*
www.lawbookexchange.com

Library of Congress Cataloging-in-Publication Data

Essays in Anglo-Saxon law.
    p. cm.
   Originally published: Boston : Little, Brown, and Co., 1876.
   Essays by Henry Adams, et al.
   Includes bibliographical references and index.
   ISBN 1-58477-435-5 (cloth : alk. paper)
   1. Law, Anglo-Saxon. I. Adams, Henry, 1838-1918.

KD554.E84 2004
340.5'5'0942--dc22   2004041804

Printed in the United States of America on acid-free paper

ESSAYS

IN

ANGLO-SAXON LAW.

———oo:o:oo———

BOSTON:

LITTLE, BROWN, AND COMPANY.

LONDON: MACMILLAN AND COMPANY.

1876.

CAMBRIDGE:

PRESS OF JOHN WILSON AND SON.

TO

CHARLES WILLIAM ELIOT,

PRESIDENT OF HARVARD COLLEGE,

THIS VOLUME, FRUIT OF HIS ADMINISTRATION,

IS RESPECTFULLY DEDICATED.

TABLE OF CONTENTS.

TITLES OF WORKS CITED.

ÆTHELWEARDI CHRONICON. In the Monumenta Historica Britannica.

ALLEN JOHN. Inquiry into the Rise and Growth of the Royal Prerogative in England. A new Edition. London, 1849.

ANGLO SAXON CHRONICLE. Edited, with a translation, by B. Thorpe. 2 vol. Published under the direction of the Master of the Rolls. London, 1861.

ASSER. Annales Rerum Gestarum Ælfredi Magni. In the Monumenta Historica Britannica.

BALUZIUS, Capitularia regum Francorum. Curante Petro Chiniac. 2 vols. Paris, 1780. Fol.

v. BAR, L. Beweisurtheil des germanischen Processes. Hannover, 1866.

BAUMSTARK, ANTON. Ausführliche Erlaüterung des allgemeinen Theiles der Germania des Tacitus. Leipzig, 1875.

BEDAE OPERA. In the Publications of the English Historical Society.

BEHREND, J. F. Zum Process der Lex Salica. Festgaben von August Wilhelm Heffter. Berlin, 1873.

BEHREND. Lex Salica. 1875.

BEOWULF. Edited by Benjamin Thorpe. London, 1875.

v. BETHMANN-HOLLWEG, Der Civilprocess des gemeinen Rechts in geschichtlicher Entwickelung. Bonn, 1868.

BLUNTSCHLI, J. C. Neuere Untersuchungen über das deutsche Sachenrecht. In the Kritische Ueberschau, VI.

BRACTON, HENRY DE. De Legibus et Consuetudinibus Angliae. London, 1569.

BRUNNER, HEINRICH. Zeugen und Inquisitionsbeweis der karolingischen Zeit. Wien, 1866.

BRUNNER, HEINRICH. Die Entstehung der Schwurgerichte. Berlin, 1872.

BRUNNER, HEINRICH. Das anglonormannische Erbfolgesystem. Leipzig, 1869.

BRUNS, C. G. Das Recht des Besitzes im Mittelalter und der Gegenwart. Tübingen, 1848.

VITA S. CUTHBERTI. In the Publications of the English Historical Society.

DIGBY, KENELM EDWARD. An Introduction to the History of the Law of Real Property, with Original Authorities. Oxford, 1875.

DU CANGE, C. D. Glossarium ad Scriptores mediae et infimae Latinitatis. Paris, 1733. 6 vols.

DUGDALE, SIR WILLIAM. Monasticon Anglicanum: A History of the Abbies and other Monasteries, Hospitals, Frieries, and Cathedral and Collegiate Churches, with their dependencies in England and Wales; originally published in Latin by Sir William Dugdale, Kt. A new Edition, by John Caley, Esq., F.S.A., Henry Ellis, LL.B. F.R.S., Sec. S. A., and the Rev. Bulkeley Bandinel, M.A. London, 1817–1830. 8 vols.

EADMERI, Monachi Cantuariensis Historiae Novorum sive sui Saeculi Libri VI. . . . Emisit Joannes Seldenus. Londini, MDCXXII.

ELLIS, SIR HENRY. A General Introduction to Domesday Book. In two volumes. 1833.

FLETA, seu Commentarius Juris Anglicani. Londini, 1685.

FREEMAN, EDWARD A. The History of the Norman Conquest of England, its Causes and its Results. Oxford, 1873. 4 vols.

GALE. Historiae Britannicae, Saxonicae, Anglo-Danicae, Scriptores XV. . . . Editi Thomae Gale, Oxoniae, MDCXCI.

GANZ, E. Das Erbrecht in weltgeschichtlicher Entwickelung. Stuttgart and Tübingen, 1835. 4 vols.

GEMEINER, A. Ueber Eideshülfe und Eideshelfer des älteren deutschen Rechtes. München, 1848.

GLANVILLE, RANULPH DE. De Legibus et Consuetudinibus regni Angliae. London, 1604.

GRIMM, J. Deutsche Rechtsalterthümer. Göttingen, 1854.

HÄNEL, A. Das Beweissystem des Sachsenspiegels. Leipzig, 1858.

HANSSEN, G. History of the Field Systems of Germany, in the Zeitschrift für die gesammte Staatswissenschaft. Vol. XXI.

HASTED, EDWARD. The History and Topographical Survey of the County of Kent. Second Edition. 12 vols. Canterbury, 1797–1801.

HEMINGI. Chartularium Ecclesiae Wigorniensis. . . . Edidit Tho. Hearnius. Oxonii, MDCCXXIII.

HEUSLER, ANDREAS. Der Ursprung der deutschen Stadtverfassung. Weimar, Hermann Böhlau, 1872.

HEUSLER, ANDREAS. Die Gewere. Weimar, Hermann Böhlau, 1872.

HICKES. Georgii Hickesii. . . . Dissertatio Epistolaris ad Bartholomeum Showere. . . . Oxoniae, MDCCIII.

HISTORIA ECCLESIAE ELIENSIS. See Gale.

HISTORIA RAMESIENSIS. See Gale.

HOMEYER, C. G. Das sächsische Lehnrecht und der Richtsteig Lehnrechts, 1842. 2 Theile. Berlin, 1861.

KEMBLE, JOHN M. Codex Diplomaticus Ævi Saxonici, Opera Johannis M. Kemble. Londini, MDCCCXXXIX. 6 vols.

KEMBLE, JOHN M. The Saxons in England. London, 1849. 2 vols.

KOENIGSWARTER, L. J. Histoire de l'Organization de la Famille en France. Paris, 1851.

KÖSTLIN, C. R. Geschichte des deutschen Strafrechts in Umriss. Tübingen, 1859.

KRAUT, W. T. Die Vormundschaft nach den Grundsätzen des deutschen Rechts. Göttingen, 1835.

KRITISCHE Ueberschau der deutschen Gesetzgebung und Rechtswissenschaft. Herausgegeben von Arndts, Bluntschli und Pözl. München, 1853–1859.

KRITISCHE Vierteljahrsschrift für Gesetzgebung und Rechtswissenschaft. Herausgegeben von Pözl. 17 vol. München, 1859–1875.

LABAND, PAUL. Die Vermögensrechtlichen Klagen nach den sächsischen Rechtsquellen des Mittelalters. Berlin, 1869.

LAMBARDE, W. A Perambulation of Kent. London, 1826.

LEWIS, W. Die Succession des Erben in die Obligationen des Erblassers nach deutschem Recht. Berlin, 1864.

LEWIS, W. Zur Lehre von der Successionsordnung des deutschen Rechtes. In the Kritische Vierteljahrsschrift für Gesetzgebung und Rechtswissenschaft, IX. München, 1867.

LEX SALICA herausg. v. J. Merkel. Berlin, 1850.

LÖNING, R. Der Vertragsbruch und seine Rechtsfolgen. Strassburg, 1875.

MAINE, SIR HENRY SUMNER. Ancient Law. New York, 1875.

MAINE, SIR HENRY SUMNER. Early History of Institutions. New York, 1875.

MAINE, SIR HENRY SUMNER. Village Communities in the East and West. Six Lectures delivered at Oxford. London, 1871.

v. MAURER, G. L. Einleitung zur Geschichte der Mark-, Hof-, Dorf- und Stadtverfassung und der öffentlichen Gewalt. München, 1854.

v. MAURER, G. L. Geschichte der Fronhöfe, der Bauernhöfe und der Hofverfassung in Deutschland. 4 Bände. Erlangen, 1862.

MAURER, KONRAD. Ueber angelsächsische Rechtsverhältnisse. In the Kritische Ueberschau der deutschen Gesetzgebung. I., II., III. München.

MAURER, KONRAD. Island von seiner ersten Entdeckung bis zum Untergange des Freistaats. München, 1874.

MAURER, KONRAD. Das Beweisverfahren nach deutschen Rechten. Kritische Ueberschau, V.

MEICHELBECK. Historia Frisingensis. Augustae Vind. 1724.

MERKEL. Lex Salica. Berlin, 1850.

MICHELET, J. Origines du Droit français. Paris, 1837.

MONUMENTA HISTORICA BRITANNICA, or Materials for the History of Britain from the earliest Period. Petrie and Sharpe. Published by command of Her Majesty. MDCCCXLVIII.

MONUMENTA HISTORIAE PATRIAE. Ed. jussu Regis Caroli Alberti. Chartarum tomus I. et II. Aug. Taur, 1836. Fol.

MORGAN, LEWIS H. "Montezuma's Dinner" and "Houses of the Mound-Builders." Articles in the North American Review for April and July, 1876.

MURATORI, Antiquitates Italicae medii aevi. 6 vols. Mediolani, 1738–1742.

NASSE, E. On the Agricultural Community of the Middle Ages and Enclosures of the Sixteenth Century in England. Translated from the German, by Col. H. A. Ouvry. (Cobden Club Publication.) London, 1871.

NASSE, E. Review of Maine's Village Communities in the Contemporary Review, May, 1872.

NENNIUS. Historia Britonum. In the Monumenta Historica Britannica.

NJALSAGA. The Story of Burnt Njal. Dasent. 2 vols. Edinburgh, 1861.

PHILLIPS, G. Versuch einer Darstellung der Geschichte des angelsächsischen Rechts. Göttingen, 1825.

PLANCK, J. W. Das Recht der Beweisführung. In the Zeitschrift für deutsches Recht, X.

V. RICHTHOFEN. Friesische Rechtsquellen. Berlin, 1840.

ROBERTSON, E. W. Historical Essays. Edinburgh, 1852.

ROBINSON, T. The Common Law of Kent, or the Customs of Gavelkind. London, 1741.

ROGGE, K. A. Ueber das Gerichtswesen der Germanen. Halle, 1820.

ROTH, PAUL. Geschichte des Beneficialwesens. Erlangen, 1850.

ROTH, PAUL. Feudalität und Unterthanverband. Weimar, 1863.

ROZIÈRE, EUGÈNE DE. Recueil Général des Formules usitées dans l'Empire des Francs du Vᵉ au Xᵉ Siècle. Paris, 1859–1871.

SACHSENSPIEGEL oder sächsisches Landrecht, mit Uebersetzung, etc. von C. R. Sachsse. Heidelberg, 1848.

SCHMID, REINHOLD. Die Gesetze der Angelsachsen. Leipzig, 1858.

SCHROEDER, R. Geschichte des ehelichen Güterrechts in Deutschland. Stettin, Danzig, und Elbing, 1863.

SIEGEL, H. Das deutsche Erbrecht nach den Rechtsquellen des Mittelalters. Heidelberg, 1853.

SIEGEL, H. Geschichte des deutschen Gerichtsverfahrens. Erster Band. Giessen, 1857.

SOHM, RUDOLF. Die fränkische Reichs- und Gerichtsverfassung. Weimar, Hermann Böhlau, 1872.

SOHM, RUDOLF. La Procédure de la Lex Salica. Traduit et annoté par Marcel Thévenin. Bibliothèque de l'École des hautes Études. Paris, 1873.

SOHM, RUDOLF. Das Recht der Eheschliessung aus dem deutschen und canonischen Recht geschichtlich entwickelt. Weimar, 1875.

Sohm, Rudolf. Ueber die Entstehung des Lex Ribuaria. In the Zeitschrift für Rechtsgeschichte, V. Weimar, 1866.

Sohm, Rudolf. Die geistliche Gerichtsbarkeit im fränkischen Reich. In the Zeitschrift für Kirchenrecht, IX.

Somner, W. A Treatise of Gavelkind. London, 1726.

Spelman, Henry. Glossarium Archaiologicum. Londini, 1687.

Stephen, H. J. Pleading. Ed. by Sam. Tayler, LL.D. Washington, 1872.

Stobbe, O. Die Aufhebung der väterlichen Gewalt nach dem Recht des Mittelalters. In his Beiträge zur Geschichte des deutschen Rechts. Braunschweig, 1865.

Stubbs, William. The Constitutional History of England in its Origin and Development. Vol. I. Oxford, 1874.

Stubbs, William. Select Charters and other Illustrations of English Constitutional History from the earliest Times to the Reign of Edward the First. Second edition. Oxford, 1874.

v. Sydow, R. Darstellung des Erbrechts nach den Grundsätzen des Sachsenspiegels, &c. Berlin, 1828.

Thorpe, B. Ancient Laws and Institutes of England. 2 vols. 1840.

Thudicum, Friedrich. Der altdeutsche Staat. Giessen, 1862.

Thudicum, Friedrich. Die Gau- und Markverfassung in Deutschland. Giessen, 1860.

Troya, Carlo. Codice diplomatico longobardo. 5 vols. Napoli, 1853.

Turner, Sharon. The History of the Anglo-Saxons. London, 1852.

Vaissette, et de Vic. Histoire générale de Languedoc. 5 vols. Paris, 1730–1745.

Wach, Adolph. Der Arrestprocess in seiner geschichtlichen Entwickelung. Erster Theil. Leipzig, 1868.

Waitz, Georg. Deutsche Verfassungsgeschichte. 2 Auf. Kiel, 1865–66.

Waitz, Georg. Ueber die Anfänge der Vasallität. Göttingen, 1856.

Walter, Ferd. Corpus Juris Germanici Antiqui. 3 vol. Berolini, MDCCCXXIV.

Walter, Ferd. Deutsche Rechtsgeschichte. Bonn, 1857. 2 vols.

Wasserschleben, H. Die germanische Verwandtschaftsberechnung und das Prinzip der Erbenfolge nach deutschem insbesondere sächsischem Rechte. Giessen, 1864.

Wasserschleben, H. Das Prinzip der Successionsordnung nach deutschem insbesondere sächsischem Rechte. Gotha, 1866.

Wiarda, T. D. Willküren der Brockmänner. Berlin, 1820.

Wiarda, T. D. Asega Buch. Berlin und Stettin, 1805.

Wilda, W. E. Das Strafrecht der Germanen. Halle. 1842.

Vita S. Wilfridi. In the publications of the English Historical Society.

Wilkins, David. Concilia magnae Britanniae et Hiberniae, a Synodo Verolamiensi, A.D. CCCCXLVI ad Londinensem, A.D. MDCCXVII. 4 vol. Londini, MDCCXXXVII.

ZEITSCHRIFT FÜR KIRCHENRECHT. Herausgegeben von Dove. Berlin, 1861.

ZEITSCHRIFT FÜR RECHTSGESCHICHTE. Herausgegeben von Rudorff, Bruns, Roth, Merkel, Böhlau. Weimar, 1861.

ZEITSCHRIFT FÜR DEUTSCHES RECHT. Herausgegeben von Beseler, Reyscher und Wilda. Leipzig, 1839. 20 Bände.

ZOEPFL, H. Deutsche Rechtsgeschichte. Braunschweig, 1872. 3 vols.

ZORN, P. Das Beweisverfahren nach langobardischem Rechte. München, 1872.

THE ANGLO-SAXON COURTS OF LAW.

THE long and patient labors of German scholars seem to
have now established beyond dispute the fundamental historical principle, that the entire Germanic family, in its
earliest known stage of development, placed the administration of law, as it placed the political administration, in the
hands of popular assemblies composed of the free, able-
bodied members of the commonwealth. This great principle
is, perhaps, from a political point of view, the most important
which historical investigation has of late years established.
It gives to the history of Germanic, and especially of English,
institutions a roundness and philosophic continuity, which
add greatly to their interest, and even to their practical
value. The student of history who now attempts to trace,
through two thousand years of vicissitudes and dangers, the
slender thread of political and legal thought, no longer loses
it from sight in the confusion of feudalism, or the wild law-
lessness of the Heptarchy, but follows it safely and firmly
back until it leads him out upon the wide plains of northern
Germany, and attaches itself at last to the primitive popular
assembly, parliament, law-court, and army in one; which
embraced every free man, rich or poor, and in theory at
least allowed equal rights to all. Beyond this point it seems
unnecessary to go. The State and the Law may well have
originated here. There is no occasion for introducing theories in regard to the development of families into tribes, of
family heads into patriarchal and tribal chiefs, of the tribe

1

into the state, of the tribal chief into the king, of the family council into the state assembly, or of family custom into public law. We know, as yet, absolutely nothing of the society from which the Indo-European family immediately sprung, or from which it voluntarily or involuntarily separated itself. But there is no sufficient reason for supposing that, within the Germanic society itself, the family was ever exclusively powerful. There is strong internal evidence in the Germanic laws to indicate that, whatever may have been the previous social condition of the race, its earliest political and legal creation was in the form of an association of small families, with or without actual or theoretical relationship, but without a patriarchal chief ; an association whose able-bodied male members, uniting, not as families, but as individuals equally entitled to a voice, formed one council, which decided all questions of war and peace ; elected all officers, civil or military, that circumstances required ; provided for the security of property ; arbitrated all disputes that were regularly brought before them ; and left to the families themselves the exclusive control of all their private affairs, as belonging to the domain of family custom. So far as concerned the purposes for which this association existed, the state was already supreme. Within its own sphere, the family was uncontrolled.

This popular assembly was the primitive law-court of the Germanic race.[1] What may have been its composition when the Germans were a nomadic race, if, indeed, they ever were a really nomadic race, is a subject of little importance. For all ordinary purposes of historical reasoning, the present division of Europe has existed from indefinite ages. The Germans have occupied the centre of Europe, so far as any thing is known to the contrary, as long as the Greeks and Romans have occupied their peninsulas. The Saxons, from whom the English sprung, have been from all historical time the inhabitants of the territory which their descendants still occupy. Their habitations have been fixed ; their dwellings have been permanent ; their boundaries have been estab-

---

[1] Compare, however, Sohm, Reichs-und Gerichtsverfassung, pp. 1-8.

lished. At the time when German law and society were first brought within the view of history, the German popular assembly consisted, and to all appearance had always consisted, of the free inhabitants of a fixed geographical district. The army, indeed, when assembled for war, was a court of law, because it was the people that were assembled ; and the people, wherever assembled, were the state. But at home the free men of each geographical district met at a fixed spot within that district, at fixed times, and formed the court of law. The idea of the State was not merely a personal but a geographical idea, if not in theory, at least in fact.

Various names were used, and are still in use, to designate this political and territorial unit. English writers have usually called it the *tribe*. They have also called it territorially a *pagus*, a *canton*, a *shire*, a *gau*. There are objections to all these terms. The territorial meaning of *pagus*, *gau*, *canton*, and *shire*, is that of a division or section of a country, whereas the idea to be expressed is that of an entire country, a territorial unit. The *tribe* is equally unsatisfactory, as expressing the political unit, for the reason that the scientific meaning attached to the word *tribe* by historians is precisely the meaning which is not meant to be here conveyed. The German organization is important only because, and only so far as, it is not a tribal but a political organization ; not a tribe, but a state. In this difficulty there seems to be no resource better than that of adopting American usage. The idea to be conveyed is entirely expressed, both in its political and territorial meaning, by the American use of the word *state*, as in the term *United States*, signifying, as it does, not merely definite territorial boundaries, but confederated political organizations. Instead, therefore, of the words *tribe* and *gau* or *canton*, the word *state* will be here used to designate the primitive political and territorial unit of Germanic society, the *civitas* of Cæsar and Tacitus.

If any correct inference can be drawn from the facts known in regard to the earlier and ruder stages of German society, it would seem that the entire race was divided into an almost innumerable variety of such petty states, varying greatly in size and customs, but each enjoying its own independence of action through its own popular assembly, and each considering itself at liberty to join or to abandon a confederation with other states, as suited its ideas of its own interests. Even when conquered in war, and held in political subjection, each state would ordinarily preserve its own powers of self-government to a degree that would render a resumption of its independence easy, and, in time, almost inevitable. Yet it is obvious that if military conquest, under the influence of foreign example, ever took the shape of consolidation, so that two or more states were united in one, and their popular assemblies ceased to exist independently, and became merged in one great assembly of the entire nation, such a change might easily give birth to a military monarchy, a territorial aristocracy, a feudal anarchy, or almost any other form of transition. Such seems, indeed, to have been the case with the most powerful of all the German confederations, the Franks, when they first appear in history. The small states of which the Frankish kingdom was composed had not confederated together, but had been consolidated. Possibly it was this policy of centralization which gave them supremacy in Europe. But in return it hastened the decay of their democratic institutions, which could only be safe in states so small that the popular assembly could actually include the body of free men in healthy and active co-operation. From the moment the small state became merged in a great nation, the personal activity of the mass of free men in politics became impossible, if for no other reason than for the mere difficulties of distance. Nevertheless, even in this case, the functions of a supreme court of law would remain vested in the great national assembly, until, with all other public rights, they fell ultimately into the hands of the king.

It seems most probable that some of these petty states were very small; so small as to need no subdivision for administrative purposes. In this case, their popular assembly must have provided, by frequent meetings, for the ordinary business of the law. But, in the rule, the state appears to have been large enough to require subdivision into administrative districts. These districts, at least in historical times, had no fixed rule of size. They varied greatly in extent of territory, and in numbers of population. Indeed, the mere effect of time and accident must soon have brought confusion into any arrangement that could have been invented. The object seems merely to have been to group together in one district such hamlets, or village communities, as lay in convenient proximity to each other.

The name by which this district was known also varied greatly among the different German states. Sometimes it was called a *gau*, or *scir*, and was translated into Latin as *pagus*, or *pagellus*, or simply as *regio ;* sometimes *huntari*, *hundred*, or *zent*. In Latin it is also known as *centena*, *vicaria*, *condita*.[1] In later times, the word *hundred* has come into general use. But, although these and various other terms show that there was no uniformity in the names of Germanic institutions, they prove even more decisively that the thing itself existed almost, if not quite, universally ; and that the district, whatever it may have been called, was the foundation of the German administrative system. For the present, it will be convenient to adopt none of these names, and to use merely the word *district* to indicate the ordinary subdivision of the state, subsequently known as the *hundred*.

The organization of the district was modelled on that of the state. Its essential characteristic was the regular assembly of all free men resident within the district. This assembly was the ordinary court of law, and provided for all the immediate legal wants of the public. It met frequently, perhaps once a month, in most cases, while the state assembly met twice a year. The district court, however, appears to have had no independent political functions. It was simply a court of justice, and an instrument for administrative purposes.

The name of the popular assembly varied nearly as much as the names of the territorial divisions. Three of these

[1] Sohm. Reichs-und Gerichtsverfassung, I. 181 ff. Thudichum, Gau-und Markverfassung, erstes Buch. Maurer, Einleitung, pp. 59–64; Waitz, Verfassungsgeschichte, I. 150 ff. ; II. 817 ff.

names, however, are alone of importance here. The Franks used the word *mahl*, translated *mallum* in Latin; while elsewhere the word *thing* was commonly employed. The English gradually adopted the word *gemot*.

The general court, or assembly of the state, and the local assembly of the district, were, therefore, the law courts of higher and lower jurisdiction throughout the north of Europe. No doubt, the pressure of circumstances did, in many cases, produce variations from this arrangement; but, amid all changes and convulsions, the state assembly still remained the one supreme court; the district assembly still remained the one district court, of what may be called the common or customary law. This is the typical form of judicial constitution among the Germans. Its variations make the judicial history of modern Europe.

The Germans who emigrated from the Danish peninsula and settled upon the south-eastern coast of England during the latter half of the fifth century belonged to the purest Germanic stock. Among all German races, none have clung with sturdier independence or more tenacious conservatism to their ancient customs and liberties, than the great Saxon confederation, which stamped its character so often and so deeply upon the history of northern Europe. Of all productions of the German mind within the domain of law, the Sachsenspiegel was the purest and the greatest. So far as the conquerors of Britain were Saxons, they could have had no notion of law that was not German; while, so far as they were influenced by their Scandinavian neighbors, they brought with them, if possible, a more archaic type of Germanic custom than the Saxon type itself.

Nevertheless, it so happens that almost absolutely nothing is known with certainty in regard to the history of England between the conquest and the introduction of Christianity, a period of more than a century. In the absence of all exact information, there has been a wide divergence of opinion among historians. One school has seen in the Roman institutions of the conquered Britons the influence which reacted upon the conquerors, and gave character to Anglo-Saxon law. The other has maintained that the conquerors swept away in one mass every thing which was British or Roman, and introduced pure German law in its place. This dispute is only interesting here, so far as it may involve the question of identity between the Anglo-Saxon law court of the later period, and the German law court already described. The mere absence of information between the years 450 and 600 would in itself create no special difficulty, in establishing this identity, if the sources after 600 gave any precise picture of Anglo-Saxon society. But this is not the case. And the question is further complicated by the fact that the Anglo-Saxon district, known as the *hundred*, appears to be a creation of the ninth century at the earliest. But if the district did not exist from the first, the district court could hardly have existed, and the historical connection with German institutions is lost. It is hardly enough to assert, with Dr. K. Maurer,[1] that such a connection must, on general principles, have existed. It is far too little to assume, with Professor Stubbs,[2] that the early arrangement of the Anglo-Saxons may have been a personal division into hundreds of warriors, and was, probably, not a territorial division into equal districts. The essence of the German district system, at least so far as it is known to history, is that it was territorial, as well as personal. It was territorial in the time of the Lex Salica, in the time of Tacitus, in the time of Cæsar.[3] The essence of the village community and the customary law is in this territorial district system. The historian cannot possibly concede that the tie which united German settlers under the law was a merely personal one, without cutting loose from all the known facts of German society. If the Anglo-Saxon system was not from its origin identical with the German system, it was something else, and owes its character to unknown influences, whether Roman, British, or merely circumstantial.

At the outset, therefore, it is necessary to prove, if possible, that the Anglo-Saxons brought with them from Germany

---

[1] Krit. Ueberschau, I. 78.   [2] Hist. I. 97, 98.

[3] Thudichum, Der altdeutsche Staat, p. 91, ff.

and established in England, not merely German law, but German courts of law, and the German territorial district which was the theatre of activity of the German district court. In the utter absence of information regarding the pagan period of Anglo-Saxon England, it will hardly be required to produce contemporary testimony to its organization. The requisites for demonstration will be satisfied by proving, if such proof is possible, that all the evidence which exists is conclusive in favor of the identity, in the seventh and eighth centuries, between Anglo-Saxon law courts and judicial districts and those of Germany.

The first and easiest part of the argument is to show the identity of the law court. No sooner did Kent accept Christianity from St. Augustine, than the process of committing the customary law to writing appears to have begun. The first collection of customary law, known as the Laws of Æthelberht, and dating, perhaps, from about the year 600, contains ninety short paragraphs, most of which merely state the amount of the money atonement which the courts were to allow in the enumerated cases of simple personal injury. These differ in no way from the similar enumerations which are to be found in other contemporary German codes. So far as these laws go, they indicate the existence of a legal system identical with that of the continent, but they nowhere allude directly to the method of judicial administration. The next collection is also Kentish, and appears to have been made towards the year 675, during the reigns of two kings, Hlothar and Eadric, who are supposed to have reigned either together, or successively, over Kent or portions of it, between 673 and 680. The eighth paragraph of this collection runs as follows : —

"If any man make plaint against another and meet him at [cite him to : Price] the *methel*, or the *thing*, let the defendant always give surety to the other and do him such right as the Kentish judges prescribe to him." [1]

---

[1] Gif man oðerne sace tihte and he ðane mannan mote an medle oððe an ðinge symble se man ðam oðrum byrigean geselle and ðam riht awyrce ðe to hiom Cantwara deman gescrifen.

This passage merely describes the ordinary procedure of German law. It is, however, peculiarly interesting here, because it gives the name by which the popular assembly was known. Grimm [1] gives a list of the terms used to designate the German court of law. The Anglo-Saxon *methel*, the Frankish *mahal*, and the Norwegian *thing*, are all synonymes. The only question that can arise in regard to the Kentish law above quoted is caused by the use of two words, neither of them commonly found in the later legal literature of the south of England, but both found among other and distant races. One is left in doubt whether to suppose that one court is meant, and that there was no settled usage in Kent, as between the two well-known words which described it; or that two courts were meant, in which case one would be the district, the other the state assembly. In either case, however, the fact of the existence of the law court, its identity, even in name, with the German law court, as well as its identity in procedure, is as firmly established for the kingdom of Kent by this passage, as it is by any contemporary record for any continental state. So far as the procedure is concerned, the same fact is supported by other passages in the same laws, which relate to a class of legal business peculiar to the district court. These, however, will find their proper place hereafter, in dealing with the subject of procedure. [2]

The next Kentish laws are those of Wihtræd, which date from the close of the same century. There is a preamble to these which declares that they were adopted by an assembly of great men, including the king, the archbishop, the bishop of Rochester, and the rest of the priesthood, acting in unison with the people. The fifth paragraph of these laws appears to give the name of *gemot* to this assembly. So far as the legal character of the laws is concerned, they throw little new light on the nature of the judicial tribunal, except that certain paragraphs point to the conclusion that the king's sheriff was already the presiding officer in the district court.

There would seem, therefore, to be no room for doubting that Kent, at least, had brought from the continent the

---

[1] Rechtsalterthümer, pp. 746–749.   [2] See pp. 189 ff.

judicial system of the Germans in all its parts, and had even
followed with exactitude the judicial development of the
Merovingian kingdom.   The evidence in regard to Wessex
is not so complete, since the earliest collection of Wessex
laws is little older than the latest of the Kentish series.   The
laws of Ine of Wessex fall, perhaps, not far from the year
690.   They include no fewer than seventy-six paragraphs,
rich in details of social life, and illustrations of legal principles,
but, as usual, offering no special description of the courts of
law.   The eighth paragraph, however, seems to confirm the
inference drawn from Wihtræd, § 22, that the king's sheriff
was already the presiding officer in the district court: "If
any man bring suit before a shireman, or other judge . . .
and the defendant will give him no surety," &c.   The case
is unmistakably in the district court, and the king's reeve
is, probably, the presiding officer.   Dr. Schmid also cites as
proof of the same point, the subsequent paragraph, § 73:
" . . . Let them make composition for the offence as they
may be able to agree with the king and his reeve."   But it
is possible that the sheriff may be acting in this case, merely
as the *exactor*, or collector of the king's fines.

The next collection of Wessex law is that of Alfred the
Great, and was published towards the end of the ninth century.   Here, again, is the clearest evidence of the existence,
in all its most characteristic features, of the German district
court, presided over by the king's reeve, and administering
law in the minutest details.   In § 34 is an example of business peculiarly characteristic of the district court: " Mer-
chants are required to produce the men who accompany
them, before the king's reeve in the folk-gemot . . . and if
they need to have more men with them on their journey, they
may do so, if necessary, by notifying the king's reeve with
the witness of the gemot."   Another instance of legal procedure in the same court is contained in § 22: "If any one
bring a charge [of theft] against another, in the folk-gemot
before the king's reeve," &c.   The distinction between
the two courts is clearly observed in Alfred's law.   When
the district court is meant, it is mentioned as the folk-

gemot of the sheriff, as above, while the old assembly of the state has now become the gemot of the ealdorman ; as in § 38: " If any one break the peace in the gemot before the king's ealdorman," &c.   The same distinction is preserved in the well-known passage in Asser's Life of Alfred, where it is said that the eorls and ceorls (nobiles et ignobiles) in the courts of the ealdormen and sheriffs (in concionibus comitum et præpositorum) would never allow that what had been determined by the ealdormen and sheriffs was true.

Finally, to carry the evidence down to the period beyond which the subject no longer admits of dispute, the laws of Alfred's son and successor, Edward, direct (§ 8) that " every reeve shall hold gemot every four weeks."   The state assembly, or what was now the ealdorman's court, was in the habit of meeting only twice a year.

The evidence seems, therefore, as conclusive in regard to the identity of the judicial tribunal, as the nature of the case admits.   The procedure, the nature of the business performed, the very names of the courts, are mere repetitions of what is found in the barbarian codes of the continent.   And as in all continental societies the great mass of ordinary business was necessarily done in the district court, so in England the same district court is seen, from the earliest recorded times, performing identically the same duties.

It is little likely, however, that this point will be disputed. The difficulty appears to be, that the existence of the court does not necessarily imply the existence of the territorial district, known as the *hundred ;* that there is no evidence of the existence of such a territorial district before the ninth century ; and that, if the district really existed, such silence in regard to it would have been impossible.

On the other hand, an opinion is advocated by Mr. Kemble and Mr. Freeman which carries precisely the opposite view to an extreme.   " We must remember," says Mr. Freeman,[1] " that the kingdom, like all our ancient divisions, from the shire, perhaps from the hundred, was formed by the aggregation of smaller divisions.   The unit is the *mark,* roughly repre-

---

[1] Hist. Norman Con. I. 96.

sented by the modern parish or manor. The shire must not be looked on as a division of the kingdom, or the mark as a division of the shire. The shire is, in truth, formed by an aggregation of marks, and the kingdom is formed by an aggregation of shires. . . . The first followers of Cerdic, no doubt, settled themselves in marks forming self-governed communities."

To both these views it is necessary, if the theory of identity with German institutions be followed, to oppose the most decided negative. Politically and judicially, there was but one unit in primitive German society, and that was the state itself. There was but one political or judicial subdivision of the state, and that was the district, known commonly as the hundred. The kingdom (state) was not formed by an aggregation of marks, or of districts of any kind, but was from the first a constitutionally complete whole. As it conquered new land, it created new districts; but, even if it were so small as to require but one popular assembly, and to require no judicial districts, it was still a state, not a hundred nor a mark. As a state it had fixed boundaries, and its subdivisions had fixed boundaries. It was territorially and politically complete.

The great obstacle to all historians in dealing with this subject has been the absence of proof that the district subsequently known as the hundred existed at all before the ninth or tenth centuries. There is no higher authority on the subject of Anglo-Saxon law than Dr. Reinhold Schmid; and Dr. Schmid in connection with this point says:[1] "Many things argue against the assumption that the hundred became a territorial division immediately on the first occupation of the land; first of all, the fact that in all the older sources, especially in Beda, although he often reckons different parts of England according to their superficial contents, the hundred is never the ground-work of the calculation, but always the hide. Also the fact that in the Chronicle, shires are mentioned, but not hundreds; and that, so far as I am aware, not one of the numerous charters of the earlier centuries

[1] Gesetze der Angelsachsen, p. 614. Gloss. s. v. *hundred.*

contains the smallest hint of their existence." These are, indeed, most serious objections; and none of the historians have succeeded in removing them. Yet, until they are removed, there must always be grave doubts in regard to the historical continuity between German and Anglo-Saxon institutions.

That the court of the district subsequently known as the hundred existed in England from the earliest Saxon times has already been proved by evidence precisely the same as that which proves its existence in the Lex Salica or in Saxony itself. This, however, is not enough. In order to leave no doubt upon the subject, it is necessary to prove the existence of the territorial district as well as of the court. The objections raised by Dr. Schmid can only be met by showing that, whatever may be the case with the mere name of the district, the district itself existed in England from the earliest recorded times.

Dr. Schmid's first statement is, that, in all the older sources, especially in Beda, the hide is always, the hundred never, mentioned as the measure of land. This statement is so broad as to weaken its force. Not only in the earlier but in the later sources, down to Norman times, the statement is equally true. The hide was always the ordinary measure of territory. But it would be quite untrue to suppose that no other division of land except the hide is to be found in Beda and the early sources. On the contrary, Beda's History swarms with references to places and districts which may have been hamlets or may have been hundreds, but which were certainly divisions of territory between the hide and the kingdom. For example: Beda speaks of a "provincia in Undalum," a province of Oundle; of a "regio in Feppingum," a district of Fepping; of a "regio in Cuneningum," a district of Cunning[ham?]; and of a "regio familiarum circiter sexcentarum in provincia Orientalium Anglorum," which he calls Elge, — that is to say, a district of six hundred hides, called Ely, in the province of East Anglia. In the ancient list of districts according to hidage, given under the word *Hida* in Spelman's Glossary, and re-

printed by Kemble (I. 81, 82), there are five which contain
only three hundred hides, and eleven which contain only six
hundred.   The Vita S. Cuthberti speaks of a "regio Henitis"
and a "regio Alise," on the road from Hexham to the "civitas Vel."   The Vita S. Wilfridi speaks of a "regio juxta
Rippel," a "regio in Gaedyne," a "regio Dunitinga," a "regio Caetlevum," a "regio Hagustaldese."   Nennius contains
a long list of *regiones*, which, it is believed, have, in a number of cases, not yet been identified.   Under these circumstances, it is obviously quite out of the question to rely on
Beda and the early sources in order to disprove the existence,
in the seventh and eighth centuries, of the district, which
subsequently appears as the hundred.

The argument drawn from the silence of the Chronicle is
still more easily met.   If Dr. Schmid had said that the
Chronicle never mentioned the hundred before the reign of
Alfred, but frequently used the term afterwards, the inference would have been inevitable.   But neither before nor
after Alfred's reign does the Chronicle mention the hundred.
Even when describing the Domesday census of William the
Conqueror, it speaks only of hides and shires.   The word
itself occurs, so far as I am aware, only once in the Chronicle, and then it is in a forged and interpolated charter of
Peterborough, bearing date in 972.   Unless, therefore, it is
argued that the hundred never existed at all, the silence of
the Chronicle leaves its existence before 900 as probable as
its existence afterwards.

Dr. Schmid finally asserts that, so far as he knows, not one
of the numerous charters of the earlier centuries contains the
remotest hint of the hundred.   This is a sweeping statement,
and can only be met by a thorough inquiry into the contents
of the Codex Diplomaticus, in the eighth and ninth centuries.
Genuine charters of the seventh century are rare.

It must, however, be confessed at the outset, that the
Anglo-Saxons had very little conception of accuracy in statement.   Their legal documents are, almost without exception,
atrociously drawn up.   To this day, antiquarians are specu-
lating as to the situation of Clovesho, a place more frequently

mentioned than almost any other in Anglo-Saxon literature. The list of places mentioned in the charters, but which Mr. Kemble was unable to identify, is appalling. Even in the later charters, no place is ever mentioned as lying in such a parish, in such a hundred, in such a county; while it is only as the Norman period is approached that the hundred is mentioned with any frequency at all.

The Formulas of the Frankish kingdom, which were used on the Continent for all ordinary legal documents, caught something of the accuracy of Roman law. They describe land as situated "in loco nuncupante illo, in pago illo, in centena illa." The usual form of the Anglo-Saxon charter was to name a place, probably the parish, and no more; as, for instance, "XL. hyde aet Alresford." If the charter was written in Latin, the words used were commonly, "in loco qui dicitur Alresford," or, in more ornate phrase, "in illo loco ubi ruricolae appellativo usu ludibundisque vocabulis nomen indiderunt aet Alresford." The chancery formula in Oda and Dunstan's time, about the middle of the tenth century, was, "in illo loco ubi solicolae illius regionis nomen imposuerunt aet Alresford." Here *regio* may mean merely neighborhood, although in Charter CCCCXXVII. (ii., 297) *regio* and *pagus* seem to be used as synonymes: "XVIII. mansas dedi in illo loco ubi jamdudum solicolae illius regionis nomen imposuerunt aet Waeligforda, pro commutatione alterius terrae quae sita est in Cornubio ubi ruricolae illius pagi barbarico nomine appellant Pendyfig." But, whether the two words are here used as synonymes or in contradistinction, there can be no doubt that both of them, as well as the word *provincia*, are common Latin translations of the Anglo-Saxon word *shire*. Asser translates *shire* as *paga;* Ethelwerd, as *provincia:* "Dominabatur rex Offa in XXIII. provinciis quas Angli Shyras appellant" (Vita Offae, Wilkins, Sac. Con. I. 156); "Regiones vel pagos" (Cod. Dip. III. 42); "Regio Suthseaxna" (Asser); "In regione Suthregie" (Cod. Dip. CCXL., I. 318, MXLIV., V. 91); "Regio Cantia" (Cod. Dip. MXIX., V. 58); "Regio Oxanaford" (Cod. Dip. DCXCVII., III. 299). Beda also speaks of Surrey as a *regio*. These citations might be indefinitely multiplied; but they are quite sufficient to show the loose legal and geographical phraseology of the Anglo-Saxons, and to explain the confusion that exists in regard to their territorial divisions. It is, however, evident, from these instances, that *provincia*, *pagus*, and *regio* are all used as equivalents for *shire ;* nor do they ever seem to be used for any smaller territorial district, such as *vill* or hamlet.

An examination of the early charters brings to light a number of cases in which the word *regio* occurs. The first that raises a doubt is the " regio Stoppingas," with its " locus Widutun," in a charter of Æthelbald of Mercia, 723–737 (I. 100). This may pass, however, for what has been heretofore called a State, if antiquarians so decide. In 847, the "senators" of Æthelwulf of Wessex grant to their king twenty hides of land in the " regio Homme " (II. 28). This also may pass as a doubtful case, although it must raise curiosity. Another charter of Æthelbald of Mercia, without date, but of course belonging to the first half of the eighth century (I. 122), grants seven hides " in provincia Middelsexorum, in regione quae dicitur Geddinges." There is still a manor or hamlet of Yeading in Middlesex; but Mr. Kemble, rightly enough, has not thought it possible that a place designated as *regio*, and ending in *ingas*, could have been a hamlet, and has therefore classed it with Stoppingas as a mark, whatever a mark may have been. There seems to be nothing unreasonable in supposing that Yeddings, or Yeading, was once a Middlesex hundred. If, however, these three cases are thrown aside as unconvincing, there remain others, which can hardly be dealt with in the same manner.

1. Cenwulf, 812 (Cod. Dip. CXCIX., I. 249), grants half a ioclet " in partibus australi in regione on Liminum, et in loco ubi ab indigenis ab occidente Kasingburnan appellatur." This would seem to be the manor of Caseborne, near Hythe. The Limen was, in that day, a port of great consequence. The Lord Warden of the Cinque Ports was formerly called the Limenarch ; and the " regio on Liminum " possibly means the ancient Liberty of the Cinque Ports, with its own jurisdiction.

2. Offa, 774 (Cod. Dip. CXXII., I. 149), grants three hides "in occidentali parte regionis quae dicitur Mersware ubi nominatur ad Liden." Here is another Kentish Liberty, enjoying its own jurisdiction time out of mind, — that of Romney Marsh.

3. Ecgberht of Kent, 778 (Cod. Dip. CXXXII., I. 160), and 779 (CXXXV., I. 163), grants half a hide "ubi nominatur Bromgeheg" and "in regione vocabulo Bromgeheg." The estate known as the manor of Bromhei was, with certain other lands, an appendage, in later times, to the parish of Frindsbury, in Shamel Hundred, in Kent. Apparently in the eighth century, it gave its name to the hundred.

4. Cenwulf, 814 (Cod. Dip. CCI., I. 253), grants one hide of land "in provincia Cantiae, in loco et in regione quae dicitur Westanwidde, ubi nominatur Cynincges cwa lond." In these early times, the influence of the Frankish chancery seems to show itself in this unusual accuracy of statement. Westanwidde is obviously Westwood, a manor in the parish of Preston, and hundred of Fevresham, in Kent. Hasted, in his admirable county history, speaks of it as an eminent manor; its court-baron enjoying a jurisdiction curiously coterminous with that of the hundred, to which it seems once to have given its name.

5. Æthelberht, 762 (Cod. Dip. CVIII., I. 132), exchanges half of a mill situated in a "possessio quaedam terrae in regione quae vocatur Cert." The hundred of Cert, in the county of Kent, is repeatedly mentioned in Domesday.

6. Eadberht, 738 (Cod. Dip. LXXXV., I. 102), grants land "in regione quae vocatur Hohg, in loco qui dicitur Andscohesham." The *regio Hohg* is still the Hundred of Hoo. The Textus Roffensis further supplies even the identification of Andscohesham. Among the manors reclaimed by Lanfranc from Odo of Baieux, in the famous suit on Penenden Heath,[1] was one called Stoke, the ancient name of which was Andscohesham. One of the parishes of Hoo Hundred is still this same Stoke, or Andscohesham; and Penenden Heath itself must be within sight of it.

---

[1] See Appendix, No. 31.

7. Offa, 788 (Cod. Dip. CLIII., I. 184), grants one hide " in provincia Cantiae, in regione Eastrgena, ubi nominatur Duningcland." Archbishop Wulfred, in 811 (Cod. Dip. CXCV., I. 238), grants three hides " in regione Easterege quae inibi ab incolis Folkwining lond vocatur, atque iterum in eadem regione Eosterge ruriculum unius aratri." The *regio Eosterge* is still the Hundred of Eastry. Possibly Duningland might also be identified. And, to augment still further this mass of cumulative evidence, there remains a charter of Cuthred of Kent, dating before 805 (Cod. Dip. CXCI., I. 233), which grants to " Æthelnotho praefecto meo " three hides at Hegythethorne. This charter, curiously enough, is indorsed by " Æðelnoð *se gerefa to Eastorege.*" Hegythethorne is to-day the parish of Eythorne, in Eastry Hundred.

Demonstration can go no further. There is ample material for argument in the same sense still in reserve, in the Codex Diplomaticus ; but it would merely encumber these pages with unnecessary matter. Not only have we here the actual hundreds themselves, unchanged in name or boundary by more than a thousand years of vicissitude, but the very hamlets and parishes into which they were then, as now, divided. Not only in the ninth and eighth, but also, at least by natural inference, in the seventh century, the actual hundred, as it still exists, is here seen in full activity, with its parishes, its reeve, and its court of law ; for, if the district was under a royal reeve, and, as seen in the laws, the court of the district was synonymous with the court of the king's reeve, the inference is inevitable that the character essential to all was that of jurisdiction.

Nevertheless, it must be conceded that, even here, Dr. Schmid is, at least technically, correct. The district described in these charters is not a hundred. Had it been so, it would have been called so, as it was on the Continent, by some name that expressed the relation, — *centena, vicaria,* or *condita.* Eastry, Hoo, and Cert were not hundreds in the seventh and eighth centuries : they were *regiones,* — shires. Æthelnoth was by no means a mere hundred-reeve : he was shire-reeve. So, in a charter of Uhtred, "regulus Huiccio-rum," in 767 (Cod. Dip. CXVII., I. 144), the grant is made to " Æthelmundo videlicet filio Ingeldi qui fuit *dux et prae-fectus* Æthilbaldi regis." In charters CXXI., CXXXVII., and CXLV. (774–781), two Brordans sign each document, — one always as *princeps;* the other, as *praefectus* twice, and once as *dux.* So, in CXXVII. (757–775), Eadbald signs as "praefectus et princeps Offae regis." The office was one of the highest dignity during the Heptarchy ; and in Kent, at least, it might be supposed equivalent to that of ealdorman in the larger kingdoms.

This conclusion in regard to the name of the district in the early centuries does not stand alone. Professor Stubbs says : " In Cornwall, in the twelfth century, the subdivisions were not called hundreds, but shires, one of which, Triconscire, now the hundred of Trigg, is mentioned in Alfred's will. . . . Of the Yorkshire subdivisions, two, Borgheshire and Craveshire, — the latter of which is never called a wapen-take, — retain the name of shire ; and it is given in later doc-uments to Richmondshire, Riponshire, Hallamshire, Island-shire, Norhamshire, and probably other similar districts. . . . It may seem not impossible that the original name of the subdivision immediately above the township was scir or shire, — a term of various application." [1]

The facts above cited authorize the assumption, as a gen-eral law, of the principle that *the State of the seventh century became the Shire of the tenth, while the Shire of the seventh century became the Hundred of the tenth.*

This degradation of the early shire in dignity and impor-tance probably accounts for another fact, which otherwise seems inexplicable. As has been above shown, all the allu-sions to these districts which are to be found in the charters date from the period of the Heptarchy. From the moment that the consolidation of England begins, — that is, from the reign of Ecgbert, — these allusions cease. It was natural that the shire should be mentioned in defining the situation of an estate. It was equally natural that, after the shire had

---

[1] Const. Hist., I. 100.

been degraded to the lower position of a hundred, it should be overlooked. The use of the word " shire," in its modern and larger signification, appears to have been introduced either during, or not long after, the reign of Ecgbert.

The origin of the modern shire in what has here been called the primitive State, will hardly be disputed. The Sumorsets, the Wilsets, the Thornsets, the South Saxons, the East Saxons, the Middle Saxons, the North Folk, the South Folk, have left traces enough on the early annals of England to show how the county system originated. The only difficulties in the history of this development are two : one of these is the origin of the hundred, which has just been explained; the other is the continued existence of the shire court in England while it was completely obsolete in the Frankish empire.

That the hundred should have been found indispensable is natural enough. The hundred and its court were, of all Germanic institutions, the most long-lived and useful, from Iceland to the Adriatic. " The hundred, and the principle that the hundred community is a judicial body, outlived the storms of the folk wanderings, the political creations of Clovis, the reforms of Charlemagne, the dissolution of the Frankish empire, the dissolution of the county system, the dissolution of public authority by feudalism, the complete beginning of a wholly new development in the isolated territories. The hundred constitution gave way at last only to a more powerful enemy, — the awakening legal science of the sixteenth century." [1]   The district court was no less necessary to consolidated England than it had been to consolidated Germany, or to the petty primitive state. It is, therefore, not merely probable — it is almost certain — that the story which attributes to Alfred the origin of the hundred must be, in one sense, true. He did not create the district, or its court (both of these were, to all intents and purposes, as ancient then as they are now ; they are among the first, if not the first, political creations of man) ; but he, or some member of his family, in reorganizing the enlarged

[1] Sohm. Altd. R.-u. G. Verf. I. 541.

kingdom, must have introduced, in imitation of Frankish usage, the name of *hundred.*

That they did not, at the same time, introduce the hundred constitution of Charlemagne, cannot but create surprise. There seems to have been no reason why the ancient state should have been allowed to preserve its state assembly when the national assembly had made it superfluous. This is, indeed, the distinctive peculiarity of England as compared with Germany; and it is a distinction rich in philosophic interest. The development of Germany was in the path of political consolidation; that of England was in the path of political confederation. England has always moved slowly, and has been reluctant to abandon established institutions. The ancient states, though degraded to the rank of shires, preserved their autonomy to the utmost practicable extent. They retained their state assembly; and it was, in fact, their supreme court of law: the king himself sat in it, as in the national assembly. It dealt with folkland, the highest act of sovereignty. In the king's absence, the ealdorman presided in it, — an officer whose dignity conforms to the dignity of the assembly. " True, the ealdorman, like the sheriff, receives his office from the king's hand. But the office of the Anglo-Saxon ealdorman is not one of service, but one of command. The ducal power among the Anglo-Saxons was not a creature of the kingdom, but was older than the kingdom. What the kingdom had won, it had won from the ealdorman. Even in historical times, there is yet living recollection of the kingless period. We see the Anglo-Saxon ealdormen return to an interregnum from the kingdom they had already introduced, and restore the old independence of the ealdormen during a series of years, with a vacant throne. The maintenance of the ealdorman's power under the royal government is a sign that the crown is not yet in full possession of the public authority. The ealdorman is a vice-king, with an *independent* power as opposed to the king. Not the king's pleasure, but a principle of the public constitution, determines the completeness of the ealdorman's authority. Not the king's pleasure, but only a lawful judgment, can strip the ealdorman of his office. The ealdorman excludes the king from the immediate government of the shire. The shire government is not royal, but ducal. The king, in truth, in appointing the ealdorman, appoints, not a servant of his will, but a 'prince' and 'lord' of the shire. . . . The Anglo-Saxon shire constitution, in spite of the establishment of the empire, is an expression of still undeveloped royalty." [1]

Under the new constitution of Alfred, therefore, the old district court was retained intact, with a mere change of name. The old state assembly was retained intact, with only a steady decline in its political powers. And a national assembly, commonly known as the *Witan*, arose to the highest authority in the United Kingdom. The Witan was in theory an assembly of the whole people, although in practice it was a highly aristocratic body. The function of acting as a judicial tribunal seems to have been inherent in the German conception of a popular assembly. The Witan, therefore, exercised judicial powers, becoming thus the highest court of law in the kingdom. But all these courts — the hundred, the shire, and the Witan — were mere adaptations of the primitive organic type of the popular assembly. Nor did the Anglo-Saxons ever entirely lose sight of this, their original democratic starting-point.

It is unnecessary to enter here upon the discussion of other varieties, real or imagined, of the same institution. The law-courts of the Anglo-Saxon cities — the burg gemot, the hustings, &c. — were but the shire and hundred courts in a slightly different form. Their origin was the same, and their procedure the same. The mark-gemot was either the hundred court under a different name, or a mere corporation meeting, whose acts were of a private nature. The various guilds were also without authority as courts of the common law. Nor is it to be supposed that there was any court of the township. Not only would such an institution be quite at variance with all that we know of German law, but there

[1] Sohm. Altd. R.-u. G. Verf. I. 25, 26. The appearance of the second volume of this most brilliant work will be expected with the greater interest as it is to contain an account of the Anglo-Saxon constitution.

is no evidence that the township ever enjoyed any judicial powers other than such as were essential to the smallest matters of police. The legal position of the township with reference to the hundred is clearly laid down in the two following extracts: —

"And whosoever goes forth after cattle [to purchase], let him make known to his neighbors the object of his journey; and, when he returns, let him also make known with whose witness he bought the cattle. But if, on a journey, he make a purchase without previous intention, let him make it known on his return; . . . and, if it is live-stock, let him bring it upon the common pasture, with the witness of his township. If he fail to do this within five days, the townsmen shall notify the hundreds-ealdor, and they and their herdsmen shall be exempt from punishment; and he who brought the cattle shall forfeit it, because he would not make it known to his neighbors; and the landlord shall receive half, and the hundred half." (Edgar, iv. 7, 8.)

"If any one should lead an animal or bring property to a vill, and should say he had found it, before he takes it to his own or another person's house, let him go to the church, and, before the priest of the church and the head-man of the vill, and as many as he can get, by the summons of the head-man, of the best men of the vill, and, when they are assembled, let him show them what has been found. And let the head-man of the vill send to three or four neighboring vills for the priests and head-men of the vills, who are to bring with them four of the best men of each vill; and, when they are assembled, they are to view all that was found. And, after they have taken view of it, the head-man of the domain to which the finder belongs shall take charge of the property till the next day; and on the next day, with some of their neighbors who have seen the thing that was found, let them go to the head-man of the hundred in which their vill is, and show him every thing. And, if the lord on whose land it shall have been found have not his customs, — namely, sac and soc, — let him deliver every thing over to the head-man of the hundred, if he wish to have it, with good witnesses. But, if the lord have his customs, let it be held to right in the lord's court." (Edw. Conf., § 24.)

The township, as is obvious from these extracts, had no jurisdiction whatever. For judicial purposes, it was but a police district of the hundred. Such it was in the Lex Salica, and in all Germanic systems; and such it always remained. Its court of law was the hundred court.

How consistently the Anglo-Saxons adhered to their legal and constitutional principles is shown by the fact that the king, like the ealdorman and sheriff, had no judicial powers separate from those of the court in which he sat. He was simply the presiding officer of that court, with executive powers to carry out its decrees. A legal opinion or decision of the king, as such, was not one which any court of law or any suitor was bound to respect, unless it were made as the result of a special agreement or arbitration, accepted by both parties in advance. A curious example of this nullity in law of the king's decision is given in the suit described in Charter DCXCIII. (Appendix, No. 22).

Further, it would be a mistake to suppose that any appeal, in the modern legal sense, lay from one of these courts to another. There is nothing in the laws or the charters to show that such right of appeal existed, or that it was ever claimed. The decision of the court was final. It was only when the court failed to decide within the time prescribed, that the case could be carried before a higher court. Against a decision incorrect in law, the suitor had no such remedy. He could then only accuse the presiding officer before the king or ealdorman, and procure his removal as incompetent or venal. To attribute a system of appeals to the Anglo-Saxon judicial constitution is to transfer the conception of a civilized age to the rude practice of a barbarous one.

More than this, and still more remarkably illustrating the conservatism of Anglo-Saxon law, it is clear that, down to the very close of the Anglo-Saxon period, the conception of equity as a part of the legal system had never taken shape even as an experiment. This is the more remarkable because the Franks, at a very early period, appear to have invested their king with equitable powers, while Charlemagne gave a remarkable development to the Frankish law in this direction. The Frankish equitable procedure, too, survived in Normandy, England's nearest neighbor, to be carried from there by the Norman and Angevin kings to England, where it made the foundation of the later development of English law. But neither equity as a system, nor equitable powers in the crown, were ever known to Anglo-Saxon England. Both king and people, indeed, seem steadily to have resisted every disposition to widen the royal jurisdiction. Instead of enlarging their own powers by encouraging suitors to seek justice directly from the crown, the king and the Witan frowned upon every symptom of popular discontent with the clumsy justice of popular tribunals, and forced suitors back upon the local courts. Instead of applying themselves to the study of practical remedies for the flagrant absurdities of their legal system, as Charlemagne had done, and as their Angevin successors were to do, the Anglo-Saxon kings adopted a series of measures which steadily tended to aggravate these absurdities, and to render them intolerable. It has been said, by some historians, that Alfred the Great showed a disposition towards the reform of legal procedure. Alfred had, indeed, the inestimable advantage of Charlemagne's example. So, also, had Edward, Æthelstan, and Edgar, his successors. But, whether it was that these monarchs, unlike Charlemagne, were constitutional kings, and were controlled in their policy by the Witan, or whether they failed to understand the necessity of reform, neither their legislation nor the records of legal administration during or after their time show any trace of a disposition to improve the law. Their whole energy was devoted to police, or at best to mere legal administration. The well-known passage in Asser's Life of Alfred is an example of the limited range of English legal ideas. Asser represents Alfred as inquiring into the correctness of his sheriffs' and ealdormen's legal decisions, and threatening them with removal for their ignorance of the law. But, as Mr. Kemble has pointed out, it is nowhere intimated that Alfred assumed the power to reverse those decisions, or that he attempted to create any judicial system more satisfactory than the one which, by common consent, even in his time, was utterly unequal to the public wants.[1] One collection of laws after another, almost in a set formula, harshly forbade the people to bring their suits before the king, unless they had previously ex-

[1] Kemble, Saxons in England, ii. 44, 45.

hausted all the tedious formalities of the local courts. Even then, if the king consented to hear a complaint of denial of justice, his power of redress seems to have gone no further than to send the case back to the ealdorman or sheriff, with the threat of punishment if justice were still denied; or, what was probably more usual, to negotiate an extra-judicial compromise between the parties. Neither at the beginning nor at the end of the Anglo-Saxon time, was the king considered in law as the fountain of justice. The law was administered in the popular courts, theoretically as the act of the freemen. It was strict law; the decision, when reached, was final in the eye of the law; and not even the Witan itself wielded any process by which the letter of the common law could be escaped.

One result followed from this absence of equitable powers, which was, perhaps, not without an ultimate influence on the fate of the whole judicial system. A very slight examination of the law cases printed in the Appendix will show how rarely the parties were allowed to push their differences to a final judgment. A compromise was always effected where compromise was possible. Arbitration was, perhaps, the habitual mode of settling disputes among the Anglo-Saxons. This arbitration might take the actual forms of legal procedure, without offering any anomaly to the Anglo-Saxon mind. In regard to more than one of the cases given in the Appendix, it is evident that the judges are mere arbiters acting in judicial form. The king seems to have habitually performed this function of *quasi* judge. The curious case before Alfred, narrated in Appendix, No. 17, seems to be an instance. If a decision were given without the previous assent of both parties to the jurisdiction, it might be rejected, and a legal trial required, as in charters MCCLVIII., DCXCIII.,[1] even though the king himself were judge. This loose habit of judicial administration, stimulated doubtless by popular distrust of the knowledge or honesty of the king's sheriffs, grew into a system, and not improbably was the germ of subsequent manorial jurisdictions. In a society which had no confidence either in

---

[1] Appendix, No. 19 and No. 22.

its judges, its judicial processes, or its very law itself, — which could devise no system of reform in the practice, nor of equitable protection against the evils, of that law, — it was certainly not surprising. that men should seek a remedy outside the public tribunals, even though the result should ultimately be more fatal to their own interests than all the immediate inconvenience or injustice they were suffering.

The three law courts thus described, with powers indistinctly defined and apparently overlapping each other, mark the whole period of Anglo-Saxon history. As they appear in the earliest times, so they appear in the latest, unchanged during six centuries, so far as their essential character is concerned, and unchanged in fact, except by the steadily increasing tendency towards aristocracy and feudalism. This tendency, though less marked and less mischievous than on the Continent, yet produced the only considerable changes that can be detected in the long history of the Anglo-Saxon judicial constitution. It only remains, therefore, to discuss the degree of influence which feudalism exerted on the judicial system of England down to the accession of William the Norman.

The origin of the English manor as a form of landed property belongs to the domain of real-property law, and will be treated hereafter in that connection. The origin of English manorial jurisdiction is a separate subject. The land and the jurisdiction do not necessarily go together. Originally, as has been seen, all jurisdiction belonged to the State. Only at a comparatively late period did the State allow its power to slip from its hands, and to become attached to the proprietorship of the land.

There is much contradiction, among the writers who have treated this subject, in regard to the stages of its development. Mr. Kemble sometimes inclines to believe that the manorial jurisdiction, as a jurisdiction in law, was of very early origin;[1] at other times, he asserts that "there is no clear proof that the immunity" of sacu and socn "did

[1] Cod. Dip. I., Introd. xliv.–xlvii.; Saxons in England, I. 177, n.

exist before the time of Cnut."[1] Professor Stubbs, without
entering into any discussion of the subject, seems to favor the
idea of an early origin.[2] Dr. Konrad Maurer, whose thorough investigation of the point leaves his successors little
more to do than to paraphrase his pages, leans also towards
the theory that the manorial jurisdiction existed in law from
a much earlier period than that to which it can be traced
back in the laws, charters, and historical literature.[3]

Only with the utmost diffidence can any new inquirer vent-
ure to differ from authority so high as this. Yet there seems
to be something forced in the assumption that an institution
so revolutionary as a private common-law court could have
existed unknown to the written law ; and the ordinary rules
of historical criticism hardly justify the historian in arriving
at such a conclusion, unless under the pressure of absolute
necessity. It is, therefore, a matter of some consequence to
ascertain whether such a necessity exists. If not, it will
certainly be safer to keep within the letter of the law.

Dr. Maurer has admirably explained and illustrated the
nature of the early immunities granted to the great landed
proprietors, and the private authority exercised by them over
the occupants of their land, and the inmates of their household. As head of the household, the land-owner was bound
to responsibility before the law for the good behavior of its
inmates. He might dismiss from his service as infamous the
man whom he could not hold to right, — a punishment which
must have been almost equivalent to outlawry. As landlord,
he might resume his grant of land, or he might simply eject
the occupant on sufferance or at will. The state supported
this power of the land-owner to the utmost, as one of its most
necessary guaranties for the preservation of social order. On
the other hand, the tenant or peasant cultivator would be
inclined to accept, or even to invite, the decision of his lord,
rather than incur the risks of a public suit without his lord's
support, or the possibility of drawing upon himself the extremity of his lord's disfavor. It was therefore natural that

---

[1] Saxons, II. 397.   [2] Const. Hist., I. 184.
[3] Konrad Maurer, Krit. Ueberschau. II. 58.

the lord should have developed, for his own use, a certain
system of law, in mediating between his own people in their
disagreements with each other, or with the public. It was
natural, too, that this system should be based upon the ordinary hundred law, — the only code known to England. Yet
all this did not create a jurisdiction in the eye of the law.
The great proprietor might discourage his dependants from
suing in the hundred court; he might assume upon himself
the responsibility for the acts of his dependants, and place
himself between them and the law, paying their fines, and
using his wealth and power to force all parties rather to accept his arbitration than appeal to legal process. But all
this did not remove his people from the jurisdiction of the
hundred court. It did not create a new jurisdiction in law.
It merely established an association analogous to the family,
which chose to settle its legal questions without bringing
them before the courts.[1]

In the tendency to establish such a private court of arbitration, the great landed proprietors appear to have been
actively supported by the crown. It is, indeed, not improbable that the large proprietors could essentially lighten the
task of the law courts, and facilitate the objects of royal policy, by looking sharply to the behavior of their dependants.
It is not improbable, too, that the lord of the manor did, on
the whole, offer more effective means for obtaining justice
and preserving order than could be possibly offered by the
hundred, with its clumsy organization and procedure. If to
these natural reasons for favoring the landlords there be
added the great pressure of the church and of the warriors
to obtain favors from the crown, it is not a matter of surprise
that the crown should have yielded to a tendency the ultimate effect of which it probably could not foresee.

The royal grants, so far as they affected the ordinary
course of justice, seem to have been double in their nature.
They were, in the first place, grants of the fines and pecuniary profits of jurisdiction, which, by the old system, fell to

---

[1] See the elaborate discussion of this subject, from the continental point of
view, in Roth's "Feudalität und Unterthanverband," Abschnitt 4, Das Seniorat.

the crown. This is entirely a fiscal arrangement, which only indirectly concerns the subject of jurisdiction. It was not intended to convey, and in fact it did not convey, the capacity of acting as a court of law.

Some examples of these grants may be given here : —

CXVI., Pilheard, 799–802. " Ego Pilheardus misellus comis . . . Cenwulfi . . . accipi eas [terras] in synodali conciliabulo . . . et per pecuniam . . . consecutus sum . . . ut ab omnium fiscalium redituum operum onerumque seu etiam popularium conciliorum vindictis nisi tantum praetium pro praetio liberae sunt in perpetuum."

CCXXVII., U Uiglaf of Mercia, 831. ". . . a pastu regum vel principum seu praefectum, ab omnique saeculari servitute notis et ignotis intus et foras liberabo nisi . . . singulare praetium contra alium.". . .

CCXXXVI., Ecgberht, 835. " Ego Ecgbert . . . dedi . . . Mercham . . . ad Abbendune . . . et sic mandamus . . . ut nullus superveniat hominum ibi superbia inflatus nec rex suum pastum requirat vel habentes homines quos nos dicimus *festigmen* nec eos qui accipitres portant vel falcones vel caballos ducunt sive canes. Nec poenam mittere super eos quoquomodo audeat nec princeps nec graphio hanc lenitatem praefatam in alicujus oneris molestiam mutare audeat . . . Si pro aliquo delicto accusatur homo dei, aecclesiae illae custos solus cum suo juramento si audeat illum castiget. Sin autem ut recipiat alienam justiciam hujus vicissitudinis conditionem praefatum delictum cum simplo praetio componat. . . . De illa autem tribulatione quae *witereden* nominatur sit libera nisi tamen singuli praetium solverit ut talia accipiant. Fures quoque quos appellant *weregeld theofas* si foris rapiantur, praetium ejus dimidium illi ecclesiae et dimidium regi detur; et si intus rapitur totum reddatur ad aecclesiam. . . . Praetium quoque sanguinis peregrinorum, id est *wergeld*, dimidiam partem rex teneat, dimidiam aecclesiae antedictae reddant."

CCL., Berhtwulf, 841. ". . . liberabo ab omnibus saecularibus servitutibus magnis vel modicis notis et ignotis regis et principis vel juniorum eorum, nisi in confinio rationem reddant adversus alium."

CCCXIII., Æthelred, 883. ". . . And nu ðaet ilce land aet Stoce . . . ic selle Cynulfe Ceoluhtes suna in ðreora manna daeg for syxtigum mancesa claenes goldes aeghwelces ðinges to freon ge wið cyning ge wið ealdorman ge wið gerefan aeghwelces ðeodomes lytles and micles butan . . ; angylde wið oðrum and noht ut to wite."

MLXXXIV., Edward, 904;[1] DXCVIII., Edgar, 978:—

". . . concessi ut episcopi homines tam nobiles quam ignobiles in praefato rure degentes, hoc idem jus in omni haberent dignitate quo regis homines perfruuntur regalibus fiscis commorantes, et omnium saecularium rerum judicia ad usus praesulum exerceantur eodem modo quo regalium negotiorum discutiuntur judicia. Praedictae etiam villae mercimonium quod Anglice ðaes tunes cyping appellatur, censusque omnis civilis... aecclesiae... deserviat.". ..

" Eadweard cyning . . . geuðe ðaet aegðer ge twelfhynde men ge twyhynde weron on ðam Godes hame ðara ylcan gerihta wyrðe ðe his agene men sindon on his agenum cynehamum; and man ealle spaeca and gerihtu on ðaet ilce gemet gefe to Godes handa ðe man to his agenre drifh, and ðes tunes cyping and seo innung ðara portgerihta gauge into ðere halgan stowe.". ..

These charters, unintelligible as their terms may appear to be, illustrate sufficiently well the fiscal side of the royal grants. They show the landlord exempted from all obligation to pay to the royal fisc, or to the ealdormen, any of those dues which the law gave them. They do not remove the occupants of these lands from the jurisdiction of the hundred court. They even expressly affirm the contrary. If such persons were convicted of a crime in the hundred or boundary court, they must, as usual, pay the *praetium pro praetio*, the *singulare praetium*, the *angyld*, — that is to say, all that atonement which the law exacted to redress the wrongs of the injured party. The exemption extended only to that portion of the money penalty which, by law, accrued to the fisc, or to the ealdorman. Nor is it to be supposed that the law here meant to benefit the criminal. It left the offender in the same position as before, except that his landlord stood, so far as the fine was concerned, in the place of the king. This process is fully described in No. CCXXXVI. There the abbot was authorized to appear for his man in the hundred court; to testify his innocence, if he could, with

---

[1] Mr. Kemble (Saxons in England, I. 177, n.) cites this charter as an admirable example of the grant of Sacu and Socn. The grant, however, is silent as to jurisdiction: it conveys only the profits of jurisdiction. See Krit. Uebers. II. 57, n.

merely his own oath; or, if he could not take the oath, to compound with the simple *angyld*. What the abbot might choose to do with the offender afterwards, did not concern the court, unless it gave rise to new proceedings at law. In regard to thieves caught with the stolen property within the exempted lands, it is by no means intimated that the abbot had the right to exercise jurisdiction over them, except so far as to admit them to ransom. By law, the thief so taken in the act necessarily forfeited his life.[1] It seems, however, to have been customary to enforce this law only against the very poor. Indeed, the amount of the *wergeld* of even the poorest freeman was enough to be an object of desire even to the fisc. Accordingly, the thief who could raise enough money to redeem himself was little likely to suffer death; and it became a question only as to the recipient of the fine. By this grant, the abbot was to receive it all, if the thief were taken in the act, before escaping from the privileged land; while, if he were caught beyond the boundary, the abbot received only half, the king maintaining his claim to the rest.

This privilege of appropriating the *wer* of thieves taken in the act is expressed in a different form in another class of charters, and has given rise to a theory which affirms the existence of a private criminal tribunal from very early times. Some eight or ten charters[2] contain passages like the following : —

". . . sint libera ab omni regali servitio, a pastu regum et principum, ducum et praefectum exactorumque, ab equorum et falconum accipitrumque et canum acceptione, et illorum hominum refectione quod nos *festingmenn* nominamus, a parafrithis, et ab omnibus difficultatibus regalis vel saecularis servitutis, notis et ignotis, *cum furis comprehensione* intus et foris, majoris minorisve." . . .

[1] See pp. 275 and n. 3, 276, 285, 286.

[2] CCXXIII., Ecgberht of Wessex, 828, I. 287; CCXLVI., Æthelwulf of Wessex, 840, II. 9; CCLIII., Æthelwulf, 842, II. 16; CCLXXXI., Æthilberht of Kent, 858, II. 64; CCC., Æthelred of Wessex, 869, II. 95; CCCXII., Æthelwulf, 880, II. 109; CCCCLXXXIII., Edgar, II. 368; MXLIX., Æthelwulf, 850, V. 95: DLV., Edgar, 969, III. 39; DCLXXXVI., Æthelred, 994, III. 275. See also DCCCLXXXVIII., Edward, IV. 228.

That a private criminal jurisdiction should be suddenly inserted in a long list of exemptions from the burdens of refection, of maintaining horses, hawks, and hounds, as well as men, of post-horses, and all other royal servitudes, great and small, would certainly be surprising. In point of fact, however, the thief caught in the act was considered here only in the light of property. His life was already forfeit. The king had the right to allow him to redeem his life,[1] and granted this right to the church, or other landed proprietors, not as a jurisdiction, but as a source of income. The idea is strongly expressed in the following charter, which, though a forgery, is good evidence for the present purpose: —

DLV., Edgar, 969. ". . . cuncta illius monasterii possessio nullis sit unquam gravata oneribus, nec expeditionis nec pontis et arcis edificamine, nec juris regalis fragmine, nec furis apprehensione, et ut omnia simul comprehendam nil debet exsolvi, nec regi nec regis praeposito, vel episcopo, vel duci, vel ulli homini, sed omnia debita exsolvant jugiter quae in ipsa dominatione fuerint ad supradictum sanctum locum." . . .

In the second place, apart from the fiscal character of these grants, it would appear that they were in some cases intended to exclude the royal officials entirely from the exempted territory, and to substitute the steward of the church or manor in the place of the sheriff, in all manner of legal acts. This side of the subject is, however, not altogether so clear as were to be wished; and its obscurity is all the more remarkable because of the distinctness with which the principle is

---

[1] The exemption finds its origin in the powers conferred by the customary law. The following paragraphs seem to explain the nature of these powers: —

Wihtraed, 26. "If any one seizes a freeman in the act of theft, let the king have power to do one of three things: either let him [the thief] be put to death, or sold over sea, or redeemed with his wer. Whoever seizes and secures him, let him have half; if he is put to death, let him [the captor] have seventy shillings."

Ine, 12. "If a thief be taken, let him suffer death, or let his life be redeemed with his wer. 28. Whoever captures a thief, let him receive X shill., and the king the thief."

Edgar, III. 7. ". . . And the open thief may seek whom he will: . . . he shall find no security for his life, unless the king grants him his protection."

avowed as the foundation of immunities in the contemporary continental charters. The formula observed by the Frankish kings is precise on this point: —

"... Nullus judex publicus ad causas audiendo aut freda undique exigendum nullo unquam tempore non praesumat ingredere ... neque vos neque juniores neque successores vestri nec nulla publica judiciaria potestas quoquo tempore in villas ubicunque in regno nostro ipsius ecclesiae ... aut ad audiendum altercationes ingredere aut freda de quaslibet causas exigere, nec mansiones aut paratas vel fidejussores tollere non praesumatis; sed quicquid exinde aut de ingenuis aut de servientibus caeterisque nationibus quae sunt infra agros vel fines seu supra terras praedictae ecclaesiae commanentes fiscus aut de freda aut undecunque potuerat sperare, ex nostra indulgentia pro futura salute in luminaribus ipsius ecclaesiae per manum agentum eorum proficiat in eternum."

This was a true immunity, clearly and fully defined in the grant. As will be seen, even this charter, wide as it was, did not create a jurisdiction. It did, however, on the one side, convey to the church all those sources of revenue which the fisc by law possessed within the church lands; while, on the other, it closed these lands to the royal officers, and gave the agents of the church the powers which the royal officers exercised. Naturally, a privilege of this sort could not fail to require continual modifications. One such is especially noteworthy. The Capitularies of Charlemagne (anno 803) define the extent of the immunity in the case of a thief or other criminal who has fled within the immunity. The sheriff is to demand his delivery, and each refusal entails on the church a heavy penalty. On the third refusal, the sheriff is authorized to enter the immunity by force; and, if resistance is offered, the offender incurs the heaviest penalty known to the early law.

If immunities like these existed in England, it would seem inevitable that they should have left indelible traces on the law. The terms of the English grants become, therefore, a subject of interest. The following are specimens of the fullest genuine powers conceded in extant charters: —

"LXIX., Æthilbald, 718. "... in omnibus rebus notis et ignotis, regis sive principis, libera permaneat." ...

LXXVII., Æthilbert, 732. ". . . jus regium in ea deinceps nullum reperiatur omnino excepto dumtaxat tale quale generale est in universis ecclesiasticis terris . . . in hac Cantia." . . .
CLXVI., Offa, 791–796. ". . . ut sit libera tam in terrarum donatione seu in omnibus causis parvis vel magnis . . . ut nullà secularis dignitas de nostra haereditate plus his in magno vel modico per vim aut petitionem aliquid exigat." . . .
CCLXXXI., Æthilberht, 858. ". . . ut omnium regalium tributum et vi exactorum operum et penalium rerum principali dominatione furisque comprehensione et cuncta seculari gravidine . . . immunis permaneat."
DCCVII., Æthelred, 1002. ". . . omni alieno permanent extranea dominio et cunctis poenalibus causis." . . .

Whether grants like these are to be understood as excluding the action of the royal officials to the same extent as is expressed in the continental grants of immunity, may be a question. The doubt is somewhat strengthened by the fact that there are charters which follow the continental formula, but which are in every instance, so far as I am aware, forgeries of a late period.[1]

So far as the charters are concerned, the evidence that private jurisdictions were known to the law of England, before the year 1000, is limited to the inferences that may be drawn from these grants. The best authorities seem now to be agreed that the argument, as based on these grants, fails to prove the existence of such private courts of law.

There is another argument, not yet so familiar, which may throw some further light upon the subject. The legal history of England, in its earlier stages, stands in curiously intimate connection with that of the Continent. English law was always more conservative than that of the Franks. It was more slowly affected by Roman jurisprudence. It adhered more persistently to the popular principles of its archaic constitution. It offered an equal resistance to the good and the bad of Frankish example, — to the equity as to the despotism of Charlemagne. But, although English law was affected slowly by that of the Continent, it was

[1] See, for example, Cod. Dip. DLV. (III. 43); DLXXV. (III. 93).

affected surely. Both in consolidation and in disintegration,
England was centuries behind the Continent; but, nevertheless, both consolidation and disintegration came at last, only
in forms somewhat less mischievous in their immediate effects, and much more beneficial in their ultimate results, than
was the case in the Empire and in France.

Yet, even on the Continent, where feudalism established
itself far earlier than in England, the creation of private
jurisdictions was a comparatively late event.[1] The first recorded attempt made to set up the authority of a private
court against that of the State tribunals was that of Bishop
Hincmar, of Laon, about the year 868. Down to this time,
there is no reason to suppose that either the spiritual or the
temporal lords had ever attempted to wrest jurisdiction from
the public courts. They had been content with the private
authority exercised by them and supported by the State, as
regarded their own families and dependants. Such authority, verging though it did upon the character of a legal tribunal, was not, as yet, recognized by the law in any other
character than that of a private association, which in no way
excluded the ultimate jurisdiction of the public courts. But
the utter dissolution of all political ties, which characterized
the condition of Northern France during the latter years of
the ninth and all the tenth century, created an absolute anarchy in the administration of justice. The public jurisdiction, in the absence of a central authority, fell into private
hands, and became an object of inheritance. The private
court of the landed proprietor acquired the character of a
court of law. The old courts of the grafs and the new courts
of the private lords became intermixed in a confusion that
was and still remains inextricable, and unintelligible to the
ordinary understanding.

But it so happened that the precise period which was so
fatal to the structure of European society was exceptionally

---

[1] Roth, Feudalität und Unterthanverband, Abschnitt IV., Das Seniorat;
Sohm, Altdeutsche Reichs-und Gerichtsverfassung, I. 351 ff. ; Zeitschrift für
Kirchenrecht, IX. 193–271, Die geistliche Gerichtsbarkeit im fränkischen
Reich; Heusler, Stadtverfassung, 17.

favorable to the quiet development of England. The struggle with the Danes, which marked the lowest point of England's power, was closed by Alfred and Guthrum's peace, about 880. Just as Northern Europe saw the last flickering ray of hope expire with the deposition of the Emperor in 887, England began to develop a degree of unity and political power which she had never before known. The partition of Mercia between Alfred and the Danes established the supremacy of Wessex beyond all future question. The abilities of Alfred, of his son Edward, and of his grandson Æthelstan, fortified this supremacy, and maintained the steady progress of national development during a period of half a century. The death of Æthelstan was followed by a moment of confusion; but the administrative skill of Oda and Dunstan soon restored order, which continued undisturbed till after the close of Edgar's reign in 975. Thus England passed in safety and content through all the darkest period of modern history, when every hope of happiness seemed extinguished in Northern France. During all this period, there was no time when the crown was in a position to make a sacrifice of its rights necessary or probable.

That private jurisdictions should have originated in England, before they existed on the Continent, is in the highest degree improbable. Not only did England take no such lead in the movement of the time, but there is not the slightest evidence of the existence of any such institution, and there is strong evidence to the contrary. That they should have originated during the vigorous reigns of the great Wessex monarchs, before 975, is also highly improbable in itself. Moreover, there is no period in all early English history when the course of law seems to have been so regular as during this century of comparative repose. The charters granted by these monarchs are dull, moderate, and uniform to the last degree. The laws are energetic, and the royal power efficient. In the absence of all evidence pointing to any collapse of the judicial constitution, and in the face of all the facts which testify to the extent and vigor of royal authority, it is mere unsupported assumption to infer that

there was any weakening in the bands of society, or any concession to private aggressions upon the rights of the crown,
before the death of Edgar, and the overthrow of Dunstan's
policy.

But, during the next half-century, the condition of England
was widely different. The reign of Æthelred the Unready was
marked by a series of disasters, each more destructive than
the last, and culminating in the absolute collapse of the royal
authority in 1013, and the deposition, or at least abdication,
of Æthelred, who retired to the Continent. Absolute political disorganization prevailed. The situation of England during these years was, in all essentials, identical with that of
the Continent one hundred years before. It is true that
neither the French nor the Germans had ever been reduced
to such humiliation as not only to depose their own king, but
to choose a Dane and a pagan to wear his crown, as was done
by the English in their submission to Swegen. It is also true
that the dissolution of all conceptions of political union was
hardly forced on the Continent to such an extremity as that
to which it was systematically carried in England by the policy of Ælfric and Eadric Streona. But, in all essentials, the
situation of England from 990 to 1017 was identical with
that of the Empire one hundred years before. It was a
situation of social and political anarchy.

It would seem natural to suppose that the effect upon the
judicial system of England must have been the same as on
that of the Continent. During these long years of disorder,
what was to prevent the great landed proprietors, with the
church at their head, from assuming powers which did not
legally belong to them? They protected their tenants and
dependants as well as they could in the absence of a protecting government. Their courts might naturally, in practice,
become courts of justice.

Nothing is known of the extent to which this movement
may have been carried before the restoration of order. When
a new government was established, the great house of Wessex no longer wore the crown. A foreigner sat on the
throne. Cnut was welcomed by the English people, who

never attempted to disturb his reign. On the other hand, he seems to have made no attempt to disturb their customs. He was not a great law-giver, like William and Henry II. He accepted the laws as he found them ; and the administration of justice remained where it was left by the wars.

Yet, notwithstanding the inherent probability of the thing; notwithstanding the contemporaneous existence of private courts of law on the Continent, with their natural influence on English society; notwithstanding the concurrent agreement of all modern writers that private jurisdictions did exist in the law of England at least from the time of Æthelred, — a careful examination of the evidence warrants the assertion that no contemporaneous evidence exists which will bear out any such theory. If such jurisdictions existed, they existed outside the law ; they existed not as a part of the constitutional system ; they received no countenance from the crown; they have left no trace on the contemporaneous records of the period.

Even a slight examination of the grounds on which the highest recent authorities have conceded the existence of private jurisdictions in the law of England, before the time of Edward the Confessor, — that is, the year 1042, — tends to raise a doubt as to their solidity. Mr. Kemble, while agreeing that there is no conclusive evidence that these tribunals existed before the time of Cnut, concludes " that they were so inherent in the land as not to require particularization " in legal documents, — a view which can hardly be considered as convincing even in regard to so defective a system of law as the Anglo-Saxon. Professor Stubbs has not expressed any very clear opinion upon the subject, but may perhaps be considered as accepting generally the views of K. Maurer and Dr. Schmid. Professor Maurer rests his argument on the following passage from the laws : [1] —

Æthelred, III. 6. " . . . And let every vouching to warranty, and every ordeal, be in the king's burg." . . .

Even from this, however, he draws only a cautious conclu-

[1] Krit. Ueb. II. 58.

sion, that at the utmost it can only be thought to imply that, in other respects than warranty and ordeal, some courts which were not the king's courts may have had competence. Even this cautious suggestion, however, can hardly be admitted. The meaning of the passage is obscure. Team and ordeal would seem to have been essential elements in every legal tribunal. They appear to have been always conveyed or implied in the subsequent grants of sac and soc. On the whole, the most reasonable interpretation of the clause would seem to be that the informal exercise of these legal processes before the manorial lords was becoming usual; and that this law of Æthelred prohibited the abuse, and enjoined upon the suitors a strict observance of the old law, which recognized no tribunal competent to administer its forms, except the courts of the hundred and the shire. Thus this passage would rather tend to prove that private jurisdictions, though beginning to exist in custom and for convenience, by consent of the parties, were not legal, and were even prohibited by law.

Dr. Schmid, however, quotes another passage from Æthelred's laws, which, at first sight, seems conclusive : —

Æthelred, III. 11. "And let no man have socn over a king's thane except the king himself."

Dr. Schmid translates " socn " here as " jurisdiction." So, also, does Professor Stubbs, and so do all other authorities. It becomes necessary, therefore, to turn aside for a moment, in order to make some inquiry into the history of this word.

The invaluable Glossary, which Dr. Schmid has appended to his edition of the Anglo-Saxon Laws, tells us that *sócn* is a derivative of *sêcan*, which is identical with our modern verb *seek*. It is frequently used in all branches of Anglo-Saxon literature, and in a number of combinations; as, for example : —

1. Land-socn, visitatio terrae, land-seeking. Caedmon.

2. Hlaford-socn, lord-seeking, the search for a lord, in order to place one's self under his protection, or in his service. Æthelstan, III. 4 ; IV. 5 ; V. 1, § 1. Alfred, 37.

3. Ham-socn, ham-fare, invasio domus, the seeking of a house for hostile purposes. Hen. 80, § 11.

4. Fyrd-socn, fyrd-faru, expeditio, army-seeking, — one branch of the trinoda necessitas. Cod. Dip. CCCXIII. 883; DCLXXV. 990; DCLXXVI. 991.

5. Ciric-socn, church-seeking, the privilege of sanctuary, sought by persons in danger of life or liberty. Ine, 5; Alfred, 5.

6. Frith-socn, peace-seeking, the general peace enjoyed by the king, the church, &c., in behalf of suppliants who sought it. Æthelred, VIII. 1; Cnut, I. 2, § 3.

It is not pretended that, in any of these cases, jurisdiction is to be understood. In fact, the terms of the law, in mentioning the ciric-socn and frith-socn, exclude the possibility of such an idea. The following passages from the laws of Æthelstan define the nature of the frith-socn for the various ranks of society who enjoyed it: —

Æthelstan, IV. 6. " Et sic fur . . . nullo modo vita dignus habeatur, non per socnam non per pecuniam. . . .

§ 1. " Si regem vel archiepiscopum requirat vel sanctam dei ecclesiam, habeat novem noctes de termino. . . .

§ 3. " Si comitem vel abbatem vel aldermannum vel thaynum requirat, habeat terminum tres noctes." . . .

In a subsequent council, further provisions are added: —

Æthelstan, V. 4, § 2. " And, if any one slay the thief within this term, then let him pay the mund-byrd of the person whom the thief sought, or take an oath of twelve that he did not know of the socn."

§ 3. " And the thief may seek whatever socn he will; yet shall he not have a right to his life, except for so many days as is above ordained." . . .

Again, in the laws of Edmund, the same use of the word is to be found: —

Edmund, II. 4. " I also give notice that I will give no socn to any one of my household who has shed man's blood, before he has done penance to the church, and has agreed with the kin for the amends." . . .

This kind of socn contains no pretence of jurisdiction. It merely invests individuals or places with the privilege of affording a limited asylum to fugitives from justice or violence, after the expiration of which the law shall take its course.

There was, however, another and wider sense in which the word *sôcn* was used. In this sense, it indicates the sum of the fiscal privileges enjoyed by lands which the king and witan had freed from fiscal burdens, and .to which they had granted the proceeds of fines, &c., as heretofore described. In this use, the word is merely synonymous with the Anglo-Saxon formula, "Mid eallan ðam gerihtum and ðam witan ðe ðaerof arisað;" as, for example: —

Cod. Dip. MCCXCVIII., 1002; DCCX., 1004. ". . . Mortun and eal seo socna ðe ðaerto hereð." . . .

A curious illustration of this meaning of the word is afforded by a diversity in the text of Cnut's law. The ordinary reading of Cnut, II. 73, § 1, is as follows: —

"And sy he his weres scyldig wið ðone cyning oððe wið ðone ðe hit geunnen haebbe."

"And let him forfeit his wer to the king, or to him to whom the king may have granted it."

Codex G. substitutes the words "*his sôcne*" as equivalent for the word "*hit*," so that socn can here only mean the right to receive the wer, — the same right which has already been described as expressly specified in the charters.

Other cases of the same nature occur, all pointing to the same conclusion: —

Cnut, II. 63. "Gif hwa reaf-lac gewyrce, agife and forgylde and beo his weres scyldig wið ðone cyningc [oððe wið ðone ðe his socne age. Codex G.]."

"If any one take by force another's property, let him return it, and its value, and forfeit his wer to the king [or to whoever has his socn. Cod. G.]."

Cnut, II. 37. ". . . Gylde ðam cyninge oððe landrican be healsfange."

Codex G. ". . . Gylde ðam cyninge oððe landrican ðe his socne ah, be healsfange."

"Let him forfeit his halsfang (ten shillings) to the king [or to the manorial lord who has his socn. Codex G.]."

In all these cases, there is no reason for supposing that jurisdiction is implied in the word *sôcn*. The idea expressed is always that of the charters. It is the profits of justice, and not the justice itself. To add to the plain statements of the charters an implied grant of jurisdiction, is mere gratuitous assumption, unsupported by a particle of evidence. The same rule of interpretation applies also to the clause cited by Dr. Schmid, as given above, — " Let no man have socn over a king's thane except the king himself." That is, let no man claim to exact a forfeiture or fine from a king's thane except the king himself. This was merely another and more concise way of expressing the same idea that is set forth in the earlier legislation of the same king : —

Æthelred, I. 1, § 14. " And let the king be entitled to all the forfeitures of such as hold book-land ; and let no man make composition on any accusation, unless with the witness of the king's reeve."

So the Latin version of the Confessor's charter to Abbot Ordric of Abingdon (Cod. Dip. DCCCXL., IV. 200) renders " swa ðaet nan scyrgerefe oððe motgerefe ðar habban aeni socne oððe gemot " by " sic ut nullus vicecomes vel praepositus ibi habeant aliquam appropriationem seu placitum." [1]

And, finally, the same meaning is perfectly appropriate to the mention in Cnut, 71, 3, of " a king's thane among the Danes, who has his socn," his freedom from fiscal burdens, and his rights to the profits of justice.

Dr. Schmid cites one more example, also from Codex G., to illustrate his view : —

Cnut, II. 62. " Gif hwa ham-socne gewyrce, gebete ðaet mid fif pundan ðam cyningce on Engla-lage [and on Cent aet ðam socne V. ðam cinge and threo ðam arcebisceope]."

Dr. Schmid considers " aet ðam socne " to mean here, again, jurisdiction. But this is obviously a very forced interpretation. A reference to the before-mentioned law of Æthelstan, V. 4, § 2, sufficiently illustrates the meaning of the later law.

In point of fact, no instance can be found, before Norman

[1] See also DCCCLXXXVIII., IV. 228.

times, in which *sôcn* means jurisdiction. *Sôcn* had a
technical meaning of its own, which is always rigorously
observed. The idea of jurisdiction, on the other hand, was
expressed by an equally technical word, the meaning of which
is also rigorously observed. This is *sacu*, a word which has
strangely vanished from our legal vocabulary, but is still preserved, even in its technical sense, by the German *sache*.
Another expression is also found, *spraec* or *spaec*, meaning
placitum, or lawsuit; but *sacu*, *saca*, or abbreviated *sac*, is
the legal term most commonly adopted. It is found in the
early laws of Kent, and in the late laws of the Norman
kings; it is used throughout the charters, and never in any
doubtful sense. *Sacu* in all the early literature, meant a
suit at law. When joined with *sôcn* in a royal grant, the
intention is to convey to the grantee *placita et forisfacturas*,
— pleas and forfeitures, justice and the profits of justice.

Dr. K. Maurer, while conceding that the evidence is far
from convincing in regard to the existence of private law-
courts before Cnut's accession, goes on to say : " But all the
more certain is it that, from the reign of Cnut, the manorial
jurisdiction appears in its most complete development; innumerable charters, from his and his successors' hands, grant or
confirm the same ; so that the expressions, sac and socn, toll
and team, aðas and ordalas, &c., occur on almost every page
of the Codex Diplomaticus." [1]

Here, again, careful criticism can only express dissent. So
far as Dr. Maurer's statement concerns the charters of Cnut,
investigation will show that it is in error. He has himself
given no instances of such charters. The Codex Diplomaticus contains only two such, which offer even an appearance
of authenticity. One of these (MCCCXIX., VI. 183) is
an evident forgery, which hardly needs notice. The other
(MCCCXXVII., VI. 190) does not even purport to be an
original document; and the paraphrase is so carelessly made
that, if Mr. Kemble's version is trustworthy, the name of the
king himself is omitted among the signatures; and that of
Earl Harold is made to appear in a charter which must have

[1] Krit. Ueber. II. 58.

been executed about the year he was born, — apparently, a copyist's mistake for Earl Hacun. Neither of these documents can be allowed to carry any weight whatever in opposition to the uniformly and rigorously conservative character of all the authentic laws, letters, and charters of Cnut's reign.

So far, then, as contemporary evidence is concerned, there is no more reason for attributing to Cnut the first legal recognition of private jurisdictions than there is for attributing it to Alfred or Ine.   The subsequent reign of Edward the Confessor must be invoked, in order to supply even the shadow of a direct proof that these private law-courts were recognized by Cnut. Here, indeed, something which seems a positive assertion of the fact may be found, as, for example, in the grant of jurisdiction to St. Austin's (Cod. Dip. DCCCXXXI., DCCCCII.): ". . . Habeo has consuetudines deo datas et sancto Augustino . . . ita pleniter et libere sicut melius habuerunt tempore praedecessoris mei Knuti regis."   And again, in the corresponding grant to St. Paul's (Cod. Dip. DCCCLXXXVII., Cf. MCCCXIX.): ". . . Let them have their saca and their socne, within burg and without, and as good laws, so full and so far as they were best in any king's day or in any bishop's, in all things."   But the force of such an expression is weakened by the looseness of its application, as, for example, in DCCCLVIII.: " . . . I have given to . . . Westminster the land at Shepperton, with all that belongs thereto, and with saca and with socne, scotfree and gafelfree, from hundred and shire, as full and as far as Saint Dunstan bought it, and granted it to the minster." [1]   Either legal memories were very short in Edward's reign, or these expressions are to be understood as mere chancery .formulas, which record the freedom of the land without pretending to record the past stages in the development of this freedom.

But, from the moment that Edward the Confessor ascended the throne, a new theory of constitutional law makes itself apparent in the form as well as in the matter of the

[1] See also Cod. Dip. DCCCXVI., IV. 190; DCCCXXVII., IV. 190.

royal charters. And, if it be remembered that the Confessor was half Norman by birth, and wholly Norman by education and sympathies; that he filled the offices in his chancery, so far as was in his power, by Normans; and that he appears, at least at times, to have attempted to make the Duke of Normandy his successor on the English throne, — it is little surprising that his constitutional practice should have been Norman also. But, apart from these Norman tendencies of the king, there were other causes in operation to. alter the English constitution. A single great English family overshadowed the whole of England with its wealth and power, and absorbed and embodied the political influence of the Witan. That Godwine and his sons were little inclined to look with favor on the foreign tastes of the king, is probably true. But their situation compelled them to yield, wherever concession was compatible with their own security; and there is nothing in the recorded character of any one of them which makes it probable that they took any wider views of public policy than such as were selfish and superficial. In the whole history of the Anglo-Saxon period, there is not one example of an original and progressive law-giver. Godwine and his sons appear to have had the virtues and the faults of their race. They were not men of that stamp of mind which would hazard power for the sake of a constitutional theory that in itself was indifferent to their own immediate interests.

A few examples of Edward's charters will show the nature of the changes in constitutional practice: —

The first of the citations to be made is interesting upon many accounts, but, among others, for the reason that, as has been already noticed, Cnut's name appears in it. Its date is between 1042 and 1050, — early, therefore, in the Confessor's reign.

DCCCXXXI.

Eadward king gret Ealsige archebisceop and Godwine eorl and ealle mine ðegnes on Kent

DCCCCII.

Ego Eadwardus dei gratia rex Anglorum Eadsio archiepiscopo et Godwino comiti et omnibus

freondlice, and ic kyðe eow ðaet ic habbe geunnen Sancte Augustine and ðam gebroðram ðe ðerto hyreð ðaet haebbe on heora saca wurðe and heora socna and griðbrices and hamsocne and forstealles and infangeneðeofes and flymenesfyrmðe ofer heora agene menne binnan burh and butan, tolles and teames, on strande and on streame, and ofer swa fele ðegna swa ic heom habbe togelaeten ; and ic nelle ðaet aeni man aeni ðing ðaron teo buton heom and heore ðienesse ðe hie hit betaeche willan, forðan ic habbe forgefen Sancte Augustine ðas gerihta minre sawle to alesidnesse swa full and swa forð swa hi hit formeste hefden on Cnutes dagum kinges, and ic nelle geðafian ðaet aeni man ðis abreca bi mine freondscipe. God eow geheolde.

suis baronibus Cantiae, salutem. Sciatis me dedisse deo ac Sancto Augustino et fratribus ut habeant eorum saca et socna et pacis fracturam et pugnam in domo factam et viae assultus et latrones in terra sua captos latronumque susceptionem vel pastionem super illorum proprios homines infra civitatem et extra, theloneumque suum in terra et in aqua, atque consuetudinem quae dicitur teames, et super omnes allodiarios quos eis habeo datos. Nec volo consentire ut aliquis in aliqua re de hiis se intromittat nisi eorum praepositi quibus-ipsi haec commendaverint, quia habeo has consuetudines deo datas et Sancto Augustino pro redemptione animae meae ita pleniter et libere sicut melius habuerunt tempore praedecessoris mei Knuti regis ; et nolo consentire ut aliquis haec infringat sicuti meam amicitiam vult habere.

This document purports to be simply a confirmation of the jurisdiction which the church of St. Austin's had enjoyed in the reign of Cnut. It does not purport to be done by the advice or consent of the Witan. It is totally different in its form, in its import, and in its effect, from any grant ever made before this time. It is Norman, not Anglo-Saxon. The writ itself was not a novelty : its use in this manner was one. But, even where the old form is retained, as for example in the royal charter to Harold's great religious foundation at Waltham, the grant is essentially different, and far more comprehensive than the old grants. Not content with conferring, in the body of this instrument, the usual jurisdiction, known as " sacha et soche, tol et team," &c., the king added

a special paragraph, apparently to extend the privileges still
further : —

DCCCXIII., 1062.   ". . . Ego Eadwardus, nutu divino rex, omnia praedia quae Haroldus comes monasterio apud Waltham subjecit,
vel quae adhuc se daturum decernit, sublevans statuo, ut ab omni servitutis jugo sint semper libera, et a shiris et hundredis, et extra curiam
sanctae crucis omnibus placitis et omnibus geldis." [1]

As the grant previously quoted purported to be a mere
writ confirmatory of prescriptive privileges, so this formal
charter may be intended only to raise the new monastery to
the same dignity as was enjoyed by the older foundations.
It is, therefore, interesting to ascertain whether the Confessor
habitually granted by simple writ, without mention of the
Witan, rights of jurisdiction avowedly new, and belonging, as
he conceived, not to the state, but to himself.   The following
writ, which must have been issued about 1045, in the earliest
years of the Confessor's reign, seems sufficient evidence on
this point.   It begins by confirming a gift of land made by
his housecarl, Thurstan, to the king's favorite foundation of
Westminster : —

DCCCXLIII.

Eadweard kyng gret Rodberd
biscop and Osgod Clapa and
Ulf sciregerevan and ealle mine
ðeignes and mine holdan freond
on Middelsexan freondlice. ic
kyðe eow ðaet ic wille and ðaet
ic ann ðaet Sancte Peter and ða
gebroðra on Westmynstre [hab-
ben] to heora bileoven ðaet land
aet Cealchylle . . . swa Ðurstan
min huskarll hit furmest of me
heold and into ðaere halgan
stowwe geaf. And ic ðaes fullice geuðe and ic an heom eoft
ealswa ðaet hy habben ðaerofer

Ego Eadwardus rex Rodberdo
episcopo et Osgod Clapae, et
Ulfo vicecomiti et omnibus meis
thanis et fidelibus amicis in Mid-
delsexia benevole salutem dico.
Vobis notum facio me velle et
consentire ut S. Petrus et fratres
Westmon. in eorum convictum habeant praedium istud quod est in
Cealchylle . . . tam plene et libere quam praefectus meus pala-
tinus Thurstanus ea primo ex me
tenuit et sacro dein loco donavit.
Quod quidem donum ego plane
corroboro, iis iterum etiam con-

[1] See also DCCCXVII. (IV. 165), grant of freedom "de schiris et hundredis." DCCCLVIII. (IV. 213); DCCCXXVIII. (IV. 191).

saca and socna, toll and team, in-
fangeneðeof and flemenefyrmðe,
and ealle oðre gerihtu on eallum
ðingum ðe ðar uppaspringað. . . .
And ic wille and faestlice be-
beode be fulre wite ðaet ðeos
mundbyrdnesse beo strang and
staðelfaest into ðaere halgan
stowe a on ece erfe. Amen.

cedens ut insuper habeant privi-
legium tenendi curiam ad causas
cognoscendas et dirimendas lites
inter vassallos et colonos suos
ortas, cum potestate transgresso-
res et calumniae reos mulctis
afficiendi easque levandi, porro
etiam ut ibi habeant in vendendis
et emendis mercibus a tolneto
immunitatem, cum privilegio habendi totam suorum servorum
propaginem ; potestatem etiam
fures in terra sua cum re furtiva
deprehensos in jus vocandi et pu-
niendi, cum privilegio fugitivos
suscipiendi et omnia alia jura
quae omnimodo exinde oritura
sunt. . . . Volo igitur et firmiter
mando sub poena gravissima ut
haec confirmatio nostra in loco
illo sancto aeternae haereditatis
vim et firmitatem semper obti-
neat. Amen.

Another expression, in a charter already quoted, is of
peculiarly Norman origin (DCCCXXXI., DCCCCII.) : —

". . . ic habbe geunnen sancte
Augustine . . . ðaet haebbe on
heora saca wurðe and heora socna
. . . ofer swa fele ðegna swa ic
heom habbe togelaeten." . . .

"Sciatis me dedisse S. Augustino . . . ut habeant eorum saca
et socna . . . super omnes allodiarios quos eis habeo datos."

Another similar charter, of a date probably not later than
1046,[1] confirms a similar gift, likewise with a special royal
supplementary grant of jurisdiction : " And icc an ðat sainte
Petre habbe ofer ðam, saca and socne, toll and team, infan-
geneðef and alle oðere richte ða to me belimpað." [2]

[1] DCCCXXVIII., IV. 191.
[2] See also Cod. Dip. DCCCLXI., IV. 214; DCCCLXII., IV. 215;
DCCCLXIV., IV. 217; DCCCLXIX., IV. 219; DCCCLXXXIX., IV. 228.

It is needless to offer further evidence on this point. The Confessor's charters frequently, not to say habitually, convey the most important rights of jurisdiction into private hands: they do so by simple writ, without suggesting the concurrence of the Witan ; and they do so on the ground that the jurisdiction is the property of the king in his private capacity, and may be alienated at his pleasure. In the same way, Edward conferred the highest offices in the church, granting investiture to the bishop by simple writ, which contained no reference to the concurrence of the Witan. Whether the Witan, in point of fact, were consulted or not, is another question. So far, at least, as the Confessor's theory of government was concerned, it seems to have been little, if at all, different from that of William the Conqueror.

Nor is it to be supposed that these grants went no further than to confer here and there, on favored religious communities, the privilege of a private court of justice. Towards the close of his reign, Edward appears to have adopted the settled policy of granting to all religious bodies the jurisdiction which had previously belonged to the state tribunals. The form of this grant was a writ, of which the following may serve as a specimen, as it happens to be given in both languages, although the omitted portions contain details more elaborate than were customary at a later day, and although this writ happens exceptionally to be witnessed, but only by the queen, her father Godwine, and her brother Harold. The presence of Godwine and the name of Archbishop Stigand show that this document belongs to the year 1052–1053. Another curious point in it is the mention of Gyrth as eorl in East Anglia, over Norfolk and Suffolk, four years before the date commonly assigned to his appointment.[1] This fact may well throw a doubt over the genuineness of the names given as witnesses to the writ, but not necessarily on the writ itself.

DCCCLIII.

Eadward cyng gret Stigand ercebiscop and Aegelmaer biscop

Eadwardus rex Anglorum Stigando archiepiscopo, Ailmaro epis-

---

[1] Freeman, Hist. Norman Conquest, II. 566.

and Gyrð eorl and Toli scirreve and ealle his ðeines inne Norð-folce and inne Suffolce and ealle his oðra witen ofer eall Ænglande hadede and leawede freondlice; . . . And in aelcer scire ðaer sanctus Benedictus hafð land inne his saca and his socne, tol and team, and infangenðeof, wiðinne burhe and wiðuten and on aelce styde be lande and be strande, be wude and be felde, swa huilc man swa ða socne ahe, sanctus Bene-dictus habbe his freodom on eal-len ðingen swa wel and swa fre-olice swa ic hit meseolf betst ahe ahwaer in Engelande. . . .

copo, Girð comiti, Toli vicecomiti, et omnibus ministris suis de Norð-folke and Suðfolke et universis aliis fidelibus suis per totam An-gliam constitutis tam clericis quam laicis, salutem. . . . In omni co-mitatu ubi sanctus Benedictus habet terram concedo eis sacam et socam suam, tol et team et in-fangeneðef, infra burgum vel civi-tatem et extra, ubique in terra et aqua, in bosco et plano, cujuscun-que fuerit soca, habeat sanctus Benedictus libertatem suam in omnibus ita bene et plene sicut ego ipse alicubi habeo in tota Anglia. . . .

Similar grants are still extant, conferring similar im-munities on the Archbishop of Canterbury and Christ's Church, Canterbury (DCCCCIX.); the Archbishop of York (DCCCXCIII.); the Abbot of Malmesbury (DCCCXVII.); the Abbey of Westminster (DCCCLXXXIX.); St. Æthil-bert's Minster, in Hereford (DCCCLXVII.); St. Paul's Minster, in London (DCCCLXXXVII.); St. Mary's, in Abingdon (DCCCLXXXVIII.); and St. Edmondsbury (DCCCXCIV.), besides those heretofore quoted. Nor was this all. So absolute was the Confessor's property in the justice of his kingdom, that he granted entire hundreds out-right into the hands of the church, as in the case of Godde-lie hundred, which was given to the Abbot of St. Peter's, in Chertsey (DCCCXLIX.). How far these grants were merely confirmations of powers already existing, in fact if not in law, and how far they were new and revolutionary, is not a point capable of exact settlement; yet the language of the charters already quoted is enough to show that the intention of the grantor was to convey new privileges, and, in a number of these writs, he gives his reasons for doing so: "forðam icc nelle geðafian ðat aenig man undo ða gife ðe icc

ðider inn geunnen habbe, oððe ðaet ðaer aenig man aenigne
onsting habbe on aenigum ðingum oððe on aenigne timan
buton se abbod and ða gebroðra to ðes mynstres nytðarflicre
neode." This purpose of rendering the churches more secure
from external encroachment, whether of the royal officials or
of private persons, is mentioned in two charters which belong to the earliest years of Edward's reign (DCCCLXX.,
DCCCLXXII.), and frequently afterwards. The adoption
of such a principle could not be limited in application. There
can be no doubt that the Confessor's love for the church and
his Norman education combined to make this application natural and easy.

To what extent Edward's sweeping grants of jurisdiction
to the church followed or preceded the silent assumption of
judicial powers by private hands, is a question in regard to
which only surmise is possible. From the evidence furnished
above, it is clear that the peculiarity of the constitutional
changes effected by Edward was, that they were not partial,
but general; that they mark an entire revolution in men's
conceptions of fundamental law, not in their mere habits;
and that they affected not one, but all classes of the community. From the moment that the state jurisdiction began
to be looked upon as property, the change was inevitable.
Down to that time, it was impossible. The Confessor was
the first English king to whom such a conception of law
would have seemed natural. His acts, not merely in reference to jurisdiction, but throughout his career, show that he
was not an Anglo-Saxon, but a Norman, king. It was he
who introduced the worst maxims of government into England ; and, whatever abuses may have existed before his time
in the practice of judicial administration, it was he and his
advisers who revolutionized the law.

There can be little doubt, however, that the actual change
produced by Edward's new principles, on the mere habits of
the people, was not a violent one. If the views above suggested are at all correct, the most potent agent in undermin-
ing the authority of the old judicial system was the loose
popular practice of administering the law. In a legal system

so crude that it was almost an invariable habit not to press suits to a conclusion, but to compromise them, in order to escape the consequences, the delays, or the uncertainties of strict law, arbitration was a more attractive resort, in nine cases out of ten, than the ordinary judgment of a regular tribunal. The collection of cases given in the Appendix shows how habitually suitors accepted the informal decision of their friends. But, apart from arbitration, they were in every way tempted to ignore the public tribunals. It required only their consent to invest the neighboring manorial lord with all the powers of a hundred court. There was no reason why the oath, the ordeal, the vouching to warranty, and all the other common forms of hundred procedure, should not take place before the lord as well as before the sheriff, if the parties so agreed ; and there was every reason why the parties, when occupants of land under the same lord, should so agree. The profits of justice already belonged to him by grant. It was perfectly natural that the mere forms of justice customary in the public courts should be adopted by him in the settlement of cases voluntarily brought to him for decision. The mere practice of these forms before him was in itself no more a violation of the law than the use of any other forms would have been. It did not exclude the authority of the public tribunal. It rested on the consent of the parties. It was probably a convenience to suitors. The settlement, when reached, was only binding in law so far as it was the result of a formal contract. In all probability, the weight of the lord's private authority was alone sufficient to enforce his decision, without the necessity of an appeal for the performance of such a contract in the public courts.

Thus, to the ordinary Englishman, Edward's reckless grants of jurisdiction to the church may probably have seemed innocent. It is very possible that they produced little immediate effect on the habits of suitors. At all events, not a whisper of complaint has come down to us against Edward on this account. Yet the revolution, however easy, was not the less fatal to the old Anglo-Saxon constitution. After Edward's reign, as before, the freemen met in their courts of law, heard pleas and decided them, as they had done from time immemorial. It mattered not so much to them whether the king's, the abbot's, or the lord's reeve presided over their court, as it did that whoever presided should not abuse his power. But the theory of the constitution was irretrievably lost. Justice no longer was a public trust, but a private property. The recognition of the legality of private tribunals for the church was a recognition of the legality of private tribunals in general. England was soon covered with new courts of law, endowed, by royal favor or by prescriptive use, with judicial functions of the most diverse nature over territories inextricably interwoven and confused. Some of these territories were complete states in themselves, like the counties palatine of Durham and of Chester. Some were completely organized as counties. Far the larger number, however, had only the jurisdiction of a hundred court. The entire judicial system of England was torn in pieces; and a new theory of society, known as feudalism, took its place.

With the hopeless confusion of jurisdictions which followed the collapse caused by the Confessor in the Anglo-Saxon system, this is not the place to deal. From the moment that private courts of law become a recognized part of the English judicature, the Anglo-Saxon constitution falls to pieces, and feudalism takes its place. Yet whatever historical interest the manorial system possesses, as a part of the English judicial constitution, is due to the fact that its origin was not feudal, but Anglo-Saxon. The manor was a private hundred, so far as its judicial powers were concerned. The law administered in the manorial court was hundred law; the procedure was hundred procedure; the jurisdiction, like that of the hundred, was controlled by the shire. The manor was but a proprietary hundred, and, as such, has served, during many centuries, to perpetuate the memory of the most archaic and least fertile elements of both the Saxon and the feudal systems.

THE ANGLO-SAXON LAND LAW.

HARDLY any branch of early Teutonic law is more obscure than that which forms the subject of this essay. Modern investigation has been comparatively slight, and, on the whole, unsatisfactory. This does not arise entirely from a lack of material. The codes, it is true, are but meagre in all that relates to the ownership of land; but the charters of the Anglo-Saxon period are numerous, and rich in detail. It is this very abundance of detail which has proved the chief stumbling-block to scholars of the present day. The intricacy and confusion in the grants, wills, settlements, and the like, are, in a measure, to blame for the faulty methods of treatment, which thus far have only brought out a few of the most prominent features of the subject. The land law of the Anglo-Saxons, like all their other law, is based on a few simple and fundamental conceptions. The extreme clumsiness of the Anglo-Saxon mind is apparent to any one who has closely studied their early legal history; and this mental awkwardness led them to cling to their primitive ideas, with a tenacity unequalled, except among the Scandinavian races, by the kindred continental tribes. Another effect of these intellectual qualities was not so happy. As society progressed, the old principles, which had been all-sufficient in the German forests, proved inadequate to the new requirements. Instead of making such additions as altered circumstances demanded, they twisted their old methods, invented numberless details, added here and diminished there, as the momentary stress impelled them, and suffered the inevitable changes and the new conceptions to work their way, without assistance, into general acceptance. The result, as might easily be foreseen, was, that the law slowly developed, more and more encumbered in each succeeding generation with a mass of contradictory and well-nigh impossible details, which at this day are absolutely appalling. The law of real property, too, was really nothing but a collection of customs. It may be fairly said that there is hardly any law, in the exact definition of the term, existing on the subject. To enhance all this, their legal thought and expression were loose, ill-defined, and clumsy to the last degree. Many eminent writers have endeavored to extract, from the authorities, evidences of a system, rounded, defined, and of arithmetical proportions. But, if contemporaneous Anglo-Saxon histories and charters show any thing, they prove that such a system did not exist, — that it was something inconceivable to the Anglo-Saxon mind.

Unfavorable as many circumstances were, the purity of the race, the isolated condition of the country, and the very slowness and tenacity of intellect already referred to, gave a scientific development to the pure Germanic law hardly to be found elsewhere. Free from the injurious influences of the Roman and Celtic peoples, the laws and institutions of the ancient German tribes flourished and waxed strong on the soil of England. If the Anglo-Saxon laws are not as absolutely untainted as those of their kindred in Sweden, Denmark, Norway, and Iceland, they developed to more purpose. Strong enough to resist the power of the church in infancy, stronger still to resist the shock of Norman invasion, crushed then, but not destroyed, by foreign influences, the great principles of Anglo-Saxon law, ever changing and assimilating, have survived in the noblest work of the race, — the English common law. The early law of real property is not so rich in marked and imperishable principles as many other branches; but it was based on certain strong conceptions, some of which have endured, while others, long since vanished, possess now only historical importance. It is the purpose of this essay to attempt a classification of these conceptions or principles, — to prove their existence, and trace the outlines, as the case may be, of their growth or their decay. Starting with the belief that the mass of intricate details in which the subject is involved are objects only of antiquarian curiosity, every thing not directly tending to the illustration or elucidation of the main and leading ideas will be rigidly excluded.

The first difficulty which meets the inquirer is to ascertain how many kinds of land resting on fundamentally different conceptions were known to the Anglo-Saxons. If difference of origin be taken as the only standard of distinction, there were two, — estates originating in a written instrument, and estates originating in custom ; or, in briefer form, estates that were created by book (boc-land), and estates that were not so created. The latter class falls into three subdivisions, — estates of the family or individual (family land) ; estates of a corporation, like the mark, thorpe, or hundred (the common land) ; finally, estates of the nation or state (the folc-land). These three subdivisions are severally so important, and so distinct from each other, that, for a complete answer to our first question, it is necessary to admit four sorts of land, — boc-land and the three subdivisions of the opposite class. An examination of these four great classes ought to result in a thorough understanding of Anglo-Saxon land law. The only portion not necessarily covered by them is the law of dower in lands, which requires separate treatment.

Before proceeding with this investigation, it becomes necessary to consider briefly two preliminary points, — the distribution of the various kinds of land with reference to each other, and taxation.

Nothing has proved a more fruitful cause of unnecessary misconception and difficulty than a failure to appreciate the relative distribution of lands. Much labor and ingenuity have been vainly expended in evolving theories as to the mode of division of the territory of Britain adopted by German invaders. Analogy with the methods in vogue among the Continental tribes is misleading, because the circumstances were different. Two theories are discussed by Dr. Konrad Maurer, — either the conquerors divided the land in accordance with fixed rule as they advanced ; or, after the first period of war and confusion, a rearrangement took place according to established forms. Dr. Maurer [1] gives his adhesion to the first of these views. Whether the first theory be accepted and the second rejected, or *vice versa*, or whether, as seems most probable, the distribution was regulated by a system which was a mixture of both, the ultimate question, and the only really important one, is as to the relative distribution of lands at the period when contemporaneous authorities begin. In order to simplify the matter as far as possible, let all England be regarded as a political unit. The whole territory may then be taken to represent a vast area of folc-land ; the lands of individuals or families, of communities and of the book, being scattered throughout its length and breadth, like oases in a desert. Roughly speaking, this represents not unfairly the geographical distribution of lands. The same person could, and often did, hold estates of all the kinds thus intermingled. One well-known example suffices to prove this statement. Duke Alfred bequeathed family land, boc-land, folc-land, or certain definite parcels of the same,[2] and appendant rights in common land, and these estates, as appears by the same document, lay in various parts of the country. It is further evident, from this instance, that the same person might be a member of several communities, all widely separated. To better illustrate this last point, a charter of Æthelwulf of Wessex, A.D. 839, may be cited. The grant is of a vill lying within the walls of Dover, and twenty-three acres pertaining thereto in various parts of the *civitas*.[3] Here the king — holding, as is shown by other charters, in all parts of England — appears as the owner of lands in various parts of Dover. Still more prolific in confusion was the growth of dependent communities.[4] There were in England many owners of large estates. The most prominent

---

[1] Kritische Ueberschau, I. 100.   [2] Cod. Dip. CCCXVII.

[3] Cod. Dip. CCXLI. See also, for grants of common land, Cod. Dip. MCCLXXVIII. and DIII.

[4] See; on this point, Robertson, " Historical Essays," Introduction, p. liii. I should have been glad to have made such use of these Essays as the patience,

were the state, the crown, and the church; but there were
also many large individual proprietors, including the king.
On these great estates, or on the folc-land, groups forming
communities, exactly similar to the pure, independent community, — except that the title to the lands they occupied
was not vested in themselves, — were seated. A community on the folc-land affords the best illustration of the
result. A large proprietor, like Duke Alfred already referred to, held extensive estates of folc-land,[1] which he let
out[2] to poor freemen, his tenants. A communal group was
thus formed, with all the usual intricate relations and customs. In the case cited, the title to the land is in the state,
the lands are *laens* as to the individual tenant, and communal
as to the aggregate of tenants, and Duke Alfred, the lord of
the land, is in turn but the tenant on sufferance of the state.
There are instances in plenty, in the later grants, of the gift
of lands and communities together. These were probably
cases where the title had never been in the commoners, or
had been lost by the growth of some great estate within
their limits.[3] To take another example, this time a description of church property: " Saeculares igitur episcoporum
ditione subjecti intra ambitum hujus spatiosae telluris diver-
sis in villis[4] degentes." [5] Again, in the case of a royal grant,
to take a very common instance, Ceoluulf, A.D. 875, grants
a vill with two small vills pertaining to it.[6] Still another
case is a grant of Offa's, A.D. 780, in which the estate, pre-

industry, and thoroughness exhibited in them well deserves; but the ideas and
any comprehensive theories that there may be are so obscured by a confused
mass of detail, and an utter absence of regard for chronological development
and change, that the student is exasperated, and not instructed. See also
Stubbs's "Constitutional History," Vol. I. p. 89.

[1] Cod. Dip. CCCXVII.   [2] *Vide infra*, pp. 84, 85.
[3] Cod. Dip., E. G., Nos. DCCCXL., DCCCXLIX., DCCCL.
[4] In this case, *villis* appears to represent a communal group. In other
cases, as in Æthelwulf's Dover grant mentioned above, it clearly means a single
house. This double signification probably arose from the fact that the villa of
the great proprietor was the centre around which the communal group gathered.
Cases occur in which its original meaning of a single house has not been lost
in its later and finally exclusive one, of a collection of houses, — a tûn, or
village.
[5] Cod. Dip., No. CCCXLII.   [6] Cod. Dip. CCCVIII.

sumably one of folc-land, is described as "rus . . . in IIII. villulis separatum."[1] The further description makes it clear that four small village communities had grown up on this one estate. These extracts sufficiently show the super-imposition of one estate upon another, no one of them being entirely destroyed. Judged by its title, the land was of one kind; by its occupiers, of another; and by the manner of dividing and using, of a third. The same person could hold lands of all the four principal classes, could be a member of several communities, and the practical proprietor of several more, and could create and hold laens. This description may possibly serve to demonstrate the relative distribution of lands, and the great entanglement of estates. It must not be imagined, however, that the various kinds of land were confused as to their fundamental characteristics. On the contrary, land changed its original legal position only by certain well-defined methods. The external confusion is of importance only in so far as it serves to explain many apparent contradictions.

Nothing exercised greater influence on the development of real-property law than the growth of the principle of taxation.[2] Treating it here as the second of the preliminary points mentioned, it is only necessary to show what taxation was in the Anglo-Saxon period, and the general direction of its development. Adam Smith divides the expenses of the sovereign or commonwealth into four classes, — the expense of defence, of justice, of public works, and of the dignity of the sovereign. In the forests of Germany, but one of these forms of expense existed. Military service was made incumbent on every freeman, and thus, in the rudest way, defence was efficiently provided for. This was the very essence of the army constitution, one of the fundamental principles of the

---

[1] Cod. Dip. CXL.; also Ibid. CXXIX.

[2] That one marked feature in the German invasion everywhere was that the conquerors brought with them no system of taxation has never been sufficiently insisted on. On the continent, they destroyed the elaborate system of the Romans, and introduced nothing. The same was true of England, except that there they found nothing to destroy. Mr. Nasse makes a slight allusion to this in an essay in the Contemporary Review for May, 1872.

Germanic system. The expenses of justice were met in an entirely similar way. The duty of military service and of attendance on the courts was based solely on personal freedom, and was universal in its application.[1] The occupancy of a country, previously inhabited by civilized people, at once produced the new expense of public works. This, too, was met in the old way. Labor on the public works, the roads, and fortifications, was added to the army service, and made compulsory on every one. This common burden was the *trinoda necessitas*, in its origin required of all people, not resting on land,[2] and therefore not the subject of immunity. But one occasion for expense remained, — the dignity of the sovereign. One of the consequences of invasion and conquest was the rise of the royal or centralizing principle. Before the "folk-wandering" the king in the monarchical tribes probably supported himself in much the same way as any other freeman. But in England, at an early period, it became necessary to provide for the expense of supporting the dignity of the sovereign, or, according to the ideas of the time, for the simple expenses of the king. On the continent, all unoccupied lands went to the king. In England, on the contrary, only certain definite quantities of land were allotted to him. The lands thus given were of two kinds, — private and crown lands. The revenues arising from these estates must have proved inadequate at a very early day, and other means were soon devised to meet the ever-growing want. In so early a stage of civilization, the readiest way to supply the royal needs was by payments in kind or services. In the proem to Wihtræd's laws, and also in the first chapter of the same code, occurs a reference to the contributions

---

[1] The researches of Sohm and Roth have settled this question beyond any doubt. Cf. Reichs und Gerichtsverfassung, R. Sohm, Vol. I. p. 833, ff., and Beneficialwesens, P. Roth, p. 42; also Roth, Feudalität und Unterthanverband, p. 322, ff.

[2] This assertion is abundantly proved by the fact that no genuine charter contains an exemption from the *trinoda necessitas*. Moreover, in all the early charters it is described as the "burden common to all people," and in some similar fashion, but never as a burden common to all lands. But also *vide infra*, pp. 92, 93.

which were made to princes and leaders in the time of Tacitus.[1] The precise meaning of these contributions, which
afterwards became the *cyninges-gafol*, is very obscure. Turner is entirely adrift on the subject, Kemble considers it a
tax levied by the king and Witan,[2] Professor Stubbs offers
no explanation, Dr. Maurer does not dispose of the difficulties, and Mr. Robertson[3] apparently regards it as a tax, but
offers no suggestion as to its origin. The only definite
opinion is Kemble's; and, though his account of the origin
of the " cyninges-gafol " is undoubtedly correct, he is clearly
wrong in considering it as a tax levied by the king and Witan.
A tax so levied would have been universal in its application.
This is a fair inference from the taxing which is admitted to
have been done by the king and representative body of the
nation. It can hardly be supposed that the practice of taxing particular articles or particular persons had then obtained.
There is certainly no proof that this was the case; and the uni-
versality of any imposition on land or the reverse offers, therefore, one test as to the nature of such imposition. The language
of Wihtræd's law is obscure, but can leave no doubt that the
gafol still retained its ancient voluntary character. Kemble re-
lies on a passage in Ine's laws as an example of this tax as he
deems it. " One must pay for the harvest-gafol for one *wyrhta*
six pounds weight."[4] Schmid[5] takes *wyrhta* to mean a laborer,
and in this instance conjectures that the intent of the law is to
regulate the commutation for rent service. Another passage
in Ine[6] is of the amount to be paid by ten hides " to foster."
This Schmid[7] concludes is a regulation of the landlord's *feorm*.
In short, both these laws are enacted for the protection of
the holders of unbooked laens. But one other passage in
Ine's laws bears on this point: " If he then fight in the
house of a *gafol-gildan* (rent-payer) or of a *gebur* (peasant)

---

[1] Germania, XV. As to the purely voluntary nature of these contributions,
cf. Peucker, Kriegswesen, I. 72, and Germania des Tacitus, Baumstark, p. 543.

[2] Kemble, Saxons in England, Vol. II. pp. 80 and 223, 224.

[3] Historical Essays, pp. 102–112 inclusive.

[4] Ine, c. 59, § 1.   [5] Schmid, Gesetze, p. 49 note, and p. 680.

[6] Ine, c. 70, § 1.   [7] Schmid, Gesetze, p. 53 note.

let him pay a fine of thirty shillings, and six to the peasant."[1] This shows that a distinction existed between the rent-paying estates and others. Therefore, if this be taken to refer to the *cyninges-gafol*, it is clear that it was not universal as a legal requisition. The reference to *gafol-land* in Alfred and Guthrum's peace[2] either refers solely to unbooked laens, or, if this be not admitted, then it would seem to follow that the *gafol* could not at this time have been universal. In the "North people's laws," referred by Schmid to the beginning of the tenth century, the "wer" of a tax-paying Welshman or foreigner is fixed according to the amount of land he pays for, but this does not aid us.[3] If Mr. Kemble[4] is right in considering the *feorm-fultum*, from which Cnut relieves his subjects, as identical with the *cyninges-gafol*, then his argument that the latter is a general tax levied by the Witan falls to the ground, as the king's farm was a well-recognized service arising from the folc-land, and of a different origin and significance from that claimed for the *cyninges-gafol*, as will be shown further on. It will thus be seen how insufficient the laws are to support Mr. Kemble's theory, or indeed any theory. Their fragmentary evidence, pieced out by the language of the charters, may, however, assist in drawing some conclusions. In a grant of Offa's,[5] A.D. 791–796, with the Witan, the usual immunity is given, with the reservation of certain revenues corresponding with the *gafol* of Ine's laws.[6] In A.D. 883, a monastery is freed from all which the monks are bound to pay as *cyning-feorm*, "bright ale,[7] &c." Instances of this sort might be multiplied ; but they all point to the conclusion, suggested by Cnut's law already men-

---

[1] Ine, c. 6, § 3 ; c. 23, § 3, of the same law, is too doubtful and general in its expressions to admit of any deduction.

[2] A. & G. fri'ð, c. 1, § 2.

[3] This law and that of Ine, c. 23, § 3, fall in with Bede's description of Æthelfrith, Hist. Aeccl., Lib. I., c. 34. He says that Æthelfrith was remarkable for his conquests, and turning the Britons into tributaries, — in the Saxon version, " to gafolgyldum gesette." These three instances, taken together, suggest one of the sources of the compulsory *gafol*, and also show its non-universality.

[4] Saxons in England, II. p. 81 note.   [5] Cod. Dip. CLXVI.

[6] Ine, c. 70, § 1.   [7] Cod. Dip. CCCXIII.

tioned, that the old voluntary contribution of Tacitus became, in the process of time, assimilated with the *cyninges-feorm.* The latter was one of the services mentioned in the charters from which immunity was given. These services were dealt with by the Witan, and assumed the form of taxation because their starting-point was the folc-land,[1] not because they were services rendered to the king. The king's revenues, considered merely as such, were purely personal, and not of necessity subject to the consent of the Witan. This is shown by the way in which the king, in certain instances, granted the revenues arising from merchant-ships, a purely royal prerogative.[2] The *cyninges-gafol,* in its origin voluntary, became compulsory first on the holders of folc-land, and in its extension followed the course of the other services, becoming finally, as in Cnut's law, thoroughly amalgamated with them, and indeed undistinguishable from one kind of service. The *gafol* was in its nature a rent, and did not differ from the rents exacted by private lessors. The other services steadily increased in number, until, under Edward the Confessor, the list had become a very long one,[3] and the old voluntary contribution, as may be learned from Domesday, had become compulsory upon every landholder in the kingdom.

But one more source of royal revenue remains to be noticed, the proceeds of justice. It does not lie within the scope of this essay to examine any but those which took the form of confiscations of land, but the charters fortunately contain a number of instances which fully illustrate this point : —

The first case is in a charter[4] of the year 737 A.D., marked

---

[1] *Vide infra,* pp. 68, 94.   [2] Cod. Dip., E. G., LXXVIII., CVI., CXII.

[3] A description of these services, and the immunities and privileges of a later time, would only burden the subject unnecessarily. Specimen lists occur in the following charters : Cod. Dip. CXLII., CXLV., CLXI., CLXVI., CLXXVI., CXCI., CCXVI., CCXXIII., CCXXXVI., CCXLVI., CCLXI., CCLXII., CCLXXVII., CCLXXXVIII., CCCX., CCCLVIII., CCCLIX., CCCC., CCCCXX. CCCCLIX., CCCCLXXXVIII., DXL., DLXVII., DCCLVI., DCCLXXI., DCCLXXXV., DCCCXLIII., MLXXXIV., MCCCXLV., DCCXIX., DCCLXXI., DCCCCII. See also Kemble, Saxons, Vol. II., Chap. 2.

[4] The charters marked with an asterisk in the following enumeration are those considered forgeries by Mr. Kemble.

by Mr. Kemble a forgery: it is said the land came to the king : —

* COD. DIP. MII. " Furti crimine a possidentibus uno eodemque tempore justo dampnatis judicio ablata est."

* COD. DIP. CLXI., A.D. 792. " Quam videlicet terram Ahlmundus abbas, expeditionem subterfugiens mihi reconciliationis gratia dabat."

COD. DIP. MXX., A.D. 799. " Sed harum post modum possessiones Offa immutavit . . . dicens injustum esse quod minister ejus praesumpserit terram sibi a domino distributam absque ejus testimonio in alterius potestatem dare."

COD. DIP. MLXXVIII., A.D. 901. " Ista vero praenominata tellus primitus fuit praepeditus a quodam duce nomine Wulfhere et ejus uxore quando ille utrumque et suum dominum regem Ælfredum et patriam ultra jusjurandum quam regi et suis optimatibus juraverat sine licentia dereliquit; tunc etiam, cum omnium judicio sapientium Geuisorum et Mercensium, potestatem et haereditatem dereliquit agrorum."

COD. DIP. MXC., A.D. 909. " Praefatum equidem rus pro stupro cujusdam militis cui accomodatum fuerat ut censum singulis annis persolverat indictum, a praefata aecclesia injuste abstractum nuper fuerat." This charter was a case of restoration. The confiscated land was redeemed from the king's hands, "licet non juste," by Bishop Denewulf, who claimed it as church property. The final restoration was in the presence of the Witan.

COD. DIP. CCCLXXIV., A.D. 938. "Istarum autem VII. mansarum quantitas justo valde judicio totius populi et seniorum et primatum ablata fuit ab eis qui eorum possessores fuerunt quia aperto crimine furti usque ad mortem obnoxii inventi sunt."

COD. DIP. CCCCXCIX. and MCCXXXVII., A.D. 961. On serious charges, Goda was adjudged at the king's suit to forfeit charters and lands.[1]

COD. DIP. MCCLVIII., A.D. 966. Widow of Ælfric on judgment of gemot forfeits land for stealing the charter.[2]

* COD. DIP. DLXXIX., A.D. 973. " Unam autem mansam quam fur quidam ante possederat, (Leofstan), a rege cum triginta mancusis auri emit."

COD. DIP. DXCI., A.D. 963 – 975. A woman and her son were

---

[1] Appendix, No. 18.   [2] Appendix, No. 19.

found guilty of witchcraft, and the former drowned at London Bridge, "but the son escaped and became outlaw, and the land went into the king's hand."[1]

COD. DIP. DCI. (about 977 A.D.) "Quo reatu (*adultery*) omni substantia peculiali recte privatus est, et praefatum rus ab eo abstractum rex hujus patriae suae ditioni avidus devenire injuste optavit." This is another case of forfeited lands claimed and redeemed by the church.

COD. DIP. DCXCII., A.D. 995. Æthelsie was found guilty of theft, and his lands adjudged to the king.[2]

COD. DIP. DCCIV., (about 1000 A.D.) Land forfeited to king by judgment of Witan for failure in army duty, rebellion, treason, &c.[3]

COD. DIP. MCCLXXXIX., A. D. 995. Land of three brothers forfeited because they defended one of their men who was a thief. This land was then granted by the king to his reeve, Winsig, with consent and witness of Witan.

COD. DIP. MCCXCV., A.D. 995. "Quae portio terrae cujusdam foeminae fornicaria praevaricatione mihimet vulgari subacta est traditione."

COD. DIP. MCCCV., A.D. 1008. Dower lands forfeited. "Qui ambo crimine pessimo juste ab omni incusati sunt populo." Church subsequently claims, and, in accordance with the composition made, buys in the lands.

COD. DIP. MCCCVII., A.D. 1012. Leofric forfeits hereditary land for rebellion, adultery, and other crimes. "Semetipsum condempnavit simul et possessiones."

COD. DIP. DCCXIX., A.D. 1012. Murder the cause of forfeiture. "Peracto itaque scelere ab eo, inii consilium cum sapientibus regni mei petens," &c.

COD. DIP. MCCCXII. Ælfric, the boy, despoiled a certain widow of lands, and was rebel. He was condemned by Witan.

COD. DIP. DCCLVII. Lands granted simply described, in setting forth title, as forfeited to the king's hand.

COD. DIP. DCCCI., A.D. 1055. "Quae mihi per judicium nobilium et principum meorum evenit ab Erusio . . . pro suo commisso."

It appears plainly by these examples that confiscated lands went into the king's hands. The criminal procedure afforded

---

[1] Appendix, No. 20.　　[2] Appendix, No. 23.　　[3] Appendix, No 26.

an ample barrier against usurpation in this direction; in almost every instance, moreover, the judgment of the Witan is expressly mentioned, and in none is there any thing to show that their consent had not been obtained. This safeguard was undoubtedly due to the anxiety to protect life and liberty, but it also served to protect property.[1]

Such, then, were the royal revenues. Confiscations and escheats are distinct from the other sources of revenue, and, in a question of taxation, may be rejected. The result is, that certain royal services, including ultimately in one form or another the ancient gratuity of the time of Tacitus, remain as the only possible form of taxation. That they are to be considered in this light at all, arises solely from the fact that they are dealt with by the sovereign power, the King and Witan. Why the disposition of these services was an attribute of the king and Witan is susceptible of very easy

[1] Entirely akin to this it may be supposed was the procedure in cases resembling escheat. There is, however, no authority, with the exception of one passage in the charters, which throws any light on the subject. This single instance is a case of escheat of boc-land to the king, the grantor (Cod. Dip. MXXXV.). There is no reasonable doubt that boc-land always escheated or more properly reverted to the donor; and the appearance of the Witan is, therefore, the only important fact. In cases of private persons, escheat of boc-land to the donor required no judgment of the Witan (Cod. Dip. MCCLXXXVIII., and *infra*, p. 111); and the fact that there was such judgment in Burghard's case must be owing to the character of one of the parties. The grantee had been guilty of no crime, and required no protection. The appearance of the Witan was therefore probably due to the character of the grantor, whose only mark of distinction, so far as concerned land, was his royalty. The fact that a king required the action of the Witan, in cases of escheat, suggests the important inference that much boc-land having formerly been folc-land, in case of escheat the right of the Witan to make an award depended on the original character of the land. The unusual absence of all authority on this question was probably due to the excessive rarity of cases resembling escheat, and this in turn was due to the Anglo-Saxon land law. All estates lying in a community reverted to such community (G. L. v. Maurer, Einleitung, p. 110); boc-land reverted to the donor, folc-land to the state, leaving only family estates, which were neither communal in their origin, nor an old estate of boc-land, liable to escheat to the crown, in the modern sense. If the size and completeness of the family organization be considered, it will not seem surprising that even in the cases where escheat was possible, arguing from the authorities, it almost never happened. It is at best a purely theoretical point. It is doubtful if any such thing as escheat was known to the Anglo-Saxon law. This solution of Burghard's case is offered as a conjecture, from unwillingness to pass it over entirely.

explanation. Before the time of Æthelred, there is no instance of a general tax levied by the Witan.[1] The *Danegeld*,
at the close of the tenth century, was a great extension of the
power of the National Assembly. It has been shown that the
only revenues of the state were those used to support the
dignity of the sovereign. The Witan, it may be supposed,
had few or no expenses, and the king therefore obtained the
lion's share of these revenues. With very few and unimportant exceptions, these services were connected with land ;
and immunity from them, if the great majority of the charters. be believed, required the presence and consent of the
Witan. This could not arise from the nature of the services,
for they were almost purely personal; and it is to their origin,
therefore, that one must look for explanation. The services
were, of their very nature, connected with land. Certain
lands known as folc-land, and no others, were under the
peculiar protection of the Witan :[2] to grant immunity from
these services was an especial attribute of the Witan ;[3] therefore the services must have originated in the folc-land.

The nature of taxation and its origin have now been
sketched, and a sure test provided by which its future course
can be followed. The history of the immunities in the grants
is the history of taxation ; and its spread from the folc-land
to all the lands of the kingdom may therein be traced. The
development of taxation with reference to each will be reserved for examination in the history of the several classes
of landed property.

Having disposed of the two preliminary questions, we are
now in a position to take up the first of the four classes
mentioned at the outset, — the family land. The designation, " family," is not altogether satisfactory, but is, on the
whole, open to fewer objections than any other. Such high
authorities as Professor Stubbs[4] and Dr. Konrad Maurer[5]
have used the name *ethel* to indicate land of this kind, and

---

[1] Professor Stubbs admits this, though in the main following Kemble on this
point (Constitutional History, Vol. I. p. 133).

[2] *Vide infra*, p. 93.   [3] Cod. Dip. CCCXVII., CCLX., and CCLXXI.

[4] Constit. Hist., Vol. I. p. 75.

[5] Kritische Ueberschau, Vol. I. p. 97.

alod is also used by the same writers. Kemble treats it as the ethel, hide, or alod. But all these terms seem to be only productive of confusion. In the family alone can be found the characteristics which define and separate it from all other estates ; and, though not including every feature, it has, for the reason just stated, been here adopted. There is no need of misconception, if it be borne in mind that the land of the family, when it comes within the range of history, was generally held by individuals, was the origin of individual property in land, and in its growth took the form of the development of individual property.

Private property in land had already made its appearance in the time of Tacitus.[1] " Suam quisque domum spatio circumdat" is the expression of the Roman historian ; and in this may be detected the first slight invasion of the communal principle. Sir Henry Maine divides the lands of a village community into " the mark of the township or village, the common mark or waste, and the arable mark or cultivated area." [2] Adopting this division, but rejecting the nomenclature for reasons to be given hereafter,[3] the lands of the communal groups fall under three heads, — the house, the arable, and the waste or wild land. The first of these — the houseland — is that to which the language of Tacitus applies. Certain portions of the land actually enclosed by the village wall or hedge always retained their communal character, as, for example, the streets, squares,[4] &c. ; but " the house-land " means the ground actually covered by the house, together with the yards, stables, gardens, &c., — in short, the curtilage.[5] This was the foundation of individual property, the

---

[1] This opinion has already been established by G. L. v. Maurer, "Einleitung," p. 10; Konrad Maurer, "Kritische Ueberschau," Vol. I. p. 99. More recently, it has been adopted by Mr. Digby, in his most admirable "Introduction to the Law of Real Property," p. 3. It seems hardly necessary to enter into an argument to disprove Mr. Robertson's theory that private property originated in boc-land ("Historical Essays," Introduction, p. lvii.). It may be conveniently said here that the expression, "private property," is used as covering lands of the family as well as of the individual.

[2] Village Com., p. 78.　　　　　　　　[3] *Vide infra*, p. 82.

[4] Von Maurer, Einleitung, pp. 86–89.　　　[5] Ibid., pp. 80–85.

land peculiarly sacred to the family, and to the communal principle the centre of opposition towards which all other lands
were rapidly gravitating. This conception was transplanted
intact to England. In one of Ine's laws it is provided : "If
a ceorl and his wife have a child together, and the ceorl dies,
let the mother have her child and feed it ; let them give her
six shillings for support, — a cow in summer, an ox in winter.
Let the kin hold the homestead until it (the child) be grown
up." [1] The English *frum-stol*, depicted in this law as the
especial care of the family, is clearly identical with the
"domus" of Tacitus, the house-land of the early Germanic
tribes. The existence of the central point once clearly
proved, the existence of all other kinds of family land, known
to us by the kindred systems, follows as a matter of necessity. Differences, if they exist, are only in matters of detail.
Family land is distinguished by four very marked characteristics from other kinds of land. It was the creation of customary [2] law, — a quality possessed also by folc-land and
common land ; but it was also an estate essentially of inheritance ; was based upon the family ; was subject to certain rights
on the part of the family ; and, finally, was, in origin and theory,
liable to no public burdens, except the *trinoda necessitas*.

It is not necessary to enter into detailed proof of its creation by custom. Family land had existed as a fundamental
Germanic institution long before the Teutonic tribes ever
conceived of any law more positive in its nature than custom.
At a subsequent period, an attempt — apparently successful
— was made to convert estates of boc-land into estates of
the family, then rapidly changing into individual property.
This new source of family estates alone requires a more
elaborate investigation before admitting the force of the first
proposition.

The well-known provision in Alfred's Laws recites that,
"If a man have boc-land, and his kin left it him, then we
declare that he must not sell it out of his kindred, if there

---

[1] Ine, c. 38; cf. Konrad Maurer, Kritische Ueberschau, p. 99.

[2] Mr. Austin's distinctions have not been forgotten. "Customary" is used
merely to denote the origin and source of the law.

be writing or witness that the man forbade who first acquired it, and those who granted it to him, that he might not."[1] A charter[2] of 804 A.D. is an example of the grants which subsequently were embodied in this law. Æthelric comes before the synodal council " cum libris et ruris . . . quod propinqui mei tradiderunt mihi et donaverunt." He then, in presence of the Witan, devises them ; and of certain lands left to his mother, he provides that she can give them up " cum recto consilio propinquorum meorum qui mihi haereditatem donabant." A charter[3] of Offa's, of still earlier date (A.D. 779), contains a limitation to the family in terms, " post se suae propinquitatis homini cui ipse voluerit." In a suit[4] of Alfred's time, the litigation concerns land granted the family on certain conditions. The reversion reserved to the church was confirmed in his will by the second holder of the lands. The family neither performed the condition nor yielded the lands ; and the consequent suit of Bishop Werfrith was for the recovery of the lands against Eadnoth, who appeared as defendant in behalf of the family. This suit may be considered to fairly represent archaic tendencies of which Alfred's law was the exponent. The law and the charters prove nothing on their face but that the conditions of books were to be held inviolable ; and the limitation cited from Offa's charter is merely an example of one kind of those limitations of which the books are full, and does not differ essentially from limitations in tail,[5] to certain individuals named, &c. Indeed, Mr. Kemble[6] classes with the one we have cited, as of similar import, another charter of Offa's, in which the lands are granted in special tail; and he considers Alfred's law a rep-

[1] Alfred, § 41; Stubbs's Documents, p. 62.   [2] Cod. Dip. CLXXXVI.
[3] Cod. Dip. CXXXVII.
[4] Cod. Dip. CCCXXVII.; also see Appendix, No. 16.
[5] The modern legal phraseology is used throughout this Essay, wherever it has been possible, to express the Anglo-Saxon estates. In almost all such cases, the modern estate does not differ, in its broad and substantial meaning, from the Saxon one. The refinements of the later principles did not, of course, exist at such early periods as those treated in this Essay ; but this did not seem to me a good ground for rejecting a convenient classification, at once clear, defined, and generally understood.
[6] Cod. Dip., Introduction, p. xxxii.; and Charter CLIII.

etition of one of Offa's now lost. But the general inviolability of the terms of a book was a well-established principle, and a law to protect terms of a certain kind would have been needless. The fact that this law was confined to limitations to the family, and the passages in the charters, especially Werfrith's case, seem to indicate the struggle, introduced by the church, which, it cannot be doubted, was in progress between the Saxon principles and those of the boc-land. Every thing points, in this, as in other branches of the law, to a revival, under Alfred, of what may be called the pure Saxon elements in law. The law as to boc-land was probably one result of this revival. The effort was made by this law to establish the principle that estates of boc-land, which had passed from one generation by testament or otherwise to another, were then to be family land. How far the principle became established is difficult to determine. In the laws [1] of Henry I., Alfred's law as to boc-land is substantially repeated in regard to a feud. This and the other laws of the same period show that the struggle of the family to hold its own was still in progress. After the time of Alfred, no assistance on this point is given by the charters; and the absence of such limitations may not unreasonably be considered to show that the principle of family rights contended for, partially triumphed; that is, as the family principle gave way to that of individualism in land, the boc-land was converted from an estate purely of grant to an estate of custom, and the tenure by virtue of and according to the terms of a book changed to a feudal and customary tenure. The estates of boc-land and the estates of the family merged, therefore, in the estate of the individual. Under the Normans, it still retained marks of its double origin, and it was for the protection of the family in estates of this sort that Henry's laws were enacted.

Estates created by book were hostile to the rights of the family, in so far as they fostered the spirit of individualism;

---

[1] Leges Hen. Prim. 88, § 14, also 70, § 21; and Glanville vii. 11, l. f. In the law of Cnut on the same point (Cnut, II. 70), the family claim is recognized, the *propinqui* being classed among the other legal heirs.

and, whatever temporary success the old Germanic principles
may have obtained, the ultimate result is indubitable. Family influence waned and disappeared. With this explanation,
one is justified in accepting the first proposition, — that family estates were the pure creation of customary law. The
attempts to extend the domain of family land in the time of
Offa and Alfred were due to the encroachments of boc-land;
and their object was simply to convert estates held by virtue of a written instrument into the old estate originating in
custom. In a word, the principle contended for was the
identity of all heritable estates with family land. The result
would seem, by the laws of Henry, to have been that the
two kinds of land merged, and became boc-land in name
and family land in principle. Any deductions from authorities of so late a period must, however, be made with great
care; for the principle of individual property must have then
been so much in the ascendant as to have reduced the family
rights to a very low point.

The second proposition — that the family land was essentially an estate of inheritance — may be readily admitted;
it is merely necessary to show that it was the only one
essentially so. Von Maurer has proved it to be the opposite
of an estate acquired by purchase.[1] It was equally opposed
to estates created by book. Boc-land might be an estate for
life or lives, limited in tail general, or tail male, and subject
to an indefinite right of alienation. The estate of the family,
on the other hand, could descend only according to certain
fixed principles; it was not alienable, and could not be, in
theory, granted by book. In the time of Tacitus,[2] the law
of intestate succession was fixed, but there were no wills.
With the introduction of written instruments by the church
influence, came, too, the introduction of wills, which were
also an invasion of the family domain, not only keeping from
its power estates of purchase or grant, but tending to infringe upon the family land itself. There are several cases[3]

[1] Von Maurer, Einleitung, p. 14, and authorities cited in note 59; K. Maurer, Kritische Ueberschau, I. pp. 97, 98.
[2] Germania, c. 20, 21.   [3] Appendix, Nos. 4–8,–10–14,–16–30.

in which the heirs are parties to suits for having broken their ancestors' will. The very name by which boc-land is usually translated shows this most vital difference. It was the *terra testamentalis*, — the land capable of devise ; while family land was purely an estate of inheritance, in theory incapable of devise.[1]

The arable lands, like the house-land, were, in their nature, lands of allotment, made on the theory that each member of the community was entitled to an equal share, in quantity sufficient for the support of his family.[2] The rights in the waste of wood, water, fishing, hunting, pasture, &c., were in a similar way allotted in proportion to each commoner's share in the arable, and rested, therefore, on the same basis as the house-land. Thus, the family estate, in the old English community, consisted of the house and arable lands, and the rights in the common land running with them, based originally on the theory of family support. It is not necessary to develop more fully this third proposition, — that the family estate rested primarily upon the needs of family. The labors of German scholars have made this allusion all-sufficient.

The estate based on the family was naturally subject to many rights and limitations in its favor. It must be borne in mind that, long before the period when laws and charters first begin, the family, as such, had ceased to hold land.[3] It was probably universally held and administered by individuals in that capacity alone, or as the heads of households. The influence of the family in historic times had been reduced to the exercise of certain rights. These

---

[1] The question of the course of descent and the methods of division is entirely omitted here, since it falls more appropriately within the province of another essay in this volume.

[2] Von Maurer, Einleitung, p. 71, *et seq.*, and p. 88.

[3] It is of course purely matter of conjecture that the family as such ever held land. It is, however, a fair inference that in pre-historic times the Germanic family was regarded more as a legal entity than as an aggregation of individuals. The course of historical development took the form of the disintegration of the family, and the further back we go the closer the bond of family becomes, and the stronger the probability that it held land in its collective capacity.

rights pertained to the whole maegth, including of course the household, as against any stranger or individual member of the family. These are the rights referred to in the fourth proposition, and of them alone is it necessary to speak. The most important doctrine, in this regard, was the inalienability of the family lands. The law of inheritance has already been alluded to as given by Tacitus. Intestate succession was fixed; and all such lands, in default of heirs, reverted to the community from which they had been derived. Without referring to that extremely indistinct cause, — the strength of the family bond, — the inalienability of the lands is sufficiently accounted for by the necessities of the communal system. Lands of a community were inalienable,[1] and all family lands were originally communal. The working of this principle in England may be traced in the efforts to break through it. In a charter made between the years 757 and 775 A.D., Abbot Ceolfrith grants land "jure paterno haereditario dono terram meam et haereditatem patris mei Cyneberhti." The royal confirmation of the grant is expressed, and then in the *si quis* clause the *parentela* are especially warned not to infringe the grant.[2] In a charter of Bishop Wulfred's, A.D. 811, it is said: "Rex Offa praedictam terram a nostra familia abstulit, videlicet quasi non liceret Ecgberhto agros haereditario jure scribere."[3] The land in question had been originally granted by Ecgberht to Aldhun, and by him to the church, from whom it had been taken by Offa on the ground stated in the text; that is, it was an infringement of the law to *book* family or hereditary lands. In another case, the family join for the purpose of protecting the church, the grantee, against future claims.[4] In still another instance, Aki, the son of Toki, breaks the will of his father, by which certain lands were devised to the church; and the latter is able to establish its claim only by paying Aki a proper compensation.[5] This last case is but one instance of the many efforts of the family to break books

---

[1] Von Maurer, Einleitung, p. 106.
[2] Cod. Dip. CXXVII.
[3] Cod. Dip. CXCV. See also Cod. Dip. MXX.
[4] Cod. Dip. MXVII.
[5] Cod. Dip. DCCCV. See Appendix, No. 30.

and wills,[1] and the law of Alfred, already cited,[2] sustains the same interpretation. The principle contended for was the inalienability of all hereditary land; and from the language used it is clear, as in the principle cited by Offa, that it was not the introduction of a new principle, but the extension of an old one to new forms of hereditary land. The doctrine of inalienability would seem to have succeeded[3] as to intestate estates, so that they were protected from the invasion of a superior, but probably broke down when the alienation was made by the possessor. The first innovation which led to this result was the establishment of the principle that lands were alienable within the limits and by the consent of the family. The non-existence of wills among the Germanic tribes in the very earliest times left no means to the individual to direct the distribution of his possessions even among his own kin. The mere fact of the introduction of wills by the church, giving opportunity for *post mortem* distribution, was, as already said, of itself an invasion of the family domain. The firm establishment of the principle of alienation among members of the same kin, the first breach in the family system, is abundantly proved. The most convincing evidence is to be found in the will of Duke Alfred,[4] the object of which is to define " which of my kin and friends are the men to whom I will my *yrfe-land* and my *boc-land*." The evident distinction between land of inheritance and boc-land is very significant. It shows that there were other estates of inheritance than those held by book: and as neither folc-land nor common land, as such, could be a heritable estate, and as laen-land is invariably so described, it follows that the pure estate of inheritance must have been family land; and, this being proved, it also follows that family lands could be legally the subject of devise. To the will of Beorhtric and Ælfswyth, members of the family exclusively give witness and consent, the same persons also taking under the will.[5] The necessity of family consent is shown by the

---

[1] See Appendix, Nos. 4, 8, 10, 14, 16, 30.   [2] Alfred, 41.   *Vide supra.* p. 70.
[3] Alfred, 41; Henry, § 88, § 14; Cnut, II. 70; Will. I. 84.
[4] Cod. Dip. CCCXVII.   [5] Cod. Dip. CCCCXCII., MCCXLII.

provision in Æthelric's will, that the land could be alienated
"cum recto consilio propinquorum."[1] In a purely family
arrangement between Cynethrith, the widow of Alderman
Æthelmod, and Eadwald, one of his kin, the contract, as
to lands left to Cynethrith by her husband, is made entirely
with a regard to the family rights.[2] The land in this case,
the disposition of which involved so closely the rights of the
family, had already been made the subject of devise. One of
two conclusions must therefore be adopted, — either family
land had been made the subject of devise, or boc-land had
been successfully converted into family land. In a contract
of the year 1046, the vendors agreed "that they would see
that all the brothers went out of the land, except one, that is
called Ulf, to whom it was bequeathed, and he should have
it for life."[3] This is another instance of the family dealing
with land already devised, in connection with family rights.
Ten years later, in A.D. 1056, Leofwine buys land of his kinsman Eadric, the son of Usic, "Ever in his kin to hold and
sell to whom best pleases him."[4] This again was a family
arrangement, and the limitation exhibits the vigor of the
family principle even at so late a date. In proportion, however, as the family gathered strength against the principle of
boc-land, they lost it by the force of individualism working
from within. This is shown by attempts like those of Ceolfrith, already cited, to bar the *parentela*. In this and similar
cases, the confirmation of the king and Witan is substituted
for that of the family, in order to give force and strength to
the instrument. There are also other cases in which family
lands are alienated, and neither the consent of the family nor
the confirmation of king and Witan is given.[5] These examples represent, in its fullest extent, the principle contended for by the church, — of barring, by the simple writing, all future claims from the family or others. Among the
family rights was also included the guardianship of the
estate of a minor. This appears from the law already cited

---

[1] Cod. Dip. CLXXXVI. ; and *vide supra*, p. 71.
[2] Cod. Dip. CCXXVIII.   [3] Cod. Dip. MCCCXXXIV.
[4] Cod. Dip. DCCCII.   [5] Cod. Dip. CCXXV.

from Ine as to the *frum-stol* passing into the hands of the kin until the child was grown up.[1]

The last proposition offered in regard to family land was that in theory and primarily it was an untaxed estate. This view has already been advanced by Dr. Konrad Maurer, who argues from the analogous Scandinavian codes, and bases on the Northern laws and history the opinion that the family land was " a full, free, and unburdened estate."[2] Mr. Kemble considered the *gafol*, already discussed, as a general tax incumbent on all estates. Professor Stubbs says : " All local requirements were met by the allodial obligations discharged by personal services."[3] If this be taken to refer to the communal duties, no exception can be taken, but such a construction seems to be scarcely borne out by the context. The passage cited occurs in a paragraph treating of the power of the Witan to levy taxes. Professor Stubbs follows Kemble, and, at the same time, is evidently troubled by the inconsistencies of that view, and adds, in explanation, what has just been cited. This explanation is so worded that it throws no light on the important question, as to whether family estates were primarily taxed or free. The analogy from the Northern law, relied on by Dr. Maurer, is not of itself sufficient to establish the existence of the same principle in England. Taken cumulatively, however, with such evidence as can be obtained from native sources, Dr. Maurer's theory may be safely adopted. The laws offer no assistance, and the proof to be drawn from the charters would be far from conclusive if unsupported by the Scandinavian practice. Taxation has already been defined as consisting of services which owed their origin to folc-land, and the test of the existence of taxation is the appearance in the charters of immunities which exempted the grantee from it. A first glance would lead one to believe that immunity was granted in all cases, and that taxation was therefore universal from

[1] Only two rights of the family as peculiarly pertaining to land have been discussed. Their powers in other directions are more appropriately treated in another portion of this volume.

[2] Kritische Ueberschau, Vol. I. p. 98.

[3] Const. Hist., I. p. 188.

the time of the earliest contemporaneous authority. A close examination alone will reveal the fact that taxation started with the folc-land, was not at first compulsory on the holders of family lands, and only after several centuries spread to all the lands in the kingdom. Before the year 1000 A.D., there are eight[1] royal grants of what may fairly be considered family land. The first three contain no reference to immunity from taxation. The fourth, a charter of Ecgbert's, grants family land which had been previously given away by the king, and, on the death of the grantee without heirs, had reverted again to him; while in the hands of the king's grantee, it is impossible to say what services were laid upon the land under the terms of the book. The fifth and sixth are likewise Wessex grants, and contain the immunity, while the seventh and eighth cases do not. About the beginning of the ninth century, the king's family estates were taxed, or, more precisely, fixed services in the nature of a tax were drawn from them; and nothing is more striking than the steady advance of the principle of taxation under the Wessex supremacy. Immunity becomes universal in the charters of Alfred and his successors. It appears, therefore, that, before the year 826, no case can be found of royal family lands freed from taxation; and it is also true that, before 798,[2] no grant of private family land occurs with any mention of taxation. Yet there are twenty-seven examples of private grants[3] before that date. Some of these are family lands; it is possible that most of them are so. In many cases they are made with the confirmation of the king and Witan, and the grantors were presumably therefore in a position to secure immunity; yet the case of Headda, in 798, is the first case in which this exemption occurs. The only inference appears to be that during the first three centuries of the Anglo-Saxon rule taxation was by no means universal. Although immunity is given in almost every case

[1] Cod. Dip. XXX., CLVIII., DLXXVIII., DCCCCXCV., MXXXV., MLVIII., MXLIV., MXLVIII.   [2] Cod. Dip. CLXIX.

[3] Those marked by Mr. Kemble forgeries, and those passed by him as genuine, are both included.

where folc-land may fairly be considered to have been involved, it occurs in none of the private grants for the same period. Whatever the conditions of original settlement may have been in Wessex, that province, when it began to assume prominence, was far more advanced than its neighbors in the development of the centralizing principle and from the time of Ecgberht, the spread of taxation, as shown by the charters, was rapid, and at an early day complete. The result of this examination, which alone serves to throw any light on this most obscure and difficult point, bears out Dr. Maurer's theory derived from the Scandinavian codes. With the analogy so supported by internal evidence, it may be fairly concluded that among the Anglo-Saxon, as among their Northern brethren, the family land was primarily a " full, free, unburdened estate."

Having attempted to trace the most prominent features of family land, it only remains to sketch the course of its development and change during the six centuries which elapsed between the landing of Hengst and of William.

In discussing the question of family rights, this has already been partially sketched, and it is only needful to complete the outline then drawn. The land of the family developed a great force in the direction of individualism, — a force which worked in two ways; urging men to redeem waste lands, and convert them from common land and folc-land into estates of inheritance, and at the same time to limit and destroy, in every way, the rights of their kindred. The first process was tolerably rapid. The second, running as it did directly counter to a cherished and ancient system, moved more slowly but not less surely. The importance of the struggle already referred to, as revealed to us in the charters, cannot be overestimated. In their origin, the terms hereditary and family, as applied to land, were synonymous. Conquest and centralization promoted in certain cases a great increase of hereditary lands, and the effort of the pure Saxon element was to maintain in its entirety the absolute identity of inheritors and family. The examples already cited are witness to this effort. The most striking evidence of the working of this principle is in

Alfred's will, the period of the Saxon revival. Alfred says: " And I will that the men to whom I have bequeathed my boc-land grant it not out of my kin after their life ; " [1] then follow elaborate provisions as to the precise course of its descent. All these provisions in regard to the family are about boc-land ; there are lands willed to his sons and others which are not so described ; but no mention is made of the latter while limiting the boc-land to the family. The only conclusion left open is, that it was not requisite to hedge in other estates of inheritance with such precautions. In entire accordance with the principles of his legislation, Alfred wished to convert all his land acquired by book into strictly family land. The principle of individualism eventually triumphed. The last effort to protect the family was Henry's law cited above ; and during the Norman and Angevin period the decadence of the family power was probably rapid. While the estate based upon the family flourished and expanded until it absorbed almost all forms of property, the family considered as a legal entity, to which that estate owed its existence, perished ; and a few ancient customs in Kent have alone survived to bear witness to the persistence and tenacity of pure Germanic principles, the last vestiges of what once was a complete system of rights and duties. The hostile element of individualism worked on the family with both interior and exterior forces. With the former it destroyed, with the latter it created and strengthened. A double process of development and transformation was therefore constantly in progress. The extension of the family principle in the direction of boc-land has been already described. Its expansion in another direction is so closely connected with the next branch of our subject that they are most conveniently treated together. The growth of the one was the extinction of the other.

" Family " was not a perfectly satisfactory name for the first class, but the description of the second class, resting on customary law, as " common " land is open to no such objection. Better than any thing else perhaps, this name illus-

---

[1] Cod. Dip. CCCXIV.

trates the advantage of clinging to general principles, and adopting comprehensive classifications in all questions of Anglo-Saxon law. The effort of most writers on the subject has been to support some one special form of organization as the typical Anglo-Saxon community, — the unit of a complicated system. The authority of Kemble is given for the mark, which is, in a measure, supported by Dr. Konrad Maurer. Dr. Gneist, followed by Professor Stubbs,[1] rejects the mark as the basis of the English polity, while the latter adopts the township as the constitutional unit. It is not within the province of this Essay to discuss the title of the township to the place of constitutional unit, but the authorities certainly do not justify its acceptance in preference to the mark or any other community as the unit of the land system. The mark, the township, the vicus, in certain cases the vill, the hundred, the thorpe or dorf, were all what are now termed village communities. Throughout all these organizations runs the one abiding principle of community of land; in all of them existed, primarily at least, the kinds of land mentioned by Sir Henry Maine, — house, arable, and wild land; and in all cases the land was held by the community in a corporate capacity. The community in its purest form had the title vested in itself; but many communities unquestionably grew up on the folc-land, the title being then vested in the state; on the crown lands, the title being in the crown; and on the private lands of the king or other large proprietor, the title being in the king or in such proprietor. In the last case, the commoners were presumably tenants of the land-owner. This was one efficient cause in hastening the downfall of the independent community. The organization of the dependent communities was nevertheless, in all their complicated internal relations, the same as that of the old independent community. For the present, it is sufficient to take only the latter for consideration. Before proceeding with this investigation, it is a necessary preliminary step to distinguish the lands of the community from the folc-land. The analogy between them is obvious and misleading. An

[1] Const. Hist. I. p. 83, note.

example from modern times best shows the difference. Here in America exist, side by side, the lands of the United States, the lands of the States, and the lands of the municipalities and townships. The land of the State, the municipality, and the township, are private, as compared with the land of the United States. As the land of the State is to that of the United States, as the land of a corporation or township is to that of the single State, so was the land of the Anglo-Saxon community to the folc-land. Another characteristic which makes plain the distinction between the common and the folc-land is the different method of treatment employed in the two cases. The lands of the folc, or people, were treated as revenue-bearing lands, as the national fund to which no individual had an inalienable right of separate enjoyment. The lands of the community were enjoyed by all in the same way, bore no revenue except the rights of user, and every commoner had an inalienable right to the enjoyment of a definite amount in severalty for a given time.

The existence of so-called village communities in England has been proved by the researches of Maine, Nasse, Kemble, Maurer, and others, and is now accepted by all leading authorities. Their organization and internal construction and relations have all been a subject of the most thorough investigation, and any further discussion on this point would be superfluous. The way in which the communal lands were absorbed by families and individuals has been traced in detail in Dr. G. L. von Maurer's admirable "Einleitung." That work treats almost exclusively of Continental development, but it cannot be doubted that the process was nearly identical in England. When Tacitus wrote, the house-land was already, in great measure, private property; the arable next became so, and last, the waste. In strict accordance with this order, the ordinary example of the communal system which has survived is in waste or wild lands. A few cases, comparatively speaking, have also remained to us of the community of the arable land. It is perfectly clear that the hereditary right to an allotment for a term of years was easily converted into an hereditary right to a certain parcel of land. The difficult point is to explain the formation of large estates, the most potent destroyers of the Germanic communal system.[1] This was chiefly brought about by the right of redemption[2] from the waste. There is no time within the historic period at which difference in rank and wealth did not exist to some degree. The rich member of the community, the owner of many slaves, in the exercise of his rights, redeemed land from the waste much faster than his poorer fellow-commoners. Conquest, too, was an important factor in the problem; for the leaders, the kings, and the crown obtained much larger estates in the conquered territory than the average freeman. Books, introduced by the church, and occasional sales, all contributed to swell the current. The large estates, once started, grew rapidly. Their development was the development of the estates of individuals, of family estates; and it was owing to the growth of the large estates, by additions from conquest, sale, &c., consisting sometimes wholly, sometimes in part, of lands not communal, and free from communal burdens, which raised one free man above another, and thus developed the lord of the middle ages and destroyed the old Germanic community, based on the system of small freeholds and equality before the law. Here, therefore, the growth of the old family estate, now the estate of the individual, and the destruction of the communal system by the large land owners become coextensive. Men found themselves the possessors of estates which they were unable to cultivate by slave labor. Sometimes these estates consisted of outlying lands[3] in the same community, and very often must have been lands scattered among many communities. In either case the utland of the proprietor needed cultivators. As estates grew, population increased, and the ancient communal system afforded no relief to the poor freeman, whose inherited share of a share no longer sufficing for

[1] See on this V. Maurer, Einleitung, pp. 203–214. Roth, Beneficialwesen, pp. 103–105.

[2] V. Maurer, Einleitung, pp. 158–186.

[3] The lands cultivated by the lords' slaves, and the outlying lands, are respectively the lands known as inland and utland. They are referred to frequently in the charters. See Cod. Dip., E. G., DCCCXXI.

his needs, naturally turned to the great proprietor to obtain
the land which neither the community nor the family could
give him. The large land-owner was thus enabled to work
all his land with profit. Lands were rented to freemen at the
close of the seventh century, as appears by the laws of Ine.[1]
" If a man agree for a virgate of land or more, at a fixed rent,
and shall plough it, if the lord wish to yield him the land for
rent and service, it is not necessary for him to take it if he
will give him no house, nor shall he lose the land." The
system of leasing land for fixed rent and services had, in
Ine's time, become sufficiently general to demand special
legislation. The personal relation between *princeps* and
comites was fundamental in military affairs. With the introduction of services in lieu of rent, the step was a short one to
extend this principle of personal relation to tenures of land.
In fact, in the same code, it appears that a freeman was liable
to a fine for working on Sunday without his lord's permission,[2] and that if a man left his lord without permission and
went into another county he should pay a fine.[3] The responsibility of the lord, instead of the personal responsibility
of the freeman, is apparent in the law against Sabbath break-
ing. In Alfred's time the powers of the lord had made such
progress that legislation had become necessary to preserve
to every freeman the right to seek a new lord.[4] In Æthelstan's time still further progress had been made. Alfred's
law as to the right to seek a new lord is reiterated,[5] and it is
made incumbent on the family to provide lordless members
of the kin with a lord.[6] This course of legislation represents
fairly the decay of the communal and free spirit, and the
establishment of the principle that every man must have a
lord. The substitution of the lord for the community in
judicial affairs is more appropriately treated in another portion of this volume, but a similar substitution in the land
system preceded it. It is only necessary here to discuss
two points, — the nature of the estates thus held of a lord by

[1] Ine, c. 67.
[2] Ine, c. 3, § 2.
[3] Ine, c. 39.
[4] Alfred, c. 37.
[5] Æthelstan, III. 4; and IV. 5.
[6] Æthelstan, II. 2.

freemen, and the manner of substitution of the lord for the community in the proprietorship of the common land.

The estates of utland held by freemen may be most concisely and exactly described as *unbooked laens*. That is, they were estates of which the title was vested in the lord, while the actual possession was conferred on the tenant by some oral form of investiture. These estates were probably held at first, as Ine's law suggests, at a fixed rent in money or kind ; but in a semi-barbarous community rents could be much more easily paid and collected in the form of services than in any other way, and the latter method no doubt prevailed. In another law of Ine's, the rent to be demanded from a certain amount of land is fixed.[1] In the " Rectitudines Singularum Personarum,"[2] it is said that the services of the *gebur* were heavy, light, and moderate in different places, and the elaborate laws of William in this direction show that the needs sought to be remedied by such legislation were as crying as ever.[3] The general similarity of the services required, and the innumerable local variations, may be gathered from an examination of the services of the tenants of Hysseburn twice given in the charters,[4] as well as from the " Rectitudines "[5] already cited. The inference to be drawn is, that rent in the form of services was practically arbitrary, and dependent solely on the will of the lessor. The only protection possible at so early a stage of civilization would be that afforded by custom.

The phrase " unbooked " is of importance. It has been usual to mix all laens together, as if no distinction existed among them. The ordinary laen from lord to man has just been described as dependent on the will of the lord, and protected only by custom ; while a laen by book, on the other hand, was held in exact accordance with the terms of the instrument, and protected by the sanctity of the charter.

" Then is three hides of the land which Oswald, archbishop, booketh to Wynsige, his monk, so as Wulfstan, his

---

[1] Ine, c. 70, § 1.   [2] Rect. S. P., c. 4.
[3] Will. I. c. 29, and III. 5.
[4] Cod. Dip., MLXXVII., DCCCCLXXVII.
[5] Schmid, Gesetze, p. 371, ff.

father had it with the witness of the chapter at Worcester."[1] Again: "Then is three hides of the land which Oswald, archbishop, booketh to Eadric, his thane, both nearer tûn and farther, as he before had it for laen-land."[2] In another grant of Oswald's to his client Ælfsige: "Also we write to him the croft within the hedge, which is by the East of Wulfsige's croft, that he may have it as freely for boc-land, as he before had it for laen-land."[3] These extracts prove the existence of unbooked laens, and of an important distinction between them and booked laens. The object of converting laen-land, pure and simple, into booked laen-land, was evidently the fixity of tenure caused by the reduction of the terms to writing. This is clear from the fact that the laens were taken on the same terms as under the purely customary tenure ; and a book was simply futile if it did not alter the old relation in some way. The terms of the lease were not altered ; therefore the only object of the book was to make the maintenance of the former terms more secure. In the laws already cited, the responsibility of the lord for the man, the reservation of the right of changing from one lord to another, and finally the absolute necessity of having some lord, all indicate the immense control exercised by the lords over their tenants, the *quondam* freemen who held their laens. The same view is borne out by passages in the charters. Towards the end of the ninth century (A.D. 880), Duke Æthelred[4] grants certain lands to the church, and, in augmentation of the gift, six men and their families ; " ut sine contradictione alicujus nobilis vel ignobilis, semper ad terram aecclesiae supradictae pertineant." This is the first instance, in the charters, of the grant of men and their families, and of the principle that men could be " adscripti glebae." It does not appear here to what class the *homines* granted belonged ; nor is this of consequence. There is nothing to show that they were slaves ; indeed, it may be fairly concluded they were not, for when slaves were intended, it was usual to say so. It is therefore evident that, in A.D. 880, freemen of some class were granted by book, and were made " adscripti

1 Cod. Dip. DCXVI. 2 Cod. Dip. DCXVII.
8 Cod. Dip. DCLXXIX. 4 Cod. Dip. CCCXI.

glebae " at the will of the grantor. About the same period, the expression *fasallus*[1] or *vasallus* appears in the charters, — a hint of the changing relations in the community. In a grant of A.D. 889, men are given with the land, and again in A.D. 902.[2] There is also a grant[3] in A.D. 975 — marked a forgery by Mr. Kemble — which speaks of lands granted "cum octodecim servis, et sexdecim villanis et decem bordis." In another grant of A.D. 987, also marked a forgery, the right to seek a secular patron is specially given by the grantor.[4] In still another forgery,[5] of a much later date (A.D. 1051), there is a grant of lands to Croyland, with the reeve, the smith, the carpenter, the fisherman, and a variety of others, presumably farmers. In a small way, this is a good example of the substitution of the lord's tenants for the old Germanic freeman, with his hereditary *status* in the community. In late charters, written in Saxon, the expression, "mid mete and mannum," is of constant recurrence, showing the ultimate establishment of the "adscripti glebae" principle. The history of the large estate, the history of the lord and tenant principle, is the history of the decline and degradation of the body of freemen which had primarily formed the state. In relation to land, the stages of the downward course may be briefly indicated as the period when one freeman rented an estate to another; when one freeman assumed a legal responsibility, and a corresponding control over other freemen; and when one freeman bought and sold other freemen with his land, and bound them to it. These were the powers gradually assumed by the great land-owners; and the unbooked laen dependent on their will gradually became the estate of the once free tenant.

This brings us to the second point, the substitution of

---

[1] Cod. Dip. MLXXX., CCCCLXII., DXXXIV.

[2] Cod. Dip. CCCXV. and MLXXIX.

[3] Cod. Dip. DLXXXVII.

[4] Cod. Dip. DCLVI.

[5] Cod. Dip. DCCXCV. It is usual to find the occurrence of phrases and customs in forged charters a few years anterior to the time when they came into actual existence. As the earliest charter cited on this point is clearly genuine, the subsequent forgeries probably do not unfairly represent a veritable legal custom.

the lord for the community. In a general way, it may be said that this substitution was due solely to the rise of large estates, which owed their existence to unequal powers of re-demption, to conquest, sales, grants, and possibly, in the tenth and eleventh centuries, to commendation with land. In a com-munity such as has been already mentioned, where the title was vested in the crown, the state, the king, or some other individual, and not in the community itself, the process of substitution was never necessary. The title was always in the crown or lord, as the case might be ; and the community, which had grown up on the land, had merely acquired cer-tain prescriptive rights, exactly similar to the communal rights in independent communities. The title was in the lord ; the rights ran with the estates held by his tenants, or, as in later times, his serfs. The same legal situation was also brought about in so great a majority of the cases of indepen-dent communities that it may be called universal. In order to understand how this was done, it is necessary first to get an idea of a freeman's estate at as early a period as may be. In A.D. 819,[1] there is a grant to Croyland, by one Fregisl, a soldier. The charter is marked by Mr. Kemble as a forg-ery, but the description of the estate granted is repeated in the same words in three or four Croyland charters ; and, whether this is a forgery or not, an estate probably existed corresponding to the description, which is as follows : ". . . totum manerium meum et villam de Langtoft, et in campis ejusdem villae sex carucatas terrae arabilis habentes in longitudine XV. quarentenas, et IX. quarentenas in lati-tudine, et centum acras prati, et sylvam et mariscum duarum leucarum in longitudine, et aecclesiam ejusdem villae, et XL. acras prati de eodem feodo in campo de Deping." Another example is of a similar gift to Croyland. Ælfgar grants,[2] in A.D. 825, " manerium meum de Baston cum quatuor caru-catis terrae arabilis . . .; et XLV. acras prati ; et mariscum . . . Et aecclesiam villæ, et unum molendinum, et dimidium alterius molendini, et totam piscariam meam in aqua a prae-dicto molendino versus occidentem." The first of these grants appears to be the case of a dependent community ;

---

[1] Cod. Dip. CCXIII.   [2] Cod. Dip. CCXXI.

the second, of lands lying in an independent community. The central and most important part is the *croft* or *toft* — the *frum-stól* of Ina's law — lying within the hedge, as described in Oswald's grant to Wynsig, quoted above.[1] Then comes the arable land, the meadow for pasture, the marsh and woodland, the fishing and the hunting. A large estate was, in the main, simply the unlimited extension of such estates as these. The principal proprietor, having obtained all the arable and house land in the various ways already pointed out, had thereby secured the rights belonging to all this land in the wild and waste. In early times, these were rights allotted, as has been said, in proportion to the amount of arable, and they obtained generally on all the common, lands. By the descriptions above cited, it will be seen that a revolution, similar to that which had taken place in the rights to arable lands, had likewise taken place in the rights over the waste and wild lands. Instead of rights pertaining generally to all the land held in common, the owners of arable had acquired certain parcels of the wild lands, definite in amount, and distinguished from the mass of communal property. The lord who had acquired all or most of the arable had likewise acquired all or most of the wild and waste land. The title in such land having passed from the community, and the community having changed from freemen to tenants, nothing remained to the holders of the lord's utland — that is, of the tenant estates — but the privilege of exercising, on the land of the lord, the rights running with their land, and which they had formerly exercised over their own communal property. In a dependent community, the title had always been in the lord, and the rights were purely prescriptive. In an independent community, on the other hand, the title to the wild and waste lands had shifted from the community to the lord; and nothing was left to the commoner but the exercise of certain rights, to all intents and purposes, of no more force or of no better title than the prescriptive rights of the dependent communities. In this way were the lands of the manor substituted for those of the community. In this way, the waste and common of the community became

[1] *Vide supra*, p. 87.

the lord's waste, and gave birth to the long controversy of enclosure on the one hand, and the maintenance of the full rights on the other. This was the history of common land in the great majority of cases. Instances were doubtless not wanting in which the lord or chief proprietor never obtained control of the arable lands. To cases of this last description the examples of community in arable land, which have survived to the present day, may be attributed. Still oftener, to judge by the modern examples, the wild and waste lands never lost their communal character, in the broadest sense of the term; and the title remained vested in the community.

The last class of lands not held by books — the folc-land — has now been reached.

The researches of Allen and Kemble first determined the true meaning of the expression "folc-land." The obvious meaning of the word was also the right one, — the "people's land," which belonged to the people in their collective capacity, forming an organized whole known as the State. This, the only correct view, has been best expressed by the first of German writers on these subjects. In the "Verfassungsgeschichte,"[1] Dr. Sohm says: "The folc-land rests on the principle in the constitution that royal and public are not the same thing; that the king, not alone, but only at the head of the whole body of the people, represents the public power; that, therefore, the public objects are the objects of all, and the public property the property of all." What was the origin of this public property? Mr. Freeman[2] concludes from a passage in Cæsar[3] that folc-land even then existed. The passage referred to can hardly be strained to support this meaning; but it will bear the interpretation that all lands at that time were common lands, — the lands of various communities, — and dealt with as such. This distinction is not

[1] Vol. I. p. 84. Dr. Sohm omits an interesting case, which shows the powers of the Witan in all grants of folc-land by the king. Cod. Dip. CCXL. Lands were claimed as unjustly booked, "Quia cum recta libertate facta non esset, quia in fugatu ejus (Baldredi regis) conscripta et concessa fuisset."

[2] Norman Conquest, I. p. 57, note 4. Cf. also Von Maurer, Einleitung, p. 84, ff.

[3] Cæsar, De Bello Gallico, VI. 22.

a merely verbal one. The conception of a great territory like the folc-land, forming a species of national fund, and representing the national property, could hardly at that early time, as it did later, have existed as a distinct conception. Something was needed to give to the people, collectively, a sense of ownership in the large tracts of land then unoccupied. The proximate causes of this sense of ownership which led to the conception known as folc-land were migration and conquest. England was won by hard fighting; and, after every man and every community had obtained all they desired, much still remained. This was as truly the land of the people, and as much the fruit of their labor, as the shares they had already received. On the continent, the unoccupied lands fell to the crown.[1] In England, the king had a large share of the conquered territory as an individual, and still more annexed to the crown; but the larger portion of the conquests remained unshared and national property. The primary use of folc-land, according to Bede's celebrated epistle to Ecgberht,[2] was to reward soldiers. This was obviously a national use and benefit. With the growth of population, more and more folc-land was probably taken, not only by individuals, but by entire communities; and thus was the national property occupied by people who had no title to the land, and with no resulting benefit to the State. The obvious way to utilize the land thus occupied was by drawing rent, which, in this case, was but another name for taxation. Taxation, it has been already said, outside of the *trinoda necessitas* consisted in services to the king, and to this all the folc-land was liable. Folc-land thus became the *ager vectigalis* of England.[3] The title was in the State, the usufruct, on certain conditions, in the occupier, and the only power capable of dealing with this land was the people in their collective capacity, or through their representatives. A well-established function of the king or other leader was to distribute the conquered lands; and in

---

[1] Roth, Beneficialwesen, p. 203, ff.; V. Maurer, Einleitung, p. 84, ff.

[2] Bedae, Opera Minora; Ad Ecgberhtum Antistitem, §§ 11, 12.

[3] K. Maurer, Kritische Ueberschau, p. 102. That services were the especial characteristics of folc-land, see Cod. Dip. CCLXXXI.

this capacity, therefore, with the witness and consent of the Witan, in theory certainly the representatives of the people, he dealt with the folc-land. This was equally true in freeing lands from services, and in restoring them. In both cases, the consent of the Witan was requisite.[1]

Folc-land taken as a whole is easy to understand; it is in discussing the nature of *estates* of folc-land that the difficulties begin. The authorities which throw any light on this point are unusually few, and the information they contain is scanty. By the will of Duke Alfred,[2] it is determined that estates of folc-land existed; that they were held by private individuals, and were not heritable nor the subject of devise. The important passage from which these facts are derived runs as follows: "and I grant to Aethelweard, my son, III hides of boc-land . . . and if the king will give him the folc-land in addition to the boc-land, let him have and enjoy it. If not, then let her [his wife or daughter] give him whichever she pleases, either the land at Horsalege or Langafield." Not only the four points already mentioned are here at once apparent, but it is evident that neither the provision in the will nor the fact that the legatee was the testator's son was of any legal value in giving a title to the folc-land. By a fundamental principle of law the folc-land reverted to the state, while boc-land followed the provisions of the book. This conclusion suggests an interesting comparison between the English estates of folc-land and boc-land on the one side, and the Frankish land-grants of the same period on the other. The Merovingian gifts of crown lands were private and heritable estates; when once created, confirmation was not necessary to prolong their existence, and was sought merely as evidence of the rightfulness of that existence.[3] The Carolingian benefice, the successor of the Merovingian gift, was on the other hand an estate which lapsed on the death of either the grantor or the grantee, and confirmation was sought

---

[1] Cod. Dip. CCLXXXI; Sohm, Verfassungsgeschichte, Vol. I. p. 34.

[2] Cod. Dip. CCCXVII.

[3] Roth, Beneficialwesen, pp. 210–216. Also, in general, Roth, Feudalität und Unterthanverband; and *contra*, Waitz, Ueber die Anfänge der Vassalität; and Verfassungsgeschichte, Vols. II. and III.

because a new grant was necessary in order to create a new title in the holder or his heirs.[1] The land conveyed by the Merovingian gift was conveyed in full and free property to the grantee. The Carolingian benefice remained the property of the grantor. In English law the boc-land is essentially the same estate as the Merovingian, while the English estate of folc-land, as shown in Duke Alfred's will, would seem to be the analogue of the contemporary Carolingian benefice. There is, however, hardly evidence enough to establish a demonstration of this theory, and the estate of folc-land must therefore remain a problem more or less undecided, but apparently furnishing another illustration of the Anglo-Saxon tendency to follow the rapid development of Frankish law only with tardy and unwilling steps. The estate of folc-land never became a favorite estate of Anglo-Saxon law.

Estates of folc-land, moreover, were not ill-defined masses of land scattered here and there in the national territory ; on the contrary, they were as carefully bounded as any other estates, and appear to have existed in the midst of other estates. In other words, the character of folc-land and its legal position remained for long periods unchanged. To demonstrate this, it is sufficient to examine those grants in which folc-land is expressly involved. In Æthelwulf's[2] celebrated grant to himself, the twenty *manentes* of folc-land there booked are as carefully bounded and described as any species of private estate could possibly be. Again, in the exchange[3] of folc-land for boc-land, made by Æthelbert of Kent, the boundaries are exactly given.

The essential feature of the estate of folc-land was the taxation of which it was the origin, and with which it was inseparably connected. It is not necessary to recapitulate here the argument already used to prove this ; it is sufficient simply to mention it as, above all, the characteristic of folc-land.

But one other form of folc-land remains to be considered. This is the laen, to which reference has already been

[1] Roth, Beneficialwesen, p. 416. [2] Cod. Dip. CCLX.
[3] Cod. Dip. CCLXXXI.

made.[1] Professor Stubbs says: "These estates of folc-land may have been for a life or lives, or subject to testamentary disposition, according to the terms of the grant."[2] Another passage[3] leads one to suppose that Professor Stubbs considers folc-land to have been converted into book-land only when the estate created was an alodial and heritable estate for ever. This opinion of the most eminent English authority has been selected as containing, in the most concrete form, the opinions in vogue. In this, as in many other cases, confusion has arisen from a misconception and misuse of the term laen. The Anglo-Saxon laen was not a leasehold estate in any sense of the word. The one distinguishing feature of a leasehold is that it must be for a term of years, — for a definite and limited period of time. The time certain is of the very essence of any estate less than a freehold. There is but one, and that a very late, example in all the Anglo-Saxon authorities of any leasehold properly so called. The inference is unavoidable that the Anglo-Saxons conceived of no estate less than an estate for life. Such an estate, it must not be forgotten, might be of the most precarious kind as an un-booked laen, or an estate of folc-land, so that the tenant, in exact language, held only on sufferance; yet, notwithstanding this, if a man had possession, it was *prima facie* a possession for life. In some cases the tenant was liable to ejectment at any moment, in others he was protected by the strength of a book; but, in the Anglo-Saxon theory, the estate was for life. The Anglo-Saxon laen meant simply an estate where the title and the possession were not vested in the same person; that is, it was a loan of land for a greater or less period, — rent sometimes being received, and as often not. Such being the definition of laens there are two classes of them, — those which are held by book and those which are not. To the latter class belong the unbooked laens of a lord's utland, already discussed, and all estates of folc-land. In discussing them, it has seemed better to treat those estates held directly of the State as estates of folc-land, and portions of such

---

[1] *Vide supra*, pp. 86, 87. [2] Constit. Hist. I. p. 77.

[3] Constit. Hist. I. p. 130.

estates underlet by the tenants of the State as laens. A position has now been reached by this explanation in which an issue can be fairly made up with Professor Stubbs. He speaks of an estate of folc-land held "according to the terms of the grant." This is a self-contradiction: if the estate were one of folc-land, then there could be no grant; and, if there were a grant in writing, then the estate was, *ipso facto*, book-land and not folc-land. In the scattered instances where folc-land is expressly mentioned, it is always in antithesis to book-land. It occurs but once in the laws, but there in opposition to book-land.[1] Duke Alfred, in his will, marks the opposition between estates of boc-land and of folc-land by his lack of power to devise the latter.[2] The instances of conversion [3] are all familiar, and all contain the same marked opposition between the two classes of land.[4] Book-land, in the ordinary acceptation of the term, unquestionably meant "terra haereditaria," or "terra testamentalis;" but no less did it mean a laen created by book. Indeed, where does Professor Stubbs intend to draw the line? An estate for two lives was, in most cases, "terra testamentalis," and always an estate of inheritance in Anglo-Saxon law. Is it therefore to be said that an estate for one life was an estate of folc-land, and an estate for two lives an estate of book-land, both being created in the same way, — very possibly by the same instrument.[5] An estate created by book, whether a fee-simple or a laen for one life, was book-land, and remained so as long as it was held by virtue and under the terms of the grant. This theory runs directly counter to Mr. Kemble's views,[6] a comparatively unimportant matter; for, great as were Mr. Kemble's services to Anglo-Saxon law, — greater than those rendered by any other Englishman, — great also as was his knowledge, the results in the shape of scientific theory were meagre to the last degree. Every thing was misty and confused. It is a much more serious matter to oppose such a writer as Dr. Konrad Maurer; but here again

---

[1] Edw. I. 2.   [2] Cod. Dip. CCCXVII.
[3] Cod. Dip. CCLXXXI.
[4] Schmid supports this distinction, Gesetze, p. 575, ff.
[5] Cf. Cod. Dip. CLXXXI.   [6] Saxons, Vol. I. chap. xi. and xii.

the opposition is to confusion of ideas[1] rather than to any definite theory. The distinction contended for goes to the root of the whole system. By applying modern legal principles in the discrimination of the various Anglo-Saxon estates, it has been attempted to prove that under all the apparent confusion a really logical system existed, elastic enough to embrace all the varied and apparently contradictory forms of Anglo-Saxon estates.

The estates of folc-land were obtained in the beginning by general and indiscriminate appropriation.[2] This was naturally a method employed chiefly by the more powerful members of the community. As Dr. Schmid has pointed out,[3] in all the cases where folc-land is expressly mentioned, it is owned by large proprietors, — the crown, the church, the king, or some duke or sheriff. Nevertheless, as time went on, small proprietors undoubtedly took estates of folc-land, and the numberless instances in the charters of grants differing from each other in no important particular, represent, as Mr. Kemble rightly concludes,[4] the steady process of conversion of folc-land into boc-land. Dr. Schmid differs from this view,[5] affirming that the most probable course was conversion from laen land to boc-land, — another instance of the confusion arising from a non-appreciation of the true nature of a laen. Dr. Schmid and Mr. Kemble in reality agree perfectly on this point. All estates of folc-land were unbooked laens, and no book laens were folc-land. If the phrase "unbooked" be· added to Dr. Schmid's "laens," a general term results perfectly synonymous with Mr. Kemble's "folc-land," even if not so exact.

These estates of folc-land were sublet, as appears by the expression in Æthelbert's charter: " cyninges folc-land quod abet wighelm and wulflaf."[6] Wighelm and Wulflaf were therefore lessees of the king; and estates of this description

---

[1] See Kritische Ueberschau, Vol. I. pp. 102–127.

[2] Beda, Op. Min.; Ad Ecgberhtum Antistitem, § 11, ff. Ibid., Hist. Aeccl. pp. 305–316.

[3] Gesetze, pp. 575–578

[4] Saxons, I. pp. 306, 307.

[5] Gesetze, p. 577.

[6] Cod. Dip. CCLXXXI.

were laens of folc-land in the narrower sense, as opposed to the general and comprehensive expression of estates of folc-land.

To recapitulate ; the folc-land, as a unit, was the national fund, — the common stock administered by the king and Witan conjointly as representatives of the whole State. The folc-land, as divided and held by individuals, was in its nature an unbooked laen ; not heritable ; not devisable ; alienable, in that the holder could grant all the right and title possessed by him ; capable of under-letting ; and, finally, the special and primary tax-paying estate of the community.[1] It only remains to discuss, as briefly as possible, the rights of the king and people over the folc-land. To enter upon a detailed proof to demonstrate that to the king pertained certain general rights in the wild land all over the kingdom is not necessary. The existence of such rights on the Continent has been abundantly proved by G. L. von Maurer, Roth, Waitz, Sohm, and others ; and Dr. Schmid,[2] Dr. Konrad Maurer,[3] and Professor Stubbs have affirmed the same fact as equally true in England. Instances occur in the charters of grants of these rights which entirely bear out this theory.[4] One of the suits[5] in the Appendix concerns these rights, which the king had granted to a bishop. The bishop brought suit to restrain the ealderman from asserting certain public rights of pasture which conflicted with the bishop's grant. To the people therefore belonged also certain general rights on the wild or waste folc-lands, as is apparent by this suit. These rights of wood, pasture, water, &c., were in strict analogy with the communal rights, as were the royal rights with those of the king or lords on the Continent. They have endured in England until a late period.[6]

---

[1] This last statement is at variance with the views of Dr. Schmid (Gesetze, p. 578). The able argument of Dr. Konrad Maurer on this point, already referred to in support of Mr. Kemble, sustains the theory here advanced. Dr. Sohm's adherence to the same doctrine is sufficient to make the settlement final.

[2] Schmid, Gesetze, pp. 575–578.   [3] Kritische Ueberschau, pp. 102–107.

[4] Cod. Dip. LXXXVI., CCCVI., DCCXXVII.

[5] Cod. Dip. CCXIX. See Appendix, No. 11.

[6] Digby, Hist. of the Law of Real Property, p. 9.

Such being the characteristics of folc-land, as far as can be known, its history and ultimate fate may be readily and briefly sketched. Bede's complaint in the early part of the eighth century is, that the folc-land had even then been so far absorbed by religious corporations and others, that nothing was left with which to reward the defenders of the country. At this comparatively early period the church was the great enemy of the national property, but laymen were not slow to follow the example of the priests. A large proportion of the first grants are made " jure aecclesiastico," or " ad jus aecclesiasticum." A grant[1] of lands in A.D. 736 is made " ad construendum coenubium," and in the indorsement it appears that this was a grant " ad jus aecclesiasticum;" so that estates of boc-land " jure aecclesiastico " were estates conditioned to found a religious establishment or perform some similar religious duty. It is the neglect of this condition which especially calls forth the invective of Bede. Apparently, about the same time, an effort was made to enforce this condition by retaking the estate on non-fulfilment;[2] and in one of the cases given in the Appendix,[3] a grant of the king, without the authority of the Witan, is annulled, with the same general object of protecting the folc-land. That grants of folc-land made in the regular way to either the church or the courtiers diminished in number or extent, however, cannot be gathered from the charters; on the contrary, such grants become more and more numerous with each succeeding reign. As the royal power grew, and the government became more centralized, the natural tendency was to throw the control of the folc-land more and more into the hands of the king. The establishment of the Danish rule under Cnut exhibits, in a few instances, a very significant change in the form of the grants for which the centralization under the Wessex kings had undoubtedly prepared the way. This change is in the mode of acknowledging the advice and consent of the Witan, and began apparently by directing grants of folc-land simply by a writ in the ordinary form addressed to the shire-

---

[1] Cod. Dip. LXXX.   [2] Cod. Dip. XLVI., DCXCIX.
[3] See Appendix, No. 13, or Cod. Dip. MXIX., CCXLV.

moot.[1] There are several instances of these grants by simple writ, and without the concurrence of the shiremoot, but there is only one genuine case of a writ directed to the whole Witan of the Nation.[2] The exception in Cnut's reign became the rule under the strong Norman influences of Edward the Confessor's. The course of legislation in regard to fines, confiscation, and escheats, has already been examined. It has been seen that in this respect the power of the Witan was recognized even in the days of the Confessor; but the conquering power of William broke down this defence against illegal and unjust confiscations of property. William, however, always paid at least an outward deference to the native laws and customs; and, if he found it so easy and safe a matter to disregard the popular rights in a question so vital as that of forfeiture, it may readily be supposed that the principle of the popular or State ownership in such folc-land as still remained offered no resistance. In fact, it had practically ceased to be of any force under the Confessor, as appears by the introduction of the system of authorizing and legalizing grants by means of a simple writ. What had happened to the Continental tribes six hundred years before, now happened in England. The still unoccupied land passed from the people to the crown. The monarchical and centralizing forces of the age proved too strong for the old Germanic principles in this as in other cases. The people's land, in William's time, is no longer heard of. The folc-land had become the *terra regis*.

The second of the two principal classes, and one utterly different in its origin from those already described, alone remains to be considered. As the others were the offspring and the pure growth of popular customs, boc-land is the offspring of the church and the enemy of customs. The estates thus created rested upon written instruments called by the Saxons " books," and it will be necessary to a clear discussion to first examine briefly the book itself.

[1] Cod. Dip. DCCXXXI., DCCLVII., MCCCXIX., MCCCXXIII., MCCC-XXV.

[2] Cod. Dip. DCCLVI., MCCCXXVI. This latter charter is by no means free from suspicion.

Proof of its introduction by church influence would be superfluous. Mr. Kemble accepted the fact long since, and it has not been disputed. Indeed, the evidence lies on the surface. The most careless inspection of the charters is sufficient to discover the religious forms persisting to the latest times, and to show that the exclusive object of all the early grants was the enrichment or endowment of the church. Nor are the causes far to seek. The church was civilizing and Romanizing in an eminent degree, and there was beside a powerful motive which impelled them to push zealously the arts of civilization in all matters relating to the conveyance of land. Under the old Germanic system, brought by the heathen Angles, Saxons, and Jutes, from their forests, no way had been devised for clerical acquisitions. What with the claims of the family, the community, and of the nation, and the nonexistence of wills, there was no room for the church under the existing methods. Books were in their essence a mode of transfer, and their introduction was rendered less difficult than it would otherwise have been, by the fact that transfer was not a new idea among the Germans. The *adfathamire* of the Salic law is an example of one Teutonic mode of conveyance; the *de Chrene-cruda*, of another; and the indications in the Anglo-Saxon charters point to a similar procedure.

Before the introduction of documents, parties went to the land, accompanied by chosen witnesses, and the transfer was completed by the actual taking possession of the grantee or vendee.[1] There was no judicial proceeding, such as came in subsequently with the introduction of documents. The locality of the *traditio* was first lost by gifts to the church; and the *traditio* at the altar gradually absorbed even the name of investiture. Scattered provisions in the laws[2] in regard to witnesses, and the language of the books[3] in one or two instances, prove that in England, as on the Continent, the old procedure by personal investiture in the presence of witnesses

---

[1] In this brief sketch of the ancient mode of conveyance, I have followed chiefly Heusler's able work on the Gewere. See Die Gewere, pp. 7, 9, 10, 11, 13, 16, 20; also Sohm, V. G., Vol. I. 525, ff.; Von Bethmann-Hollweg, Civil Process, 493.

[2] E. G., Æthelred III., 3.   [3] Cod. Dip. LII. and CLVII.

once existed; but the books had so far superseded the old
method as a means of transfer that, in historical times, traces
of even the later stage of development — the placing the book,
a turf, or some other symbol on the altar — occur only in a
few early cases.[1] The main object of the new system of
books was to secure better and more enduring evidence, by
the superior nature of which, and by the solemnity and sanctity of a written instrument, signed by numerous witnesses,
the claims of the community, the nation, and, above all, of
the family, were to be most effectually barred.

Mr. Kemble divides a book,[2] as distinguished from a will,
contract, or synodal decree, into six parts, — I. The Invocation; II. The Proem; III. The Grant; IV. The Sanction;
V. The Date; VI. The Teste. The first, second, and fourth
of these divisions are purely religious, and require no detailed
examination.[3] Five and six are merely formal, useful only in
questions of chronology and genuineness, or as proof of the
presence of a Witan. The third division is the grant, which
contains all the important legal matter of the charter. Before discussing the grant, it will be well to sketch briefly the
general history of the book as a documentary whole, and its
various changes in the period from Æthelbert to Edward the
Confessor. Down to the time of the Wessex supremacy,
the books present great diversity both in the manner and
kind of grant; and the religious portions of the books are
short and simple. From the time of Alfred, the character of
the books changes very noticeably, great sameness taking
the place of the former variety. One charter in arrangement and language so closely resembles another that, in the
case of Bishop Oswald's grants, and even of all Edmund's,
it seems probable, as Mr. Kemble suggests, that blank
forms were used, to be filled up simply with the name of the
grantee. The religious portions of the grant increase im-
mensely both in obscurity and verbiage, until, during Dun-

---

[1] Cod. Dip. XII., XXXVII., CIV., CXIV., CLXXVII., MXIX. The latest
instance of placing a turf on the altar is in a forged charter, A.D. 799.

[2] Cod. Dip., Introduction, p. ix.

[3] One or two cases of a temporal sanction occur, but only in forged charters,
and for the benefit of the church.

stan's period, they become little more than magnificent nonsense, written in very bad Latin. The facts of interest in legal
history to be drawn from the books at this time are very few.
With the advent of Cnut, and in the subsequent reigns, the
charters again become simple ; and there is a very healthy diminution of bad paraphrases and doubtful extracts from the
Vulgate. The private grants increase in number ; and, were
it not for the general air of Norman influence and monkish
fraud which surrounds every thing connected with Edward
the Confessor, the charters of his reign would be almost as interesting as the earliest ones. It is very striking that, in all
these centuries, there were no fundamental legal changes in
the books, and scarcely any new clauses. It was sometimes
deemed necessary to insert a clause [1] barring other charters,
and declaring such other charters null and void ; and this
was almost the only innovation on the earliest form.

The grant usually begins by naming, either in the first or
third person, the grantor and grantee. Any free man or free
woman [2] could be either a grantor or a grantee,[3] and was entitled to appear in either capacity ; so, too, was any religious
corporation, and any dignitary, noble or royal, spiritual or
temporal. Grants also could be made by which land was
conveyed between members of the same family.[4] As every
one who was free was capable of making a book, so was the
law equally liberal in the subjects of grant. Not only lands,
and all the rights, privileges, or immunities connected with
them, were made, individually and collectively, the subject of
written grant, but also every description of personal property,
and revenues arising from ships [5] and the like, were conveyed
in this way. There was always a consideration expressed, in
most cases of a purely religious kind : " pro remedio animae
meae," " pro redemptione criminum meorum," and similar

---

[1] Cod. Dip., E. G., MCCXVII.

[2] For the *status* of women as exhibited in the books, *vide infra*, p. 113 ff.

[3] There is no evidence to contradict this general statement. I have found
no case of a grant to a slave. " Cliens," which sometimes occurs, appears to
be used in the same sense as " minister."

[4] Cod. Dip., E. G., CCXXIX.

[5] Cod. Dip. LXXVIII., MCCXXXIX.

phrases, are the most usual forms. In some cases, the consideration was, in modern language, a purely valuable consideration; and, except for the formal religious invocation and proem, books of this sort differ in no essential respect from a modern conveyance. In many cases, the valuable consideration is united with a religious one; but this does not practically change the legal significance of the instrument. The estate conveyed is always carefully expressed; and the numerous limitations, of which examples are found, served to create a great variety of estates, which correspond very nearly with some of those familiar to the law to-day. The estate most commonly conveyed was the largest possible, and corresponds almost exactly to our estate in fee-simple: "quam is semper possideat et post se cui voluerit heredum relinquat"[1] is one of the simplest forms. A more elaborate example is as follows: "Liberam per omnia habeat potestatem ad habendum, possidendum, perfruendumque seu vendendum aut commutandum, vel cuicumque ei herede placuerit derelinquendum perpetualiter habeat potestatem."[2] One form of limitation created estates in special tail. The grant[3] was to a man and wife, " et si contigerit ut vobis filius aut filia nati fuerint," then to the children. Estates in tail male were not uncommon: —

COD. DIP. CXLVII., A.D. 784. "Rus etiam hoc modo donatum est ut suum masculum possideat et non femininum."

COD. DIP. CLXIX., A.D. 781–798. "Donabo meam propriam haereditatem; tali conditione adfirmo quod mei haeredes in mea genealogia in aecclesiastico gradu de virili sexu percipiant."

A much commoner estate than any yet mentioned, except the largest, was an estate for life or lives. The collection of charters abound in cases of this sort. These grants are usually for one life or three lives, but instances of grants for two, four, and even five lives are not wanting; and it was

[1] Cod. Dip. CXVII.
[2] Cod. Dip. CCXXVII. Numerous examples of this, the largest, and of the other more limited, estates are collected by Mr. Kemble, in his Introduction to the Codex. Selections are given here for the sake merely of convenience and clearness.   [3] Cod. Dip. CLIII.

not unusual, at the expiration of the lives as provided in the grant, to obtain a renewal for a certain number more. It has already been stated that, in all the documents and codes of the Anglo-Saxon period, there is but one example of a true leasehold estate : —

COD. DIP. DCCCCXXIV. (after 1058). " Here is it declared about the contract which was wrought between the chapter at Worcester and Fulder. That is, that he have the land at Ludinton three years, for which he pays three pounds, and let him enjoy the land for three years, and within three years give the land to the chapter."

This example is given as more appropriately coming under the description of the various estates conveyed by book. As a factor in the argument on laens, it has already been sufficiently noticed.·

Other kinds of limitation and condition were not uncommon. An estate limited to the family has been the subject of discussion. Another hereditary estate was granted " eadem libertate qua illi concessum est;"[1] " this is the land booked to Wynsige as his father held it."[2] " This is the land booked to Eadric as his father held it."[3] Besides these, there were the numberless instances of lands conditioned to pay rent.

In the case of every estate thus far mentioned, except the first and largest, it will be seen that there must have been a remainder, and all the remainders thus left by the estates created are duly provided for.· This fact, omitted to avoid confusion in the general argument on laens, is finally destructive of the statement of Professor Stubbs. The provision for remainders, which completes the alienation of the estates, and renders them as entirely alienated from the folc-land, or any other kind of land, as the allodial and hereditary grants which Professor Stubbs considers distinctively book-land, is universal. Many grants are apparently made simply for the purpose of providing for the remainder. Another use of the books was the confirmation of estates where any cloud rested on the title, or where the protection of the king was necessary to the

[1] Cod. Dip. CXLVIII.   [2] Cod. Dip. DCXVI.   [3] Cod. Dip. DCXVII.

holder of the estate confirmed. One very striking instance of this latter use is the case of three sisters who inherited certain lands. The lands were confirmed to them by the king and Witan; one sister withdrew any claim on her part to a share, and the lands were then reconfirmed, and partition ordered by king and Witan.[1] One form of confirmation very common during the tenth century, and subsequently, was the restoration of charters which had been either lost or destroyed, and it curiously shows the strong respect for customs, that in the new charters it is often simply said that the lands are to be held as they were under the old charter.[2]

Thus far only grants, or confirmations of grants, have been dealt with; and, though these form a large majority of the charters, there are also found books which contain marriage settlements, mortgages, and wills. The first of these may be conveniently left to the last division of this Essay, which treats of the rights of women in land. Mortgages[3] occur in at least two charters, and are sufficiently well defined to put their existence beyond doubt, but not well enough defined to determine with any exactness the state of the law in regard to them. The most important example occurs in one of the cases given in the Appendix (No. 18), from which it is clear that the land mortgaged was in the actual possession of the mortgagee; that on payment of the money loaned, the mortgagee, having found his profit or interest on his loan in the use of the lands, was to render back the property at once to the mortgagor, and that the failure so to do was good ground of action. The other charter referring to a mortgage is a deed by Æscwine, bishop of Dorchester, granting certain lands to the church (A.D. 995), "quam videlicet terram Sigericus archiepiscopus ejusdem aecclesiae Christi, praedecessor praefati archiepiscopi Ælfrici, dedit mihi in vadimonium pro pecunia quam a me mutuo accepit."[4] Here the mortgagee

---

[1] Cod. Dip. CCXXXII.

[2] Cod. Dip. MLXXX., MLXXXI., CCCXXXVIII., CCCXL. are instances of restorations.

[3] I have used this modern term here simply as meaning land pledged for the payment of money, and not as involving any of the refinements of a later time.

[4] Cod. Dip. DCXC.

deeds away the mortgaged land, showing that at some time, or in some way, the title could vest in the mortgagee unconditionally. The facts brought out in these two charters are the sum and substance of our knowledge as to the Anglo-Saxon mortgage. Slight as the result is, it becomes of interest as showing a pledge of lands for money borrowed to have been a conception quite distinct from the taking pledges[1] of other kinds for debt; the latter required legal formalities, no trace of which is found in our cases of mortgage.

In proportion as the sources of information are meagre as to mortgages, they are voluminous on the subject of wills. One of the few perfectly undisputed passages in Tacitus is that in which he declares that there are no testaments among the German tribes. Wills, however, were introduced at an early period by church influence. No simpler or more profitable way to temporal possessions was open to the church than through the superstitious fears of dying men and women; and if the extent to which this practice was carried on the Continent, in the very infancy of the church, be considered, it is wonderful, relying on the examples which have survived,[2] that so little was effected in England. Fresh proof of the strength of the pure Germanic principle in England, and of its resistance to the hostile system, is afforded by the fact that, despite the creation of a class of estates especially distinguished as " terra testamentalis," comparatively so little devise by will seems to have taken place. Out of thirty-six examples, no less than twenty-six are after the beginning of Æthelred's reign, when the Anglo-Saxon power rapidly began to break up ; and, of these twenty-six, sixteen are of the reign of Edward the Confessor. Down to the middle of the tenth century, there are but four examples of wills in existence, and in these there is no reference to royal permission, or to those gifts to a superior, afterwards known as a heriot. After that time, the permission of the king or lord occurs in almost every

---

[1] Cnut, II. 19. But see Schmid's note, p. 642, where all the law on the subject of pledges is collected.

[2] As the wills were mostly in favor of the church, probably a fair proportion have been preserved.

case, and there is mention of being declared testament-worthy. This fact is susceptible of very simple explanation. It merely indicates the extension of the system of unbooked laens with the accompanying growth of the lord's power, until, in Cnut's time, the gift to the lord and the permission to devise property had changed to the heriot, the relief of the next conqueror. Every form of property was made the subject of devise. Already it has been shown, from the descriptive phrase in Duke Alfred's[1] will, "my yrfe-land" and "my boc-land," that all lands of inheritance were not boc-land, but, in many instances, family land, and, as such, matter of bequest. The probable necessity of family consent has also been shown, both from the appearance of kinsmen as devisees and witnesses, from the attempts of members of the family to break wills, and from the analogy with the grants. These wills were made with all possible solemnity and publicity, as in Duke Alfred's case, before king and Witan. The principal devisee, in all the later examples and in many of the early ones, was the church. The chief peculiarity of the earlier wills is, that they make provision in the first place, and most fully, for the wife and children, with remainders to the family; while, in the later cases, the church and the king or lord get a large share, and the remainders generally are to the church, and not to the family. Originally, every free man and free woman could make a will, and could take under a will. Not only could witnesses take under the will, but the principal devisees sometimes acted in that capacity.[2] That it was ever an undisputed principle of law, that family lands could be alienated from the family by will, seems improbable. On the other hand, it is almost certain that an individual possessor could direct the course of descent of family lands within the limits of the family.

That the church should also have encouraged nuncupative wills would have been natural; but there are only two instances in the charters, both of which are mentioned and described in cases given in the Appendix.[3] The first will

<hr/>

[1] Cod. Dip. CCCXVII.   [2] Cod. Dip. CCCCXCII., MCCXLII.
[3] See Appendix, Nos. 14, 28.

was made in the presence of churchmen only, and was apparently the chief support of the widow in the litigation which ensued. The second is two hundred years later, and, like the first, seems to have been supported by the judgment and authority of the Witan; but in this instance the witnesses of the declaration were not churchmen. It can hardly, then, be doubted that nuncupative wills, properly witnessed, had perfect validity, but, as they were less secure, held a very inferior position to that occupied by written wills.

This concludes the list of uses to which books were generally put by the Anglo-Saxons; and it only remains to point out the distinguishing characteristics of book-land, and briefly to trace its history down to the period of the Norman and Angevin kings. The first marked feature in an estate of book-land, its origin in a written instrument as opposed to the estates originating in custom, has been sufficiently dwelt upon. The second important quality is, that an estate created by book was only held in exact accordance with the terms of the written instrument to which it owed its existence; and, theoretically if not always practically, any departure from the terms worked forfeiture. Passages can be cited in which it is especially provided that any infraction of the terms or conditions of the grant should, *ipso facto*, forfeit the estate;[1] but the proof rests much more strongly on the evidence afforded by the general tone adopted in all the charters, and especially in those where rent was reserved. In all grants, the most terrific spiritual penalties are invoked against the presumptuous man who dares infringe the terms of the book; and, in cases where rent is reserved, this is applied to non-payment, and the more practical remedy of forfeiture by default in the stipulated rent is often expressly added.[2] This shows clearly the prevailing usage, and the sanctity attached to the terms of the book. It has been already said that the book, as a mode of transfer, presents none of the peculiarities which belonged to the archaic method, or to the one which arose from a combination of the old method with document-

---

[1] Cod. Dip. XLVI., CCCCVI., DCXLI.

[2] Cod. Dip., E. G., DCLXI., MXLIII. See also the cases of confiscation cited *supra*, pp. 65, 66, Cod. Dip. MXC. and DCI.

ary evidence, and which were preserved in numerous charters, laws, and formularies on the Continent. Except in the few early examples of placing a turf on the altar, there is no trace of either the *traditio* or the *investitura*.[1] Both the right of possession and the actual possession seem to have been conveyed by the simple modern process of passing the books, or mutual exchange of deeds; *e.g.* : —

" Libros quos ante non habebat in eodem concilio illi reddebat."[2]

" Duasque scripturas per omnia consimiles hujus reconciliationis conscribere statuimus, alteram habeat episcopus cum telligraphis aecclesiae, alteram Egberht et Æthelwulf reges cum haereditatis eorum scripturis."[3]

In two cases in the Appendix, the right of possession and the title passed by the simple delivery of the books; and in others the same effect is apparent from the manner in which possession of the books is treated.[4]

The manner in which a grant was declared is described in a late example, reciting the agreement between Oswulf and his wife Æthelitha and Abbot Leofstan. After stating the subject and terms of the agreement, "Ad quorum uocem, imposito silentio, coram omni populo episcopus Wulfwius alta uoce respondens dixit, Quicunque hoc dono sanctum priuauerit Albanum sciat se," . . . then the spiritual sanction, " Cui cuncti qui aderant Amen responderunt."[5] This or some similar formal recitation before the Witan, the witnesses, or the chapter, as the case might be, probably gave to the book its binding force, and was equivalent to putting it upon record.[6]

---

[1] Heusler's work on the Gewere, already referred to, is an able and exhaustive treatise on these points in continental procedure. In one case (see Appendix, No. 27), a reference occurs to taking possession in the presence of witnesses; but this has been rejected on the ground that the land in question was the subject of litigation, and the witnesses were probably official, in order to see the decision of the court carried out.

[2] Cod. Dip. CCXX.

[3] Cod. Dip. MXLIV.

[4] Appendix, Nos. 5, 6, 9, 13, 15, 17, 18, 23, 25, 27. All these cases show very clearly the position and legal force of the book; particularly No. 18. See, especially, Cod. Dip. CCCXXVIII., CCCCXCIX.

[5] Cod. Dip. DCCCCXLV.

[6] In many cases, reference is made to putting the books in churches and other safe places.

But one point remains to be noticed, — the escheat of boc⌐ land, already partially discussed in the note on the subject of escheat in general.

Cod. Dip. MXXXV., A.D. 825. "Hanc quippe tellurem fidelissimus quidam praefectorum meorum vocabulo Burhghardus olim me donante possedit, sed ille postmodum sine liberis defunctus eandem terram sine haereditaria sententia nemine sibi superstite existente dereliquit, sicque tellus ipsa cum omnibus finibus ejus, optimatum meorum decreto adjudicante, michi, qui eam antea possedi restituta est."

Cases of escheat, as already said, if such a thing existed at all, were certainly rare, owing probably to the family organization; but it may be inferred, from this and the example about to be discussed, that estates of book-land always reverted to the donor. The theory that all land, of book or otherwise, escheated to the king, is disproved by the case of Ælfeh.[1] If this had been a simple case of intestacy in ordinary lands, the family generally would have come in; but, on the contrary, all the land given by Ælfeh reverted to him on the death of the donee, Eadric, intestate and without children. This points to the conclusion that the prevailing principle was the reversion of all book-land, on the death of the holder childless and intestate, to the grantor and his heirs; and therefore estates of book-land could not escheat to the king, except in the rather improbable case of the extinction of the families both of grantor and grantee.

Another important fact as to books, bearing on the sanctity attached to them, is their influence in litigation. In a case under Offa,[2] the holders of the books prevailed against the parties in possession. In another case,[3] four years later, the grantees made no attempt to recover the land of which they had been disseised, until the books, which had been stolen from them, were recovered; and, when they had obtained the charters, they, as possessors of the documentary evidence, were sustained by the Witan against the party in possession, although the latter was the king's grantee. In another

[1] See Appendix, No. 21.
[2] Appendix, No. 5, Cod. Dip. CLXIV.
[3] Appendix, No. 6, Cod. Dip. MXIX.

·case [1] (A.D. 840), the claim of the holders of the books was again sustained against the king and his grantees. In still another instance,[2] which illustrates also the rigid adherence to the terms, the suit went against the holder of the land for a slight infringement of the conditions of the grant. In a case [3] about the year 1000, a claim founded on the possession of books was sustained against the person in actual possession of the land. The retention of charters also, in two cases,[4] carried with it the right of possession. These citations [5] show, better than any thing else, the legal force of a book.

A few words suffice to tell the history of book-land. The system of making grants by written instruments went on unchecked until, with the advent of the Normans and the system of feudal tenures, the old significance of the Anglo-Saxon book, as well as the name, almost disappeared. The importance of the book primarily lay in its opposition to the old Germanic customs and principles, and in the protection it afforded against the claims recognized by that system. When each and every estate formed but one link in the great feudal chain, there was no longer any use in the book as the Anglo-Saxons conceived it. The only characteristic it retained was as an evidence of title. Charters and title-deeds went on accumulating in great abundance, but the old Saxon book perished with the Conquest. In all Domesday, there is but one estate of boc-land mentioned. The cause of this sudden disappearance is obvious. The book had been introduced and used to supply certain needs and bar certain claims. When those needs and claims no longer existed, the vital force of the principle of boc-land was extinct. There was but one object left for a written instrument, to evidence title ; and the Norman charters fulfilled that object. If the Norman charters preserved in Dugdale, the Abingdon Chronicle, &c., be examined, it will be found that the religious portions of the

---

[1] Appendix, No. 18, Cod. Dip. CCXLV.
[2] Appendix, No. 15, Cod. Dip. CCCXXIII.
[3] Appendix, No. 25, Cod. Dip. DCCCXXIX.
[4] Appendix, Nos. 17 and 18, Cod. Dip. CCCXXVIII., CCCCXCIX.
[5] Already referred to with others. *Vide supra*, p. 110, note 4.

book are gone, and that the consent of the Witan very soon disappears. The keen legal spirit of the new conquerors soon reduced the charters to the simplest form in which they could serve as evidence. They differed as essentially from the books, as we see them in the Codex Diplomaticus, as the system of William differed from the system of Alfred. The ultimate position of boc-land as the family land, under the laws of Henry, has already been pointed out.

In treating of family land, no attempt was made to deal with the question of inheritance. Under the customary law, males were preferred to females, and nothing more; and difference of sex did not work absolute, but only conditional,[1] exclusion. The theory that, in respect to the legal position of women, the Anglo-Saxon conception did not differ in principle from that of the pure Germanic codes of the North, is abundantly proved by the books. The charters are full of cases in which women are grantors and grantees,[2] vendors and vendees,[3] plaintiffs and defendants,[4] devisors and devisees,[5] without a variation in the terms of the instrument which could raise a suspicion of difference in sex. In all the law to be drawn from the books, women appear as in every respect equal to men. To women and men are given the same immunities and the same privileges, and on them are laid the same legal and political burdens.[6] A woman was as good a witness,[7] and as good a helper in the oath[8] as a man. There is no occasion to enter into a detailed proof of all this. The fundamental principle of the equality of women before the law, in every thing relating to land, except the family land, is indisputable, and is apparent on the face of the charters. A much more difficult question to answer is that in

[1] *Vide supra*, p. 74.
[2] Cod. Dip., E. G., CCXXIX., DXXXV.
[3] Cod. Dip., E. G.. MCXXIII., DCCLXXXIX.
[4] Cod. Dip. E. G., DCXCIII., DCCIV. See also Appendix, Nos.
[5] Cod. Dip., E. G., CCXXXV., DCLXXXV.
[6] From this it would seem that military service must have been commuted at quite an early period.
[7] Cod. Dip., E. G., DCXCIII., DCCIV. See also Appendix, Nos. 23 and 26.
[8] Cod. Dip., E. G., CCCIV., DCXCIII. See also Appendix, No. 22.

regard to the position of married women, and the law of dower. As to the former, it appears, from a grant A.D. 855, that a man could convey land by book to his wife.[1] Examples also occur in which husband and wife join as grantors,[2] devisors,[3] and vendors;[4] and, in other cases still, they are joined as grantees,[5] vendees,[6] and devisees,[7]—the law of survivorship sometimes being duly enforced by the terms of the instrument. This is evidence that in England, as in Iceland, husband and wife held and administered property in common; but no light is thrown by these cases on the law of dower. In the charters, there are eight references to dower or morning gifts, and two to marriage settlements:—

COD. DIP. MCCCV., A.D. 1008. Deditque conjugi suae Ælfgife sub haereditario datalicii dono." On the death of the husband, the widow again marries, and carries to her second husband these lands given in dowry, which are subsequently forfeited for the crimes of the woman and her second husband.

COD. DIP. DCCCCXXVI. (before A.D. 1069). "Ego Gytha comitissa concedo aecclesiae . . . terram meam de Scireford quae est de dote mea."

COD. DIP. CCCXXVIII. (after A.D. 900).[8] "Then it was the opinion of all of us that Helmstan might go forth with the charters, and prove his right to the land, that he held it as Æthelthrith gave it to Oswulf, in full property for a fair price; and she told Oswulf that she was fully entitled to sell it to him, because it was her morning-gift when she first came to Athulf."

COD. DIP. MCCLXXXVIII., A.D. 965–993. Ælfeh booked to his nephew, Eadric, certain lands. Eadric died childless and intestate; and all these lands reverted to Ælfeh, who confirmed one of the estates, Cray, to his nephew's widow, because it had been her morning-gift, and kept the other two estates, Erith and Wouldham. The nephew's widow married again, and, aided by her second husband,

---

[1] Cod. Dip., E. G., CCLXXVI.
[2] Cod. Dip., E. G., DCCLXVI., MCCCXL.
[3] Cod. Dip., E. G., CCCCXCII., DCCCCLXXI.
[4] Cod. Dip., E. G., CCXC., CCXCIX.
[5] Cod. Dip., E. G., CCCXLV., DCXXXVII.
[6] Cod. Dip., E. G., CCLXXIX.
[7] Cod. Dip., E. G., CCCXIV.
[8] See Appendix, No. 17.

entered upon and claimed Wouldham, as well as Cray, on Ælfeh's death. But Ælfeh's will was sustained on trial.[1]

Cod. Dip. MCCXC., A.D. 995. Wynflaed devises certain lands to Eadmer, to whom she also devises the remainder in certain other lands " at Faccancumb, her morning-gift."

Cod. Dip. DCCIV.[2] (after A.D. 1000). " Then the widow prayed Archbishop Ælfric, who was her intercessor, and Æthelmere, that they should pray the king that she might give her morning-gift to Christ's church, for the king and all his people, on condition that " [3] . . .

Cod. Dip. DCCXXXII., A.D. 1016–1020. " Here is declared by this writing the contract which Godwine wrought with Beorhtric when he married his daughter ; that is, first, he gave her one pound's weight of gold for that she received his will ; and he gave her lands at Street, &c." This was before the king and Witan, whose names follow, and then the names of those who made the wedding-feast at Brightling. " And so whichever survives shall hold all the lands I gave her and every thing."

Cod. Dip. DCCXXXVIII., A. D. 1023. " Here is it declared by this writing about the contract which Wulfric and the archbishop wrought when he got the archbishop's sister to wife ; that is, that he promised her the land at Alderton and at Ribbesford for her life ; and promised her the land at Knightwick, that he would obtain it for her for three lives from the chapter at Winchcombe ; and granted her the land at Eanulfintum, to give and to sell to whomever she most pleased during her life, and, after her life, as she most liked ; and he gave her fifty mancuses of gold, and thirty men and thirty horses."

In the laws, the principal passages on the subject of marriage occur in Appendix VI. of Dr. Schmid's collection, " De sponsalibus contrahendis," — popularly known as " The Kentish Betrothal," and attributed by Dr. Schmid to the reign of Æthelstan. Two paragraphs only in this Appendix throw even a side light on the subject of dower in lands : —

C. 3. " Then afterwards let the bridegroom declare what he gives her that she chooses his will, and what he gives her if she survive him.

[1] Appendix, No. 21.   [2] Appendix, No. 26.
[3] See also Cod. Dip. DCLXXXV. and DCCCCLXVII.

C. 4. "If it be so agreed, then is it right that she be worthy half the inheritance, and all, if they have a child, unless that she afterwards choose again."

It is shown elsewhere that, if a widow married within a year after her husband's death, she was considered unchaste, and forfeited all rights in his property. From the passages here collected, it may be inferred that it was a common practice to dower with lands, and that dower might be the subject of contract.[1] It is not apparent that there was any legal difference between the lands of dower, and those of the morning-gift. In both, the woman's power was absolute, as may be seen from the case where she carried the lands "ex datalicii dono" of her first marriage to her second husband. Ælfeh's case does not militate against this theory of absolute power on the expiration of the first year. In that instance, the law of reversion of book-land prevailed over the law of dower. The discussion has been confined to those facts which are solely to be drawn from the native sources, but these few facts are sufficient to bear out fully the analogy with the Northern codes.

An essay on the Anglo-Saxon land law cannot be fittingly concluded without some reference to the feudal system, and the subject of military tenures. The researches of Thudichum and Hanssen have established the fact that personal freedom did not primarily, among the German tribes, rest on the possession of land. The opposite view is that supported by Waitz,[2] and has been completely overthrown by the able arguments of Sohm[3] and Roth.[4] The latter have further shown that the attendance on the court and service in the army were, under the pure Germanic system, incumbent on every freeman, and therefore not on the possession of land. This view is also adopted by Dr. Schmid[5] and Professor Stubbs.[6] It will not at this day be disputed that the same

---

[1] *Vide infra*, p. 175.   [2] Waitz, V. G., Vol. I. § 120.

[3] Sohm, R. G., VI. p. 133.

[4] Roth, Feudalität und Unterthanverband, pp. 322–335. Beneficialwesen, pp. 42 and 182–200.

[5] Gesetze, p. 587.   [6] Constit. Hist. I. p. 189.

system existed in England. The only question is one of
time. When did the Germanic army constitution break
down and make room for the purely feudal system? In
answering this question, it must not be forgotten that the
personal relation of *princeps* and *comes* was brought to
England; and the extension of this relation to matters involving the holding of land has already been shown. Moreover, another prevailing cause of feudalism, large estates, had
existed in England from the earliest period, spreading slowly,
until, under the Confessor, they must have been almost universal. Beneficial tenures of a modified form also prevailed
in later times,[1] and, therefore, all the factors necessary to
produce feudalism were present, except the all-important one
of the army constitution. The old Germanic system of universal military service was but a form of taxation,[2] and the
feudal system which replaced it was simply another clumsy
kind of taxation imposed for the same objects. The germs of
feudalism had all existed in England, and had there slowly
expanded; but, as has just been said, the degree of development can be determined only by fixing the introduction of
military tenures; or, more explicitly, the period when land
is held on the condition of military services and personal
relations is the true feudal period. In the time of Ine, the
old Germanic system still prevailed. His laws provide that:
" If a gesithcund man forego the fyrd, let him pay one
hundred and twenty shillings, and lose his land; having no
land, sixty shillings. A ceorl, thirty shillings for fyrd-wite
[army fine]." [3] At the beginning and during the first half,
therefore, of the eighth century, it is absolutely certain
that the old system prevailed. The theory of Dr. Konrad
Maurer has met with general acceptance. He concludes
from two passages in fragments of the Northumbrian Codes:
" That, at least since the beginning of the tenth century, the
higher military service was connected with the possession
of five hides of land "[4] (a rather misleading statement), and
that this was a reform introduced by Alfred. This arrange-

---

[1] *Vide supra*, p. 95.   [2] *Vide supra*, p. 60.   [3] Ine, c. 51.
[4] Kritische Ueberschau, II. 408, 409.

ment of Alfred's introduced no new principle, but merely strengthened a connection which already existed. The *trinoda necessitas* is mentioned in the earliest grants ; and in Ine's law, just cited, the office of land in connection with military service is perfectly clear. Confiscation of land was a means of enforcing attendance which a pecuniary fine might have failed to effect. The expression, " five hides to the king's utware, or army summons," relied on by Dr. Maurer, is simply used as a badge of a certain rank liable to certain kinds of military equipment [1] and service. It cannot be inferred that five hides were more liable to confiscation than one. Grants of less than five hides are frequent, and always liable to the *trinoda necessitas*, and to confiscation for failure in army duty.[2] Five hides were simply a qualification for a degree in the kinds of army services. As the small freeholders gradually sank in the social scale, land became more and more the badge of freedom. The expression of the Northern laws — and this is absolutely the only authority suggesting military tenures to dispose of [3] — does not represent the really vital change at work in the English army.

It is not within the scope of this essay to discuss the changes which had actually taken place in the army constitution, and had insidiously undermined its strength. At the time of the conquest, the feudal system did not exist except in embryo. The army which fought at Stamfordbridge and Hastings, with the exception of the mercenary household troops, was the "fyrd," the militia of the shires. With this militia, army duty was an individual responsibility inseparably connected with the status of every freeman, did not differ from the early Germanic system, and had no con-

[1] Robertson, Hist. Essays, pp. vii.–x. Stubbs, Constit. Hist., 189.

[2] See cases of confiscation given above, pp. 65 and 66.

[3] Cod. Dip. CCXIV. In this charter of Coenulf's, the phrase occurs : " Expeditiones cum XII. vassallis et cum tantis scutis exerceant." The whole charter seems to me, from internal evidence, a very late and clumsy forgery, although passed by Mr. Kemble as genuine. Admitting, however, that it is genuine, it in no way militates against the statement in the text. The phrase occurs in the usual exception in favor of the *trinoda necessitas*, — the universal and common duty, and can therefore be most naturally construed as referring to the number of free tenants on the estate liable to fyrd.

nection with land as has just been shown. The great features of the feudal system in its complete development were the military tenures of land; and without them no perfect system, such as afterwards existed, was possible.

If the course of native development had not been changed, feudalism would have followed sooner or later in England, as a natural out-growth, just as surely as night follows. day. Whether a purely English feudalism would have been the same as that of the Continent, or whether it would have been more modified or more extreme, no one now can say. This alone is certain, that the slow, strong progress of England was rudely broken, and on the nascent feudalism of the Anglo-Saxons was superimposed the full-grown system of William and Normandy.[1]

[1] The following note was omitted until the plates of the work had been partly cast, and could not, therefore, be inserted in its proper place on p. 67, where it was said that "the *Danegeld*, at the close of the tenth century, was a great extension of the power of the National Assembly." The ship-money assessed in 1008 was of the same nature as the *Danegeld*. It was an extraordinary levy for purposes of defence; and the first trace we find of it dates from the same period as the *Danegeld*. Archbishop Ælfric's will (Cod. Dip. DCCXVI.) only proves that, at the close of the tenth century, shires were expected to furnish ships. To say that the fleets of Alfred and Edgar were the same thing in principle as the ship-money of Æthelred is like saying that the military service of the Germanic freeman was the same thing as the *Danegeld*. The fleets of Alfred and Edgar were perhaps raised by voluntary contributions, or, more probably, were included in the *trinoda necessitas*, as a part of the duty of every freeman in providing for defence. Every thing on the point is, however, wholly conjectural. At the close of the tenth century, the shires were apparently responsible for ships; and this was made the excuse for commuting this provision for defence into a tax, like the Danegeld, liable to abuse, and which led to the most unjust extortion. There is no trace that it was any thing but a new and extraordinary extension of power on the part of the Witan, or that, before the period of weakness and disintegration at the close of the tenth century, it was any thing but one of the fundamental duties of every freeman. As to Alfred's fleet, see Asser, A. 877, Sax. Chron.; and Florence, 897. This view is opposed to that taken by Mr. Freeman, Vol. I. p. 228 and note L. L.; cf. Dowell's History of Taxation in England, p. 23.

THE ANGLO-SAXON FAMILY LAW.

THE principal difficulty in dealing with Anglo-Saxon Family Law is occasioned by lack of material. The legal sources of the Anglo-Saxon period contain little pure family law, and even the main outlines of the family system of the Anglo-Saxons would be difficult to determine without a knowledge of the kindred systems of the continental Germans. The reason is not far to seek. The earliest collections of written laws among the Germans were not comprehensive codes, designed to cover the whole region of law, but in the main only records of new principles introduced by specific legislation or through the medium of the courts. With the migration of the tribes a rapid development of law began, but at first only particular branches of the law were affected. Family law, belonging entirely to the domain of custom, opposed the most stubborn resistance to innovation, and remained longest outside of this development. Dealing with the intimate relations of private life, and administered within and by the family, its rules formed part of the daily habits and of the common sense of the community. Family law, therefore, offered little occasion either for judicial decisions or legislative enactments. In certain cases the violation of family rights and obligations entailed legal penalties, but more frequently family custom and public law are found opposed. In two directions, however, the family system was gradually modified. On the one hand, the old independence of the family in private feuds, dangerous to the peace of the state, was gradually limited by the growing power of public law; and, on the other, the church exerted its influence to soften the harsher features of the old system. Most of the provisions in the laws relating specially to the family are innovations in one of these two directions. Few as these are, they are sufficient to prove that the family system of the Anglo-Saxons was essentially the same with that found existing in all other German tribes.

The importance of the family in all early societies of the Indo-Germanic race has been so often dwelt upon, that a long discussion of it here would be superfluous. Saxon England formed no exception to the rule. The family was not only the most important institution of private law; it stood also at the bottom of the whole police and criminal system. In the earliest times it was upon the family that the state chiefly depended for the maintenance of peace and the punishment of crime. It was to the family first of all that every member of the community owed the protection he enjoyed. In childhood the family watched over and protected him, even from his father. Members of the family were his witnesses and sureties at his marriage. Before the court they swore for him either to support his claim as plaintiff or his denial as defendant; and, in case of necessity, they were obliged to pay his fines. In the blood-feud they stood beside him to defend him even with their lives. Even after his death, their guardianship did not cease. If he were murdered, they avenged his murder or exacted compensation for it. They acted as guardians of his widow and children, and took charge of his estate till his children came of age. All of common blood were bound by these ties of mutual right and obligation. If these ties had been somewhat loosened, if the bond of kinship among the subjects of Ine and Wihtraed was no longer what it had been among their ancestors at some remote past, it was far from being the mere nominal connection that it has since become. Though the family no longer owned and administered its property in common, the traces of the older system were still seen in the right of heirs to prevent the alienation of the family estate, a right not limited to descendants, but extending to more remote kinsmen. In the Anglo-Saxon period only the first steps had been taken in that development which has continued to modern times, exalting the individual at the expense of the family as a whole.

What, then, was this formidable association? There were two groups of individuals in the Anglo-Saxon community, to which the word family may be applied, but, for the sake of clearness, it will be better to give them specific names. The first and larger group, including the whole body of the kindred, is called in Anglo-Saxon the *maegth* or *maegburh*. Of course, in speaking of the whole body of the kindred, reference must be made to some one person as the starting point. In the course of this essay, therefore, whenever the *maegth* is mentioned, it must be understood to mean the *maegth* of some one person, the *propositus*. The second and smaller group, including only the husband, his wife, and children, may be called the household. That these two groups were really distinct, and that the smaller was not merely a portion of the larger group, follows from the relative position of husband and wife. Nothing is more evident in the laws than that the wife is not regarded as kin to her husband's kin. The wife, at marriage, did not become one of her husband's *maegth*, but remained in her own. If she committed a wrong, neither the husband nor his *maegth* were in any way responsible. Her kindred alone bore the feud or made compensation.[1] If the husband committed a crime without the cognizance of his wife, the wife and her kin were free from any obligation either to bear the feud or to make compensation.[2] It follows, as a matter of

---

[1] Schmid, Anh. VI. § 7. "But if a man desire to lead her out of the land into another thane's land, then it is advisable that her friends have there an agreement that no wrong shall be done her, and if she commit a fault, that they may be nearest in the bot if she have not wherewith she may make bot." Hen. I. 70, § 12. "Similiter, si mulier homicidium faciat, in eam vel in progeniem vel parentes ejus vindicetur, vel inde componat; non in virum suum, seu clientelam innocentem."

[2] Ine, 57. "If a husband steal a chattel and bear it to his dwelling, and it be intertiated therein, then shall he be guilty for his part without his wife, for she must obey her lord. If she dares to declare on oath that she tasted not of the stolen property, then let her take her third part." Cf. Aethelst. VI. 1, § 1; Cnut II. 76; Will. I. 27. That the wife and her kin were not responsible for a homicide committed by the husband needs no proof.

course, that the wergeld of the husband was paid to his
maegth, as the wergeld of the wife to hers.[1] Moreover, the
wife had no rights of inheritance from the husband or his
maegth, and he could not inherit from the wife or her
maegth.[2] The household was formed by the alliance of two
persons, who had different *maegthe*. The *maegth* of the
woman intrusted to her husband the guardianship over her,
which they, up to that time, had exercised. He became her
active guardian; but her *maegth* constantly watched over his
administration of his trust, and interfered to protect her if
necessary. This guardianship exercised by the husband over
the wife and her estate was essential from the nature of the
marriage relation, but it did not place the wife in her husband's *maegth*. It did not create between husband and wife
the mutual rights and obligations arising from the blood-feud
and from inheritance, and it was these rights and obligations
which especially characterized the *maegth*. These existed
only between those of common blood. To make the household therefore a portion of the larger group of the *maegth* is

[1] It was an invariable principle that those who would have to pay the wergeld, if their kinsman committed homicide, should receive it if he were slain.
Hen. I. 75, § 8. "Si quis hujusmodi faciat homicidium, parentes ejus tantum
werae reddant, quantum pro ea reciperent, si occideretur." The *healsfang* was
paid to the father, children, brothers, and paternal uncles. There is never any
question in pure Anglo-Saxon law of its payment to wife or to husband. The
wergeld belonged to blood relations. Schmid, Anh. VII. c. 1, § 5; Hen. I. 76,
§§ 4, 7. The passage in William's Laws (I. 9), "De were ergo pro occiso soluto,
primo viduae x sol. dentur, etc.," cannot be accepted as evidence against the
earlier and more reliable passages. It is not without significance that the
wife's wer was estimated by the position of her father, not of her husband.
Hen. I. 70, § 13. "Si mulier occidatur, sicut weregildum ejus est reddatur, ex
parte patris, sicut observamus in aliis."

[2] It was a general principle of German law that the widow was not heir of
her husband. If she is sometimes spoken of as sharing in the inheritance, it is
only that her morning-gift might be considered as in fact forming part of the inheritance. That she was not legally heir is evident from the fact that if she
died before her husband her heirs got through her no right in the inheritance of
the husband, which they must have done if she were herself heir. Cf. Schroeder,
Geschichte des ehelichen Güterrechts, I. p. 166. That the husband was not heir
follows from the custom of gifts *mortis causa* of wife to husband. If he were
heir these would be superfluous. The passage in Hen. I. 70, § 23, which speaks
of the husband as sharing with the children in the inheritance of the wife, is of
too doubtful authority to be relied on. Cf. Schroeder, I. p. 168, n. 6.

to include in the *maegth* a person who distinctly did not belong to it, and so to confuse the whole subject. The children,
of course, belonged both to the *maegth* of the father and to
that of the mother. Every person had two *maegthe :* that
of his father, the *faedren maegth, paterna generatio,* or paternal kin, and that of his mother, the *mêdren maegth, materna
generatio,* or maternal kin. These groups, entirely distinct
before his birth, unite in his person, and become only subdivisions of his general *maegth.* Both have with him the
rights and duties of kindred, but in different degrees, as will
appear later.

Accepting the *maegth* and the household as distinct groups,
the subject of family law in the Anglo-Saxon period naturally
divides itself into two branches : the law of the *maegth* or
kindred, and the law of the household ; in other words, the
laws regulating the relations between members of the same
maegth, and the rules obtaining when an alliance was formed
between persons having different *maegthe.* Of course these
two systems of law are closely connected. The relations
between husband and wife, father and child, were modified
by the fact that each member of the household was subject
to the general law of the *maegth ;* the husband to that of his
maegth, the wife to that of her *maegth,* and the children to
that of both. And on the other hand both the *maegthe*
forming the alliance had rights and obligations toward the
household.

The law of the *maegth* will first be considered, then the
law of the household. In treating of the law of the *maegth,*
these questions will demand attention : who were a man's
kindred ; how were the degrees of kinship reckoned, and what
was the order of succession among the kin ; what was the
relative position of the paternal and maternal kin ; within
what degree, if within any, was kinship limited ; how was
the tie of kinship ended ; finally, what were the rights and
obligations of the kindred ?

Those are kindred and belong to the same *maegth* who
have common blood with each other or with a third, originating in lawful marriage. This is the only basis of the tie of

kinship known to the German law. It is true that adoption was often practised among the continental Germans. An instance of this adoption occurs in Beowulf,[1] and the occurrence of the phrase "adoptivo parenti meo," in an Anglo-Saxon charter,[2] proves that it existed in Anglo-Saxon law. But the early German adoption did not even place the one adopted under the parental authority of the adoptor. Much less could it create the ties of kinship between the one adopted and the kin of the adoptor. Its only effect was to give the adopted son rights of succession from his adopted father. The legitimation of natural children was permitted in none of the early German codes, except the Lombard, and was strongly opposed to the whole spirit of German family law. That the father, by symbolic forms, could acknowledge his natural child, and give him a place and protection within the household, is proved from German and Scandinavian sources.[3] That a similar practice was known to the Anglo-Saxons may be inferred from Ine, § 27: "If any one beget a child secretly, and conceal it, let him not have the wer for his death, but his lord and the king." Clearly by acknowledging the child the father could protect him, and avenge his murder or exact satisfaction for it. If the father did not acknowledge him, the child was in the guardianship of the lord and the king. This passage, however, gives no argument for the existence of any rights of the natural child toward the father or his kin, and it is impossible that any such could have existed. Natural children could not have been reckoned among the *maegth*. That children born in unlawful marriage had no rights of inheritance is expressly stated in the laws of Alfred,[4] and it may be inferred that all other rights of kindred were denied them except that of protection. If slain, their wergeld was paid to the paternal kindred and the king.[5] Those then only were of kin, and belonged to

---

[1] Thorpe's Beowulf, 1897–1905.   [2] Cod. Dip. MCXCVI.; ib. MCXCVII

[3] Grimm, Alterth. p. 463; Ducange s. v. pallio coöperire; Koenigswarter, De l'Organization de la Famille en France, p. 142; Michelet, Origines du Droit Français, p. 11.

[4] Alf. 8, § 2.   Cf. Phillips, Geschichte des Angelsächsischen Rechts, p. 127

[5] Alf. 8, § 3.

the *maegth*, who had common blood originating in lawful marriage.

The method of reckoning the degrees of kinship must next be considered. In reckoning the degrees of kinship in the direct line, all systems agree in assigning one degree for each generation. The early German method of reckoning the degrees of side relationship is described in the Sachsenspiegel, in the first half of the thirteenth century. Sachsensp. I. 3, § 3: " Now mark we where the sippe begins and where it ends. In the head it is ordered that man and wife do stand, who have come together in lawful wedlock. In the joint of the neck stand the children born of the same father and mother. Half brothers and sisters may not stand in the neck, but descend to the next. . . . Full brothers' and sisters' children stand at the joint where shoulder and arm come together. This is the first grade of the sippe which is reckoned to the magen, — brothers' and sisters' children. In the elbow stands the next. In the wrist the third. In the first joint of the middle finger the fourth. In the next joint the fifth. In the third joint of the finger the sixth. In the seventh stands a nail, therefore ends here the sippe, and this is called the nail-mage."

Here the degrees of kinship are reckoned by reference to the joints of the arm and hand. The common ancestors and their children standing in the head and neck are not reckoned among the *magen*. The first grade of the *sippe* is formed by cousins, who are, therefore, in the first degree of side relationship to each other. The *sippe* includes in all seven degrees. The family as a whole, therefore, includes nine generations.

In the Anglo-Saxon laws, two passages throw light on the method of reckoning the degrees of collateral kinship. Aethelr. VI., 12: " And aefre ne geweorðe þaet cristen man gewifige in vi. mánna sib-faece on his agenum cynne, þaet is binnan þam feorðan cneowe." " And let it never happen that a Christian man marry within the relationship of six persons of his own kin, that is within the fourth joint."[1] If, in

---

[1] Cf. Schmid, Anh. II. § 61; Cnut, I. 7.

counting six persons, only four degrees of side relationship are
reckoned, it is clear that the first two generations, the common ancestors and their children, are omitted in computing
the degrees, and that brothers' and sisters' children form the
first grade. Schmid, Anh. VII., c. 1, § 5: "Healsfang gebyreð bearnum, broðrum and faederan; ne gebyreð nanum
maege þaet feoh, bute þam þe sy binnan cneowe." "Healsfang belongs to children, brothers, and paternal uncles. This
money belongs to no kin except to those who are within the
joint."[1] Thorpe's translation of *cneowe* in this passage by
knee is misleading. As applied to relationship, *cneow* means
always joint or degree, as in the first passage quoted above.[2]
The passage must mean those who are within the first joint:
that is, those who are not counted on the joints at all, and
who, therefore, are not reckoned among the degrees of collateral kin. These would be the descendants, the common
ancestor, and his children, or (omitting the common ancestor,
who would naturally be already dead) precisely those mentioned in the passage, — children, brothers, and uncles.

These passages prove that the Anglo-Saxons employed the
same method of reckoning the degrees of collateral kinship
as the continental Saxons. They began with brothers' and
sisters' children; these formed the first grade. The use of
cneow to designate grade of relationship, together with the
language of the second passage quoted above, makes it
almost certain that they computed the degrees by reference
to the joints of the arm and hand, and if we accept the probable derivation of *healsfang* or *halsfang*, from *hals* meaning
the neck, so called because it was paid to those standing in
the neck, this conclusion becomes irresistible.[3] Of the distinction made in the Sachsenspiegel between the full and the
half blood, the Anglo-Saxon law shows no trace. The distinction is not found in the earliest German codes, and is
probably only a refinement of a later time.

[1] Cf. Hen. I. 76, § 4; ib. 76, § 7, mentions also the father.

[2] So in Conf. Ecgb. § 28 (Thorpe II. 152 and note), where *gradus* of the
Latin version is in the Anglo-Saxon rendered by *cneow*. Schmid, Gloss, s. v.
cneow.

[3] Schmid, Gloss. s. v. halsfang.

By the method just described, it is possible to determine the grade of relationship between two persons descended from a common ancestor: cousins were in the first grade, cousins' children in the second grade, and so on. Or the grades might be unequal: if A's grandfather were great-grandfather of B, A would be in the first grade, B in the second grade. But the rule does not suffice to determine the relative position of two persons to a third, and this must be known before the order of inheritance can be determined. According to the rule, all ancestors of a man deceased stand in the head; all children of ancestors stand in the neck; all grand-children of ancestors stand in the shoulder, that is, in the first grade of side relationship; and so on. Did all in the same grade stand in the same position; or, if not, what rule determined their relative position? Did a nearer grade from a more distant ancestor precede a more distant grade from a nearer ancestor, or was the opposite the case? In short, what was the order of inheritance?

This question has been the subject of a controversy in Germany, which in its extent, and in the heat with which in some quarters it has been carried on, has been rarely equalled in the history of German legal science. The theory of the so-called *parentelen-ordnung*, first established by the writings of John Christian Majer at the end of the last century,[1] obtained general recognition, and for half a century was regarded as one of the most firmly established points in the history of German law. Within twenty years, however, the writings of Siegel[2] and Wasserschleben[3] have thrown much discredit on this theory, and have deprived it of many of its supporters. But Siegel and Wasserschleben, united in opposing the

---

[1] Brunner, Das Anglonormannische Erbfolgesystem, p. 7.

[2] Siegel, das deutsche Erbrecht nach den Rechtsquellen des Mittelalters 1853, and Die germanische Verwandtschaftsberechnung mit besonderer Beziehung auf die Erbenfolge 1853.

[3] Wasserschleben, Das Princip der Successionsordnung nach deutschem insbesondere sächsischem Rechte, 1860. (Reviewed by Siegel in östr. Vierteljahrsschrift für R. u. St. W. VI. 21); Die germanische Verwandtschaftsberechnung und das Prinzip der Erbenfolge nach deutschem insbesondere sächsischem Rechte, 1864.

old theory, differ as to the theory that must replace it, each introducing a theory of his own. The result has been a triangular contest between the supporters of the three theories, which, until recently, seemed likely to be interminable. At last, in the contributions of Lewis and Brunner, the bewildered and exhausted student may find some ground for hope that the controversy will have an end.[1] It is not the purpose here to take part in this controversy. Indeed, if one asks what ground there is in Anglo-Saxon law to support either of the theories advanced, the answer must be: None whatever. Only a single passage in the laws has any reference to the points in dispute, and this, a passage in the so-called Laws of Henry I.,[2] is only a copy by a Norman writer of a passage in the L. Ripuaria, and is of no value as evidence of Saxon law. Moreover, each of the parties finds in the corresponding passage of the L. Ripuaria, evidence to support its theory. Whatever system is finally accepted as the prevailing one in early German law must be accepted also for Anglo-Saxon law. It will only be useful here to describe the various theories, and to state the present situation of the controversy.

According to the theory of the *parentelen-ordnung*, the kindred are divided into *parentelae* or classes: the first parentela including the deceased and his descendants, the second parentela including the parents of the deceased and their descendants, the third including the grandparents of the deceased and their descendants, and so on. The members of the first parentela are first called to the inheritance ; if none of these are living, then the members of the second parentela, and so on. The members of any one parentela are not called till all the members of all the preceding parentelae are dead. Between members of the same parentela the nearness of grade decides, except in so far as difference of sex and the right of representation introduce modifications. In general, therefore, the nearest in grade belonging to the nearest parentela will be the nearest heir.

Siegel and Wasserschleben both reject the division of the

---

[1] Brunner (p. 7 note) has given a summary of the literature on this subject.
[2] Henry I. 70, § 20 ; cf. L. Ripuaria, 56.

kindred into parentelae, and make the nearness of grade
alone decisive. According to them, a nearer grade from a
more distant ancestor precedes a more distant grade from
a nearer ancestor. But they disagree about the mode of
counting the degrees where the deceased and the heir are in
unequal grades of kinship to each other; that is, when the
generations between the deceased and the common ancestor,
and between the heir and the common ancestor, are unequal.
Siegel maintains that the degrees are counted always on the
longer side; Wasserschleben, on the other hand, that the
degrees are counted only between the heir and the common
ancestor, and that no account is taken of the number of degrees on the side of the deceased. To make their theories
consistent with the evidence in the sources, both are forced to
introduce modifications which need not here be mentioned.[1]
In an exhaustive article[2] Lewis sums up the arguments
hitherto advanced by each of the parties to this controversy.
After examining the evidence in Tacitus, in the folk laws,
and in the Sachsenspiegel and other legal sources in the
middle ages, he concludes that no sufficient evidence can be
found in them to prove the *parentelenordnung;* but at the
same time he thinks the theories of Siegel and Wasserschleben are themselves inconsistent with these sources. At the
close of his article he says: "If now, as we have seen,
the *parentelenordnung* cannot be proved from the sources,
the question remains whether other grounds speak for its
existence in pure German law. And here the consideration
seems to me to be very important that, as Homeyer has
already suggested, the rules of succession among the higher
nobility are based throughout upon the principles of the
parentelenordnung. . . . In this circle of society, the old
German institutions maintained themselves longest." Lastly,
Brunner[3] has shown that the *parentelenordnung* forms the
basis of the laws of inheritance in the Anglo-Norman and

[1] They are given by Lewis on p. 32 of the article cited in note 2.

[2] Zur Lehre von der Successionsordnung des deutschen Rechtes: Kritische
Vierteljahrsschrift für Gesetzgebung und Rechtswissenschaft, IX. p. 23.

[3] Das anglonormannische Erbfolgesystem.

Norman laws, and in the Customs of Bretagne, "three laws of undoubted German origin." Brunner accordingly throws the great weight of his authority on the side of the old theory.

One fact is made evident by this controversy, that no system can ever be found which will be in all respects consistent with all the sources. The German laws of inheritance were not the results of legislation based on philosophic principles, but rather the slow outgrowth of custom adapting itself to special needs. It is useless to expect that uniformity of system and logical application of fundamental rules which characterize Roman law. The most we can hope for is that some general system may be found which in the main prevailed in early German law, but always with different modifications in different tribes. Such a system, lying at the basis of custom, may be discerned in the rules of succession applying to near kindred. The order of succession among these, which has been quite generally agreed upon by German writers, is as follows: 1, sons; 2, daughters; 3, grandchildren, etc. After descendants fail: 1, father; 2, mother; 3, brothers; 4, sisters.[1] A modification of this system was early introduced by the right of representation, grandsons from a deceased son being allowed to succeed to their father's share, in concurrence with the surviving sons; but this innovation was stoutly resisted. In the time of Otto I. its legality was still disputed in Germany, and it was not till the beginning of the sixteenth century that the rule became firmly established there.[2] In England the right was disputed in Glanville's time, but in the time of Bracton was generally recognized.[3] It could hardly have existed in Anglo-Saxon law. It cannot be doubted that the order of succession among the nearest kin in Anglo-Saxon law was substantially that given above, although there is evidence only for the first two classes.[4] That sons were the nearest heirs, and

[1] Wasserschleben, however, makes all ascendants precede brothers and sisters.

[2] Von Sydow, Erbrecht, pp. 77–80.

[3] Brunner, Anglonorm. Erbfolgesystem, pp. 82, 83.

[4] Rüstringer Land-recht, XVI.: "This is the 16th land-recht: whenever a man

shared equally, appears from Will. I. 34, "Si quis paterfamilias casu aliquo sine testamento obierit, pueri[1] inter se hereditatem paternam equaliter dividant."[2] After the sons came the daughters, who, like the sons, shared equally. In the Kentish Custumal, it is said: "E clament auxi, que si ascun tenant en Gavylekende murt, et seit inherite de terres e de tenemenz de Gavylekende, que touz ses fitz partent cel heritage per ouele porcioun. Et si nul heir madle ne seit, seit la partye feit, entre les females, sicome entres les freres."[3] The evidence of the Kentish Custumal is confirmed here by Glanville and Bracton. Glanv. lib. 7, c. 3: "Si vero fuerit liber sokemannus, tunc quidem dividetur haereditas inter omnes filios quotquot sunt per partes aequales, si fuerit socagium *et id antiquitus divisum.* . . . Sin autem plures filias tunc quidem indistincte

or woman dies and leaves their land [erve] and other property, and after them live neither father nor mother, brother nor sister, child nor child's child, nor any of their six next of kin [sibbostâ sex honda], then let the equally near relations make claim to the estate, who reckon relationship, taking equally with equally near hands [or: let all the near relations who claim the estate reckon their relationship thereto; if they are all related alike, let them share equally]; unless there come one who is nearest of all to the estate, in which case this hand shall take the inheritance. But if this do not happen, then shall the relations divide amongst themselves according as they are related and can prove their relationship." The Frisian law is so closely allied to the English that, for purposes of argument, it is almost as good as pure Saxon. The six next of kin are therefore the father, mother, brother, sister, child, and child's child.

1 "Enfans," in the French version. For the relation of the different texts, see Schmid, Einl. p. lvi.

2 Cnut, II. 70, is often referred to in discussing the laws of inheritance among the Anglo-Saxons. The passage is as follows: "And if any man depart this life intestate, whether because of carelessness or of sudden death, let not the lord take more from his property than his lawful heriot, and by his direction let the property be distributed justly to the wife, the children, and the near kin, to each according to the degree that belongs to him." The allusion here to the partition of the inheritance is only casual, and, as being evidently in general, not in precise language, cannot be accepted literally. A partition by which the near kin shared with wife and children is, for the period of Cnut at least, inconceivable, though it is not impossible that it might have existed in prehistoric times. The passages in Henry I.'s laws, relating to inheritance (1, § 7; 70, § 20; 70, § 23), are worthless as evidence of Anglo-Saxon law, and no consideration is taken of them here.

3 Lambarde's Perambulation of Kent, p. 518; Robinson's Common Law of Kent, p. 285.

inter ipsas dividetur hereditas sive fuerit miles sive sokemannus pater earum," etc.   Bracton follows Glanville. Bracton,
lib. 2, c. 34: " Si liber sockmannus moriatur pluribus relictis
haeredibus et participibus, si haereditas partibilis sit et ab
antiquo divisa, haeredes quotquot erunt habeant partes suas
aequales."   The feudal principle of primogeniture had completely changed the rules of succession to lands held by military tenure ; but lands held by socage tenure, for the most
part, still descended according to the ancient custom of partition, first among the sons, then among the daughters.   It
cannot be doubted that this custom goes back to Anglo-Saxon
times, and that the Gavelkind lands in Kent, and the *socagium antiquitus divisum* of Glanville and Bracton are monu-
ments of the endurance of the old system in customary law,
where special needs had not forced the adoption of new principles.

The case might be allowed to rest here, were it not that
in the Kentish Custumal, as well as in Glanville and Bracton,
a different order of inheritance is given for movables : —

" Ensement seient les chateus de Gavylekendeys parties en treis
apres le exequies e les dettes rendues, si il y eit issue mulier en vye,
issi que la mort eyt la une partie, e les fitz e les filles muliers lautre
partie, et la femme la tierce partie.   Et si nul issue mulier en vie ne
seit, eit la mort la meite, e la femme en vye lautre meytie." [1]

The chattels were divided into three portions: one-third
went to pay the legacies of the deceased, or, if he had made
none, were devoted by his executor *in pios usus ;* one-third
went to the wife ; and one-third was distributed among the
children, daughters as well as sons.   It is necessary to decide
whether this is Anglo-Saxon custom, still in force throughout
most of the kingdom under the Norman and Angevin kings,
or whether it is only a later introduction, which has forced itself even into Kent.   The passage quoted contains three things
quite distinct: a limitation of the right to devise by will ; a
provision for dower; and, lastly, a regulation of inheritance.

[1] Lambarde, Peramb. of Kent, p. 520; Robinson's Com. Law of Kent, p. 287;
cf. Glanv. lib. 7, c. 5.

The triple division has no necessary historical connection with the equal division among the children, irrespective of sex. The two things must therefore be considered separately. As regards the triple division, it is first of all interesting that the old lawyers could never agree whether the writ corresponding to it, *de rationabili parte bonorum*, lay at common law or by custom.[1] In the next place it is certain that the limitation of the right to dispose of personalty by will is not Saxon law. In the Saxon period this right was unlimited. It is not impossible that in some parts of England, even in Saxon times, customs may have arisen by which movables were always willed in certain proportions to certain classes of persons. In this connection Somner quotes an interesting passage from Beda, Ecc. Hist. lib. 5, c. 12: " Omnem quam possederat substantiam in tres divisit portiones, e quibus unam conjugi, alteram filiis tradidit, tertiam sibi ipse retentans statim pauperibus distribuit." The Saxon version has in place of the words *sibi ipse retentans*, the words ðe him ge-lamp, "which belonged to him." Somner remarks on this passage: " The third part is there said to belong to himself, plainly insinuating that the other two as rightly apperteined to his wife and children, each of them a third. But withall observe that this is the act of an housekeeper in the Province or Region (as there called) of Northumberland, . . . and such a testimony indeed it is as makes much (I confesse) for the antiquity of that custom [of a tripartite division] yet surviving and currant in those northern quarters of the Kingdome."[2] If such customs existed in Saxon times, they might, in the end, have acquired the force of law, and have influenced the laws of intestate succession. But, if so, this must have come after the conquest. In London, at the time of Bracton, the right to dispose of personalty by will was unlimited, but later the custom of a tripartite division was introduced.[3] The limitation of the right to dispose of personalty by will may then be rejected as not being Anglo-Saxon law. Of the chattels not granted by will, the wife

[1] Somner's Gavelkind, p. 96.   [2] Ib., p. 92.
[3] Ib., p. 98.

receives half, and the children half. The share of the wife corresponds to the half of the realty granted her as dower, and is undoubtedly derived from the legal dower of Anglo-Saxon law, which included half of the husband's property, real and personal. The remaining third of the chattels is the only portion which can properly be said to be inherited, and the children are the only persons who are legally heirs. This third part of the chattels is shared by the children irrespective of sex. This part of the passage suggests the inquiry whether it is not derived from some earlier law, by which the personalty was inherited by all the children, without precedence of sons before daughters, and, if it is derived from such a law, whether the law is to be found among the Saxons in England. Is it necessary to modify the previous statement of the order of succession, and to lay down different rules of inheritance for personalty and realty ?

In the laws of the continental Saxons, certain classes of personalty were subject to peculiar rules of succession. Things specially adapted to the use of the man, the best weapons, the best war-horse, with his equipments, etc., were set apart from the rest of the inheritance, and were called collectively the *hergewäte*. These fell to the nearest male of the paternal kindred. Things specially adapted to the use of women were called *gerade*, and were inherited by the nearest female of the maternal kin. No trace of the *gerade* is found in Anglo-Saxon law. The heriots paid by the heir to the lord may have had, probably did have, their origin in the *hergewäte*,[1] but of the *hergewäte* in its original form, as inherited by the nearest male of the male stem, there is no trace. Apart from these special rules, applying only to a small number of objects of little value, the law of the continental Saxons made no distinction between realty and personalty. The *erve* of the Saxon *landrecht* included both. It was only in the *lehnrecht* that the two classes of property were distinguished.[2] At the period of the folk laws a distinction between movables and immovables in the laws of

---

[1] Schroeder, I. p. 144 ; Kemble, II. p. 98.
[2] Von Sydow, Erbrecht; Zoepfl, Deutsche Rechtsgeschichte, III. p. 241.

inheritance is found only in the Thuringian and in the Salic law. In the Thuringian law, land is inherited only by males of the male stem, while personalty falls first to the sons, then to the daughters. In the Salic law, sons precede daughters in succession to land ; only women are excluded from succession to the *terra Salica*, but daughters share with sons in movables.[1] This custom of the Salian Franks presents the only analogy in continental law to the Kentish custom of an equal division of chattels between the children, without regard to sex; and even here this seems to have been an innovation. It is impossible that it should have passed into Anglo-Saxon England from the Franks, while it might easily have come through Normandy into England, after the conquest. If then the Anglo-Saxon law of inheritance made a distinction between movables and immovables, the distinction must have originated with them, and as an innovation of the first importance would appear prominently in their laws ; but in fact there is not the slightest evidence of such a distinction, and the silence of the laws in this respect is conclusive proof that the distinction did not exist.[2]

The preceding inquiry has been directed only to the establishment of the order of succession among the *maegth*. What classes of property were heritable, and what not, is a different question, the investigation of which does not fall within the purpose of this essay. Undoubtedly, all personalty which was not paid to the lord as heriot, or given to the wife as dower, if not disposed of by will, was inherited by the *maegth*. The relation of land to the laws of inheritance is discussed in another part of this volume.

Although kinship was traced equally through females and through males, a marked distinction was made between the paternal and the maternal kin, and the rights and obligations of the former were much more extensive than those of

---

[1] L. Sal. 59; Schroeder, I. p. 113.

[2] No importance can be given to the use of the word *yrfe* (literally pecus, pecunia) to designate inheritance. It is so used because originally only personalty was heritable at all. In the Anglo-Saxon period, it applies as well to land as to personalty, as in the expressions *yrfe-boc*, a charter, *yrfe-land*, hereditary land, &c. Cf. Grimm, Rechtsalt. p. 467.

the latter. Certain rights, as the guardianship of orphans,[1] and the right to receive the *healsfang*,[2] belonged only to the paternal kin. In the blood-feud, the rights and obligations of the paternal kin stood to those of the maternal kin in the ratio of two to one. Two-thirds of the wergeld were paid by the *faedren maegth*, one-third by the *mêdren maegth*.[3] When an oath was to be taken by the kindred, two-thirds of the compurgators were taken from the paternal kin, one-third from the maternal kin.[4] It follows, as a matter of course, that two-thirds of the wergeld were paid to the paternal kin, one-third to the maternal kin.[5] Phillips[6] infers from this that the male stem had a proportionate advantage in inheritance, but there is no evidence to support this view, and it is opposed to the whole spirit of the Saxon family law.

It does not appear from the sources whether the *maegth* was limited to any fixed number of degrees of kinship. Some limitation of kinship, within a fixed degree, is found in most of the German tribes, and Von Sydow,[7] on the authority of a passage in the laws of Henry I. (70, § 20), assumes that the Anglo-Saxon *maegth* was, in like way, limited to five degrees of kinship. The worthlessness of this passage as evidence of Saxon law has already been alluded to. No argument can be derived from the prohibition of marriage within the fourth degree,[8] as this is purely church law, and we have direct evidence that the Saxons, in early times, allowed marriage even between cousins.[9] As each grade of side-relationship was assigned a place on some joint of the arm or hand, the means of computation must have failed with

---

[1] Hlot. and Ead. § 6.

[2] Schmid, Anh. VII. c. 1, § 5; Hen. I. 76, § 7.

[3] Alf. 27; Hen. I. 75, §§ 8, 9.

[4] Schmid, Anh. VII. c. 1, § 3; Aethelst. II. § 11. Cf. Hen. I. 74, § 2; 76, § 1.

[5] Alf. 8, § 3; Hen. I. 75, §§ 8, 9.

[6] Ges. des Angels. Rechts, p. 146. Cf. Ganz, Erbrecht, IV. p. 308.

[7] Erbrecht, p. 127.

[8] Schmid, Anh. II. § 61; Æthelr. VI. § 12.

[9] Beda, Ecc. Hist. lib. I. c. XXVII.; Ecgb. Excerpt. CXXXII. (Thorpe II. p. 117).

the seventh degree, and even before this the proof of common blood must, in most cases, have become practically impossible. The question is important chiefly in its bearing on the laws of inheritance. The estates of those dying without heirs fell to the king, or to the community, as the case might be. Was there any limit beyond which common blood ceased to give a title to the inheritance? In the absence of any evidence, it may fairly be inferred that the limitation did not exist, and that, in any event, if common blood could have been proved in any degree, it would have given a title to the inheritance, if no nearer heirs existed.[1]

In the Anglo-Saxon, as in all early societies of German origin, the degree of security and of distinction which each member of the community enjoyed depended chiefly upon the number, wealth, and power of his kindred, and there was little temptation to any one to separate from the family. But if the tie of kinship created rights, it involved also obligations which might easily become burdensome. As civilization advanced, and individual members of the *maegth* became wealthy and powerful, or attained a higher position in society, a tendency appeared on the part of the rich to discard their poorer kin. Thus a freeman need not pay the wergeld with a slave, or with one who, for any cause, forfeited his freedom.[2] In the latter case, the kindred lost the right to share in the wergeld if they did not free their kinsman within a year.[3] Moreover, every tendency to weaken the tie of kinship was encouraged by the state, which had much to fear from the independence of powerful families,[4] and whose peace was endangered by the continuance of the old system of private vengeance. King Edmund tried to break down the old system entirely, by permitting the *maegth* to abandon their kinsman, guilty of homicide, and to force him

[1] Von Sydow and Von Ludewig are of the opinion that the limitation of the family within a fixed degree of kinship was not archaic German law; but an innovation from Roman law, through the influence of the church. *Vide* Von Sydow, Erbrecht, p. 129, and the passage there quoted from Von Ludewig.

[2] Ine, 74, § 2; Edw. II. 6; Æthelst. VI. 12, § 2.

[3] Ine, 24, § 1.

[4] Æthelst. III. 6; IV. 3; VI. 8, §§ 2, 3.

to bear the feud alone.[1] The subsequent laws of Æthelred and Cnut prove that this measure was ineffectual, and was afterward abandoned by the state itself.[2] The influence of the church contributed also to weaken the tie of blood. The rights and duties of kindred were inconsistent with the duties of monastic life, and those who became monks lost all rights of kin. The secular clergy, however, were not separated from their kindred, and retained their rights in the *maegth*.[3] If accused of homicide, they must clear themselves with the help of their kin.[4] In one or two instances the loss of family rights occurs as a legal penalty.[5] Thus, in Alf. 42, the man who attacks his foe, after he has yielded, forfeits his rights in the *maegth;* and in Alf. I. §§ 4–5, a man who proves false to his lawful pledge, and resists imprisonment, forfeits his property, and, if slain, lies unavenged. These passages prove, what also is only natural, that outlaws, in general, were deprived of family as of civil rights. Elsewhere, the man who refuses to aid against an outlaw, who is his kinsman, incurs a heavy fine.[6] It is not clear from the laws whether separation from the *maegth* at will was permitted, or what the effect of the dissolution of the tie of kinship was. A passage from the laws of Henry I. would answer both these questions, if its evidence could be relied on ; but it is only a copy of a passage in the L. Salica, and is worthless, therefore, as evidence of Anglo-Saxon law.[7] With regard to the first point,

---

[1] Edm. II. 1.

[2] Æthelr. II. 6; VIII. 23; Cnut, I. 5, § 2.

[3] The same distinction between the regular and the secular clergy is found among the continental Saxons. Sachsensp. I. 25, § 1: "With the brothers shares the priest, and not the monk." The gloss gives the reason : "Warum nimmt denn der Mönch nicht Erbe? Diess geschieht darum dass man ihn in der Welt für todt achtet." *Vide* Von Sydow, p. 63.

[4] Æethelr. VIII. 23 ; Cnut. I. 5, § 2.

[5] Cf. Hen. I. 88, § 15.

[6] Edg. III. 7 ; Cnut, II. 25, § 2.

[7] Hen. I. 88, § 13 (L. Salica, 60, Merkel) : "Si quis propter faidiam vel causam aliquam de parentela se velit tollere et eam forisjuraverit, et de societate, et hereditate et tota illius se ratione separet; si postea aliquis de parentibus suis abjuratis moriatur vel occidatur, nihil ad eum de hereditate vel compositione pertineat; si autem ipse moriatur vel occidatur, hereditas vel compositio filiis suis vel dominis juste proveniat." Dr. Schmid thinks there are "inner grounds"

it is significant that all the laws which speak of a separation from the family are special provisions, where the dissolution of the ties of kinship is either permitted as a privilege, or incurred as a penalty in special cases. It is only a fair inference that the arbitrary separation from the *maegth* was not permitted. Of the effects of the dissolution of the tie of kinship, the laws mention only the freedom from obligations in the blood-feud, with the loss of the corresponding rights. The obligations and rights of kindred were, however, so indissolubly connected in all Teutonic custom, that it is impossible to suppose one right or obligation lost, and the rest retained. A partial separation from the *maegth* is inconceivable. Freedom from the blood-feud must have carried with it the loss of rights of inheritance, of guardianship, and of all that belonged to kin.

The various questions of the constitution of the *maegth* have been considered, and it is now possible to state in brief its general characteristics. In a general sense, the *maegth* means simply the kindred, — all of common blood through lawful marriage. But, when one person is taken as a starting-point in the reckoning, his kin form a definite group, which, as having a certain organic form, is called, in a restricted sense of the word, " the maegth." All of common blood with him, in whatever degree, whether on the father's or on the mother's side, have their appointed place in this group, according to the established order of succession. The *maegth* is subdivided into two groups, — the paternal and the maternal kin. Both are important portions of the general *maegth*, the rights of the former being only somewhat more extensive than those of the latter. The tie uniting the members of the *maegth* cannot be broken arbitrarily; but in certain cases, by law, a withdrawal from the *maegth* is permitted. The man who thus renounces his family loses every right that belongs to kinship.

which speak for the applicability of this passage to Anglo-Saxon law, and so far as concerns the effect of separation from the family on the rights of inheritance, the point he had in mind when he wrote, no one will be disposed to dispute his view.

Such was the Anglo-Saxon *maegth*. It remains to consider the laws regulating the relations between the members of this group, — to describe, so far as is possible from the sources, the various rights and obligations which together made up the *maeg-lagu*, the law of the kin.

If all the laws which speak of the obligations of kin be compared, it will be found that, however these obligations differ in form, — whether it be to serve as guardian, to fight in the blood-feud, or to assist with oath before the court, — one idea lies at the bottom of all, — the idea of protection. Some forms of this protection, as the guardianship of orphans, are common to all stages of society, and to all laws. The peculiarity of early law here is only that, by custom, this protection is always exercised by the kindred. Other forms of this protection, as the pledge to mutual assistance in the blood-feud and before the court, are peculiar to primitive societies where a strongly centralized public law has not yet been developed, or where the principles of feudalism have not yet corrupted the earlier law. In those early times, personal safety could only be secured by a system of mutual guaranty ; and the organization of the *maegth* offered itself naturally for this end. For here, to the advantages of the protection which each enjoyed was added the additional incentive of affection for his own blood. In the earliest laws of the Anglo-Saxons, this system of mutual guaranty is seen in its purity ; and it maintained itself throughout the Anglo-Saxon period, though under the later kings it was much weakened, on the one hand, by the increasing force and widening range of public law, and, on the other, by the development of the *quasi* feudal relation of man to lord.

To this difference in the nature of the protection afforded by the kindred corresponds a difference between those who enjoyed this protection. In the Anglo-Saxon community, all free persons — and it is only with free persons that this essay is concerned — were divided into two classes, — the legally independent and the legally dependent ; those who could act for themselves, and those who needed a guardian to act for them. The obligations of kindred may therefore be divided into obligations between those legally independent, and obligations of those legally independent toward those legally dependent. The first have their ground in the peculiar constitution of early German society. With regard to the second class, a distinction must be made. That those legally dependent must be protected by those legally independent is a principle of all laws. But certain persons are legally dependent for natural reasons, and in all stages of society; and others are legally dependent for artificial reasons, peculiar to a particular constitution of society. So women of full age were legally dependent in Anglo-Saxon law, for reasons peculiar to the constitution of Anglo-Saxon society. Apart from the right of inheritance, which has already been discussed, the rights of kindred will be considered, in connection with the obligations to which they correspond.

The obligations between kindred legally independent may be classed under the two heads of, — 1. Obligations arising from the blood-feud; and, 2. Obligations to defend a kinsman before the court, and to become responsible for him to the state.

A full description and history of the blood-feud does not fall within the scope of this essay. As one form of the right of self-help, its details and its limitations belong more appropriately to the subject of criminal procedure. Here it is only necessary to state what the rights and duties of the kindred in the blood-feud were.

In one of Æthelred's laws [1] it is said: "If a breach of the peace be committed within a burh, let the inhabitants of the burh themselves go and get the murderers, living or dead, or their nearest kindred, head for head." If this were changed so as to describe a simple murder, it might read: "If a murder be committed, let the kindred of the slain themselves go and get the murderers, living or dead, or their nearest kindred, head for head." This would be an exact description of the primitive form of the feud. Unlike some of the continental tribes, the Anglo-Saxons did not permit the exercise

[1] Æthelr. II. 6.

of the right of feud for simply corporal injuries, but limited
it to the single case of guilty homicide.   When a man was
slain, his kindred must avenge the murder by slaying an
enemy or enemies of equal value.[1]   The obligation of the
slayer's kindred was simply to defend his life.   But already,
in the time of Tacitus, and in the earliest laws of the Anglo-
Saxons, the system of money compensation had been developed, although it is uncertain whether, before the laws of Ine
and Alfred,[2] the kindred of the slain were obliged to accept
the composition, or whether they were still free to choose the
feud, if they preferred.   Under the system of money compensation, the kindred of the slain must demand payment of
the wer, or prosecute the feud.[3]   They had the right to the
wer when paid,[4] and must by oath release the slayer and his
kindred from the feud.[5]   The first instalment of the wer —
the *healsfang* — was shared equally between the father, the
children, brothers, and paternal uncles.[6]   The rest of the wer
was shared by the kindred, but exactly by which of the kindred does not appear.   Evidently two-thirds were paid to
the paternal kin, and one-third to the maternal kin : beyond
this, nothing can be proved.

The kindred of the man accused of homicide must, first of
all, free him from the charge, if he be innocent, by an oath
of his paternal and maternal kin.[7]   If this is not possible,
they must negotiate with his foes for a release from the feud
by payment of composition, or they become personally responsible for his act, and are liable to be slain in the feud.
If he is captured by his foes, the kindred have thirty days in
which to release him by payment of composition.[8]   They
must become his sureties for payment of the *wer*, — eight of

[1] Schmid, Anh. VIII. c. 1 ; Æthelr. II. 6 ; Cnut, II. 56.

[2] Ine, 74 ; Alf. 42, cf. Schmid, Gloss. s. v. Fehderecht.

[3] Ed. Conf. 12, § 6 : " Emendationem faciat parentibus, aut guerram patiatur, unde Angli proverbium habebant: *Bicge spere of side other bere*, quod est
dicere, lanceam eme de latere aut fer eam."

[4] Schmid, Anh. VII. 3, § 4.

[5] Schmid, Anh. VII. 1, § 4 ; Edm. II. 7.

[6] Schmid, Anh. VII. 1, § 5 (quoted above, p. 128) ; Hen. I. 76, § 7.

[7] Æthelr. VIII. § 23 ; Hen. I. 64, § 4.

[8] Alf. 42, § 1.

the paternal kin, and four of the maternal kin;[1] and must take an oath that peace shall be preserved.[2] He must pay from his own property, if he can.[3] If he cannot, the kindred must pay; the paternal kin paying two-thirds, and the maternal kin one-third. If he cannot pay, and his kindred cannot or will not pay for him,[4] he becomes an outlaw. If he voluntarily leaves the land, the obligation of the kindred is limited to half the wer, in Æthelbirht's laws;[5] but apparently, in Alfred's time, they must pay the whole. Only, if there were no paternal kin, the obligation of the maternal kin did not extend beyond the payment of their share. The guildbrethren paid a third, and for a third the slayer fled.[6] In the same way, the obligation of the paternal kin was limited to the payment of two-thirds, even when there were no maternal kin.[7]

It has been said above that the only lawful ground of the exercise of the right of feud was the guilty murder of one's kinsman. In certain cases, slaying was permitted, and the kindred could not avenge the slain. Thus, a man might fight "orwîge," — that is, without incurring the penalty of murder, — if he found another within closed doors with his wife, daughter, sister, or mother.[8] So also the thief caught in the act might be slain with impunity, only the slayer must prove on oath that he was a thief. If he did this, the kindred of the slain were forced to release the slayer from the feud.[9] But, if he concealed the act, the kindred of the slain were permitted to clear their kinsman if they could.[10] If they succeeded, the slayer must pay the wer.[11] But, if

[1] Edm. II. 7; Schmid, Anh. VII. 1, § 3.
[2] Edm. II. 7; Schmid, Anh. VII. 1, § 4.
[3] Æthelb. 30.
[4] It has been shown above (see p. 139) that, in certain cases, the kindred might abandon their kinsman, if they chose to do so.
[5] Æthelb. 23.
[6] Alf. 27; Hen. I. 75, §§ 8, 9.
[7] Hen. I. 75, § 8.
[8] Alf. 42, § 7. Cf. ib. id. § 5.
[9] Wiht. 25; Ine, 12, 16, 35, Pr.
[10] Ine, 21, § 1.
[11] Ine, 35, Pr.

they undertook to do so and failed, they incurred a heavy fine, and their kinsman lay unavenged.[1] The method of proof was by oath of two of the paternal kin, and one of the maternal kin,[2] or by ordeal.[3]

Besides the obligations arising from the blood-feud, the kindred were, in general, bound to assist their kinsman in an oath before the courts, whether he appeared as plaintiff or defendant. Their share in the oath against a charge of homicide, and in the oath to clear their kinsman slain as a thief, has been mentioned. A case entirely apart from the blood-feud occurs in the Law of the Northumbrian Priests, where it is said that a king's thane must clear himself from a charge of witchcraft or idolatry by an oath of twelve of his kinsmen.[4]

If the organization of the *maegth* offered itself as a natural means of the mutual guaranty needed in early times, the state found it equally useful as a police organization, enabling it to hold lawless men to right. It was one of the duties of the kindred to see that their landless kinsman had a lord in the *folk-gemot*, or else themselves to become responsible for him to the state. If they did not do this, he became an outlaw, and might be slain by any one as a thief.[5] If any one was imprisoned for theft, witchcraft, &c., his kindred must pay his fine, presumably if his own property did not suffice, and must become surety for his good conduct on his release.[6] A notorious thief found guilty at the ordeal could be slain as an outlaw, unless his kindred paid his fines and became his sureties. If, afterward, he committed theft, they must pay for him, and bring him again into prison.[7] If the kindred found a lord for their kinsman, the lord seems not to have been bound to assume these obligations of the kindred. He might do so if he chose, or might return the man to the

1 Æthelst. II. 11; Æthelr. III. 7.
2 Æthelst. II. 11.
3 Æthelr. III. 7.
4 Schmid, Anh. II. § 51.
5 Æthelst. II. 2; II. 8.
6 Æthelst. II. 1, § 3; II. 6, § 1; II. 7.
7 Æthelst. II. 1, § 4; VI. 1, § 4; VI. 9, cf. ib. VI. 12, § 2.

charge of his kindred.[1] From the time of Edgar, the *maegth*, as a police organization, no longer existed. It had been superseded by a system of police organizations of a purely political nature ; and the police duties hitherto exercised by the kindred had passed to the members of these political organizations.[2]

Lastly, it was the duty of the kindred to protect all of their kin who were not legally capable of protecting themselves, and who were not members of a household where they could be protected by the head of the household. This protection exercised by the kindred is only a substitute for the protection exercised by the head of the household. The law of guardianship is therefore only an artificial extension of the law of the household, and, as such, will be more conveniently considered when the law of the household is known.

The various laws of the kindred, which have formed the subject of the previous pages, gradually — many of them very soon after the close of the Saxon period — fell into disuse, and were superseded by other rules, more adapted to the changed circumstances and needs of society. The necessities of feudalism forced an entire change in the laws of inheritance, though here the older system maintained itself, for some classes of property, to quite a late period. Under the influence of Roman law, the Roman system of computing degrees of kinship, more accurate and precise, and capable of wider application, had already, in Glanville and Bracton, replaced the older system, more clumsy if more picturesque. Already, in Saxon times, the responsibility of the kindred in matters of police had passed to other organizations, founded upon more advanced political conceptions. The right of private feud, with the rights and duties growing out of it, maintained itself against every hostile effort of the Saxon kings ; but, with the rapid growth of a strong, centralized state power under the Norman kings, it could not but early succumb. Even the rights of guardianship the kindred eventually lost,

[1] Edw. II. 3, cf. Ine, 74, § 1.
[2] Edg. III. 6, IV. 3 ; Æthelr. I. 1, Pr. ; Cnut, II. 20, Pr. ; Wil. I, 25.

and the customary guardian gave way to one appointed by the court. The rules of the *maeg-lagu* have left no lasting trace on English law. But the case is far different with the law of the household. Here we have to do with an institution now as then, and as far back as we know any thing of Aryan society, the basis, the corner-stone, of that society; and it is not too much to say, that, however outward appearances have changed, the household is still what it was when the Teutonic race first appears in history. Not that the law of the household has not undergone many and important modifications. Fathers no longer sell their daughters into marriage, or their infant sons into slavery. But the essential characteristics of the modern household already existed in the earliest Teutonic law; and daily occurrences remind us of the most archaic institutions of our heathen ancestors. The bridegroom who places the ring upon the bride's finger, and speaks the words, "With this ring I thee wed," stands very near to the old Saxon who gave to the bride's father the money of which the ring is but the representative,[1] with a *wed* or surety to bind the contract; and the widow's third, of English common law, is more true to its early original than the words of the marriage service, "With all my worldly goods I thee endow."

But the old German law of the household is not merely interesting and important as showing the origin of modern laws and customs: it is even more important, for the student of comparative history, as furnishing a type — perhaps the most archaic type of which we have any knowledge — of a primitive Aryan institution. It has long been the fashion to regard the Roman family, with its rigid conception of a single head, to whose absolute will, wife and child, slaves and cattle, were all alike subjected, as the typical form of the primitive Aryan family, and to study the German family from the light of the Roman. Few questions, certainly, offer greater difficulties than this of the relation of the German to

---

[1] The ring was originally only one form of the *arrha* or *handgeld*, a small sum of money paid to bind the contract. Hence, originally, only the bridegroom gave a ring: there was no exchange of rings. (Sohm, das Recht der Eheschliessung, p. 55.)

the Roman family. Were they essentially the same? If not so, in what did they differ, and which was the earlier and purer type? These are questions about which students are far from being of one mind; it would be much beyond the present purpose to attempt to answer them; but some suggestions of the main differences between the German and the Roman family will serve to make clearer the real character of the German household.

It has already been remarked that, in early German law, kinship was not, as in Roman law, limited to the agnates, or those tracing their descent from a common ancestor through males. The mother's kin, if in some respects less favored than the father's kin, were still an important part of each man's family, and were united to him by close ties of mutual right and obligation. The wife, after marriage, remained in her own *maegth;* her husband merely became her guardian. Her children were as much kindred of her kin as of their father's kin. This difference between the German and the Roman institution is radical, and most important consequences result from it. The wife was not under the absolute power of her husband, but was protected by her kindred from his abuse. Even the children seem to have found, in their mother's kin, a protection against the abuse of the parental power. The members of the German household had rights even against the head of the household, rights made effective by the intervention of the maternal kin, — an arrangement impossible under the Roman system, which regarded the mother's kin as legally not kindred at all. This is something quite different from the Roman *patria potestas*, where the children, during the lifetime of the father, were theoretically little better than slaves, except in so far as they had potential rights. Sir Henry Maine, in speaking of the *patria potestas*, says : " It is obvious that the organization of primitive societies would have been confounded if men had called themselves relatives of their mother's relatives. The inference would have been that a person might be subject to two distinct *patriae potestates;* but distinct *patriae potestates* implied distinct jurisdictions, so that anybody amenable to two of them at the same time would have been under two different dispensations. As long as the family was an *imperium in imperio*, a community within a commonwealth, governed by its own institutions, of which the parent was the source, the limitation of relationship to the agnates was a necessary security against a conflict of laws in the domestic forum." [1] The justice of this remark is obvious at once: the absolute power of the father over wife and children could not exist where the mother's blood-relations were acknowledged as kin. The natural and only inference is, that, where we do find men calling " themselves relatives of their mother's relatives," the *patria potestas*, as known to the Romans, could not have existed. This argument may be extended even farther to show that, if a patriarchal system is ever possible in any stage of society where law can be said to exist, — a point by no means clear, — it can only be where a limitation of the family to the agnates exists. When Sir Henry says (Anc. Law, p. 138), "All the Germanic immigrants seem to have recognized a corporate union of the family under the *mund* or authority of a patriarchal chief, but his powers are obviously only the relics of a decayed *patria potestas*," he is as much in error as when he ascribes the Roman agnation to the primitive German system. Nothing rests upon more certain evidence than that, in all German law, the maternal kin were a very important portion of the family. Wherever a preference for the male stem is shown, this either lies in the necessities of the case, as in the succession to the *hergewäte*, or else bears all the marks of an innovation, as in the preference of the male stem in succession to land in the Salic and Thuringian law. It must be remembered that the inheritance of land among the kin was a comparatively modern institution when the German folk-laws were written, — that this was a time of migration and conquest. It would not be strange if a limitation of inheritance to land to the male stem should, under such circumstances, have been introduced, from motives similar to those which afterward, in feudal times, gave rise to primogeniture. There is quite as much evidence

---

[1] Ancient Law, p. 144.

in early German law to support the theory that the primitive
German kinship was limited to those descended from a common ancestor through *females* as that it was a system of
agnation. Witness the statement of Tacitus (Germania, c.
20), " Sororum filiis idem apud avunculum, qui apud patrem
honor," and the preference given by the Salic law to the female kinship in the succession to movables.[1]

It is the more important to call attention to these points
here, because, in his last published lectures ("Early History
of Institutions"), Sir Henry has given the sanction of his
great authority to the view that private property in land in
England was derived originally from the ownership of the
patriarchal chief. It is certainly not meant that a patriarchal organization, or any thing like one, ever existed among
the Saxons in England. The Anglo-Saxon *maegth* was not
a distinct group, composed of certain definite persons, all
under a single head. The *maegthe* were inextricably interwoven. It is only· when some one person is taken as a
starting-point in the reckoning, that the *maegth* assumes a
defined form, and the several kin can be assigned to their
proper place. Cousins were in the same *maegth*, but the
mêdren-maegth of one did not belong to the *maegth* of the
other. Moreover, already, in historic times, the individual
predominated over the family. The rights of the kin in
Anglo-Saxon law were individual rights. The duties of
the kin were individual duties, enjoyed by, or binding upon,
the nearest three, or the nearest six, however near or distant these might be. In the earliest system, however, it
seems to have been common for the children and grandchildren of a man deceased to live together without a division of

---

[1] L. Salica, 59, cf. Schroeder, Geschichte des Ehelichen Güterrechts, I. p. 114.
The American Indians seem to have reached a stage of social development as
nearly resembling that· immediately preceding the Aryan as any thing we are
likely to discover. Among them, both systems of kinship existed, — that
through males and that through females; but the latter seems to have been
more common. *Vide* Mr. Lewis H. Morgan's article ("Montezuma's Dinner")
in the North-American Review for April, 1876. Mr. Morgan's contributions to
the history of early society are among the most valuable that have yet appeared. His forthcoming work on "Ancient Society" will be looked for with
interest by all students of comparative history.

property; and probably, in prehistoric times, large bodies of kindred did so. But even here there is no patriarch. All of mature age in this group stand legally on the same footing. It is not the subjection of all descendants to the will of one ascendant, but the voluntary association of near kindred; and the control exercised by the family council in such a group as little resembles the despotic power of a patriarchal chief, who " disposed absolutely of the persons and fortune of his clansmen,"[1] as the free democratic constitution of primitive Germany resembled the highly aristocratic constitution of early Rome.[2]

Another important difference between the German and the Roman household was, that in German law sons did not remain under the parental authority during the lifetime of the father, but became independent at an early age, — whether at a fixed age, or only upon separation from the father's household, will presently be considered. Here again the German system is utterly opposed to the patriarchal theory. It is essential to that theory that the power of the father over his descendants should continue during his life. In short, under every aspect of the case, the German household presents itself as something radically different from the Roman, and the German family system as something entirely different from any thing resembling a patriarchal system.

But to return to the subject in hand, — the Anglo-Saxon law of the household. Under this head must be considered the relations of the father to his children, marriage, and the relations of husband and wife. It is, first of all, to be remarked that the father's power extended only over children born in lawful wedlock.[3] The father, by acknowledging his

---

[1] Ancient Law, p. 140.

[2] Mr. Morgan, in the article above referred to, tells us that, among the American Indians, it was customary for the members of a gens to occupy a house in common, under the leadership of an *elected* head. The organization of the gens and of the tribe was democratic. Such a system might degenerate into a tribal system like the Celtic, or develop a democratic system like the German. There is no place for a patriarchal system between democratic Germany and a democratic system like the Indian.

[3] Cf. Alf. 42, § 7.

natural child, could give him a place and protection in the household, and, by so doing, acquired a right to 'his wergeld, if he were slain; but he could not give the child rights of inheritance or of kinship. The power of the father was not of the nature of property, but of guardianship; it was not *gewere*, but *mund*.[1] And this *mund* of the father was not absolute, but limited, inasmuch as the children had rights made effective by the intervention of the kindred. It does not appear that the father ever had the power of life and death, except over children who had not tasted food.[2] Even this limited right is found only among the Frisians. The right to sell children into slavery was limited to cases of necessity, and, in Anglo-Saxon law, applied only to children under seven years of age:[3] even when sold, they were to be treated differently from other slaves.[4] The power to chastise the children is a natural power, inherent in all parental authority: in the Anglo-Saxon, as in many of the folk-laws, it is expressly ascribed to the father.[5] It was also the natural right of the father to exact obedience from his children. In the earliest Anglo-Saxon period, he could give his daughter of immature age in marriage against her will. Poen. Theod. XIX. § 27: "Puella vera XVI. vel XVII. annorum sit in potestate parentum; post hanc aetatem, non licet parentes ejus dare eam in matrimonium contra ejus voluntatem." But already, in the tenth century, the father's power in this respect was limited to a veto on the marriage.[6] A right analogous to that of giving the daughter in marriage was the right to send her to a convent,[7] or to prevent her entering one. It is not clear how far the parental authority over sons in these respects extended. The father certainly could forbid his

---

[1] Kraut, Vormundschaft, I. p. 287 ff.

[2] Vita S. Ludgeri, Lib. 1, c. 2: "Semel gustantes aliquid infantes apud paganos necari illicitum erat." *Vide* Kraut, I. 45.

[3] Poen. Theod. XIX. § 28 (Thorpe, II. p. 19).

[4] Alf. Ecc. L. c. 12.

[5] Ecgb. Excerp. c. 96 (Thorpe, II. p. 111).

[6] Schmid, Anh. VI. § 1: "If a man desire to betroth a maiden or a woman, and it so be agreeable to her and to her friends," &c. Cnut, II. 74: "And let no one compel either woman or maiden to whom she herself dislikes," &c.

[7] Poen. Theod. XVI. § 24; Kraut, II. p. 604.

marriage, or his entrance into a convent,[1] and probably had, at first, the right to send him to a convent.[2]

An important right or duty of the father was to represent his children before the courts, to prosecute any injuries done to them, and to make amends for injuries committed by them. These rights and duties were so inherent in the German system that they are not once mentioned in the laws of the Anglo-Saxons: the absence of such mention is perhaps the strongest argument for their existence. Finally, the father had the right to administer the property of his son. Of course this applies only to such property as the son might acquire from some source other than the father, as, for example, by inheritance from the mother or her kin. The Anglo-Saxon, in common with all the earlier and purer German laws, contain nothing that throws any light on the father's power in respect of the property of his son; and recourse must be had to late continental sources, like the Sachsenspiegel, or to codes more or less influenced by Roman law, like the Westgothic. This much, however, can be safely asserted, — the father had the *gewere*, the legal possession, of his son's property, and, as a consequence of this, the usufruct. His power of alienating such property was restricted to cases of necessity.[3] Beyond this, the evidence will not warrant any conclusion.

The paternal authority ended necessarily when either the son became a monk, or the father became a monk, or otherwise legally incapable. In the former case, the son passed into the guardianship of the church; in the latter case, into the guardianship of the next of kin. When and how, apart from these special cases, parental authority was ended, is a question of great difficulty, and various views have been held by German scholars with regard to it. In the time of Tacitus, there is not room for much divergence of opinion. At that period, sons were freed from the parental power, not at a fixed age, but when they were physically mature, and capa-

---

[1] Poen. Theod. XIX. § 26; Conf. Ecgb. § 27; cf. Liut. 129.
[2] Kraut, II. p. 604.
[3] Kraut, II. p. 608 ff.

ble of bearing arms.[1] The emancipation required a formal
ceremony, which consisted in conferring arms upon the youth
in the assembly.[2] This could be done either by the father,
or by a third person with the father's consent. In the latter
case, it was preceded by a tradition of the son by the father
to this third person ; and the emancipation then had the
effect of creating, between the emancipator and the one
emancipated, a special personal relation, the nature of which
depended upon the previous contract of tradition. The ordinary purpose of such an emancipation by a third person was
to create between him and the one emancipated the relation
of lord and personal follower ; but it might also create the
paternal relation. In this case, the emancipator would become the adopted father, but he would not acquire parental authority. The effect would be merely to give the
adopted son rights of succession from his adopted father. In
exactly the same way as sons, wards became legally independent when the guardian conferred arms upon them in the
assembly. These three cases are all contained in the much-
quoted passage of the Germania (c. 13) : " Sed arma sumere
non ante cuiquam moris quam civitas suffecturum probaverit.
Tunc in ipso concilio vel principum aliquis vel pater vel propinqui scuto frameaque juvenem ornant." The gift of arms
by the *princeps* made the youth a personal follower of the
princeps. The gift of arms by the father — the ordinary case
— simply freed the son from parental authority, and made

---

[1] It is difficult to see exactly wherein Professor Sohm differs from the ordinary view which regards this emancipation as marking the term of majority.
He says (Altdeutsche Reichs- und Gerichtsverfassung, p. 545) : " The gift of
arms did not have the object to produce majority." And yet he says that it
was "regularly occasioned by majority." What would have happened if the
father had refused to emancipate his son after the son became physically mature ? The answer must be that custom was so strong as to compel the father
to emancipate in such case. Why not, then, say at once that, by custom, — a
custom as rigid as law, and in fact at that time the only law, — sons were regularly emancipated by their father when they became physically mature, — i.e.,
when they attained majority physically, the only majority known at that
period ?

[2] For a full account of this form of emancipation, see Sohm, R.- und G. V.,
Beilage I.

him legally independent. The gift of arms by the *propin-quus* is regarded by Sohm as an adoption, preceded by a tra-dition of the son by the father to the *propinquus ;* but it seems more natural to consider it as the means of freeing an orphan ward from the guardianship of his next of kin. As, at that time, a fixed age of majority was not established, some method of this kind would be necessary to terminate the guardian's authority.

The special act by which the father's power was terminated has been called an emancipation, but it must not be supposed that it had any thing in common with the Roman *emancipatio.* The latter removed the emancipated son from his family, and destroyed the tie of kinship and all rights resulting from it. Thus the emancipated son lost all rights of inheritance in his natural family. The German emancipation was nothing more than our majority, or coming of age. A special act was necessary, because, as yet, no legal term of majority was fixed ; but the emancipation had no effect on the tie of kin-ship, or the rights resulting from it. It simply made the son an independent member of the community ; effecting what, in Roman law, was only effected by the death of the father. This is only another result of the radical difference between the Roman and the German family, and, in so far, another proof of that difference.

In the law, as it stood in the time of Tacitus, a change would first be demanded for the case of wards. As the guardian had the use and enjoyment of his ward's estate, the temptation would be strong to keep the ward depen-dent as long as possible. This evil would be met by enact-ments fixing the legal age at which the ward should become legally independent ; and, in fact, such enactments are found in all the folk-laws. This change could not but have an effect on the relations of father to son. It would become the rule to make the son independent at the same fixed period. The difference between the ward and the son would be only that, while the ward became independent *ipso facto* on attaining majority, the son still needed to be emancipated by a special act, which, however, regularly took place at or about the same period.[1]

From this point two lines of development are conceivable. Either the father's power would be assimilated to that of the guardian, and so would end *ipso facto* when the son attained majority, or the two powers would be kept quite distinct, and a special act would continue to be necessary for the emancipation of the son. The former is the view of Kraut;[2] the latter the view of Stobbe.[3] Putting aside for the moment all questions of Anglo-Saxon law, and considering only the law of the continent, it is clear that Stobbe has proved his view for several of 'the continental tribes, — for the Franks, the Alamannians, and the Westgoths. In these tribes the emancipation of the son, still at the period of the folk-laws, required a special act. Besides the old ceremony of the gift of arms, other forms appear, as, among the Franks, cutting the boys' hair. Marriage also appears as *ipso facto* making the son independent. Stobbe admits, however, that still at the period of the folk-laws the emancipation of the son, by a special act, was regularly occasioned by majority.

At the period of the early middle ages, the period of the Sachsenspiegel, the old forms of emancipation by cutting the hair or by gift of arms had fallen into disuse, as must inevitably have occurred before an advancing civilization. Unless, therefore, parental authority was now assimilated to guardianship, and made to end like it, with the attainment of majority, some new ground of emancipation must be found. Such a ground Stobbe finds in the separation of the son from the household of his father, which took place as a rule at the marriage of the son, and which was regularly accompanied by a division of property between the father and the son. It has already

---

[1] Greg. Tours. Vit. Patr. 9, 1. A Roman father emancipates his son, *ten years old*, by commendation. Sohm remarks: "This passage . . . contains a new proof that there were Romans who emancipated in the German form, — at the term of majority fixed by German law." R.- u. G. V., p. .547, n. 7. Cf. West. Goth. formula 34, quoted by Stobbe, Beiträge, p. 12.

[2] Vormundschaft, II. 590, ff.

[3] Die Aufhebung der väterlichen Gewalt nach dem Recht des Mittelalters (in his Beiträge zur Geschichte des deutschen Rechts).

been remarked that marriage was always regarded as *ipso facto* terminating the parental authority over sons. In the earlier law, however, marriage does not appear as a prominent form of emancipation, except in laws where a late period was established for majority. In laws where the earlier age of ten, twelve, or fifteen years was still the rule, the son would naturally be emancipated before the ordinary age of marriage. Kraut, of course, maintains that, for the later as for the earlier period, the father's power ended when the son attained majority. It would not be useful, for the present purpose, to enter at length upon the merits of the discussion for the period of the law-books. This would require a minute examination of a large number of passages in the various legal sources of that period. A single suggestion only may be permitted. After studying the arguments of Kraut and of Stobbe, one cannot help thinking that, so far as the period of the Sachsenspiegel is concerned, their views are not so much at variance as, at first sight, they seem to be ; and that, after all, the difference may arise from ignoring the fact that parental authority was not among the Germans, any more than it is to-day among us, a distinct, clearly defined right, like the Roman *patria potestas*, which must necessarily end entirely or not at all. Parental authority was not (to borrow the terms of Roman law) a *jus*, as *patria potestas*, in Roman law, was a " right over persons, analogous to rights of property." The law said, the father shall have certain powers over his son. When the son comes of age, certain of these powers shall cease. When a division of property takes place between father and son, certain other powers of the father shall cease. Kraut, while holding that parental authority ended with the son's attainment of majority, admits that, even after this period, the father continued to administer the common property, and, as head of the household, to represent his son before the courts. The father could even require such obedience from his son as was necessary for the well-being of the household. On the other hand, it cannot but be admitted that the father's control of his son's person was reduced to a minimum, after the son attained majority. The father could no longer chastise his son, nor forbid his becoming a monk, nor prevent his marriage. Stobbe even admits that, for the private property of the son, that which he had from sources other than the father, the father was only guardian, and was subject to the same pledges as other guardians.[1] In Westgothic law, at least, this included the pledge to restore a portion of such property to the son, when he came of age, whether married or not.[2] That even, as regards the father's property, the attainment of majority had an important effect is admitted by Stobbe. Before majority, the son had no right of veto in alienations by the father; after majority, he acquired this right.[3] In some laws also the son, after majority, had the right to demand a division of property.[4] Finally, the son was always at liberty, after he attained majority, to leave his father's house, and go where or do what he chose.

All this points to a possible solution of the difficulty. One is left by Stobbe to infer that emancipation in the time of Tacitus and of the L. Salica had the same effect as the later separation from the father's household. But was this the fact? Did the son, when his hair was cut, get control of his share of the common property, or, if he remained in the house of his father, is it supposable that the father, as head of the household, should have had no control over his behavior? The emancipation by special act in the early law was an emancipation of the person. The son became legally independent, possessed of political rights and subject to political and military duties; but he continued to hold his property in common with his father until his marriage. The difference between his position before and after majority is well shown by the fact that, before majority, he had no voice in the administration of the common property; after majority his consent was necessary to all acts affecting this property. He was then, after he was emancipated, not under the father's power, but he was associated with the father, who, as the elder, had the active administration. Now, as the power of

[1] Stobbe, p. 16, n. 18.   [2] Stobbe, p. 11.
[3] Stobbe, p. 21.   [4] Kraut, II. p. 595.

the father over the person of his son ceased in the time of Tacitus and of the L. Salica, when the son was emancipated by special act of commendation, &c., so in later law, when these customs had become obsolete, it ceased when the son attained majority. On the other hand, as the common ownership of father and son, their common life in the same household, and the rights of control necessarily given to the father as the elder of those living in the same house, were not extinguished, — let us not say by commendation (for this supposes a separation from the household), but by the ceremony of the gift of arms or of cutting the hair, *performed by the father himself;* so, in later law, they were not extinguished by the attainment of majority, but continued till the son separated from the father's household. In fine, as the powers of the German father did not form any thing at all resembling the Roman *patria potestas*, is it not after all futile to seek in German law for any thing having the same effects as the Roman *emancipatio?* The very expression " emancipation " is as little suited to express what really took place in primitive Germany as it would be to express what happens to-day.

If we turn now to the Anglo-Saxons, it is, first of all, very significant that no mention is made anywhere in their laws or history of any ceremony of emancipation of the son by commendation, by cutting the hair, or by any special act. Only in Norman times does such appear in the *foris familiatio*, which is undoubtedly of Norman origin, and is entirely analogous to the separation of households in the later law of the continent. The silence of the Saxon sources in this respect gives, at the outset, a strong presumption that already from the first the father's power in Saxon England was assimilated to guardianship, and ended like it when the son attained majority; and evidence is not lacking to make this presumption a certainty. The period of majority in Anglo-Saxon law was first fixed at the completion of the tenth year ;[1] but, later, the period of dependence was lengthened to twelve years.[2] Even this came in time to be regarded as too early

[1] Hl. & Ead. 6 ; Ine, 7, § 2.
[2] Æthelst. II. c. 1 ; Cnut, II. 20, 21.

an age to assume the responsibilities of manhood, and the later law shows a tendency to prolong the period to the completion of the fifteenth year,[1] though there is no sufficient evidence that this ever became law in the Saxon age. Throughout Norman times, however, and still in the time of Glanville, this was the age of majority for all except those holding knight's fees.[2] For these the Normans had introduced the period of twenty-one years.

That the father's control over the person of his son ended at the period of majority is clear from the following passages in the sources. Poen. Theod. XIX. § 26 : " Puer usque in xv. annos sit in potestate patris sui ; postea seipsum potest facere monachum si vult."[3] Ecgb. Excerp. c. 96 (Thorpe II. p. 111): " Parvulus usque annos xv. pro delicto corporali disciplina castigetur ; post hanc vero aetatem, quicquid deliquerit, vel si furatur, retribuat, seu etiam secundum legem exsolvat." Ine 7, § 2 : " A boy of ten years may be privy to a theft." Æthelst. II. 1. Pr.: " That one spare no thief taken in the act over twelve winters and over eight shillings." Cnut II. 20 : " And we will that every freeman be brought into a hundred or a tithing, who wishes to be entitled to satisfaction and to wer, if any one slays him after he is twelve winters old." Cnut II. 21 : " And we will that every freeman above twelve years make oath that he will neither be a thief, nor cognizant of a theft." Evidence more conclusive could not be desired. It is impossible to restrict the application of these passages to wards. They are general provisions applying to all freemen, whether orphans or sons of fathers still living. The boy, ten or twelve years old, can become a monk; can sell himself as a slave ; can no longer be chastised. Henceforth

[1] Æthelst. VI. 12.

[2] Hen. I. 70, § 18 (cf. L. Ripuaria, 81); 59, § 9 ; Glanv. VII. c. 9. Fifteen is also the age in the Kentish Custumal. Lambarde, p. 522; Robinson's Com. Law of Kent, p. 289.

[3] The number xv. here is without doubt an error of the transcriber. Another MS. has " quatuordecim annorum homini licet se servum facere." See note to Conf. Ecgb. § 27 (Thorpe II. p. 153). In two MSS. it is said : " Puella autem xiii. annorum sui corporis potestatem habet.' See note to Poen. Theod. XIX. § 26 (Thorpe II. p. 19). As the tendency of the law was to lengthen rather than to shorten the period of dependence, it is probable that the smaller of these numbers is the correct one.

he acts for himself, and is himself responsible for his acts. He must take oath to observe the laws, and enroll himself in one of the organizations provided for that purpose. What better commentary could be found on the words of Tacitus, "Ante domus, mox reipublicae"? And this personal and legal independence of the son, which Tacitus tells us was in his time acquired by the gift of arms in the assembly, is now acquired *ipso facto* by the attainment of majority. There is here no commendation, or cutting of the hair; no emancipation, *scuto frameaque;* no mention of a separation of households. Before the completion of the tenth or twelfth year, the boy is legally dependent. After the completion of the tenth or twelfth year, the boy is legally independent. He is no longer a boy, but a man possessed of all the rights and subject to all the duties that belong to complete manhood.

Nothing is said of the property relations between father and son. On this point, the Anglo-Saxon sources leave us entirely in the dark. Any control of the father over property acquired by the son would be inconsistent with the personal independence, which it has been shown the son enjoyed. It is clear from the charters that sons acquired a right of veto in alienations of the family estate. Probably until marriage sons continued as a rule to live with their father; and it would not be unnatural that the property of the mother, which during her life the father had administered as guardian and which after her death was inherited by the sons, should continue to be administered by the father until the marriage of the son led him to reclaim it. This administration would be in no way a right inherent in parental authority, but only a result of the custom of living in common: it would be dependent entirely upon the will of the son. There is nothing to show that the father had any legal rights over his son's property after the son attained majority.

As all women were legally dependent by reason of their sex, the attainment of majority could not have the same importance for girls that it had for boys. Daughters remained under their father's power until they married or went into a convent. Still the laws made a distinction between girls and adult women,[1] and this distinction was not merely nominal, but had a legal effect. The age of majority for girls was probably the same as that for boys. The Penitentials of Theodore and Ecgberht give various ages of majority;[2] and, if we assume the earlier of these to be the correct one, girls attained their majority at the completion of the twelfth year, — the ordinary majority for boys during the greater part of the Saxon period.[3] The effect of majority for women was to free their persons from the arbitrary disposal of the father.[4] They could enter a convent if they chose, and they could no longer be sent to a convent or given in marriage against their will.[5] This last, however, was the effect of majority only in the early law. It has been shown that in the later law even girls under age could not be married against their will. All other powers of the father over his daughter continued until she married or went into a convent. He administered her property as guardian, and had the use and enjoyment of it, and he represented her in court. But by far the most important power of the father was in the marriage of his daughter. Here the rights of every guardian of an adult woman unmarried were the same as those of the father, and what is said of the one will hold of the other. What these rights were will appear presently in the course of the discussion of marriage, — a subject which must now engage our attention.

In the earliest Anglo-Saxon laws, marriage[6] appears in the form of a sale by the father or other guardian to the bridegroom. Ine, 31: "If a man buy a wife and do not pay the purchase price ...;" Æthelb. 83: "If she is betrothed for money to another man ...;" id. 31: "If a freeman lie with

[1] Alf. 26, *ungewintraedne wifmon*; *i.e.*, women under age.

[2] Poen. Theod. XIX. §§ 26, 27; Conf. Ecgb. § 27 and note.

[3] In the Continental law the age was the same for both sexes. Kraut I. p. 124 ff.

[4] Poen. Theod. XIX. § 26 and note; Conf. Ecgb. § 27.

[5] *Vide supra*, p. 153.

[6] The early German marriage has been so thoroughly treated by Schroeder (Geschichte des ehelichen Güterrechts) and Sohm (das Recht der Eheschliessung) that it is now only necessary to present their conclusions so far as they relate to Anglo-Saxon law. Some peculiarities of the Anglo-Saxon development must, however, be considered.

a freeman's wife, let him purchase her with his wergeld and let him provide another wife with his own money and bring her to him." Whether marriage was ever an actual sale of the woman's person, treated as a chattel, may be doubted. The high estimation in which women were held among the Germans, when they first appear in history, proves at least that, if this was ever the case, it must have been in very remote times. The mere fact that marriage took the form of a sale proves nothing. In a primitive society, legal conceptions and legal forms are few and simple. The same word is used to designate things in fact different. Thus, all kinds of protection were included by the Germans under the designation *mund*, but it does not follow that this protection was in all instances of the same nature. Paternal authority, power of husband over wife, of guardian over ward, may in the beginning have been alike, but it is not necessary to assume this from the use of *mund* to designate them all.[1] The use of the form of sale for marriage does not prove that marriage was ever an actual sale, like any ordinary sale of chattels. This one legal form may have served several ends. It may have been used for contract, for conveyance, or for marriage, without its being necessary to assume that these were all of precisely the same nature. In fact, in the earliest Anglo-Saxon laws, marriage has a twofold aspect. In part, it exhibits the characteristics of an ordinary sale; in part, it differs very much from other sales, and appears as a transaction not merely of a mercantile, but of an ethical character. In the first place, it is certain that in historic times the thing transferred was not the person of the woman, treated as a chattel, but only the rights of guardianship. For these rights a real price was paid by the bridegroom to the guardian, and so far marriage resembled an ordinary sale. The strict formalities of a sale were also, throughout, observed.[2] On the

---

[1] The *mund* exercised by the king over ships of war (Æthelr. VI. 34) is an instance in point. This, certainly, was different from parental or marital authority.

[2] The contract of betrothal seems also to have included a warranty like any contract of sale. Æthelb. 77 : "If a man buy a maiden, let it be paid for in cattle, if it be without guile; but, if there be guile therein, let him bring her

other hand, the price was not the subject of bargain as in
ordinary sales, but, like the wer, was fixed by law, according
to the rank of the woman.[1] Again, an ordinary contract of
sale gave a right of action against the vendor to compel him
to deliver the thing sold.[2] The guardian who had contracted
to give the girl to the bridegroom could not be compelled to
this by an action. He could only be sued for breach of contract.[3] The ethical nature of marriage was already recognized
in the earliest historic times, and the history of marriage in
early German law is the history of its gradual enfranchisement
from the forms of a sale, and the substitution of other forms
more consistent with its ethical character.[4]

The price paid by the bridegroom to the guardian was called
the *weotuma*.[5] This word is connected with the Gothic root

home again and let his property be restored to him." Cf. Ine, 56 : " If a man
buy any kind of cattle, and he then discover any unsoundness in it within
thirty days, then let him throw the cattle on his hands, or let him swear that he
knew not of any unsoundness in it when he sold it to him."

[1] Sohm, p. 23 : " The *pretium puellae* is the analogue of the composition which,
according to German conceptions, is not the penalty for a wrong, but a repara-
tion for an injury to rights inestimable in money (body and life, freedom and
honor)." The proofs of this view are adduced by Prof. Sohm, in his article,
" Ueber die Entstehung des L. Ribuaria," in the Zeitschrift für R. G., V. p. 419,
ff. Æthelb. 82, as translated by Schmid, seems to contradict this view. Schmid
renders it thus : " If a man carry off a maiden by force, let him pay fifty shillings to the owner, and afterward let him buy her according to the will of that
one to whom she belongs." It is at least doubtful whether this is the true
meaning of the passage. Price (Thorpe, p. 25) translates "let him buy the
object of his will of the owner." But, even accepting Schmid's rendering, the
passage may be explained on the ground that it is an illegal marriage, and that
in such case the guardian could exact what he chose. In the Mosaic law there
was no bargaining about the price. *Vide* Exod. xxii. 17 : " If her father utterly
refuse to give her unto him, he shall pay money according to the dowry of
virgins." Alfred, in translating this passage, uses the word " weotuma." Alf.
Ecc. Laws, § 29.

[2] Laband, Vermögensrechtliche Klagen, p. 149, ff.

[3] Poen. Theod. XVI. § 29 : " Illa autem desponsata si non vult habitare cum
eo viro cui est desponsata, reddatur ei pecunia quam pro ipsa dedit et tertia
pars addatur. Si autem ipse noluerit, perdat pecuniam quam pro illa dedit."
That this is a real contract is proved by the fact that the price is prepaid. The
version of Ecgberht belongs to a later period. (See below, p. 171.) Cf. Löning,
Vertragsbruch, I. p. 142 ff.

[4] Cf. Sohm, p. 24.

[5] Alf. Ecc. L. 12, 29. In one passage the word *gift* or *gyft* occurs in the same

vidan, to bind. The *weotuma* was the payment which bound the contract; it was also that which gave the marriage its character of legality. Without payment of the *weotuma* there could be no legal marriage. All marriages without such payment and all violations of the woman's person were violations of the rights of the guardian, and were punished by a fine called *mund-bryce*. Schroeder[1] has shown that this fine had the closest connection with the legal *weotuma*, and was generally in amount either equal to the *weotuma*, or some multiple of it. The reason of this connection between the two is obvious. As the rights over the woman were something for which a price was regularly paid, to seize upon these rights without the consent of the owner and without paying for them was to steal; and the fine was proportioned to the value of the thing stolen, — the value, in this case, being the amount of the legal *weotuma*. The amount of the *weotuma* in Æthelbirht's laws appears from the following passages, — Æthelb. 75: "For the mund of a widow of the best class of the eorl's degree, let the bot be L shillings; of the second class XX shillings; of the third XII shillings; of the fourth VI shillings." Æthelb. 82: "If a man carry off a maiden by force let him pay L shillings to the owner," &c. The fine of fifty shillings, in the latter passage, must be regarded as a single *mund-bryce*, equal to the *weotuma*. For the forcible abduction of a widow the *mund-bryce* was equal to double the value of the *weotuma*. Æthelb. 76: "If a man carry off a widow not belonging to him, let the mund be twofold." In Alfred's time the amount of the *weotuma* was apparently sixty shillings for a woman of the lowest rank. For if, in Alf. 18, § 1, the woman untrue to her betrothal pays a fine of sixty shillings, while in Poen. Theod. XVI. § 29 (Thorpe, II. p. 11) it is said in like case, "reddatur ei pecunia quam pro illa dedit," it is probable that the two are identical.[2] So in Alf. 11, § 2, the violation of a maiden of the lowest rank is punished by a *mund-bryce* of

sense. *Vide* Ine, 31, with Schmid's note. *Weotuma* is kindred to the Burgundian, *wittemon;* Frisian, *wetma;* Alamannian, *widem;* Mod. Ger. *witthum.* Sohm, p. 23; Schmid, Gloss. s. v. *weotuma.*

[1] Schroeder, I. Einl. § 2.
[2] Schroeder, I. p. 15.

the same amount. For women above the rank of ceorl, the *weotuma* increased according to the wer.[1] Sometimes the *mund-bryce*, proportioned to the *weotuma*, was replaced by the wer of the guilty party,[2] and, later, when the *weotuma* was no longer a price to the guardian, but a gift to the bride of no fixed value, this became the rule.[3]

For the full completion of marriage in all its effects, two acts were necessary, — the *beweddung*, or betrothal; and the *gifta* (plur. of *gift*), the delivery of the woman, or nuptials. Schmid, Anh. II. § 61: "And we prohibit with God's prohibition that any one have more wives than one, and let her be lawfully betrothed and given (*beweddod and forgifen*)."

The betrothal was the promise, on the one hand, to give in marriage, — on the other, to take in marriage, and to pay the purchase price. But the mere promise was not enough. As marriage was a sale, so betrothal was a contract of sale. To understand the nature of the betrothal, it will therefore be necessary to speak of the early German law of contract.[4] In the earliest German law, there was no consensual, but only a real or a formal, contract. In other words, a mere convention was not binding: it must be accompanied by some formal act, or by performance on one side. But when this act had been performed, or payment had been made on one side, the contract was not binding merely as giving a claim for damages against the debtor: it effected an actual transfer of title. It transferred the negative effects of property, — the *jus vindicandi* and the *jus abutendi* of the Romans. The positive effects of property — the power to use and enjoy the *jus utendi fruendi* — were transferred when the actual delivery took place. The contract — not the delivery of actual possession — was the ground of the title of the purchaser, donee, &c. Hence, in a contract of sale, the purchaser who had paid the price had an action to obtain the thing from the vendor; and, in a contract for the sale of immovables, he

---

[1] Alf. 11, § 5.   [2] Æthelb. 31.

[3] Cnut, II. 52; Will. I. 12; Schmid, Anh. II. § 63.

[4] In this description of the early German law of contract, Sohm has been closely followed throughout. But see Löning for a contrary view.

could recover even from third parties to whom the vendor had alienated the property. The delivery was only the accomplishment, in fact, of what was already effected in law by the contract.

In the earliest Anglo-Saxon laws, the betrothal appears as a real contract of sale, binding when the *weotuma* was paid by the bridegroom to the guardian. That the *weotuma* was regularly prepaid, appears from Poen. Theod. XVI. § 29 (Thorpe, II. p. 11): " Illa autem desponsata si non vult habitare cum eo viro cui est desponsata, reddatur ei pecunia quam pro ipsa dedit, et tertia pars addatur. Si autem ipse noluerit, perdat pecuniam quam pro illa dedit." When the *weotuma* was paid, the contract was binding, and, like other real contracts, gave the purchaser the rights of a legal owner, so far as this could be done consistently with the ethical character of marriage. Sohm divides the effects of marriage, like the effects of property, into positive and negative effects. The negative effect of marriage was to establish between husband and wife the pledge of fidelity. The positive effect of marriage was to transfer the wife into the actual power of her husband, — to give him control of her person and property. The former was the effect of betrothal; the latter, the effect of the delivery of the woman, — the *gifta* or nuptials. The gift of the woman was only the completion, in fact, of what was already accomplished in law by the betrothal. The betrothal, not the gift of the woman, was the ground of the husband's title. The man and woman were therefore married when they were betrothed.[1] Hence any violation of the betrothal by a third person was a violation of the rights of the bridegroom,[2] and was punished by a fine paid to him.[3]

Thus far, Sohm's view is entirely in accordance with evidence, and presents no difficulty. The betrothal was the transaction which gave marriage its effect in law; and it con-

[1] The English " wedding " is derived from the Anglo-Saxon " beweddung," which meant, not the nuptials, but the betrothal. So a " wedded " wife, — *i.e.*, a wife promised or betrothed. Cf. Sohm, p. 56.

[2] Poen. Ecgb. II. § 12: " Si mulier aliqua desponsata sit non est permissum ut aliquis alius vir illam ei auferat."

[3] Æthel. 83.

ferred the rights of a husband on the bridegroom, so far as third parties were concerned. But was the case the same as between the wife or her guardian and the bridegroom? It has been shown above that the contract of betrothal, unlike other real contracts of sale, did not give the bridegroom an action to compel the delivery of the bride, as this would be contrary to the ethical character of marriage.[1] If the guardian refused to deliver the woman, or she refused to be delivered, the bridegroom had only a suit for damages, to recover the *weotuma* previously paid, and an additional fine of one-third.[2] On the other hand, a breach of betrothal by the man was punished by loss of the *weotuma*. That he also had to pay an additional fine appears from Ine, 31: "If a man buy a wife, and do not pay the purchase price, let him give the money and pay *compensation*, and make bot, to the sureties, according to his infraction of his pledge." The bridegroom, like any purchaser, could be sued for the price; but the guardian, unlike other parties to a contract, could not be compelled to delivery, but could only be sued for damages.[3] From the point of view of the legality of the marriage, of the violation of betrothal by third parties, even of its violation by the bridegroom, the contract of betrothal was still, like other real contracts, a ground of acquiring the title. But, from the point of view of the breach of betrothal by the woman or her guardian, the contract created only a relation of obligation, and in no way differed from the Roman contract. It was not conveyance, but contract, in the modern sense.[4] Sohm has shown that the ethical character of marriage was the means of the first introduction into German law of a contract in favor of a third party.[5] If the view here taken be correct, it was also the means of the first introduc-

---

[1] There are some indications that in the oldest German law the bridegroom had a right to compel delivery. Cf. Löning, I. p. 145, n. 10.

[2] Poen. Theod. XVI. § 29. Conf. Ecgb. § 20; Alf. 18, § 1.

[3] This was the most that was ever allowed in the oldest Latin law. The Roman law did not even allow this, but permitted a suit only where there was an express penal stipulation. Puchta, Inst. II. p. 801.

[4] It is difficult to see, therefore, why Professor Sohm, in common with all the German writers, denies to the early German law the idea of a contract *in specie*, in the Roman or modern sense.   [5] Sohm, p. 84.

tion into German law of the idea of a contract *in specie*, in the Roman sense, as distinguished from a conveyance.

Such was the betrothal in the earliest Anglo-Saxon period. The passage above quoted from Ine (§ 31) points to a change which had already taken place in the law of betrothal, corresponding to a development in the law of contract. In the earliest form of real contract, the purchaser, forced to pay in advance to make the contract binding, incurred the risk of non-fulfilment by the other side. This evil was remedied by the introduction of a new principle. The contract was held to be binding, if the purchaser had paid only a small nominal sum as earnest-money. This is the German *handgeld*, *arrha*, — the Lombard *launichild.* The *handgeld* was not, in any sense, payment or partial payment. It was the representative, not of a money value, but of a juridical effect. It only served to preserve the appearance of a real contract, without the necessity of prepayment by one side. Ine, § 31, and Alf. 18, § 1, show that already, in the time of Ine and Alfred, the price was no longer paid at betrothal, but only promised. Immediately another change in the law of betrothal became possible. The price was no longer paid to the guardian, but was given to the woman herself after marriage. Alf. Ecc. Laws, § 12: ". . . let him see that she have raiment, and that which is the value of her maidenhood, — namely, the *weotuma.* . . ." The betrothal was no longer a true contract of sale : it was only a fictitious contract of sale. The form of a sale was preserved : the contract remained a real contract, by payment to the guardian of the *handgeld ;* but the bridegroom contracted to give the price, not to the guardian, but to the woman.[1]

The betrothal once freed from the character of a true contract of sale, the next step was easy to take. The betrothal ceased to be a real contract even in form, and became a formal contract, — that is, a contract which derived its binding force, not from payment of the price or of the *handgeld*, but from the performance of some solemn act. The formal con-

---

[1] The earliest case in German law of a contract in favor of a third party. Sohm, p. 34.

tract of German law was the *fides facta*,[1] or *wette*. It consisted in the giving and taking of the straw, *festuca*. *Wette*, like *witthum*, is kindred with the Gothic *vidan*, to bind. "It is that which binds, and, as applied to the contract, the contract which binds."[2] The principal cases of the application of the *wette* were, — 1. In procedure where the party adjudged to make payment, or to give proof, promised to fulfil the judgment; 2. Where one person became surety for another; 3. In the promise of a penal sum.[3] From the beginning of the tenth century, the Anglo-Saxon betrothal appears in the form of contract, made binding by the giving of sureties both by the bridegroom and the guardian. That a penal sum was also promised, appears from Conf. Ecgb. § 20 (Thorpe, II. p. 149, note) :[4] "Si puella desponsata cum eo esse nolit cui voluntate sua desponsata erat, tunc reddat pecuniam quam antea accepisset, cui talem addat accessionem qualis tertiae parti pecuniae aequalis sit et solvant propinqui suum wedd."[5] Fortunately a full description of the betrothal in this form has come down to us in an Anglo-Saxon formula, commonly called the Kentish Betrothal, belonging probably to the tenth century. This interesting and important document deserves to be quoted entire : —

SCHMID, Anh. VI., § 1 : "If any one wish to betroth a maiden or a woman, and it so be agreeable to her and to her friends, then it is right that the bridegroom, according to the law of God and the customs of the world, first promise and give a *wed* to those who are her guardians that he will keep her according to God's law, as a man should his wife ; and let his friends be sureties for that.

§ 2. "After that, let it be known to whom the *foster-lean*[6] belongs.

---

[1] For a different view of the *fides facta*, see Löning, I. p. 3 ff. Cf. Sohm, p. 36, n. 27.

[2] Sohm, p. 35.   [3] Sohm, pp. 36–46.   [4] Sohm, p. 47, n. 47.

[5] This passage is only a copy of the passage from Theodore quoted above (p. 168). The Penitential of Theodore belongs to the seventh century ; the original of that of Ecgberht, to the eighth, but, in the form in which it has come down to us, probably to a somewhat later period. The passage from Theodore (XVI. § 29) shows the betrothal as a real contract, with price paid in advance to the guardian (pecuniam quam *pro illa dedit*) : there is no mention of a *wed*. The passage from Ecgberht shows the betrothal as a formal contract with *wed ;* and the woman, not the guardian, receives the *weotuma*.

[6] What the *foster-lean* was is doubtful. The word means "money for nour-

Let the bridegroom give *wed* for that, and let his friends be sureties for it.

§ 3. " Then let the bridegroom declare what he will grant her if she choose his will, and what he will grant her if she live longer than he.

§ 4. " And if it be so agreed, then it is right that she shall be entitled to half of the inheritance, and to all if they have children in common, unless she again choose a husband.

§ 5. " Let him confirm all that which he has promised with a *wed*, and let his friends guarantee it.

§ 6. " If, then, they are agreed in every thing, let her kinsmen take it in hand, and betroth their kinswoman to wife, and to a righteous life, to him who desired her ; and let him undertake the surety who has control of the *wed*.

§ 7. " If, then, he desire to lead her out of the land into another thane's land, then it is right that her friends have there an agreement that no wrong shall be done her ; and, if she commit a fault, that they may be nearest in the bot, if she have not wherewith she may make bot.

§ 8. " At the nuptials, there shall be a mass-priest by law, who shall, with God's blessing, bind their union to all prosperity.

§ 9. " It is also well to be looked to that it be known that they, through kinship, be not too nearly allied, lest that be afterwards divided which before was wrongly joined."

As it appears here, the betrothal is not a sale, real or fictitious, but a formal contract, made binding by the *wed*. All the formalities which concern the legality of marriage are attached to the betrothal. It, and not the gift of the woman, is the legal act of marriage. The unimportance of the gift of the woman, as compared with the betrothal, appears clearly from the small account taken of it in the formula. The nuptials are now, however, celebrated in the presence of a priest, and hallowed by the blessing of the church, — almost the earliest example of any religious ceremony of marriage in German law, but still a religious ceremony having no effect

ishment." Schroeder (I. p. 51, n. 13) regards it as a pledge to maintain the children by the marriage. Sohm (p. 317, note) considers it as a *handgeld* which is not paid, but only promised, at betrothal, — a supposition rendered probable by the fact that the *handgeld* was ordinarily spent in the purchase of beer or wine for the entertainment of those present, or distributed to the poor.

in law.[1] The *weotuma* is no longer a purchase price paid at
betrothal to the guardian, but a gift to the woman, promised,
with sureties, at betrothal.   It appears in the formula in the
words, " what he will give her if she choose his will." [2]   As
a gift to the woman, the *weotuma* is of small importance as
compared with the morning-gift.   Thus, in one deed of betrothal, a *weotuma* appears of one pound of gold by the side
of a morning-gift composed of extensive grants of land.
Cod. Dip. DCCXXXII. : " Here appeareth in this writing
the agreement that Godwin made with Byrhtric when he
wooed his daughter ; that is, first, that he gave one pound's
weight of gold for that she should choose his will.   And he
gave to her the land at Street, with all that belonged to it,
and at Burwaramesc another half-hundred hides ; and therewith thirty oxen, and twenty cows, and ten horses, and ten
theow-men.   This was promised at Kingston, before Cnut, in
the witness of Archbishop Lyfing, &c. . . . And that they
would conduct the maiden to Brightling, all became surety
for this. . . . And whichever of those two lives longer shall
have all the property, as well that land that I gave to her
as every thing," &c.   To the close of the Anglo-Saxon
period, the *weotuma* seems to have remained a separate gift,
of little intrinsic value, serving only to mark the legality of
the marriage.[3]   In the time of Cnut, the sale of the rights of
guardian in the old way was forbidden by law (Cnut, II. 74) :

[1] Sohm, p. 162, 317.

[2] Schroeder has shown this clearly, I. p. 54.

[3] On the continent, the purchase price became a gift to the bride of considerable importance, and often consisting of realty.   Schroeder (I. p. 54, n. 22)
ascribes the same development to the Anglo-Saxon *weotuma*, and finds examples
of a *weotuma*, consisting of realty, in Cod. Dip. DCCXXXVIII. (*vide supra*
p. 115), and in Cod. Dip.·MCCCV. (*supra*, p. 114).   These two cases are rather
to be regarded as morning-gifts.   The use of the word *dotalicium* in the one
case, and the fact in the other case that the gift was made to induce the guardian to give his consent, are not sufficient to separate these cases from that in
Cod. Dip. DCCCCXXVI. (see below, p. 176 n. 1), which is an undoubted case of
morning-gift.   Another consideration deserves mention.   As the old *weotuma*
was a fixed sum of money, it was only natural that, after it became a gift to
the woman, it should remain a gift of money (as in Cod. Dip. DCCXXXII.,
quoted in the text) ; preserving the remembrance of the older form, and serving
only to mark the legality of the marriage.

"And let no one compel either woman or maiden to whom she herself dislikes, nor for money sell her, unless he shall be willing to give something voluntarily."

The Kentish Betrothal speaks of two gifts to the bride. The bridegroom declares "what he will give her if she choose his will, and what he will give her if she live longer than he." The former gift has been identified as the *weotuma;* the latter is the *morgen-gifu,* or morning-gift.[1] The general history of the morning-gift, in German law, is in brief this:[2] Unlike the *weotuma,* the morning-gift had at first no connection with the legality of the marriage. It was a free gift of the husband to his wife on the morning after the bridal night.[3] At first it consisted of movables probably of no great value. Later, it became a gift for the widow's maintenance; consisting as a rule of realty, and granted at betrothal, with a written document to be used as proof after the husband's death. If no morning-gift was granted at betrothal, the law assigned a certain portion of the husband's property to the widow for her maintenance. This was the legal morning-gift, — the Lombard *quarta,* the Frankish *tertia.* So the *weotuma* and the morning-gift came to be promised at the same time, and naturally in the same document, and both were secured by sureties. The two gifts were merged, and became the *douaire* of the *Coutumes,* — the *dos ad ostium ecclesiae* of the later law. The *douaire, dos,* or dower had in common with the old *weotuma,* the time and manner of its establishment, and the close connection with the legality of the marriage. In common with the old morning-gift, it had the amount and the character of a widow's maintenance. The dower of English common law is derived in an unbroken historical development through the *dos ad ostium ecclesiae* of Bracton and Glanville, the Norman *douaire* and the Frankish *tertia,* from the purchase price or *weotuma* and the *morgen-gifu* of the heathen Germans.

[1] Schroeder (I. p. 96) has shown this clearly.

[2] Schroeder, pp. 84–112, has here been followed throughout.

[3] Cod. Dip. CCCXXVIII. : "It was her morning-gift when first she came to Athulf." Cod. Dip. DCCCCLXVII. : "And I announce what I have given my wife as morning-gift. . . . And I gave her these when first we came together."

In the Anglo-Saxon period this development did not reach its completion; the *weotuma* and the morning-gift were still in the eleventh century separate gifts;[1] but the various steps of the development appear clearly.

ÆTHELB. 78: "If she bear a live child, let her have half the property, if the husband die first." Ib. 79: "If she wish to go away with her children, let the husband have half the property." Ib. 80: "If the husband wish to have them, (let her portion be) as one child." Ib. 81: "If she bear no child, let the paternal kindred have the *fioh* and the morning-gift."

The morning-gift is here spoken of only in connection with a childless marriage. In marriages with children, it has already given way to the "higher principle of community of property" between husband and wife.[2] The law of Ine shows the progress of this principle, since the time of Æthelbirht. Community of goods between husband and wife exists in all marriages, childless or not. Ine, 57: "If a ceorl steal a chattel and bear it to his dwelling, and it be intertiated therein, then shall he be guilty for his part without his wife; for she must obey her lord. If she dare to declare by oath that she tasted not of the stolen property, let her take her third part." Æthelst. VI. 1, § 1: . . . "and first take the *ceap-gild* from the property, and after that let the surplus be divided into two parts, one to the wife, if she be innocent, and not privy to the crime, etc."[3] The exact proportion assigned to the widow seems to have varied, but was generally a half.[4] In the later period it was ordinarily fixed by agreement at betrothal.[5] But this conversion of the morning-gift into half the property of the husband did not take place when a morning-gift was granted, consisting of realty and

---

[1] See above, p. 173 and n. 3.

[2] Schroeder, p. 97. The Anglo-Saxon law is here entirely in accord with that of the Westfalian Saxons. *Vide* Schroeder, I. pp. 98–108.

[3] Cf. Will. I. 27; Ed. Conf. 19; Cnut, II. 76.

[4] So in the Kentish Custumal: Et si il eit femme, maintenant seit dowe per le heir, sil seit dage, de la *meytie*, de touz les terres e tenemenz quo son baroun tient de Gavylekend en fee." Lambarde, p. 516; Robinson's Com. Law of Kent, p. 283. See above, p. 186.

[5] Kentish Betrothal, § 4. *Vide supra*, p. 172.

secured by a written document. For the richer classes, this was ordinarily the case in the later law, and numerous examples of such grants appear in the charters.[1]

In some of the continental laws it was customary for the father or guardian to make a gift to the bride on her marriage. This gift appears most clearly in the Lombard law, under the name *faderfio*. No evidence of such a custom appears in the Anglo-Saxon sources,[2] and one passage says expressly that daughters were given in marriage without a *dot*. Hist. Rames. 4: "Factum est ut exteri reges et principes sorores ejus (King Æthelstan) quas pater indotatas reliquerat, etc."[3] From the time of the conquest such a gift was customary under the name *maritatio* or *maritagium*,[4] — the frank-marriage of the later law.

During marriage,[5] the wife was under the guardianship of her husband. She must obey him in general;[6] but, in her own sphere as housekeeper, she was independent. Cnut, II. 76: "And, if a man bring stolen things home to his cot, it is right that he [the owner] have what he went after. And, if it was not brought under the wife's custody, she shall be innocent. But she shall guard the keys, that is, of her store-room, and her chest, and her press. If it is brought into

---

[1] Cod. Dip. CCCXXVIII. (App. No. 17); *ib.* MCCLXXXVIII. (App. No. 21); *ib.* DCCIV. (App. No. 26); *ib.* MCCXC. (*supra*, p. 115); *ib.* DCCXXXVIII. (*supra*, p. 115); *ib.* DCCXXXII. (*supra*, p. 173); *ib.* DCCCCLXVII. (above, p. 174, n. 3); *ib.* DCLXXXV.; *ib.* DCCCCXXVI.: " Ego Gytha comitissa concedo aecclesiae . . . terram meam de Scireford quae est de *dote* mea." *Dos*, in the Latin sources of the Anglo-Saxon period, means always morning-gift. Thus Cnut II. 73, "let her lose her morning-gift," is translated in the Latin (Cod. Colb.) "careat dote."

[2] Schroeder (I. p. 119) has shown that the *fioh* in Æthelb. 81 is not the *faderfio* as many have assumed. The word means simply property, and can apply as well to inherited property as to property given at marriage.

[3] Cf. Albert Krantz (Wandalia, 1, 13): "Valet hodie (15th century) ea ut ferunt consuetudo in Thietmarsis, gente palustri ad exitum Albis fluminis, ut nuptui tradant filias indotatas, etc.," quoted by Schroeder, I. p. 49. The Diethmarsen belonged to the Saxon stem.

[4] Hen. I. 1, §§ 3–4; ib. 70, § 22; Ed. Conf. 19. See Charter of Mathilda de St. Liz. (A. D. 1100) in Dugdale's Monasticon, III. p. 473: "quod est liberum maritagium meum."

[5] Cf. Schroeder, p. 126 ff.

[6] Ine, 57 (quoted above, p. 175).

one of these places, then is she guilty. And no wife can forbid her husband to lay in his cot what he will." The husband, as guardian, was co-possessor with his wife of her property, — that is, property inherited by her, or given to her, including her morning-gift.[1] Neither could alienate such property without the other's consent. Sometimes, in alienations, the husband and wife acted together;[2] sometimes the husband was the acting, and the wife the consenting, party;[3] but generally the wife was the acting, and the husband the consenting, party.[4] In general, the husband had the free disposal of his own property, so far as concerned the wife. But, where a specific morning-gift had not been granted to the wife, she had, in law, a right to an undivided portion of her husband's property, and regularly appears as a consenting party to all alienations by him.[5] From the analogy of the continental laws, it is probable that the marriage acquisitions — property derived from the common labor or common property of husband and wife; not property acquired, by one of the two, by gift or inheritance, or from the proceeds of his or her own property — belonged to the husband: but, after his death, these formed part of the estate from which the legal morning-gift was granted.[6] Gifts were regularly made to husband and wife together,[7] and gifts between husband and wife were common.[8] The wife's property was not answerable for the debts of her husband, nor his property for the debts of his wife.[9] Here the rights of over-guardianship exercised by the wife's kindred appear clearly. A homicide committed by her must be atoned for, not by her husband,

---

[1] Hist. Rames, 85: "Cnutonis ergo regis tempore quidam Dacus cum memorata muliere, ex permissione regis, connubium trahens, praedictae villae dominium jure conjugis est adeptus." Cf. Phillip's Gesch. des Angelsächsischen Rechts, p. 143.

[2] Cod. Dip. CLXXVII.

[3] Cod. Dip. LXXVI.

[4] Cod. Dip. CCXCVIII.

[5] Cod. Dip. CCVI. et multa alia.

[6] Schroeder, I. p. 137.

[7] Cod. Dip. CXX.; ib. CCLXXIX.; ib. CCCLXVIII. et al.

[8] Cod. Dip. DXXIV.; ib. DCXLI.

[9] Vide supra, pp. 123, 175.

12

but by her kin.[1] Other fines incurred by the wife were probably paid by the husband, as her active guardian, from her
property. But, if this property did not suffice, not the husband, but the wife's kindred, were liable for the rest.[2] The
wife's kindred seem also to have protected her property from
alienations by the husband;[3] and probably, if she were
abused by him, they could interfere to divorce them, and to
bring their kinswoman home.[4]

At the dissolution of marriage by the death of the husband,[5] the wife was entitled to all property belonging to her
by inheritance or gift, and to her morning-gift, either one
specifically established by a grant of realty with a charter,
or, in lack of this, to half the husband's property.[6] The wife
had the full ownership in the morning-gift, unless her husband had expressly limited her to a life-estate,[7] and she could
dispose of it, during her life[8] or by testament;[9] and, if she
died intestate, it was inherited by her heirs. She forfeited
it, however, to her husband's next of kin, if she violated her
year's fidelity.[10] It follows that, by keeping her year's fidelity, she could take it with her to a second marriage.[11] Ordinarily, a partition of the property did not take place on the
death of the husband, but the widow held the property in
common with the heirs;[12] and her morning-gift seems, like
the rest of the husband's property, to have been liable for

[1] Hen. I. 70, § 12 (*supra*, p. 123).

[2] Schmid, Anh. VI. § 7 (*supra*, p. 123).

[3] It was customary to deposit with the wife's father a copy of the deed of
gift when the morning-gift was granted. Cod. Dip. DCCXXXII. *in fin.*

[4] Æthelr. 79 (*supra*, p. 175).

[5] Schroeder, I. p. 143 ff.

[6] Æthelr. 78–81 (*supra*, p. 175), Kent. Betroth. § 4.

[7] Hist. Rames. 29.

[8] Cod. Dip. CCCXXVIII. (*vide* App. No. 17); *ib.* DCCIV. (App. No. 26);
ib. DCCCCXXVI.

[9] Cod. Dip. DCLXXXV.; *ib.* MCCXC.

[10] Cnut, II. 73.

[11] Cf. Cod. Dip. MCCLXXXVIII. (*vide* App. No. 21).

[12] Cnut, II. 72. Wherever the wife is mentioned as having the whole of her
husband's property (as in Kent. Betroth. § 5), it is only because of this custom
of living in common without a partition of the property. Schroeder, I. p. 98,
n. 14.

the debts of the estate.[1] But the widow was never heir of
her husband,[2] though gifts to her in her husband's will were
common.[3]

At the dissolution of marriage by the death of the wife,[4]
such property as belonged to her by inheritance or gift was
inherited by her heirs. The husband was not heir, and got
no right in the property of his wife, except through the children. These were the first heirs of the wife ; and after their
death, if they left no children, their father would be their
first heir. As the morning-gift was a grant to the wife " if
she lived longer than he," it follows that, if the wife died
before her husband, the morning-gift remained with the husband.

Divorce by mutual consent seems to have been permitted
in the early law.[5] In such case, the wife received half her
husband's property, if she took the children with her, or a
child's portion if these remained with the husband. If the
marriage was childless, she simply received her morning-gift
and her inherited property. The husband was permitted to
divorce his wife for infidelity or desertion.[6] If for infidelity,
by a law of Cnut, all her property was forfeited to the husband.[7]

It remains only to consider the subject of guardianship.
Here the extreme meagreness of the evidence permits only
the most general conclusions. The grounds of legal dependence were four, — age, sex, physical defects, *status* or social

---

[1] Hist. Eliens. I. 11 : " Ubi inter alia judicatum est, ut Sifled Relicta Lessii,
et haeredes sui, Deo et Episcopo praedictam rapinam emendare deberent, sicuti
ipse, si vixisset, facere debuisset." Cf. Phillips, p. 144.

[2] *Vide supra*, p. 124. Phillips (Angels. R. G. p. 147) and Ganz (Erbrecht, IV.
p. 808) assert that the widow inherited in want of other heirs. The passage relied
on by them proves the exact contrary, — Hist. Rames, 85 : " Cui cum natura liberos invidisset, sine haerede mortis legem subiens, conjugi suae superstiti eam
reliquit dotis nomine possidendam." The widow received *dotis nomine*, not *haereditatis nomine*.

[3] Cod. Dip. CCCIV. *et al.*

[4] Cf. Schroeder, I. p. 167 ff.

[5] Æthelr. §§ 79, 81 ; Poen. Theod. XIX. § 20.

[6] Poen. Theod. XIX. §§ 18, 23.

[7] Cnut, II. 53.

condition. All these have their origin in the more general ground of incapacity to bear arms. As the courts were, at first, assemblies of all the armed freemen, no one not a member of the army could appear in court; and, of course, no one not able to use weapons could fight in the blood-feud. But the capacity to bear arms, as the criterion of legal independence, belongs only to the earliest period. As the blood-feud weakened and judicial processes superseded it, and as the courts became purely judicial bodies, we find women acquiring a legal independence which would have been impossible under the earlier law.

As the guardianship over those legally dependent by reason of their *status* was not a family guardianship, it does not concern us here. Persons dependent by reason of physical defects — the lame, blind, dumb, insane, &c.[1] — were under the guardianship of their father, or, if he were dead, of the nearest male of the paternal kindred. The guardian paid their fines, protected them and their property, and doubtless had the use and enjoyment of their estate.

When the household was broken up by the death of the father, the children passed into the guardianship of the nearest male of the paternal kindred. Hl. and Ead. 6: " If a husband die, wife and child yet living, then it is right that the child follow the mother; and let sufficient security be given from among his paternal kindred to keep his property until he be ten years of age." Ine, 38: " If a ceorl and his wife have a child between them, and the ceorl die, let the mother have her child and feed it; and let VI. shillings be given her for its fostering, a cow in summer and an ox in winter; and let the kindred take care of the homestead until it be of age." From these passages, it is clear that the control of the child's person did not belong to the guardian, but to the mother. It was the guardian's duty to supply nourishment for the child, to take care of the estáte, and to represent the child in the courts. In return, he had, without doubt, the use and enjoyment of the estate during the child's minority.

---

[1] Alf. 14; Hen. I. 78, §§ 6, 7.

On coming of age, wards could sue for property wrongfully withheld by the guardian, or alienated by him to third parties.[1] Boys became independent on attaining their majority; but girls continued under guardianship until their marriage, or entrance into a convent. Of the powers of the guardian over women of full age, nothing is said; and it only remains to suppose that they were the same as those of the father.

That widows, in the early law, were under guardianship, is clear from Æthelb. 76: "If a man carry off a widow not belonging to him, let the mund be twofold." It is not clear whether they were under the guardianship of their own kin, or of the husband's next of kin, as in most of the continental laws, but probably the former. In the later law, widows were practically independent. Æthelr. V. 21: "And let every widow who conducts herself lawfully be in God's peace and the king's. And let every one continue twelve months husbandless; afterwards, let her choose what she herself will."[2] The latter clause has generally been taken to mean that the widow might follow her own will in marrying. But it means more than this. She was free to enter a convent. Cnut, II. 73, § 3: "And let not a widow take the veil too precipitately." It has already been shown that she had the free disposal of her property; and it appears, from some passages in the charters, that she was free to choose her "forespeca," or guardian, to represent her in the courts. In Cod. Dip. DCLXXXV., Ælflaed gives certain lands to Æthelmere, the ealdorman: "þæt he min fulla freond and mundiend beo on minum dege," &c., — "that he be my full friend and guardian during my life;" and, again, "þaet he beo on minum life min fulla freond and forespreca and mira manna," — "on condition that, during my life, he be my entire friend, my advocate, and that of my men." So, in Cod. Dip. DCCLV. (vide App. No. 28), a widow appears as party to a suit brought by her own son, who would necessarily be her guardian if the old rules of guardianship were in force. This necessity of a *forespeca*, or representative before the courts,[3]

---

[1] Cod. Dip. LXXXII. (vide App. No. 1).   [2] Cf. Cnut, II. 73.
[3] Cod. Dip. DCCIV. (App. No. 26); ib. CCCCXCIX. (App. No. 18).

was all that remained of the old guardianship of widows; and even this does not seem to have been always necessary in later times. In one suit, not only is the plaintiff a woman, who prosecutes her suit before the king and in the shire court, but many "good women" take part in the oath.[1] Nothing shows more clearly the enormous change that had taken place in the position of women, and in the character of the courts, since the settlement of the Saxons in England.

In want of male kindred of the male stem, the duties of guardian, in some of the continental laws, passed to the nearest male of the maternal kindred; in others, to the king. The Anglo-Saxon laws throw no light on this point; but it is clear that the king was guardian for all who had no kindred, including natural children[2] and foreigners.[3]

[1] Cod. Dip. DCXCIII. (App. No. 22).

[2] Ine, 27.

[3] Ed. and Guth. § 12; Æthelr. VIII. 33; Cnut, II. 40.

THE ANGLO-SAXON LEGAL PROCEDURE.

I.

A GERMAN scholar has well illustrated the distinction between the suit of modern times and that of the primitive German period by comparing the former to a syllogism, in which the body of judicial rules is the major, and the declaration of facts the minor premise; while the latter, without any such structure, might be but a simple demand on the defendant for compensation. The democratic character of German political institutions finds a parallel in the large judicial powers vested in the individual (*Selbsthülfe*). Many evidences point to the supposition that, in the most archaic German procedure, even seizure — the distress of the common law — was permitted to the individual without intervention of the court.[1] Whether this was true or not, it is at all events certain that, in the earliest known German sources, permission of the court was always necessary before proceeding to execution.

The early legal system, which existed throughout the period closed by the Salic law, and which will be designated as the Executive Procedure, in opposition to the enlarged procedure which arose about the time of Childebert, in the sixth century, was pre-eminently a procedure of coercion, as distinguished from that of proof known to later times. A strict exactness existed in the relation between law and procedure, as shown in the case where, when the defendant repeated the claim of the plaintiff and denied it word for word, he lost his suit if he stammered in the repetition. And

---

[1] This was true in old Roman law in the Pignoris Capio, which was at first a wholly extra-judicial proceeding. Maine, Early Hist. of Instit. p. 258.

this strict formalism gave to the individual a means of procedural coercion, fortified, in case of resistance, by a legal sanction. The distinction, for example, between the executive procedure and the procedure in regard to land which arose later, consisted in the narrowness and limited character of the department of proof and judgment in the former, and the absence of any examination of the material basis of the action.

The old Germanic law recognized no *causae cognitio;* the plaintiff's material right was not examined. Nor did the legal conceptions of the early Germans recognize the distinctions of Roman law between real and personal actions. To the Romans, a real right was original, unlimited ownership (*dominium*), from which parts could be separated and conveyed to another (*jura in re*); while, to the German mind, the material possession of, and the right over, the thing were bound closely together. The conception of the thing as an abstract quantity was foreign to their modes of thought. The right to a movable could not be acquired by a contract *in genere*, but only by the actual delivery of possession; while the real right was acquired by a contract *in specie*, without delivery. But private property in land was unrecognized. In the early executive period, there was no action for inheritance, or real property; and the civil procedure was essentially one for debt.[1] As legal conceptions advanced and new needs were felt, there arose a pressure for additional judicial aid, and an extension of the procedure. The *Lex Salica* stood out to mark the close of the old executive period in German law, although even in the *Lex Salica* the introduction of the action for movables had already widened the old procedure, following a development which was always an extension, but not a destruction, of the old system. To this later period belong the codes of the Ripuarian Franks,[2] the Burgundians, the Visigoths, and the Lombards.[3]

[1] The Swiss law of debt is not a civil procedure, but a transcription of the *Lex Salica*, 50, § 1, and 52. Heusler, Gewere, p. 489.

[2] This law was a revision of the *Lex Salica*, section for section, and was written to adapt itself to the progress in the procedure.

[3] This law is especially valuable, both because the Lombards came south later than other tribes, and retained the pure Germanic law in greater complete-

To this period also belong all the sources of Anglo-Saxon law; the earliest laws — those of Æthelberht of Kent — having been written about 600 A.D. But, to justly estimate the Anglo-Saxon laws, appeal must be made to the Saxon law of the continent, and to other German codes; and the primitive German procedure must be kept clearly in view. Thorpe is, of course, in error when he says that the original institutes of the English were "little beyond that portion of the laws of Æthelberht which contains the penalties for wounds and other bodily injuries."[1] Before discussing the separate divisions of the procedure, it will be best to sketch briefly an outline of the German suit,[2] and to explain with care the means of proof and the law of evidence.

The regular characteristic of the old German law was pre-eminently an iron rigorism of form, and a minute attention to external observances. The free judgment of the court was limited within such narrow bounds as were set by the forms and maxims of the old procedure. The independence of the individual in the sphere of self-help found its counter-poise in the severe constraint of the procedural forms.

The introduction of the procedure lay in the hands of the person seeking justice, whether in civil or criminal actions; and he summoned his opponent with prescribed and rigorous formalities. At the court, the plaintiff declared the subject of the suit in solemn words, directed, not to the court, but to the individual defendant; and on the defendant's answer depended the further procedure. The judgment which followed brought the assertion of the plaintiff or the denial of the defendant to the proof; and was found, not by the magistrate, but by the whole community in court assembled, who adhered with painful precision to the strict interpretation of the letter and externalities of the procedure. It was not a judgment according to their opinions or conscience; it was not declaratory, but constitutive; nor did it aim at an analysis of the contested question of law. The judgment determined how the question of proof should be decided, and settled the

ness, and because the Lombard law was scientifically studied at Pavia in the eleventh century.   [1] Anc. Laws and Inst., Pref. p. 8.
    [2] Heinrich Brunner, Die Entstehung der Schwurgerichte, pp. 43–59.

question of law by declaring what would happen even after
the completion of the proof.[1] The party could, if dissat-
isfied, challenge the judgment as not according to law ; and
then a penalty was, in most German codes, exacted from the
judges if he succeeded. The judgment not only settled how
the proof should be given, but also who should give it ; and,
as a rule, it was awarded to the defendant. But, when
no relevant objection could be made against his claim, the
plaintiff himself came to the proof. Then, on the performance of the proof, if no default was made, the procedure
ended.

The chief importance of the procedure centred in the
means of proof allowed by the German law. The proof did
not pass under the consideration of the judges, but by it was
settled, once for all, the conditions according to which the
judgment could be carried out. In the proof, the formalism
was most severe ; a natural consequence of the fact that by
it the community, perhaps for the first time, placed their wills
over the will of the individual. The three[2] means of proof
allowable were Oath, Ordeal, and Documents ; and the former
might be accompanied with (1) the oath of compurgators, or
(2) of witnesses. The first oath was *promissory*, in which
the compurgators swore as to their belief in the credibility of
their principal, and not as to the truth of their principal's
assertion. The number of compurgators varied "secundum
qualitatem ac quantitatem causae atque personae," and were
often chosen by the party himself from his kinsmen, who
were his usual oath-helpers. In the Norman period, this class
of proof gave way to the *legis vadiatio* (Wager of law) in
cases where documents could not be used.[3] The second oath
was *assertatory*. The witness-proof of the old law is not to
be compared with the modern legal conceptions of evidence.
Since personal knowledge did not in itself form the legal capacity of a witness, no one, however much he knew of the
transaction, could act as such. He must have been produced
by the party himself. A one-sided means of proof, the wit-

---

[1] H. Brunner, Schwur., pp. 45, 46.
[2] K. Maurer, Krit. Uebersch. V. p. 185.
[3] H. Brunner, Schwur., p. 398.

ness swore only to the assertion of his chief. This species of proof by oath drew its witnesses from two classes,—Transaction and Community witnesses. Those called Court witnesses were unknown to the early law,[1] and there seems to be no trace of them in Anglo-Saxon law. In the absence of records, judicial acts were established by the party through the normal forms of proof.[2] This was shown by:

WILL. I. 24: "In omni curia, praeterquam in praesentia regis, si cui imponitur, *quod in placito dixerit aliquid*, quod ipse negat se dixisse, nisi possit *per duos intelligibiles homines de (visu et) auditu* convincere, recuperabat ad loquelam suam."

Transaction witnesses were brought to corroborate business transactions of sale, gift, exchange, &c. These witnesses existed in Anglo-Saxon law, as in all the folk-laws.

EDG. IV. 4: "To every 'burg' let there be chosen thirty-three as witness;

5: "To small 'burgs,' and in every hundred, twelve, unless ye desire more.

6: "And let every man, with their witness, buy and sell every of the chattels that he may buy or sell; . . . and let every of them . . . give oath that he never . . . will declare any other thing in witness save that alone which he saw or heard: and of such sworn men let there be at every bargain two or three as witness." [3]

These laws simply set apart certain men who should be capable of bearing witness.

Community-witnesses were produced by the party, as were Transaction-witnesses, and they testified concerning circumstances, long-continued relations, and occurrences known to them as neighbors, or members of the community. The Community-witnesses were chiefly employed in actions regarding real property and status. From this class of proof arose the "inquisitio per testes" in the Norman period, and the jury of English law; but no trace of the *inquisitio* was to

[1] K. Maurer, Krit. Uebersch. V. p. 192. [2] H. Brunner, Schwur., p. 50.
[3] Æthelst, V. 1, § 5: "Et nominentur in manunga singulorum praepositorum tot homines, quot pernoscuntur esse credibiles, qui sint in testimonio singularum causarum. Et sint eorum juramenta credibilium hominum butan cyre, id est sine electione." Cf. H. & E. 16; Ine, 25; Alfr. 34; Edw. 1 (Pr.); Æthelst. II. 10, 12; Edm. III. 5; Æthelr. I. 3; Will. I. 45, III. 10. For their oath, *vide infra*, p. 195.

be found in Anglo-Saxon or in Frisian law, which throughout retained their old Germanic procedure.[1] In fact, one is
struck, in the study of Anglo-Saxon law, with the persist-
ency with which forms peculiar to the old law continued
throughout this period.

When the church introduced the use of documents, they
were employed as a means of proof of the same character as
the proof of witnesses : a document was only by its nature a
better witness, since it was imperishable. This could be
drawn up by a notary, or before the court.[2]

The proof of last resort, standing behind the former methods, was the ordeal, or judgment of God. In cases where,
for any reason, no decision could be reached by the other.
means of proof, God was himself appealed to in aid of the
innocent, that He would reveal the truth after the manner of
a miracle.

At a certain period after the judgment, the term was fixed,
and the party gave pledge for the giving of the proof.[3]
The old German procedure was especially distinguished
from that of to-day by the fact that the proof came *after*,
not *before*, the judgment. By adjudging the means of proof,
the judgment at the same time settled the legal question ;
and the subject of the judgment was, at the same time, the
subject of the oath ; and this was first limited by the word-
ing of the plaintiff's assertion. The subject of the proof
itself was not limited to facts, but extended over into the
domain of legal judgment.[4] The proof was regarded as a
satisfaction to the claimant, and therefore was not directed
to the court, but to the opponent; the principle of the business transaction was thus carried even into the procedure of
proof. The contents of the witness-oath furnished no new
material to the proof : each witness reiterated the points of
proof declared by the judgment ; he appealed to his knowledge of the thing, and invoked the Deity to the truth of his
statements. The power of the proof lay in the fact that
the statement was in the form of an oath.

---

[1] H. Brunner, Zeugen und Inquisitionsbeweis, p. 41.
[2] K. Maurer, Krit. Uebersch. V. p. 196.
[3] This was called "Arramatio testium." Cf. App. No. 11.
[4] E.g., they swore that a man ought to be a slave rather than free.

The Anglo-Saxon sources group themselves into these divisions: Action for Debt; action for Movables; action for Real Property; and Criminal Procedure. These shall be examined in the order named.

II.

The earliest procedural needs of the Germans seem to have been for Debt; and this procedure was of the most limited range, and stamped with the characteristics of the executive period. It recognized no examination of material right in the suit; and in cases to which it did not apply, scarcely any medium of justice was furnished except that which the warrior dealt out with the spear. And this early system, common to the German races, probably before the wandering, gave its limitations to subsequent development.

The German civil actions were founded on contracts.[1] A contract in German law was not binding through the mere agreement of the wills of the contracting parties; but, as in the old Roman law, only by the performance of a fixed formality, or a fulfilment by one party.[2] Hence, among the Germans, there were, according to Sohm, no consensual, but only real and formal, contracts. In the contract of sale, in which the seller was bound to the buyer only if he had received payment, the contract was not consensual, but real, and conveyed a title to ownership. But to free the buyer from the risk of making actual payment, while yet preserving the efficacy of the contract, German law introduced, instead of the payment, the earnest money (*handgeld*), the equivalent of the arrha[3] of the Lombard law, with the effect,

---

[1] Sohm, Das Recht der Eheschliessung, pp. 24–46, 78–87, has further enforced the views of Laband.

[2] Loening, on the other hand, holds that the "fides facta" was a simple, one-sided promise, based on the will of the party bound, and unrestrained by outward form, p. 7 ff. Cf. also Behrend, for an argument against Sohm, on the question of the "fides facta," p. 81 ff.

[3] The arrha was called "weinkauf," because it was usually spent for wine drunk by the witnesses of the sale; or "God's penny," because it was devoted to charity. Sohm, p. 30. The "arrae," in Roman law, however, were deposited with the seller as a proof that the purchase had been made, — e.g., a ring (D. XIX. 1. 11, 6).

not of strengthening the contract, as in Roman law, but of concluding it. The arrha was relatively worthless, and was not in fact payment, or part payment; but it was the means of judicially binding the agreement made by the parties, and a real right arose therefrom.

The formal contract of the Germans was not concluded, as in Roman law, by the use of writing, or a fixed form of words; but, on the continent, by the delivery of the straw (festuca). Instead of the straw, a glove,[1] an arrow, a stick, or any other object, could be used. This was the German " wette," wadium (wadia) of Lombard law, and the Anglo-Saxon " wed; "[2] being derived from the root *vidan* (obligare), it signified the means of legally binding the agreement of the parties.[3] The formal contract was used in a unilateral case, such as the Anglo-Saxon " borh," or " plegium," or the Frankish " fides facta," where the party promised to bring proof, or make payment; or in the security of bail (Bürgschaft). As the institution of private law, it was the basis of marriage and of all bargain and exchange, and was concluded in the presence of witnesses.

ÆTHELR. I. 3: " And let no man either buy or exchange unless he have borh and witness." [4]

By means of the clergy, religious pains and formalities might be added to the pledge, as in " god-borh " (Alfr. 33, Æthels. VI. 51). As an institution of public law it played a large part in Anglo-Saxon procedure: (1) pledge was demanded of every accused to insure his presence before the court (de judicio sisti);[5] and (2) to fulfil the judgment (judicatum solvi).

HLOTH. & EAD. 8: " If one man make plaint against another in a suit, and he go with him to the " methel," or " thing," let the man

---

[1] Cf. App. No. 85.

[2] Compare the language of Anh. VI. 5: "Let him confirm all that he has promised with a wed [mid wedde]."

[3] Sohm, Das Recht der Ehesch. p. 35.

[4] Cf. Ed. Conf. 88.

[5] This pledge was required of (1) a defendant in a case already pending, or (2) as a security against all charges which might be brought against him. But this latter, in its connection with the " frithborg," was merely a police regulation.

[defendant] *always give borh to the other,* and do him such right as the Kentish judges prescribe."[1]

Another use of the German formal contract found its employment in the security of the fidejussor as shown in:

INE 62: "When a man is charged with an offence, and he is compelled to give pledge, and he has not himself aught to give for pledge, *then goes another man and gives his pledge for him,* as he may be able to arrange.

In the Lombard law the debtor passed the "wadia" to the creditor, and the latter then gave it into the hands of the fidejussor.[2] This explains the principle of German law, that the fidejussor was bound primarily to the creditor, and the debtor but subsidiarily; since the obligation rested against him who held the arrha. If the debtor could not pay, the fidejussor stood in his place, paid the fine for non-observance of the demand (borh-bryce), and suffered execution. The two points of the formal promise essential to the procedure were, the establishment of a fixed term for payment, and the strictly unilateral character of the obligation entered into by the defendant.[3]

The Roman ideas of contract can no more be applied to German law than the Roman conceptions of actions *in rem* and *in personam.* The Germans made use of a contract *in genere,* and one for a fixed and individual object (*certa species*), to which corresponded the actions for property. To the contract for the performance of a thing settled *in genere,* corresponded the action for debt, arising from the obligatory nature of the obligation. It aimed not at a recovery of the property, but at indemnification; for the contract on which it was founded carried with it an obligatory but *not* a real effect. And, following the established principle of German law, the burden of proof rested on the defendant, while in the Roman system, it rested on the plaintiff. It was the individual, who, through the principle of self-help, was

---

[1] Cf. H. & E. 9, 10; Ine, 8; Henr. 61, § 17, 62, § 3.

[2] Sohm, Das Recht der Ehesch. p. 38.

[3] Sohm, La Procédure de la Lex Salica, p. 13, Paris, 1873, trans. by M. Thévenin.

placed in the foreground of the procedure, and it was he who proceeded to an extrajudicial seizure. At the end of the term fixed by the obligation of payment, the defendant was called on by the plaintiff to fulfil his promise ; if the defendant obeyed the demand, the procedure was at an end. Discussion before a court was unnecessary, unless brought about by the acts of the parties. Only in case the defendant refused to perform his obligation, was the matter introduced before the court ; and here the plaintiff rested his claim on a simple extrajudicial promise, and not on a " causa debendi," or assertion of right. The judge pronounced no judgment on the validity of the obligation, or whether it was a real ground of action. It was not a suit in the modern sense, but an application to the court to carry out a judgment made by the plaintiff. When the debtor refused payment after the demand, he was thereupon fined for " borh-bryce," which corresponded to the fine of the *Lex Salica* for disobedience to the formal *testare*. This is evident in the regulations of the marriage contract.

INE 31 : " If a man buy a wife, and the marriage do not take place, let him give the money, and make bot to his byrgea, *as his borgbrice may be.*" [1]

The summons to the court was conducted under solemn formalities. The postponement of a fixed term for a suit, which was manifestly conducted under the same formalities as the summons itself, is thus described in :

HENR. 59, § 2 : " Pridie ante solis occasum ad domum suam si residens est cum quo agitur, et per bonum testimonium vicinorum et aliquorum, quos secum habeat, qui placitum contramandat, ipsi respectetur [*i.e.* postpone] si domi est; uxori, dapifero vel praeposito et familiae ejus dicatur intelligibiliter, si idem abfuerit; et hoc iterum et tertio licet continue sive interrupte."

The time and manner bear an interesting resemblance to the same ceremony of the Salic Law, if not taken from it.

---

[1] Cf. also Alfr. 1, § 8 : "If, however, there be another man's borh, let him make bot for the borh-bryce."

The plaintiff summoned the defendant to appear usually at a term of seven days.[1]

The first mention of the procedure before the court is in:

HLOTH. & EAD. 10: " If one accuse another, after he [defendant] has given him borh, and then they have sought out the judge after three days, unless a longer time is satisfactory to the one who makes complaint; then let the man [defendant], if the case has been decided, do the other his right in seven days, in goods or by oath, whichever suits him more."

In his claim the plaintiff made no proof of his right, but opened the procedure by a fore-oath.

ANH. X. 10: "In the name of the living God, as I money demand, so have I lack of that which N. promised me, when I mine to him sold."

If the defendant did not appear,[2] or did not make answer, the plaintiff could proceed to execution.[3] This was shown by an injunction against its abuse in:

INE 9: " If any one take satisfaction before he demands justice, let him return and pay for what he has forcibly taken, and pay a fine of thirty shillings."

But there is more explicit evidence of extrajudicial seizure in:

CN. II. 19: " Let no one levy execution, either within or without the shire, before he has three times demanded justice in the hun-. dred. If, the third time,[4] he shall not obtain justice, let him go the fourth time to the shiregemot, and let the shire set him a fourth term. If he then fail of justice, *let him take leave*, either from hence or thence, *that he may seize his own.*"[5]

---

[1] Hen. 51, § 2: Et submoneatur comitatus VII dies antea." Cf. H. 7, § 4; 41, § 2; 46, § 1.

[2] Cf. Hen. 49, § 3.

[3] Vide Krit. Uebersch. VI. 270.

[4] Cf. Hen. 60, § 2; 52, § 1.

[5] Certainly the strongest grounds on which Sir Henry Maine has urged the alliance of early Irish law with that of other Aryan communities, and especially the Teutonic, are the comparisons in regard to distress (Early Hist. of Inst. Chaps. IX., X.). The Senchus Mor required that:

" The plaintiff or creditor, having first given the proper notice, proceeded, in the case of a defendant or debtor, not of chieftain grade, to distrain. If the

This law was repeated in William I. 44, and again declared by :

HENR. 51, § 3 : " Et nulli, sine judicio vel licentia, namiare liceat alium in suo vel alterius." [1]

When the defendant made answer, he need not show reason why he was not indebted. He did not oppose the facts on which the plaintiff rested his claim, since the plaintiff brought forward no such facts ; he only attacked the assertion that he was indebted. And as the court had no means of proving the correctness of the defendant's answer it accepted his oath as verification of his non-indebtedness. It was a fundamental principle of German law that the defendant, where he denied having received property, or given a promise, could establish his denial by oath.[2] As in the criminal action it was but natural justice to give the proof to the defendant, and there was no presumption that the defendant was indebted to the plaintiff. The defendant with his single oath swore alone, and freed himself from the charge, no oath-helpers being used ; since, although in the criminal action oath-helpers might have full faith that he would not

defendant or debtor were a person of chieftain grade, it was necessary, not only to give notice, but also to ' fast on him.' The fasting on him consisted in going to his residence, and waiting there for a certain time without food. If the plaintiff did not within a certain time receive satisfaction for his claim, or a pledge therefor, he forthwith, accompanied by a law-agent, witnesses, and others, seized his distress."

But this distinguished writer cannot say (p. 284) that the Irish procedure, like the English (meaning thereby early English), required "neither assistance nor permission from any court of justice." For, although the practice of private seizure was a part of the Teutonic principle of self-help, like feud, and must have been the primitive procedure, yet, after the executive period, and when courts began to regulate the activity of the individual, and even in the Lex Salica, distress required the permission of a court of justice. And this has been shown to be the case in Anglo-Saxon law. This works against the "greatest resemblance of all " in his comparisons.

[1] Stat. Rob. I. 7 : "Nullus de caetero capiat namos in alterius terra vel foedo pro debito suo sibi debito sine balivo domini regis vel balivo loci." Cf. Henr. 2, Cart. Libert. Lond. §§ 13, 14, where one was permitted to seize property in the city, or in the county where the debtor resided. Cf. also Ine, 49, as an example of the working of self-help.

[2] V. Bethmann-Hollweg, Der Civilprocess des gemeinen Rechts, p. 88.

commit a crime, in the suit for debt they could hardly be allowed to prove a relation existing between two persons, as that the defendant had *not* agreed to pay the settled sum.[1] His neighbors and friends could in but few cases have had certain knowledge as to whether the defendant had accepted such an obligation. But this oath might be made as the simple negation of the whole debt, or as an *exceptio*, *i.e.* claiming that he had paid it. The Anglo-Saxon oath was as follows : —

ANH. X. 11 : "In the name of the living God, I owe not to N. sceatt or shilling, or penny, or penny's worth ; but I have discharged to him all that I owed him, so far as our verbal contracts were at first."

It is here seen that no actual facts were brought forward ; and the proof having been given the defendant, he answered by his oath simply.

In the suit for indemnification, as in the case of a buyer, who found his property unsound after he had received it, the plaintiff declared as follows : —

ANH. X. 7 : "In the name of Almighty God, thou didst engage to me sound and clean that which thou soldest to me, and full security against after claim, on the witness of N. who then was with us two."

The witnesses employed were the Transaction-witnesses, who were present at every legal sale. The oath of the witnesses is given in :

ANH. X. 8 : "In the name of Almighty God, as I here for N. in true witness stand, unbidden and unbought, so I with my eyes saw and with my ears heard, that which I with him say."

The course of the procedure unrolled itself as before ; the judgment awarded the proof to the defendant, who gave the clearing oath if he could. As in the Lombard law, the defendant aimed by his single oath at the establishment of his *bona fides*,[2] and averred that at the time of the sale he had no knowledge of the unsoundness.

---

[1] V. Bar, Beweisurtheil des germanischen Processes, p. 93 ff. ; and, for the whole discussion, pp. 92–130.

[2] Zorn. Das Beweisverfahren nach langobardischem Rechte, p. 17.

ANH. X. 9: "In the name of Almighty God, I know not in the thing about which thou suest, foulness or fraud, or infirmity, or blemish, up to that day's-tide that I sold it to thee; but it was both sound and clean, without any kind of fraud."

Then the buyer had no further claim on the seller; but, if the latter could not take the above oath, he must receive back the property and make full compensation.[1] A striking illustration of this principle, as well as of the fact that marriage was a contract of sale, is found in the Kentish code of:

ÆTHELB. 77: "If a man buy a maiden with cattle, let the bargain stand, if it be without guile; but if there be guile, let him bring her home again, and let his property be restored to him."

In case of a disregard of justice, and if the defendant would give no " borh," he was fined thirty shillings, the usual fine for contempt of the hundred court, and was further required to do justice in seven days.[2] The legal essoins which excused the neglect of a summons were: *infirmitas, domini necessitas, exercitus, causa suorum hostium*, or *justicia regis*.[3] But contumacy rendered the defendant "*tiht-bysig;*" he was seized and his property confiscated.[4]

It is to be seen, then, in conclusion, that this procedure was founded on a unilateral obligation arising from a contract *in genere*, and it shows fully the part which the individual played in the sphere of self-help. On refusal of payment, the defendant was subject to a fine for *borh-bryce;* the summons was made by the plaintiff under solemn formalities, and the defendant must usually appear in seven days at the court. Without a substantiation of the suit, the plaintiff made a simple statement of his opponent's indebtedness; and from this the latter could clear himself by his single oath, and establish his *bona fides*. But, if the defendant could not take the clearing-oath, or failed to answer, the plaintiff received permission of court to proceed to private execution.

---

1 Ine, 56.   2 Ine, 8.
3 Henr. 59, § 1.
4 Alfr. 1; Æthelst. II. 20; Edg. III. 7; Æthelr. I. 4; Cn. II. 25, 33.

III.

German writers, before Laband, have made a distinction in the German law of movables between actions *in rem* and *in personam*, claiming that the action against the borrower was purely personal, and that the one against the third possessor was a real action ; and that, both in the procedure begun by the *Anefang*, as well as in the " simple suit," the real right was used as a defence against an obligatory claim for the surrender of the object. But they have committed the great mistake of trying to engraft on German law the judicial conceptions of the Romans, with whom this distinction was original, — a development which was never reached by the German law of the middle ages, and which, moreover, is opposed to the fundamental principles of German procedure. This fact has been most clearly and fully shown by a distinguished scholar, Dr. Paul Laband.[1]

A real action may be defined as one which exists only for the enforcement of a real right. In the German vindication procedure, begun by the *Anefang*, the plaintiff proved neither ownership nor a real nor *quasi*-real right to the thing which could form the subject of the action. Could it, then, be classed as a real action ?

But Hänel[2] and Bluntschli hold the untenable theory that the action for movables was a real action, and was based on the fact that the plaintiff " laid his hand on the object itself ; " that the action aimed only at the return of the thing, and that it could only be directed against the real owner of the thing. But this Roman conception stands opposed to the German action for chattels, which was based both on obligatory[3] and real claims, as will be shown hereafter. Moreover, it is not disputed that no suitor, however clearly he might prove his ownership, could require from any third possessor the return of property which had passed out of his own hands with his

---

[1] Die Vermögensrechtlichen Klagen, Berlin, 1869, p. 51 ff.

[2] Hänel, Beweissystem, pp. 137, 138 ; Bluntschli, Krit. Uebersch., VI. p. 197.

[3] Laband, p. 54 ; Sohm, Das Recht der Ehesch., p. 80. The Roman real action must not be confounded with the English real action, which was brought for the specific recovery of lands, tenements, or hereditaments.

consent; the rule "Hand wahre Hand" forbade. That the German action for movables was a "real action" cannot possibly be admitted.

The divisions of the Sachsenspiegel, which set the actions "umme gut, umme varende have" in opposition to the actions for debt, are evidently correct. The action for movables, then, included obligatory as well as real claims.[1] It is true that a real right could be the subject of the action, and that upon its establishment the procedure depended; but a real right, as well as any right of obligation, was good only as a title to retain the object.

Having pointed out the nature of the action for movables, it will be necessary to show clearly to whom the action was given, and discuss the rule "Hand wahre Hand," or "Where I have left my trust, there must I seek it."[2] This rule meant that only in case of *involuntary* loss of possession could any one claim the object from any holder, wherever he may find it. If he surrendered the object of his own will to another, as in case of loan or deposit, his judicial relations were confined to him who received the property; but, if the object was stolen from the borrower, he only, and not the owner, had the action against the thief. But it is not that the owner is deprived of an action founded on a material right. That the action is given to the borrower is not to cut off the owner's right of prosecution; but, since the action was, in its origin, so closely allied to delict, it was an enlargement of the old procedure, since it gave even to the borrower the only action which could be given in the narrow sphere of the executive procedure. But, in cases where a family inferior, who had physical authority over the object, alienated, the owner could claim it from any possessor. This was no exception to the rule "Hand wahre Hand," since there was no *willing* surrender by the owner.[3] By the later Saxon law,

---

[1] Sohm has added the weight of his high authority to this division in his last work, referred to above, p. 80.

[2] Cf. the "Biens meubles n'ont point de suite" of the French law, and "Mobilia non habent sequelam," and "Habe hat kein Geleit."

[3] If the wife alienated, the Sachsenspiegel allowed the husband to reclaim the property; but the possessor had an action for indemnification.

there was an exception to the rule, on principles of equity, when the property of the depositee had been confiscated for crime. But, in the case of inheritance, the exception was only apparent, and based on a wrong view of succession. If A intrusted property to B, and B died, A could claim the property from B's heir, C ; for the heir stood in the exact position of the devisor. The heir was not a third possessor, because succession was not alienation.[1] This principle is conclusively shown from the Sachsenspiegel, where, if C had conveyed the property to D, A had undoubtedly no action against D.[2] William (I. 6) enacted that an object found could not be claimed after a year and a day ; limiting the operation of the rule by a fixed term, in the interest of trade. But any such prescription was unknown to the Anglo-Saxons.

With this preliminary, the action for movables will be divided into two sections, —

1. The action for the return of an object (*certa species*), arising from an obligation to restore, when the object had passed out of the owner's hands with his consent.

2. The action, with the *Anefang*, for the recovery of an object from the possessor, accompanied with the charge of dishonesty, when the object was lost against the owner's will. This division will be treated in the following section (IV.).

1. In the action for the return of a fixed object, which has been loaned or deposited, Hänel's distinction between an obligatory and a real right is untenable. The plaintiff in his claim asserted neither ownership nor a real right, in opening the procedure, nor named the obligation arising from the contract. It was immaterial whether the object passed out of his possession as a *commodatum*, *depositum*, pledge, for inspection with purpose of sale, or for repair. As in the case of debt, a simple claim, without any statement of the legal obligation, set the procedure in motion.[3] The Anglo-Saxon

---

[1] Laband, p. 88 ; Lewis, Succ. des Erben, p. 98 ff.

[2] The "sessio triduana" in German law aimed to exclude all demands of the seller of real estate after that time ; and that this institution was unnecessary in receiving property by inheritance is a proof that inheritance was not alienation.   [3] Laband, p. 133 ff.

sources, while showing the existence of this procedure, are not full in regard to it. As to the proof, the decision rested on two fundamental principles, —

a. If the defendant was no longer in possession, he went to the proof by single oath, and swore, without compurgators or witnesses, that without his connivance the specified object had perished, or been stolen, or burned.[1]

ALFR. (Einl.) 28: "If any one intrust property to his friend, if he [the friend] steal it himself, let him pay for it twofold. If he know not who has stolen it, let him clear himself that he has therein committed no fraud. If, however, it were live cattle, and he say that the 'here' has taken it, or that it perished of itself, and he have witness, he need not to pay for it. But if he have no witness, and he [the owner] believe him not, then let him swear."

If the defendant were no longer in possession, and his *bona fides* had been established by oath, it was a relevant defence to the claim of the plaintiff for return. The same principle was shown in the case of carriers.

WILL. I. 37: "Si quis in periculo maris ad navem exonerandam, metu mortis, *alterius res* in mare projecerit, si suspectum eum habuerit, *juramento se absolvet*, quod nulla alia causa nisi metu mortis fecerit." [2]

b. If the defendant was in possession of the object, the plaintiff went to the proof. Homeyer asserts that this was due to an assumed lack of a real defence on the part of the defendant.[3] Von Bar holds that, when in possession, the defendant could answer by showing his own right to the thing, as by original acquisition, or inheritance, or that he held the object from a third person; but if the defendant could not assert a particular right, it was probable he had none, and therefore the plaintiff showed a right by contract, which proved that the defendant was not the owner.[4] But this does not explain why the defendant had the right of proof,

1 V. Bar, p. 98.
2 The Norman text of this section is a personal reply of the defendant.
3 Richtst. p. 492.
4 V. Bar, p. 106.

when the object was lost. Laband has shown[1] that the defendant had the oath in regard to an obligatory claim only if there were an act of the defendant in question, or an explanation of his will to be made, wherein his *bona fides* could be shown. In an assertion of the plaintiff in regard to an act performed by himself, as that he gave this very object to the defendant, the defendant could not disprove this by his oath of *bona fides;* but, by denial, he simply forced the plaintiff to the proof. The oath of the defendant was sworn without oath-helpers, or witnesses, since it was not of a character to admit them. Even when in possession, however, the defendant had the proof, if he could make a relevant defence such as a claim to the object by original acquisition, by inheritance, or that he held from another, his warrantor. This action was given also for the case where the heir claimed his inheritance from his guardian.

The contract for an individual, fixed object (*certa species*) had not merely a contractual or obligatory effect, but a real effect in acquiring a title; not giving merely a personal, but a real, right against the promisor. To this contract corresponded the action founded on both a real and obligatory right, gained without transfer of possession. That is, a contract of sale, where the seller had not yet delivered the article, conveyed a legal title; and the seller stood, then, exactly in the position of a depositee, subject to the same responsibilities and demands.[2] The proof was assigned according to the purport of the plaintiff's assertion. According to the Sachsenspiegel, if it was a question whether the buyer had already fulfilled the contract on his side, the buyer (plaintiff) had the right to prove by the men present at the giving of the arrha.[3] If the seller asserted that the property sold had perished, or had been lost, and so was not in his possession, he could take the oath to the fact, and, by proving his *bona fides*, escape payment of its worth.

[1] Laband, p. 139.
[2] Ibid. p. 151 ff.
[3] Ibid. p. 153 ; also cf. art. 1654 Code Civil : " Si l'acheteur ne paye pas le prix, le vendeur peut demander la résolution de la vente."

This procedure, then, founded on a contract *in specie* for the return of a specified object, was used also in a contract of sale already fulfilled by one party, or in a suit for inheritance retained by the guardian. The simple claim of the plaintiff opened the procedure, and the defendant must establish his *bona fides* by the clearing oath, if the object was not then in his possession. If, however, he possessed the object, and could not claim in his defence original acquisition, inheritance[1] (if at the same time he could show his devisor's ownership), or vouch in a third person from whom he held the object, the plaintiff received the proof, and established the truth of his assertion.

IV.

The property of the early Germans being chiefly in cattle, a judicial need arose for the claim against the (third) possessor, when their property had strayed away, or was stolen. Rooted in the old condition of the law, the action for movables necessarily retained the limitations of the old executive system. Originally, it is probable that the pursuit of stolen movables was only permitted by the delict procedure, with which restitution of the thing was joined. Therefore, this procedure, in its origin, was unfavorable to the owner, but favorable to the commodatar, from whom the object had been taken. This theory is clearly explained by Lombard law.[2] When a thief stole an object from the house of the commodatar, the latter must account to the owner; if the thief was found, the action against him belonged to the commodatar, on the ground that, if the thief were accountable to the owner, the commodatar would have a claim against him for house-breaking, " et non possumus in una causa duas calumnias imputare." Arising between the existing procedure of debt and the delict procedure, it partook of a double character. It was an advance on the old procedure in that it was not wholly executive in character, but only partially so. The plaintiff was not required to bring forward his right for

---

[1] Laband, p. 141.
[2] Ed. Luit. 131. *Vide* Heusler, Gewere, p. 492.

examination; but the defendant must show how he acquired the object. And, if he could not, the course of the plaintiff, in primitive times, was simply executive again. The action for movables was an extension of the old procedure to meet cases of involuntary loss, and a new exterior form through which a suit might be introduced for goods in case of a denial of possession by the defendant.[1] As a means of satisfying private right to the property, it was a means of gaining possession; while, at the same time, the plaintiff rested his claim on the commission of a theft. The combination of the judicial procedure with the old executive forms, distinguished this from purely executive actions, and was doubtless the cause of its persistent vitality. The character of the defendant's defence brings it closer to the procedure of proof, as we know it to-day. As yet, however, no judgment was rendered on the strength of proof offered to the decision of a court. The first act of the procedure was extrajudicial; and when the plaintiff seized the thing, he said: " The object is mine: it has been stolen from me." The defendant replied: " I have bought the object." This claim and counterclaim was followed by a promise of the possessor to furnish proof. The procedure introduced proof of such a nature that it raised questions of material right and ownership, but not as the subject of the judgment. The counterclaim of the defendant was a negation based on facts which would invalidate the claim of the plaintiff.

Of an executive nature, and possessed by the commodatar, the action was not based on the establishment of a material right by the plaintiff. To give the owner an action on the ground of ownership was not allowed. Therefore the owner, who had himself voluntarily parted with the possession of his property could not vindicate, simply because the narrow, executive character of the procedure did not base vindication on the examination of a material right. Although the German conception of possession involved the legal power over the thing, it is not to be supposed that when the object passed out of the owner's hands voluntarily, he thereby gave

---

[1] Heusler, Gewere, p. 488 ff.

up his ownership; but the old form of the law gave no
action in the Roman or modern sense. In movables, —
sheep, horses, cattle, clothing, and slaves, — no legal protection of possession, as preparatory to an action for ownership, existed. Detention and seisin existed together over
movables; and detention needed no other legal means of
protection than was furnished by gaining the object. So the
action was given to the person most closely affected, not that
it was a limitation of the action for property, but on the ground
that in general no action for property was given. And it
was natural that the action should be given, not to the
owner, living on a distant estate perhaps, but to the one
from whose possession it was taken. And, in case of sale,
which, after fulfilment on the part of the buyer, presented
the same conditions as deposit, if A had sold, but not
delivered, a thing to B, and A then sold and delivered it to
C, B had no action against C for the return of the object:
his action was against A for indemnification, according to the
procedure of debt.

In this division of the procedure, there existed a settled
judicial rule, governing the action for lost movables. In
stolen goods no possessor could acquire an effectual right
which could work against the claim of the owner. This
rule decided on the relevancy of the defendant's exceptions,
and the distribution of proof. The foundation of the suit
was the unwilling loss of the plaintiff; and it was immaterial
what right the plaintiff had to possession, whether as owner,
mortgagee, depositor, commodatar, or finder who was looking
for an owner. An earlier possession was no basis of the
suit.

The defendant could raise no plea of honest possession, if
that possession did not exclude the possibility of a loss to
the plaintiff against his will. The defence of purchase, gift,
or finding in his inheritance was irrelevant if the thing had
been lost to the plaintiff against his will. The principle
drawn from German law by some writers, that the relatively
better title to possession gave an advantage, was fully denied
by the action for lost movables.

Then after the claim and counterclaim came the assignment of proof. Dr. Laband has here given the best solution of a difficult subject. The usual theory has been that the defendant came to the proof with two witnesses by virtue of his position as defendant. But Laband shows that an assertion of possession by the defendant was irrelevant, and he could not on that ground retain the right to prove. So, from a lack of a relevant defence on the part of the defendant, the plaintiff went to the proof. But if the defendant raised a relevant objection, which would destroy the possibility of unwilling loss of the plaintiff, he went to the proof. These general principles will now be shown in the course of the procedure.

The vindicatory procedure, from its original twofold character, aimed at the recovery of the property, and the imposition of a fine for theft. And the presumption was that he who possessed the stolen property was the thief, unless he could prove otherwise. So rigorous was the principle that the finder of cattle, or the one into whose possession they had strayed, must give public notice of the fact, even to a foe.[1] But with this presumption of guilt was connected the corresponding right of the accused to the clearing oath, and the proof of his innocence, although he must give up the property.

The first steps of the procedure belonged to the individual, not to the tribunal. When the owner had lost his property, the discovery of the thing and the detection of the thief belonged to him; and for this purpose he called on his neighbors to aid him in following the trail (*vestigium minare*).

ÆTHELST. VI. 4: "That every one who hears the call (bannum) should be ready to aid another in pursuing the track, and in riding with him, as long as he knows the track; and, after the track has failed, always let one man be found where there are many people, as well as from a tithing where there are less people, for the riding or going, — unless there is need of more, — wherever it is necessary, and where all choose."[2]

[1] Alfr. Einl. 42; cf. Edg. I. 4, IV. 8–11; Æthelr. III. 5; Will. I. 6.
[2] Cf. Æthelst. VI. 5.

Every possible assistance was to be given to the search; and where the track was doubtful, there the accusation of theft rested.

EDW. II. 4: "Also I wish that every one have men ready on his land to lead those who wish to search for their property."

EDM. III. 6: "And it has been decreed, concerning the pursuit and search of stolen cattle, that the pursuit be carried to the vill (villa), and that there be no foristeallum, or any prevention of the way or of the search. And, if the track cannot be traced out of the land, let the accusation be made wherever there is suspicion and doubt." [1]

In the special laws for the city of London, the loser gave the pursuit into the hands of the city, if he could not find the stolen property himself within three days.[2]   The claimant having by these measures found the property, without the aid of the court, the first step of the procedure by which he seized the property was extrajudicial.

The *Anefang* of the continent was found in Anglo-Saxon law, both in the use of words [3] and in its usual procedural meaning.   The claimant formally laid his hand upon the object, and declared it was his own (Æthelst. II. 9).   Its character was essentially executive, and in its nature was a speedy means of satisfaction, having for its especial object the forcing of the accused to surrender the goods; and, in the barbarian codes, a fine was imposed for the simple refusal to

---

[1] Anh. I. 1 (Dun-Sct.): "If one follow the track of stolen cattle from one boundary into another, let him give up the tracking to the men of the land, or let him, through proof, show that he follows lawfully."   If the owner claim that the track is pursued wrongly, the pursuer makes oath, with five community-witnesses, that the cattle went up there.

[2] Æthelst. VI. 8, § 7: "Also we command our hiremen that every one know when he has his cattle, and when he does not have them, with the witness of his neighbors, and show us the track, if he cannot find them within *three days;* because we believe many men are careless how their cattle run, because they are over-trustful in our peace."   Cf. also 8, § 8.

[3] The Anglo-Saxon equivalents are: *aetfōn, befōn, aet-befōn, aetfangan, gefon, anefáhen,* and *widerfáhen.*   The Latin expressions are: *deprehendere, percipere, capere, intercipere,* but generally *interciare.*   " Manum mittat ad propria " is used in Æthelst. II. 9, and shows that it was the same as in other German law; but William I. 10, § 2, says it was customary only in Danish law.

surrender the object, apart from the fine for theft.[1] The claim of the plaintiff to the property, made at the place where the goods were attached, contained in itself an executive power of coercion. The reply that he had bought or exchanged the object had no value, for no title could be acquired in stolen property. The accused must surrender the goods, or appear before the court with the vindicator. If he surrendered the goods and confessed the theft, he must pay the fine to the claimant. Will. I. 45: "Quod si aliquis rem postmodum calumpniatus fuerit, et nec testes habuerit, nec warrantum, et rem reddat, et forisfacturam, cui de jure competit." If he claimed his innocence, the plaintiff made a fore-oath of his honest intention, to prevent evil-minded men, as the following passage states, from making a charge of theft against another in order to put his property under pledge.

Edw. I. 1, § 5: "Also we have decreed, if an evil man should wish to put the property of another under pledge by false accusation, let him confirm with an oath that he does it not out of fraud, but with full right, without deceit or craft; and then let him (defendant) do as he can, in case one (plaintiff) lays claim to the thing, be it that he (defendant) either proves his ownership, or vouches to warranty."

This oath was to be made with one of five men, who accompanied the claimant.

Æthelst. V. 2: "Et si investigetur pecus in alicujus terram, educat terrae dominus vestigium illud extra terram suam, si possit; si non possit, stet *ipsum vestigium pro superjuramento*, si aliquis compelletur ibi." [2]

Æthelst. II. 9: "Si homo pecus aliquod intertiet, nominentur ei v vicinorum suorum, et de illis quinque perquirat *unum, qui cum eo juret*, quod in recto publico *manum mittat ad propria*." [3]

---

[1] Lex Salica, 30 sol; Lex Baiuv., 12 sol; Lex Alam. 40 sol.

[2] It is exceedingly interesting to compare the provisions of the Frankish code on this point. Lex Rib. 33, 1: "Si quis rem cognoverit, mittat manum super eam. Et si ille super quem intertiatur, tertiam manum quaerat, tunc in praesente ambo conjurare debent cum dextera armata, et cum sinistra ipsam rem teneant. Unus juret quod in propriam rem manum mittat et alius juret quod ad eam manum trahat, qui ei ipsam rem dedit."

[3] In the laws regarding the Dun-Setas, Anh. I. 8, if A attached B's cattle, A

From these passages we have no difficulty in recognizing the oath itself.

ANH. X. 4: "By the Lord, I accuse not N. either for hatred or for envy, or for unlawful lust of gain ; nor know I any thing soother : but, as my informant to me said, and I myself in sooth believe, that he was the thief of my property."

Consistent with the whole spirit of German usage in regard to the oath, it established the *bona fides* of the claimant, and was followed by the counter-oath of the defendant, who thereby asserted his innocence, and showed his intention to bring his proof to the court, as follows : —

ANH. X. 5 : " By the Lord, I am guiltless, both in deed and counsel, of the charge of which N. accuses me."

Then the defendant must give proper pledge for the further course of the procedure : —

ÆTHELR. II. 8 (Pr.) : "Si quis deprehendat quod amisit, advocet inde ille, cum quo deprehenditur, unde venerit ei, *et mittat in manum et dat plegium*, quod adducet advocatum suum." [1]

The *agramire* of the Frankish codes has been shown by Sohm to be the equivalent of the Latin expression, *fidem facere ;* and so corresponds to the Anglo-Saxon giving of " borh," or pledge. The security given was the *borh* " de judicio sisti," mentioned above, to cause the matter to be brought to the court, "ut placitum illud finem habeat," and that the defendant might produce his defence. By putting forward a claim to the property, and giving *borh* to present his proof, the defendant prevented the plaintiff from realizing immediately. If he did not follow this course, the plaintiff gained the property, and the fine for theft (Cn. II. 24, § 1). This also acted as a means of fixing the term at which he

must make oath with five others "quod ita sibi attrahat, sicut ei furatum fuit." A law of William changed this number to seven men. Will. I. 14 : "Et appellator per VII legales homines ex nomine jurabit, quod nec ex odio nec alia aliqua causa hoc ei imponit, nisi tamen ut jus suum adipiscatur."

[1] Anh. I. 8 : "Si pecus intertietur et ultra flumen advocetur, tunc *ponatur in borh vel underwed mittatur, ut placitum illud finem habeat.*" Cf. also Will. I. 8, as showing the universal use of this part of the procedure.

must appear, being usually seven days,[1] and, when a charge of fraud could be made, not less than six months.

The latitude given to the accuser of charging a man with theft, and the presumption that the charge was true, naturally led to abuses. To counteract this evil, if the accused could show that the claim against him was fraudulent, he was relieved from any obligation to prove his property: he thus presented an exception, which rebutted the plaintiff's claim of an unwilling loss, and stopped the procedure.

CN. II. 24, § 3: "And it does not seem to us right that any one should be compelled to prove property when there is testimony of, and it can be proved, that there is fraud. And let no one be required to prove that property before six months after it was [claimed to be] stolen."[2]

The accused, therefore, was not required to prove property if he could bring proof of fraud. The term of six months is well explained by:

HEN. 5, § 25: "Quidam *ad repellenda imperitorum machinamenta*, et suas rationes praeparandas, et testes confirmandas, et consilia quaerenda, annum et sex menses concedi mandaverunt; quidam annum, in quo plurimi concordant, *minus vero quam sex menses non reperi.*"

Having now carried the procedure to a point where the term was fixed, and the subsequent steps took place before the court, it will be necessary to discuss a very wide distinction as to the course of the procedure; resting on the fact whether the stolen goods were found by the claimant *within* three days, or *after* that period. In the first case, according to the procedure of the *Lex. Salica* as shown by Sohm, "A

---

[1] Æthelr. II. 8, § 3: "Si advocet ultra unam sciram, *habeat terminum,* — i.e., *ebdomadam.*"

[2] Cn. II. 24, § 3: "Et nobis non videtur rectum, ut aliquis *propiare cogatur, ubi testimonium est et cognosci potest, quod ibi hrede sit.* Et nemo *illud* propiare debeat ante sex menses postquam furatum est." Cf. Will. I. 46: "Absonum videtur et juri contrarium, ut probatio fiat super testes, qui rem calumpniatam cognoscunt, nec admittatur probatio ante terminum statutum, scilicet VI mensem, ex quo furatum fuit quod calumpniatur." Also Hen. 64, § 6 (end): "Et nobis non videtur rectum secundum legem, ut aliquis, si propriare velit, compellatur, ubi cognosci potest, quod et testis intersit, saltem ante VI menses postquam furabitur."

14

(plaintiff) conducts the procedure; *after* the third night, it is B (defendant); while the *agramire* is made by A *alone*, or by B *alone*. One of the two is admitted to act *in judicio*, to the exclusion of the other; while, by the *agramire* of B, the vindicator has lost his position of attack, likewise, by the *agramire* of A, the possessor loses his position of defence." That is, in the first case, the plaintiff went to the proof; in the second, the defendant. While the explanation of this position is necessary, its solution will give a clearer comprehension of the procedure.

This distinction in the procedure was peculiar to the Frankish law, and no similar provision was known to the Anglo-Saxons. But the term of three days was familiar to the old codes in many ways.[1] In this case, the term of three days was set as a period within which the thief was regarded as "handhabbende," or "caught in the act."[2] But the thief's life was not forfeit, as in the case of one caught in the act. Sohm's argument is based on:

LEX SAL. 37: "Ille qui per vestigium sequitur res suas per tercia manu debet agramire . . . Si vero jam tribus noctibus exactis qui res suas quaerit eas invenerit, ille apud quem inveniuntur *si eas emisse aut cambiasse dixerit: ipse liceat agramire.*"

Agramire is the equivalent of *fidem facere;* in the first passage "*per* tercia manu" is, as he shows, equivalent to "*de* tercia manu," *de* meaning "about" or "concerning," and "tercia manu" the object of the *agramire*. And Siegel[3] has shown that the expression "tercia manu" undoubtedly means the procedure of vindication, which conducts to the "third hand." Then, by Sohm's showing, the passage should read: "The plaintiff ought to give pledge to proceed according to the vindication procedure." And this is unquestionably the meaning.

---

[1] The Lex Allem. gives the buyer of an animal three days for avoidance of a sale on account of a defect in the thing sold. Cf. also the *sessio triduana* in regard to land. Also Alfr. 2: three days of protection in the sanctuary for criminals. Cf. Cn. II. 28.

[2] Heusler, Gewere, p. 490.

[3] Geschichte des deutschen Gerichtsverfahrens. p. 87, ff.

To this case it is possible now to apply the principles already laid down as the governing rules of the procedure. The foundation of the suit was the unwilling loss of the plaintiff, and no exception made by the defendant was relevant which did not refute this claim.   That a thief caught in the act could not maintain any such exception, it is unnecessary to state.   And only when the defendant, as shown by Laband, could bring forward a relevant exception was he admitted to the proof.   Therefore, in a lack of such a position on the part of the defendant, the plaintiff went to the proof.   So that the case of *agramire* by the plaintiff meant simply that he went to the proof as was understood in the vindication procedure.   When the thief was caught, the owner[1] received the goods, of course.   But it is natural and reasonable to expect that he who came forward and claimed to be the owner should, to prevent fraud, show his *bona fides* by the oath.   It was not to be allowed that any man claiming to be owner should be given the goods, unless he had indicated his ownership by oath.   Such was required in:

INE, 17 : "Qui furtivam carnem invenerit occultatam, *si audeat,* licet ei inveritare jurejurando quod sua sit."

An irresponsible assertion was not allowed even in the case of cattle which had strayed away and had been claimed by the owner; for the claimant must give pledge to the finder to secure him from loss in case any one else should claim the cattle within a year and a day.[2]   Laband says that suits for debt, movables, and immovables in German law rested on a rational foundation, and that the distribution of the one-sided right of proof was always connected with the substantiation of the claim or the objection.   In regard to this peculiarity of the Lex Salica, Bethmann-Hollweg[3] holds that the plaintiff promised to make oath with three witnesses that the lost property was in his possession three days before the *Anefang*.   But to make "per tercia manu agramire"

---

[1] Will. I. 27.   [2] Will. I. 6.
[3] Civilproc. IV. p. 432. *Vide* also North American Review. Apr. 1874, pp. 420, 421.

equivalent to "agramire ut tercia manu juret se rem furto perdidisse" is, as Heusler suggests, hardly to be allowed. It is to be concluded, then, that this case was but one manifestation peculiar to the Lex Salica, of the usual laws governing this procedure. Next must be treated the course of the procedure before the court.

The Sachsenspiegel required that the plaintiff's claim should include both the fact of his unwilling loss of possession, and that the object belonged to him. It has been strongly claimed that the basis of the action was the ownership of the plaintiff. That the claimant must include his right to possession is true; but that this must be ownership could not be true, since the right to bring the action was given to the commodatar, or even to a finder from whom, while waiting for the owner to claim his property, the object had been stolen. Of the two requirements, it was the unwilling loss of possession which was the essential and only basis of the action. Any assertion of the defendant was relevant which excluded the possibility of the object having been lost against the will of the plaintiff. If the theory were correct that the right of property was the sole foundation of the suit, as alleged by Bruns,[1] the defendant could dismiss the action by showing that the plaintiff was not the owner, or that a third person was the owner. But the sources never allowed this; nor was the plaintiff's right of possession ever a subject of contradiction. The emphasis in the old law on the necessity of showing the property to be "his" did not mean, therefore, a right of ownership; but required him to show his right of possession, chiefly to identify that chattel as the one which he had unwillingly lost.[2] The Sachsenspiegel required that the plaintiff must go to the proof, in case the defendant raised no counter-objection; i.e., when he could not oppose the unwilling loss of the plaintiff, and only said he found or bought the thing. For in the refusal of the defendant to give up the object, even if he offered no relevant exception,

---

[1] Recht des Besitzes, p. 315. Also cf. Sohm, Proc. de Lex Sal. p. 36, note 3.
[2] Lex Sal. XXXVII. 47; Lex Rib. XXXIII. 1, XLVII. 1, LVIII. 8, LXXIX. 2; Lex Burg, LXXXIII. 1; and also, later, Brünner Schöffenb. c. 104.

was contained an opposition to the claim of the plaintiff of a
loss against his will. And only, as an exception to the rule,
could the property be awarded to the plaintiff without de-
manding from him the proof. This has been shown true of
the finder of stolen flesh in a previous argument. According
to the Sachsenspiegel, the plaintiff must go to the proof with
two witnesses who knew the thing to have been in his possession, who knew of his unwilling loss, and who could
identify the object. These witnesses could become oath-
helpers and swear to the plaintiff's credibility.

To the double claim of the plaintiff, the defendant must,
to make a full defence, oppose both the return of the object,
and the charge of illegal possession, to which last a fine was
attached. The procedure, then, varied accordingly as:

A. The defendant proved an original title; *e.g.*, the object
was born his.

B. The defendant cleared himself from the fine for theft, but
gave up the property.

C. The defendant vouched to warranty.

(A.) The defendant entered an exception which worked
against the claim of the plaintiff for return of the goods, as
well as the assertion of unwilling loss. If he could assert
facts which, if proved, would rebut the plaintiff's claim, he
went to the proof; that is, by proving that the cattle were
his by birth, or that the object was his by manufacture, he
maintained a defence which opposed the possibility that it
was taken from the plaintiff against his will.[1]

EDW. I. 1, 5: "And then let him (defendant) do as he can, in case
one lays claim to the thing, be it that he either *prove his ownership* or
vouch to warranty."

WILL. I. 21: "And if he (defendant) can *prove that it is of his
own raising by three of his neighbors, so has he cleared himself.*"

ÆTHELST. II. 9: "Et qui hoc propriare sibi voluerit, nominentur

---

[1] The Sachsensp. provides that the proof should be so framed that, if one had
alienated an animal born his, and it had strayed back to him, he could not make
a relevant defence. Nor was manufacture a relevant defence if the material
(*e.g.*, wool) out of which it was made was stolen.

ei xi homines, et ex illis adquirat duos, et *jurent, quod illud pecus N. intertiatum in peculio suo natum sit,* sine rimaþ, et stet thes cyreaþ, — i.e., hoc jusjurandum electum, super xx den."

The oath to be sworn by the defendant is as follows: —

Anh. X. 3: "By the Lord, I was not at rede nor at deed, counsellor nor doer, where were unlawfully led away N——'s cattle. But as I cattle have, so did it come of my own property, and so it by folkright my own possession is, and my rearing."

The words of the oath show most conclusively that the defence aims chiefly to disprove the possibility of the theft and unwilling loss, and establishes this by the fact of original ownership. The oath must be made with two witnesses, which is the number prescribed by Æthelstan, and confirmed by the Sachsenspiegel. The case was not that of a plain clearing oath where the accused only freed himself from the charge of theft, as when the accused was only the finder. That was a matter of simple negation; but when the defendant advanced a claim of ownership, co-swearers were also necessary.[1] At least in Anglo-Saxon law, the simple oath[2] of the defendant alone was not sufficient in proving his ownership in the property. The general belief that the defendant, as such, went to the proof, is shown to be wrong; he could not prove unless he offered a relevant objection. But yet the defendant, as such, had a procedural advantage, in that to him was given the *power of rebutting* the plaintiff by a relevant defence.

But in a case where two men were equally positive of their ownership, and each could furnish witnesses, and each party claimed that the object was stolen, who would be awarded the *rôle* of the defendant? Who would be given the oath

---

[1] Edw. I. 1, §§ 3, 4 : "Also we have likewise decreed, concerning the claim for ownership, that he (defendant) should bring therefor credible witnesses of it, or find an unchosen oath, if he can, to which the plaintiff is bound [to acquiesce] : if he cannot, then let there be named to him vi men of his neighborhood where he is resident, and let him select, from these vi, one for an animal or a thing, according to its worth ; and then let there be an increase according to the value of the goods, if more men should be present."

[2] Anh. I. 8 (Dun-Set) : "In case one over the boundary proves property, he must do it by the ordeal."

for proving property, and gain the thing, since the oath was uncontestable? In such a case the court decided that he who seemed to have the better testimony was allowed the advantage of the proof: .

HENR. 64, § 6: "If certain men desire to prove property in a thing in common, and there are witnesses on both sides, and it is claimed that it is stolen, he who shall have the better testimony shall be nearer the proof; and let him alone prove with the broken oath that it is his own, and let his witnesses confirm it with a plain oath."

But if it were impossible to decide as to which party had the better testimony, the law, as usually in German codes, gave a presumption in favor of the possessor:

§ 6: "If this cannot be done, the possessor shall always be nearer [the proof] than the claimant; and let him have [the oath], or let him, if he can, make defence by warranty,[1] which goes no farther than the fourth vouching."[2]

And this was the common rule of procedure in real property. Not that possession was a relevant defence in itself, but it gave ·the first power of bringing forward such a defence when the claims were equally balanced. This is confirmed in speaking of the right of a warrantor to prove property: —

ÆTHELR. II. 9, § 4: "Etiam inter advocandum, si quis hoc incipiat, nec ultra advocet, si propriare sibi velit, non potest hoc ei jure denegatur, si credibile testimonium locum ei accedendi, *quia propriatio propinquior semper est possidenti quam repetenti.*"

The defendant by this procedure proved his ownership to the property, and thereby rebutted the plaintiff's claim of unwilling loss of possession.[8]

b. If the defendant could not oppose to the double claim of the plaintiff facts which worked *wholly* against that claim, he could adduce facts which would rebut only the charge of theft; and so. not opposing the claim for the return· of the

---

[1] Thorpe says (p. 623): "*Werminga* is supposed by Somner (note) to be a mistake for *cenninga.* The whole passage is obscure and unintelligible"! Cf. Edg. I. 4.

[2] The remainder of the law is a repetition of Cn. II. 24. Cf. Henr. 5, § 25.

[8] I have used the term "relevant" to include such defences as would be denominated in the Common Law, a *traverse* or *exceptio*, as the case might be.

goods, he dismissed the action by their surrender. It was for the purpose of establishing such a defence, that the Anglo-Saxon laws so bristle with injunctions requiring the presence of witnesses at every bargain, sale, or exchange; in order that the buyer might repel the charge of theft in receiving goods which once may have been stolen, and in which no title could be acquired. The chief object of such a defence was to vouch in the warrantor; but this will be reserved for a separate division. If the defendant could not show from whom he purchased the object, but yet was innocent, he could still establish his *bona fides* by taking the clearing oath, as given in :

ANH. X. 3 : "By the Lord, I was not, at rede nor at deed, counsellor nor doer where were unlawfully led away N.'s cattle. But as I cattle have, so did I lawfully obtain it; and as I cattle have, so did he sell it to me who had it to sell."

This oath was sworn with oath-helpers, according to the value of the fine.

INE, 25, § 1 : "Si quid furtivum intercietur super mercatorem, et hoc coram bonis testibus non emerit, *juret secundum witam, quod nec furti conscius vel coadjutor fuerit in eo*, vel emendet XXXVI. sol. witae, — *i.e.*, forisfacturae vel emendationis."

The " secundum witam juret " is explained to mean an oath of sixty hides, or sixty sol., the usual *wita* for theft.

INE, 53 : "Et *juret per LX hidas*, quod ea mortua manus vendidit ei; et per hoc jusjurandum *wita remeneat*, et reddatur interciatus domino suo." [1]

A " twelve-hynde " man was, however, reckoned the equal of six ceorls, and could swear for LX hides.

INE, 46 : "Quando aliquis inculpatur, quod furtum fecerit vel furtivum aliquid firmaverit, tunc *debet per LX hidas*, — i.e., *per VI homines abnegare*, si juramento dignus sit." [2]

This explains the earliest mention of the vindication pro-

---

[1] Cf. Ine, 7 : "Si quis furetur sic ut uxor ejus nesciat hoc et pueri sui, reddat witae LX sol."

[2] Cf. Ine, 19.

cedure (H. & E. 7 and 16), which allowed this defence of clearing from the charge of theft, and required the oath of his witnesses, or the wic-reeve.

HLOTH. & EAD. 16: "If any Kentish-man buy a chattel in Lunden-wic, let him then have two or three true men to witness, or the king's wic-reeve. . . . If he cannot [vouch to warranty], let him prove at the altar, with one of his witnesses or with the king's wic-reeve, that he bought the chattel openly in the wic, with his own property; and then let him [plaintiff] be paid its worth."[1]

The reeve, as a "king's geneat," could swear for sixty hides, or the whole of the fine.

In the later laws[2] the accused must swear the "plain oath."

WILL. I. 21, § 1: "And, if he have neither a warrantor nor a heimelborh, and he has witnesses that he bought it in the king's market, and that he knows not his warrantor nor his pledge, neither living nor dead, — so let him swear to it with his witnesses, or with a plain oath (jur. planum)."

This "juramentum planum" evidently corresponds to the simple oath of the earlier laws, as the following passages show : —

CN. II. 22: "Et *sit omnis credibilis* . . . vel juramentum vel ordalium in hundreto, *simplici lada*[3] dignus."

---

[1] Cf. Ine, 57.

[2] But, in the laws of William and Henry, a nominal change in the nomenclature was introduced in regard to oaths. The terms "juramentum frangens,""juramentum fractum vel observatum," and the "juramentum planum" were used. The want of the wager of battle in the Anglo-Saxon system of proof caused the oath to be especially extended in regard to severity; and hence the "juramentum frangens," which was awarded only for the worst crimes. The same reason probably introduced the "juramentum fractum," sworn "in verborum observantiis," which Schmid says is opposed to the "juramentum planum," but that it cannot be said what difference existed between them. The "juramentum planum" seems to correspond to the "simplex juramentum." Why does the "juramentum fractum" not correspond to the "triplex juramentum"? *Vide* H. Brunner, Schwur., p. 308 ; Schmid. p. 617.

[3] Schmid. p. 283, Cod. Colb.: " Qui autem conquirere debet simplicem purgationem, simplici sacramento hoc faciat, hoc est ; accipiat duos et ipse (sit) tertius, et sic jurando adquirat. Triplex vero juramen tum sic conquiratur: accipiat quinque et ipse (sit) sextus, et sic jurando adquirat triplex judicium, aut triplex juramentum."

WILL. I. 14: "If any one accuses another of theft, and he is a free man, and *has witnesses of his legality* (si *bonae famae* hucusque fuerit), then let him purge himself with a *plain oath* (*jur. planum*)."

In this clearing oath the witnesses swore as to the statement of the accused in regard to what they "have with their eyes seen, or with their ears heard;" but they ceased to be witnesses, if they became compurgators, and swore only to their belief in the defendant's assertion.

The defendant, although he had now cleared himself of the charge of theft involved in the accusation, had offered no relevant objection to the unwilling loss of the plaintiff. Therefore the plaintiff must go to the proof, and continue the procedure. The defendant desired only to clear himself of the presumption that he was the thief, rising from the fact that the property was found in his possession.

In conclusion, he who had in his possession by sale, exchange, inheritance, &c., an object which had been previously stolen, could not set up such a title against the claiming owner. If he could not present at the court his warrantor, who had sold him the object, he could still clear himself by an oath of his *bona fides*. In the early law the oath was sworn according to the *wita* of sixty sol.; but there can hardly have been any persistent uniformity in this regard, since the *wita* must often have varied according to the value of the stolen goods. In the later law, the oath was defined as a "juramentum simplex," or "planum." After the defendant established his *bona fides*, the plaintiff went to the proof, and the property was surrendered by the defendant.

c. By vouching to warranty, the defendant did not aim at rebutting the claim of unwilling loss suffered by the plaintiff; but by introducing his auctor, he was freed from the suit and the warrantor was substituted in his place. That such a proceeding was allowed by German law shows, perhaps more conclusively than any other argument, that ownership was not the essential characteristic of the procedure, nor the basis of the action. In the Roman *rei vindicatio* the defendant could oppose his ownership to the claim of the plaintiff; and the original defendant remained the chief party to the end of the procedure. It was to prove his right of ownership, that he proved his acquisition from the auctor. In German law, the defendant withdrew from the procedure, if his auctor accepted the obligation of warranty. The distinction is well expressed by the Lombard law: "Langobardus semper dat auctorem et numquam stat loco auctoris; Romanus semper stat loco auctoris et numquam dat auctorem." It is the purest German law, the established procedure of the Sachsenspiegel and later German jurisprudence, as well as that of the Lex Salica, the earliest law extant. This earliest code provided [1] that, if A sold a horse to B, and it was attached in B's possession on the ground that it was stolen, B summoned A as his warrantor; and to the same term, if A wished to escape the charge of theft, he must summon his seller, C, as his warrantor; and this process was continued until the thief was found. And, whoever, in the chain of warrantors, refused to appear at the fixed term, was held to be the thief unless detained by some lawful essoin. And this was the procedure of Anglo-Saxon law also.

The first mention of it is given in

HOTH. & EAD. 7: "If any man steal cattle from another, and the owner afterwards lay claim to it, let him [the defendant] vouch to warranty at the king's hall, if he can; and let him bring there the person who sold or gave it to him. If he cannot, let him give it up, and let the owner take possession of it."

The fundamental rule held that no right of possession could be acquired in stolen goods; nor could the defendant show by an acquisition from a seller that the object was his, since that gave him no title, and did not rebut the claim of unwilling loss of the plaintiff. He produced his auctor, not to prove the tradition of the goods, as in our day; but that he might escape the charge, and put it upon his auctor. The defendant summoned his auctor to appear at court, and he thereby turned the charge of theft from himself to his auctor; and gave the object into his possession. If the

[1] Chap. 47.

auctor denied any such relation by oath, the charge fell back on the defendant, and he was held guilty.[1] The Sachsen-.spiegel prescribed that the plaintiff must again repeat the formalities of the action, and begin anew against the auctor. The auctor now stood in the position of a defendant in the action for movables, and had any of the defences allowed to the latter. He could prove his original title to the property in question, as the defendant might have done.

ÆTHELR. II. 9, § 4 : " Etiam inter advocandum, si quis hoc incipiat, nec ultra advocet, *si propriare sibi velit, non potest hoc ei dene-gari*, si credibile testimonium locum ei faciat accidendi."

Or, more usually, he himself vouched in his own auctor.

ÆTHELR. II. 8, § 2 : " Si [auctor] recipiat, tunc acquietat eum, cum quo fuerat deprehensum. *Appellet deinceps unde venerit ei.*"

The vouching proceeded until an exception was raised which opposed the unwilling loss of the plaintiff. If the auctor proved his property, this was a relevant objection, and the procedure ended as far as concerned the plaintiff ; if the first auctor brought in his auctor, the chain of auctors continued until a relevant objection was made, or the thief was found. The last in the series of auctors, who could not put the charge upon another, must make good his defence, or stand convicted of theft. By the Anglo-Saxon as well as the barbarian laws, the warrantor who refused to appear was regarded as the thief; and the defendant, in order yet to clear himself,[2] must swear with three witnesses that the defaulter was really his auctor, and that he had summoned him in due form.

At the court, since the defendant was both under a charge for theft, and an obligation to restore the thing, the defendant, as shown by the oath, formally placed the object in the hands of the auctor.

ANH. X. 3 : " By the Lord, I was not at rede nor at deed, neither

---

[1] By the Lex Ribuaria, the auctor could free himself by oath, and then the defendant was held to be thief.

[2] Æthelr. II. 9, § 2 : " Manifestet hoc cum testibus, si posset, quod recte advocat."

counsellor nor doer, where were unlawfully led away N.'s cattle.
But as I cattle have, so did I lawfully obtain it. And as I vouch it
to warranty, so did he sell it to me *into whose hand I now set it.*"

Then the witnesses swore : —

Cn. II. 23 : " Et veritent hoc ipsi testes in fide Dei et domini sui,
quod ei in vero testimonio sint, sicut oculis superviderint et auribus
superaudierint, quod recte hoc adquisivit."

If a series. of auctors appeared, the object passed from
hand to hand, following in an inverse order the way by which
it had come to the present possessor.[1]

In case the warrantor, B, was dead, the defendant vouched
in the tomb of B, by swearing with an oath of sixty hides,
the usual clearing oath for theft, that B sold the slave to
him when alive.[2] Then having cleared himself of theft, he
surrendered the object to the plaintiff. The charge of theft
now lay on the dead warrantor ; but, as showing the regular
succession of the heir to the same position, and the legal
persona of the devisor, if B left an heir, C, C could take up
the procedure as B would have done.

Ine, 53 : " Si tunc sciat, quis mortui pecuniam hereditavit [defend-
ant] *appellet in ipsam pecuniam,* et roget ipsam manum, ut hoc capitale quietum ei faciat, vel ostendat, quod nunquam ipsius mortui
pecunia fuit."

Æthelr. II. 9, § 2 : " Si mortuum hominem advocet, si non habeat heredes, qui purgent eum, manifestet hoc cum testibus, si possit,
quod recte advocet, et id per se purget. Tunc erit mortuus in culpa,
nisi amicos habeat, qui eum mundificent, *sicut idem faceret, si posset
et viveret.*"

§ 3 : " Si tunc amicos habeat, qui audeant hoc facere, *tunc deficit
advocatio, sicut ille viveret ac negaret.* Et habeatur furti reus ille, qui
in manibus habet, quia semper est negatio fortior quam affirmatio."

Laband has shown from the Sachsenspiegel that the heir
was not the third possessor, but that he continued the possession of the original receiver. Sachsensp. II. 60, § 2 : " If
the tenant of the lord die, *his heir steps into his place,* and
pays ' from the property ' that which he should. If the lord

---

[1] Lex Rib. 72, 1 : "De manu in manum ambulare debet, usque dum ad eam
manum veniat quae eum (*i.e.,* the slave) inlicito ordine vendidit vel furavit."

[2] Ine, 53.

also die, likewise the man gives his rent to whom the property falls, as he had promised to the lord."[1]

This has been already discussed, and it would seem that the Anglo-Saxon laws just quoted make the position so clear that it would hardly need more than the statement. But so high an authority as Sohm,[2] in his "Procedure of the Salic Law," has declared that acquisition by inheritance was a relevant defence in the action for movables, and that it worked like the proof of "title to property." He claims, with Stobbe, that the German inheritance formed a "particular succession," in which the heir stood a step after the devisor, and not a "universal succession," as existed in the Roman law, in which the heir stood in the *place of* the deceased. But the passage of the Salic Law[3] on which he grounds this defence required that the defendant should prove that he found the object in question in the possession of his devisor, and then show how it came into the possession of his devisor. But from the laws above quoted, from the passage of the Sachsenspiegel, and the discussion above on the rule *Hand wahre Hand*, it results that the heir occupied in the procedure exactly the *same legal position* which the devisor would have taken, were he alive; and the inheritor acquired only those rights over the thing which the devisor had before him. And that this is the conclusion to be drawn from the expression of the law above in which, if the defendant knew the heir of his warrantor, he vouched in the "property of the deceased," is without doubt. Then the heir, like any auctor, must, according to the passage quoted by Sohm, prove how the object became property of his devisor, if he would retain possession; *i.e.* he might prove his devisor's original production, and then it would work as a relevant exception for his own possession against the plaintiff. Or, as any

[1] Cf. Cn. II. 72: "Et ubi bonda, *i.e.*, paterfamilias, manserit sine compellatione et calumpnia, sint uxor et pueri in eodem sine querela. Et si compellatus in vita sua in aliquo fuerat, *respondeant heredes eius, sicut ipse deberet, si viveret.*   [2] P. 72, and n. 1.

[3] C. 101: "Debet ille, super quem interciatur, tres testimonia mittere quod in alode patris hoc invenisset, et altera trea testimonia, qualiter pater suus res ipsas invenisset."

auctor, he could deny by oath that the property, or the devisor's legal *persona*, was under the obligation of warranty; *i.e.*, in the usual expression, he did not "accept," and then the imputation of theft recoiled on the original defendant. And there is no reason to suppose that the heir could not vouch in a warrantor for the object; but rather a presumption that he could, from the passage of the Lex Salica given above. But this could not often happen; since, if the devisor was dead, it would be difficult also to find the warrantor. But the rule that no title could be acquired in stolen property, no matter how far it had gone from hand to hand, and the full rigor of the vouching existed even in this case by the showing of Sohm's own passage. For if he could not have shown how the object came into the hands of his devisor, *i.e.*, if he could not vouch in the devisor's warrantor, according to the usual rules of this procedure, he lost the object, but was freed from the charge of theft.

Then it is to be concluded that the claim of inheritance was not a relevant defence, and did not act as a title to ownership; but that the heir stood, in regard to the procedure, in the same position as his devisor.

The Sachsenspiegel and later German law required the plaintiff to follow the warrantor to his court, except over the sea; and that the object should be presented at the court of the warrantor. This was also the practice in the earlier Anglo-Saxon law, but was changed by Æthelred, who directed the warrantor to appear at the court where the object was first attached. Although formerly the vouching went as far as the third warrantor at the place (forum) of the *Anefang*, and then the plaintiff followed the warrantor, Æthelred required the whole chain of warrantors to appear at the court of the defendant, as was the rule in the Lex Salica.

Æthelr. II. 9 (Pr.) : "Aliquando fuit, quod ter advocandum erat, ubi prius aliquid interciabatur, et deinceps eundum cum advocante, quocunque advocaret. Unde consulerint sapientes, *quod melius erat, ut saltem advocaretur ubi deprehendebatur*, donec innotesceret, in quo stare vellet, ne forte impotens homo longius et diutius pro suo laboraret, et ut vexetur magis, qui injuste conquisitum habeat in manibus et minus qui juste prosequitur." [1]

And no subsequent law [2] changed this provision.

After the warrantor was summoned he was allowed the usual term [3] of one week in which to make his appearance at court, if he lived in the next shire; and an additional week for each shire farther distant. Æthelr. II. 8, § 3: "Si advocet ultra unam sciram, *habeat terminum, i.e. ebdomadam;* si advocet ultra duas sciras habeat duas septimanas de termino. Et ad quot sciras cennabit, totidem habeat septimanas de termino; — *et veniat ubi primitus fuit interciatus."*

The old law required that warranty should go on until the person was found who could make no defence, and was, therefore, the thief; or until one was found who produced a relevant objection. But the severity of the old law was limited as to the number of warrantors by:

Cn. II. 24, § 2: "Si testimonium habeat, sicut praediximus, tunc liceat inde *ter advocari, et quarta vice proprietur aut reddatur ei, cujus erit."*

If by the third warrantor the exception was not established, the defendant was cleared from the theft, and gave up the object. But it is hardly to be supposed that the third warrantor was held to be the thief. This is confirmed by:

Henr. 64, § 6: "Aut ille, si potest, werminga [warranty] resistat, *quae ultra tertiam vicem non procedit."* [4]

In the early law [5] a slave could not be vouched in as a

---

1 Cf. Edw. I. 1, § 1.

2 Henr. 57, § 4: "Si eum aliquo inventum sit, unde culpatus sit, ibi necesse est causam tractari, et ibi purgetur, vel ibi sordidetur."

3 The Lex Salica (47) gave the warrantor forty or eighty nights, according as he lived this side or beyond the Leye and the Carbonaria Forest. The Lex Ribuaria gave fourteen, forty, and eighty nights respectively, according as he lived within or without the "ducatum," or outside the kingdom.

4 Colb.: "Quod si testes habuerit, quales supra diximus uuarantum (A) vocet, et ille vocatus (B), vocet alium (C), si potest, et tertius (C) adhuc tertium (D), si potest, et tertius suum faciet, si valet; quod si non valet, reddatur ei quod juste habere debet."

5 Inc, 47.

warrantor, as having sold him goods; but this was permitted by Æthelstan,[1] and confirmed by Henry.[2]

After this examination of the plaintiff's position in the procedure of warranty in relation to his defendant and warrantors, aiming at the discovery of the thief and the establishment of an objection, the original defendant should now be considered in his relation to the warrantor. It is now easy to understand the necessity of having borh and witnesses at every transfer of property, as directed in:

ÆTHELR. I. 3: "And let no man either buy or exchange, unless he have borh and witness."

The peculiarities of the action for movables made the presence of witnesses indispensable, in order to provide for the case that a stolen object had been sold. And this accounts for the large number of directions in the laws concerning witnesses, and the great precautions required for the publicity of all chattels brought into a village, and the finding of cattle.[3] The witnesses served not only to prove that the defendant vouched in the right warrantor —

ÆTHELR. II. 9, § 2: ". . . manifestet hoc cum testibus, si posset, quod recte advocet."

— and so escaped the theft; but they also served as the witnesses of the action for indemnification against the warrantor, in which the defendant was plaintiff in the action based upon the borh given by the seller, and which followed the procedure for debt, as previously described. And then, if the first warrantor was a *bona fide* purchaser, he had a like action against his own warrantor, until the thief was found.

The later Saxon sources vary greatly as to the length of time of unconcealed possession, which would act as a suitable defence; but they all agree that such possession for some period gave a right of defence, mention being made of six weeks, and of a year and a day. Perhaps nothing shows

---

[1] Æthelst. II. 24.
[2] Henr. 43. Sic potest ei warrantus esse, qui in servitio suo est.
[3] Hloth. & Ead. 16; Ine, 25; Alfr. & G. 4; Edw. I. 1; Edg. IV. 8-11; Æthelr. III. 5; Cn. II. 23, 24; Ed. Conf. 22; Will. I. 45, III. 10.

better the freedom from Roman influences enjoyed by Anglo-Saxon law than the fact that no such period existed. It was, however, set by:

WILL. I. 6: "Si quis averium errans recollegerit, vel rem quamcunque invenerit, denunciet illud per tres partes visneti villis proximis, ut sint in testimonium inventi. Quod si quis venerit, rem ut suam clamans, det vadium et plegios, quod eam judicio sistet, *si quis infra annum et diem eandum requisierit*, et suum recipiat."

Unconcealed possession for a year and a day was then held to be a defence by William.

In conclusion, it is clearly seen that, in the procedure of movables, the action for stolen goods stood opposed to the action for the return of a movable which passed out of the owner's hands with his consent. The action for lost property belonged to the depositee, (B), if the goods were stolen from him, and not to the owner (A), according to the rule *Hand wahre Hand;* but if A had lost possession of the property against his will, in any way, whether his cattle had strayed, or been stolen, he had the action against any possessor. Nor was this to be distinguished as a *real* action, as some writers hold. From its origin in the delict procedure, this action was rather an action of theft than one aiming at the recovery of the object. And it was this union of both objects, giving it a double character, which caused the claim of the plaintiff, based on the unwilling loss of the property, to be most emphasized, although the claim also included a demand for the return of the property. The extrajudicial act of the *Anefang* consisted in the assertion of a formal claim to the property by laying hold with the hand, followed by rendering the fore oath of *bona fides* by the plaintiff; if the defendant refused to give up the object, he raised the following procedure before the court, after having given a pledge to make his defence. If he could not make any defence, he lost the object, and paid a fine. It was a settled principle that no right could be acquired by any possessor in an object previously stolen. The defendant could (1) make a full and relevant defence against both the charge of theft, and the return of the object, by proving the property to be his own by original acquisition. (2) By giving the clearing oath, he purged himself of the charge of theft only; but as yet having made no relevant exception to the chief charge of the suit, the plaintiff went to the proof, and gained the property. (3) By vouching to warranty, the defendant accomplished the same object as in (2); but, knowing who his seller was, he withdrew and brought the auctor into his place in the procedure. (4) William allowed unconcealed possession for a year and a day as a defence.

V.

In comparison with movables, immovables very naturally presented great procedural similarities, and also very marked differences, arising from their peculiar nature, and from legal development. Private property in land was not recognized in the earliest German period, since land belonged as property in partnership to the community, each partner having rights of use in wood, field, and arable. But when property in land was recognized, the previous conditions of its holding naturally exercised an influence on the land procedure; the action in regard to land, therefore, belonged originally to the community; and every alienation must have taken place in the court of the community, or, instead of that, before a chosen number of witnesses as representatives of the folk community. But when a new form of property arose, and contests sprang up concerning the rights of individuals over that property, such disputes would naturally have been regulated by the forms of law already existing. This could not be otherwise, however narrow the existing procedure was in its examination into the material rights of the contesting parties.

Cn. II. 24 (Pr.) : " Et nemo aliquid emat super iiii denariorum valens, *mobile vel immobile*, nisi habeat credibile testimonium iiii hominum, sit in civitate sit extra civitatem."

But although, from their preponderating importance as
property, and the powerful interests thereby affected, immovables did not continue to be regulated by the laws of
the narrow, executive system which admitted no questions of
justice and material right, yet their procedure was closely
connected with the principles of law already known concerning movables, and was shaped by them; and only from
this starting-point is to be sought a proper conception of the
various elements of change and progress afterwards introduced. In unwritten law, the judges easily applied to land
the only known rules of property, until this want in the laws
was supplied.

Yet there were essential differences existing in the pro-
cedures of movables and immovables. 1. When property
was given in trust, a difference existed in regard to the
admission of the owner's action. If the trustee lost or alienated a movable, the owner could not proceed against the
third possessor, as already shown. These limitations of the
action for movables in regard to the right of the owner, arose
from the narrow character of the old law;[1] but in real property they did not obtain. If a vassal conveyed real estate to
a third party, the owner could have an action against the
third party for recovery.

2. And a similar difference existed in regard to purchase,
which was but one form of deposit, if the contract had been
fulfilled on one side. If A had purchased a movable of B,
it has been shown that if B, failing to deliver the object to
A, sold and delivered it to a third party, C, A had no action
against C for the return of the object. But if the seller of
real estate, before delivery or investiture, again alienated
and delivered the same property with investiture to a third
party, the buyer still had an action against the third party,
and could obtain possession.

3. In the action for movables, apart from the case where
the defendant was bound by an obligation *ex contractu* for
the return of the property, he could only be held to answer,

[1] Heusler, Gewere, Excurs. II., pp. 487–502. The chief authorities followed
in the procedure of real property are Laband, Heusler, and Sohm.

if the plaintiff had advanced a claim of loss against his will; for it was not necessary that he should show the justice of his possession, since no question of material right was examined. In land procedure the defendant was required to make answer, without its being asked how the plaintiff was deprived of his property.

These characteristics of the procedure of movables have been shown to arise from the peculiar origin and limited structure of the old executive law of proof; while these marked differences in the land procedure stamp it as the production of a later time, when closer attention was given to establish the material rights of the contestants. For the procedure of movables was less perfect than that of land in regard to the judgment and means of proof. These differences point to the rise and development of the procedure after land became property.

Land must be looked to for the element which raised the procedure from the limited system to a more extended view of private right in property. From the very limited actions of debt of the earliest time, through the better system of the movable actions, one is brought by the action of immovables nearer to the more perfect system of to-day. It is through the procedure for land that a break was made with the narrower conditions of the old law, and that questions of right were decided on wider principles of justice, and opened to larger influences of jurisprudence. The procedure for movables had its origin in the old executive period; but the action for real property, having arisen at a time when property in real estate was finally recognized, when documents were admitted as proof, and when the need of a wider procedure was pressing, was as a consequence freed from the narrowing influences which shaped the action for movables, and was based more nearly on an examination of material right. The rule *Hand wahre Hand* resulted from the conceptions of the old law; and found no application in land. On the founding of estates on conquered ground, and especially on the rise of large gifts to the Church, and other circumstances of that time, the old procedure was of course inadequate. No *causae cognitio* being allowed, a buyer of real estate under the old procedure would have had but the action arising from the formal promise (contract) against the seller alone, and not the action for delivery of possession against a third possessor. But this did not happen. A remarkable revolution in the procedure took place, by which the old executive system was brought under the direction of the court, and followed more nearly a judgment on proof.[1] It has been pointed out that the Lex Salica marked the close of the old executive period, and remained as the only monument of that otherwise prehistoric time ; and Sohm has explained[2] that the Lex Ribuaria is the working over of the Lex Salica to adapt it to the new order of things. It was then in the time of the Austrasian king, Childebert II., in the end of the sixth century, that this turning-point was found in the development of the German procedure. The Lex Ribuaria gave a new character to the procedure, especially by the introduction of documents as proof which were wholly unknown to the old law. Written documents were largely introduced through the influence of the Roman church, and became the strongest and most natural means of proof. This was the innovation which gave an additional impetus to the legal development of the land procedure, and aided the separation from the narrowness of the old law ; while the latter, by the corresponding lack of such means of proof, remained unexpanded. The Lex Ribuaria regulated the framing of the documents for transactions concerning land, and their employment ; and introduced documentary proof in its perfected form.

Lex. Rib. 59, § 8 : " Si quis interpellatus chartam prae manibus habuerit, nulla ei malo ordine invasio requiratur, quia dum interpellatur, respondeat ad interrogationis, et sine tangano loquatur et dicat : Non malo ordine, sed per testamentum hoc teneo." [3]

---

[1] Heusler, Gewere, p. 497, ff.　　　　[2] Zeitschr. Rechtsg. V. 394, ff.

[3] Meichelbeck, No. 122 : " Pater Wagoni portionem suam ad S. Corbinianum tradidit, unde et chartas traditionis eius in praesente attulerunt." Muratori, Antiq. I. 495 : " Habeo, sed non contra legem, eo quod ecce cartula, qualiter mihi quondam Eriprandi res dedit." Monum. hist. patr. Chartarum I. p. 74 : " Non contra legem, quia cartula firmitatis per manibus habemus." Baluz. Capit. App. No. 98 : " Teneo per chartas legibus factas, quas fecit Eldebertus." Vaissette, Hist. de Languedoc, I., No. 88 : " Retineo, quia scripturam emtionis habeo."

Not that the appeal to the oath and the use of witnesses were laid aside ; but the document was not only a more serviceable, but also as good a means of proof as these. The contents of the document supplied the defence which was hitherto incumbent on the defendant, and which required a showing of his derived or original acquisition by his warrantor or witnesses. Documentary proof was given by all the early German codes, which stood in the period later than the executive, such as those of the Allemanians, Bavarians, Burgundians, Lombards, and Visigoths. And, in England, documents could have been used only after writing had been introduced by Augustine, late in the sixth century ; in fact, the earliest charters of the Anglo-Saxons belong to the seventh century.

Heusler [1] has explained that farther progress in the legal development arose from the confusion of ideas in the German mind between documents as a means of proof, and as the actual ground of acquisition. It was as possible for the plaintiff as for the defendant to make use of documents, and two documents thus were opposed to each other, as in the case of "duo testamenta regum de una re." [2] Here the folk-laws [3] permitted the plaintiff's document not only to destroy the efficacy of the one produced by the defendant, but also to establish the plaintiff's own effective right. In the old one-sided form of proof by warrantors or witnesses, if the defendant did not establish his right, he gave up the property ; but the question of the plaintiff's right was not brought into the procedure. [4] But now the document of the plaintiff not only confuted the right of the defendant, but was in itself the

---

[1] Gewere, pp. 496–500.

[2] Lex Rib. Tit. 60, § 7.

[3] L. Alam. Cloth. I. 1 : "Per cartam firmitatem faciat et super altare ponat, et proprietas de ipsis rebus ad ipsam ecclesiam in perpetuum permaneat." Cf. L. Baiuv. I. 1. Cloth. 19 : "Ut res Ecclesiae de laicis absque carta nullus praesumat possidere," &c. Cf. Ed. Luit. 22, 54. L. Burg. Add. XII. 1 : "Si quis agrum . . . comparaverit, jubemus et si non habuerit cartam . . . pretium perdat." Cf. 43. 2, and 51. 1.

[4] The plaintiff's claim is shown in this formula : "Malo ordine et injuste contra legem detines, mitte mihi responsum, pone rationem."

establishment of a ground of acquisition, and the plaintiff's right. This being the interpretation of a document, it was but natural that the plaintiff would claim this advantage as proof of his right[1] as well as the defendant, for a protection of his right. As a buyer, or receiver of a gift, was secured against attack by the document (" Haec donatio ut firmior sit, cartam scribere jussi "), so not only the buyer would use the documents in bringing an action against a third party, but also the receiver of a gift would do so in an action against an heir of the donor who had denied the gift. In such cases where the defendant or plaintiff might produce documents, the whole weight fell on the question whether the formal and material *charta* was tenable or not. Here it is to be seen that finally the old one-sided procedure, in which no *causae cognitio* was allowed, gave way to a contradictory procedure which involved the examination of the plaintiff's right. An interesting case of this period is given where both parties held documents from the same person;[2] but the defendant called in the auctor, only to vindicate the legality of the document (" testamentum defendere debet." L. Rib. 59, 6). But the Lex Ribuaria (60) required one who did not acquire by documents to secure to himself the proof by procuring witnesses. Then as long as these men lived, or their memory remained, they performed the same service as documents.[3] The point has now been reached where the *contradictory* procedure has finally parted with the *executive*.[4]

A question may have arisen as to the reason for the absence

---

[1] Vaissette, I. No. 88: " Res, quas Petrus et uxor sua tradiderunt per ipsam scripturam, injuste retinet." Bouquet, Script. IX. p. 706: " Res quas Bligardis per scripturam ecclesie donaverat, Genesius invasit."

[2] Vaissette, I. No. 88: " The monastery of St. Johannis, at Carcassonne, plaintiff, *vs.* Duvigeld, defendant. Both claimed certain goods under charters of the same seller, Petrus. The latter should act as warrantor to defendant, but said, " Ipsam scripturam ego feci, sed legibus eam auctoricare non possum, quia ego et uxor mea *antea* tradidimus res per scripturam donationis ad jam dictam casam Dei."

[3] Cf. Troya, Cod. Dip. Longob. V. No. 763.

[4] It is also an interesting fact that in England the " inquisitio per testes," and thereby the English jury, arose from that class of the Anglo-Saxon and Norman proof, community-witnesses, which were chiefly used in regard to land.

of an assertion of property in German pleading. It is clearly seen that the cause, as regards movables, existed in the conditions of the old law, which separated the idea of protection in possession, from any consideration of the right over the thing. Detention and seisin[1] existed together over movables;[2] and the owner did not have the action against a third hand, as was expressed by the rule *Hand wahre Hand*. There was no decision as to the question of possession preparatory to a procedure in regard to ownership. But this did not hold of land. In the German land procedure seisin was contested by both parties sometimes, not with any effect upon the legal title, but only to gain the *rôle* of the defendant in the proof. The legal question, whether of inheritance, gift, &c., was always examined. And the right of him who had a real title in land gave him an action against any third acquirer. This shows the wide difference which existed between the conception of movables and of land, and the consequent differences in the pleading.

Although the German conception of ownership in land approached the Roman *dominium* in an absolute right to the thing, yet in other respects the two ideas were essentially different. The German allowed a division of the right of possession in such a manner, and with such a combination of real and personal rights as was not possible in the Roman jurisprudence. As *possessio* was the correlative of Roman *dominium*, so was seisin related to German ownership.[3] It is not necessary to follow the reasoning by which it has been indisputably proved that the seisin of the Germans was not for land, as it was for movables, the actual physical detention; but that it included the employment of the revenue and fruits of the land. The Roman conception of *possessio* did not stop with the physical power over a corporeal thing, but gave the word a judicial meaning by assuming the existence of possession in the absence of physical detention, and

[1] I shall use the word " seisin " as the equivalent of the German word " Gewere."

[2] Heusler, Gewere, p. 92.

[3] Heusler, p. 65.

by excluding possession in spite of actual physical power over the property.   How did seisin compare with this? German law came somewhat near this conception when the owner, although giving up naked detention and allowing another to cultivate the land, still retained seisin ; and sometimes it denied seisin to the one in physical possession.   But seisin, *manifesting itself in the use of the profits of the land,* is the judicial possession of the German law, analogous to the Roman *possessio.*   They were, of course, not synonymous, but seisin occupied the same position in German, which *possessia* occupied in Roman law; and as the judicial *possessio* is the only one recognized by law as giving a claim to legal protection, so, with the Germans, seisin was the only legally recognized possession.

But Roman law in its judicial possession united actual power over the thing with the *animus domini.*   If the proprietor gave up the usufruct, the usufructuary was not regarded as the possessor ; and no delegated possession, existing by the side of the owner's possession, could exist.   Yet just as the Germans defined seisin as possession united with actual use, so also the Romans, in the Twelve Tables, spoke of possession as *usus ;* but the Germans held more firmly to the idea than the Romans.   The seisin of movables was entirely lost by loan or deposit, and in case of loss by theft the borrower only had the action against the thief for recovery.   The seisin of immovables was widened, and the Germans carried to its full consequences the identification of use and seisin ; they recognized the usufructuary as the only possessor, instead of the owner, and conceived the possibility of various seisin in case of various uses of the same thing.   The seisin of the user did not absorb that of the proprietor, but existed side by side with it, and caused a division of the possession.

Seisin of movables only existed when one had them in his house or on his estate, so that he could at any time have actual influence over them, and exclude the influence of another.   But in land, he had the seisin who drew revenue from the estate ; and so seisin was not lost by lease.   The lord, as well as the vassal himself, had seisin of land given to the vassal in return for specified services; while the latter, who again granted the land out of his possession for a fixed rent, did not lose his seisin. If a contest arose between the vassal and lord for the possession of property, he only had the seisin who exercised the derived right; but in a contest with a third person, not thus bound, the seisin belonged to the first holder, who had transferred the possession. The seisin, or legal possession, of the German law, can then be defined as the actual exercise of a right of possession,[1] whether this existed in the immediate physical detention, or in the right to the revenue.

As has been stated in the procedure of movables, the actions of German law were largely based on contract. In regard to land, the contract for an object settled *in specie* conveyed a real title, without transfer of possession, as soon as one party had fulfilled his part. From this point of view, Sohm has first given a rational explanation of *traditio* and *investitura*. *Traditio* was a contract, like *venditio* or *donatio*, and on the payment of the earnest-money, or arrha, ownership arose; while *investitura* was but the execution and accomplishment of the acquisition of ownership. Since the beginning of the sixth century, *traditio* appeared only as a contract (venditio, donatio, concambium); while the church, to whom gifts were almost solely made, looked to it that this acquisition of ownership was made through documents, and should be thereby capable of proof at any future time. Investiture has only been mentioned ·since the eighth century in Frankish documents; and a document has *never* since been received as conveying investiture. A writing to be sure was received; but this "notitia" or "breve" was only in the manner of an appendix to the contract document, and without signatures. The documents with which parties came forward in the procedure to establish ownership were always contracts, and the fulfilment of their right (investiture) was adjudged on these. He who had gained a real title by *traditio* was, by investiture, placed in the enjoyment of seisin. The acquirement of possession (investiture) was sometimes an advantage in regard to the distribution of

---

[1] With this, cf. Sohm, Ehesch. p. 86, and p. 37, note 28.

proof; but it possessed no importance whatever in respect of the right of the parties. Then *traditio*, but not investiture, was the legal transaction of the German law; and the formalities which developed in the giving of possession in real estate had their origin in the fact that German law united to the *formal* requisites actual acquirement of possession.[1] The "book" of the Anglo-Saxon sources was the contract or document by which ownership was gained. Symbolical forms of transfer were probably customary in the early Anglo-Saxon period, but there are few traces of them.[2] A strikingly clear proof of the effectiveness of the *traditio* exists in the fact that the whole importance was attached to the drawing up of the documents, and their delivery. Investiture, then, was not a title to the land, but merely a "modus acquirendi" for gaining a more complete ownership.

In the procedure of debt and movables, the claim of the plaintiff was clearly distinguished from the exceptions of the defendant; but in land this was not always possible. There are cases, of course, in which the claimant asked for a change in the existing relations, and sought the co-operation of the court, as when a buyer claimed surrender of purchased real estate. Here the line between claim and objection can be clearly drawn. But there are cases in which a party simply asked the recognition of a right, in whose practice he is, or claims that he is, in order to make defence against another's attack, or insure himself against such claims in the future. Here the judgment was not a condemnation, but the sanctioning of a hitherto doubtful right; and it was decreed that he who was awarded the legal possession should keep

[1] The most essential element of investiture was known on the continent as "Auflassung." Sohm, opposing Laband and Heusler, has shown this to be the equivalent of *resignatio*, or a renunciation of possession by a formal casting of the straw. "Per festucam se exitum dicere" was named "exfestucatio," or "warpitio," and indicated the act. This was performed by the seller, and was necessary to the buyer, that he might acquire possession in a legal sense (seisin, or gewere). *Auflassung* occurred not only in cases of sale, etc., but when ownership was transferred by a decision of court; which proved it to be a transfer, not of ownership, but merely of possession.

[2] Schmid, Gloss. p. 537, also says that the ancient runic letters were rarely used in the affairs of common life. *Vide supra*, p. 101.

the property, and exercise all rights over it.   Such an example is found in Charter CLXXXVI. (App. No. 8): Ætheric, when about to dispose of his lands by will, was opposed, and, on application to the court, he received an affirmation of his right.   The objection might have been raised on the basis of:

ALFR. 41: "The man who has boc-land, and which his kindred left him, then ordain we that he must not give it from his 'maegburg,' if there be writing or witness that it was forbidden by those men who at first acquired it, and by those who gave it to him, that he should do so; and then let that be declared in the presence of the king and of the bishop, before his kinsmen."

Therefore, in such a procedure, which admitted a double claim, — we might say, two plaintiffs, — the consequences of contumacy befell the plaintiff as well as the defendant; for its object was the admission of one claim, and the establishment of peace.   In the Roman vindication, the non-possessing owner was the plaintiff, and the possessing non-owner the defendant.   But, in the German procedure, one or both the parties claimed the property through seisin; and it was accidental whether the real possessor sued or was sued, although, since the possessor as a rule had no motive in beginning the suit, he was usually the defendant.

The rule for the distribution of proof has been formulated by Homeyer and Planck as follows: He who appealed to seisin had the precedence in the right to prove his assertion; and, "generally from the differences of the assertions *concerning the Gewere*, one party gained a better right to the proof." [1]   And so, when both parties asserted a like seisin, the best title decided. [2]   But there are many cases in which the one who did not have the seisin undoubtedly acquired the right of proof, and gained the suit by raising a claim by which the possessor was forced to surrender.   This shows that it was insufficient to appeal to the seisin as a decision of the right of proof.   In opposition to this theory, which is held by most German writers, Hänel [3] and others assert

---

[1] Homeyer, Sachsensp. II. 2, p. 618.
[2] Planck, Zeitschr. f. D. R. X. p. 284 ff.   [3] Beweissys. p. 182 ff.

that the claim of a stronger right gave the right of proving; and that, in a claim of an equally strong right by both parties, the seisin decided. Laband has pointed out that, if "stronger right" means, in the abstract sense, more legal power than any other right, as that ownership is a stronger right than loan or annuity; that loan is a stronger right than inheritance, lease, &c., — then the position hardly needs refutation. For it was one of the undoubted points of German law that, the right of proof was given to the holder of property by loan, and not to the plaintiff who asserted ownership. But if it mean that an examination was made in each case as to which party brought forward the right, stronger " in regard to the actual relations and the legal questions applicable thereto," the rule was partly true. It is true so far as it assigned the proof to that assertion which was *relevant* for the decision of the contest according to the actual situation of the case; but it is not true that *in all cases* that party gained the proof, and therefore the decision on which the procedure hung, by raising the assertion of a stronger right. No rule can be laid down by which the weight and importance of an assertion could be abstractly established. Cases are given in which the fact of possession was decisive; and, also, cases in which the seisin of one party yielded before the right of the other. Whether the one or the other went to the proof depended on the kind of claim, and the manner in which it was advanced by the non-possessor. The latter's simple claim to the legal possession acted only as an opposition to the assertion of a right of possession by the actual possessor.[1] If one of two parties laid claim to the property as his own, the other must prove his right of possession, no matter what right of possession he advanced. It was not how he came into possession, but by what right he exercised it. If the plaintiff made a positive assertion, which would break the seisin of the possessor, he must prove this; and such an assertion was decisive.

Seisin did not, then, unconditionally give the right of proof; nor if both parties claimed the same title did the

[1] Cf. Æthelr. II. 9, § 8. "Quia semper est negatio fortior quam affirmatio."

seisin give one the precedence. But its important meaning in the procedure lay in the fact that without it the claimant who wished to acquire the right of proof was forced to substantiate his claim by a very different process from that which he would have followed had he enjoyed seisin.[1] Seisin was not the central point on which the law of proof hung; but there were suits about seisin which followed the common principles of German law. The Roman system laid the burden of proof on the plaintiff; but the German, on the defendant. If the plaintiff asserted no facts by which the right of the defendant could be attacked, the defendant swore to his right, and the case ended there. Where the simple assertion of one stood opposed to the assertion of the other, the seisin of the defendant gave him an advantage in the proof. Heusler has formulated the rule for the distribution of proof in actions for land as follows: By means of his possession the defendant rebutted the claim by an oath to his right, so long as his right was not, on the part of the plaintiff, assailed by a fact which overcame it. If this occurred, and the plaintiff proved his claim, the defendant was only freed by opposing to the plaintiff's claim a proof of his superior right. Seisin, then, had only a negative value in that it freed one in possession from a proof of his right as long as an effectual right was not advanced by the plaintiff. In German[2] as in Roman[3] law, the position of the possessor was advantageous; and the general principle of both laws, " melior est conditio possidentis," is the same as that in: —

ETHELR. II. 9, § 4: " Propriatio propinquior semper est possidenti quam repetenti."

But it can be seen how little seisin acted as a proof of material right. In movables, as well as immovables, seisin

---

[1] Laband, p. 172.

[2] " Cum ambae partes nullum testem habere professae sunt, judicatum est, ut advocatus, *qui ipsam habebat vestituram*, diceret juratus," &c. Heusler, Gewere, p. 87.

[3] " Commodum possidendi in eo est, quod etiamsi res eius non sit qui possidet, si modo actor non potuerit suam esse probare, remanet suo loco possessio." Just. de interd. IV. 15, § 4.

had no effect on the decision as to material right. But while there were no legal means for the protection of possession over movables, this was not true of land. There are examples where the suit was begun by a possessory claim, in order to gain the advantages in the suit that would be given by possession. Yet often the defendant did not answer the claim of possession, but proceeded at once to show his own legal title, or the defect in the plaintiff's. This went to the proof because it was a relevant objection, and rendered a decision on the seisin useless. There was, then, a legal protection of possession over land, but only to give the possessor the defence in the petitory claim; but in German law there was no marked distinction between the possessory and petitory claims involved in the action.

It will now be possible to lay down the rules for the distribution of proof.[1] Neither seisin nor the "stronger right" always decided the right of proof. If the plaintiff asserted his own right, and denied the defendant's possession, the latter was simply required to prove his right to possession, no matter what right of possession the plaintiff claimed. But if, from the questions involved, the plaintiff advanced a claim which would invalidate the right of the defendant, — whether by contract, or ownership, by an abstractly greater or less right, it mattered not, — he went to the proof. Yet the defendant had the proof, if he could advance a *relevant* objection, according to the special relations of each case in question.

In regard to a classification of suits for land, much confusion has prevailed from a belief that there was no settled basis of division. It is true that suits for land contained very largely an element of equity; but a basis of division is to be found in the giving of proof. There are, on the one hand, cases in which, from the claim raised against the possessor, he came to the proof of his right of possession; and, on the other hand, cases in which a claim was established for the legal surrender of the land, which claim went to the proof. In the former class, the aim was to defend and secure the

[1] Laband, pp. 166–172.

possession in which the party was, or from which he had been illegally ousted; in the latter, to bring the possessor to surrender the land.   From the peculiar character of the German judgment, the award of proof to either party practically amounted to a decision of the case; so that the above division is really one to be sustained by examples, showing in what cases Anglo-Saxon law allowed one party to *retain* the present state of possession, and in what cases the other party could *gain* possession.   In the first class, the claim of the non-possessor was not a matter of discussion and proof; but the procedure was concerned only with the establishment of the real state of possession, and the right of the possessor to it.   In the second class, the right claimed by the possessor was not a question of discussion; but the claim of the non-possessor, who demanded surrender, was alone subject to decision.   Accordingly, without using the terms in the sense of the canon law, these divisions will be designated as : —

(A) Judicia retinendae vel recuperandae possessionis.[1]

(B) Judicia adipiscendae possessionis.

The judgment was not concerned with the fact as to which party was in actual possession, but to which the possession legally belonged; and the right of possession was definitely adjudged to one of the two parties.   So by this division it matters not whether a party was in possession or not, or what right of possession was claimed by the parties, be it ownership, or a derived right, of a real, or personal character.

The first class (A) admits of two subdivisions : —

(*a*) When one party was admitted to be in actual possession.

---

[1] Vide Laband, p. 174. cf. Bracton, 103, a : "Earum quae sunt *in rem*, quaedam proditae sunt super ipsa *possessione*, et quaedam super ipsa *proprietate;* est enim possessio rei, et proprietas."   Glan. lib. 13, c. 1 : "Placita de *recto* — placita super *seisinis.*"   Fleta, lib. 4, c. 1 : "Est jus *possessionis* et jus *proprietatis.*" The historical connection between Anglo-Saxon jurisprudence and the English Common Law is manifest in this classification.   The action brought in the Anglo-Saxon procedure for land is the equivalent of the real action of the English law, which was brought for the specific recovery of lands, tenements, or hereditaments.   But, "again in [English] real actions there is a division between those founded on the *seisin* or *possession,* and those founded on the *property* or the *right.*" Stephen on Pleading, p. 89.

16

(*b*) When both parties claimed the actual exercise of possession.

The second class (B) admits of three : —

(*a*) The plaintiff's claim, after the manner of a personal action, obliged the possessor to a surrender; *e.g.*, as in contract.

(*b*) The possessor's right was disputed, because his auctor was not capable of passing possession to him.

(*c*) The plaintiff claimed a right of inheritance superior to that of the possessor.

A (*a*) In this procedure the mere assertion of the plaintiff in itself, without substantiation, of a right to the possession of the property was sufficient to introduce the procedure. And the defendant must answer such a claim, or expose himself to the consequences of contumacy. But to such a claim, accompanied with no farther substantiation, the defendant, without proving his means of acquisition, received the oath on simply replying that he had a right to the possession. The procedure aimed directly at the establishment of the rightful possession ; and in this case seisin brought the advantages of the one-sided means of proof, in that the defendant simply swore to the right which he exercised.

Charter CCXIX. (App. No. 11) furnishes an example of this procedure. The bishop of Worcester, being seised of certain rights of pasture at Sutton, was annoyed by attempts of the shire-officials to encroach on these rights, and brought his complaint before the Witan. Here the ealdorman maintained the claim on behalf of the shire.

" Then said the bishop and the chapter's counsellors that they did not confess more to them [the bailiffs] than as it was administered in Æthelbald's day."

The simple claim of the ealdorman stood opposed to the simple denial of the bishop, who upheld his claim to " two-thirds of the wood and the mast." The advantages of seisin appeared in that the case was ended by giving to the bishop the proof of his right by oath.

" Then Archbishop Wulfred and all the Witan decreed that

the bishop and chapter might declare on oath that it *was so administered in Æthelbald's day*, and that he claimed no more."

This was the judgment; and then the bishop bound himself by formal contract to the plaintiff for the performance of the proof at a fixed term. After thirty days, the oath was given by the defendant as he had promised. This is a good case, not only as showing the regular course of a suit at German law, and the office of the judgment and proof; but also, that the claim of the plaintiff was not made a subject of contradiction, but that the defendant simply rebutted the claim by an oath to his right of possession.

Another example of the same procedure is given in Charter DCCLV. (App. No. 28). Eadwine, the plaintiff, claimed certain lands of his mother, Eanwene, — probably on the ground that they belonged to his inheritance. The defence was made by Thurkil White, her legal representative. A proceeding was adopted, which points to the use of apparitors, as in the Saxon law of the continent, by choosing men to ride to Eanwene and hear her defence. To the simple claim to the land, Eanwene " said that she had no land that belonged to him in any way." As in many cases, the full course of the procedure is wanting. The remainder of the charter is occupied solely with an account of the nuncupative will. But since Eanwene was allowed to devise all her property, including the lands in dispute, it is easy to see that Thurkil White undoubtedly made oath for Eanwene, as defendant, to her right of possession; and that the men despatched by the court were " witness to this " as declared in his oath.

But although simple demand and simple denial were sufficient to decide the course of the procedure, yet they were not the sole elements. After the denial of the defendant, the plaintiff might then judge that he could advance a claim which could not be opposed by the defendant; and then the suit would pass under division B. But the claim of the plaintiff might contain an assertion of right to the land, which, although unsubstantiated, implied a superior right;

and so, to make a relevant objection, the defendant was
required to show such a right of possession as would be a
just defence. In Charter CIV. (App. No. 2), Catwal sold
land to Wintran, but did not deliver to him the original
charter with the description and signatures which he had
received, granting a new one instead. The monastery of
Catwal subsequently brought suit against that of Wintran
for the land. The plaintiffs claimed the land by virtue of
the original charters which they still held, knowing that
by the death of the witnesses to the sale between Catwal
and Wintran they might present a better title to the land.
Then the decision must have been on the tenability of the
charters. The possessors were allowed the proof by oath,
since their charter was not effective; proof by oath serving
the purpose of the document. But this was effected by extrajudicial compromise, " in part money being given, and in part
an oath added in evidence." This last must have been given
by the defendants as explained. While the claim to possession
meant only an assertion opposed to the actual fact of possession, the claim to possession on higher grounds forced the
defendant to show that his right was superior. The law here
broke down ; and from the justice and equity of the case was
it to be decided whether the defendant's objection was relevant, and whether the plaintiff's claim was such in strength
as to preclude the proof to the other. In this case, the right
to the land resulting from retention of the original charter
and description was opposed to the assertion of a *bona fide*
sale ; and such a decision would have implied an examination
of material right, which was unknown to the rigorous conditions of the old law.

It has been elsewhere shown in this volume that com-
promises were frequent; but these proceedings were always
conducted after the manner of the regular, legal procedure.
Such a case is that of Charter CCCXXVIII. (App. No. 17),
where Æthelm claimed the land of Helmstan. The defendant averred that Æthelthrith, who had received the land as
her morning-gift from her husband, sold it to Oswulf in full
right, and that he held it from Oswulf. The plaintiff had

asserted no facts which invalidated this, and the oath was awarded to the defendant.[1]

So in this procedure when one party was in undisputed possession, and the plaintiff simply contested this right without substantiation, the defendant proved his right by an oath. In the Saxon law of the continent, he went to the oath with six others of the same circle of land-possession. But if the assertion of the claimant implied a better right to the possession, no defence was relevant but a proof of his own superior right by the defendant.

A. (b.) In this procedure each party might demand that the other should not obtain the seisin, and might wish to prove his own right of possession and to be protected therein. But neither would desire to show that the other's acquisition of possession was ineffectual, since each denied that the other was possessed. Two parties, indeed, might appeal to seisin of the same property; since the possession of land, from its nature, did not imply the necessary exclusion of all influence by another person over the thing possessed. With movables where seisin and detention coexisted, the case was different. Two persons might both claim the actual seisin of a strip of border-land between two estates, or a part of the meadow or wood-lot, and unhesitatingly swear to his actual enjoyment of possession with a sincere belief in his right. Or, again, one party might have claimed that he was forcibly dispossessed, and so both parties might claim seisin. The rule in these cases was simply that, after one of the claims to seisin had been set aside as illegal, the procedure resolved itself into the case described in the preceding division. This division, then, is concerned with the manner in which such a result was brought about. Not that there was a separate division of possessory and petitory suits, for in German procedure these are but parts of the same suit. The decision of the question to whom the seisin belonged

---

[1] A notice of Charters CCLVI. (App. No. 14) and CCXVIII. (App. No. 9), which properly belong to this division, has been referred to the subject of inheritance, B. (c), p. 257.

was part of an unfinished judgment, which simply pointed out who should receive the advantages of possession in the subsequent stages of the procedure. There are cases,[1] however, in which the possessory claim was decided in favor of one party, and then the petitory in favor of the other; but the sole object of a special proof of possession was the settlement of the rôles of the parties to the procedure.

In regard to forcible dispossession, it has been established, as a general principle of German law, that this did not give to the forcible holder the advantages of seisin, although he was in the actual exercise of the right. Transfer of possession (resignatio) was accompanied by the formalities of investiture; and investiture was necessary for the establishment of full legal possession. Therefore, a possession forcibly acquired would not have the force of seisin. A good illustration of this procedure is found in Charter DCXCIII. (App. No. 22). Ælfric had exchanged land, under proper witness of Archbishop Sigeric, Bishop Ordbyrht, and others, with Wynflaed. The right of Wynflaed was evident; for " Archbishop Sigeric sent his evidence thereto, and Bishop Ordbyrht his." No separation of the possessory from the petitory claim was made; but, on the general rule above noted, Wynflaed was held to have the seisin, and the procedure now went on without division to the petitory claim. " Then Wynflaed was instructed that she must prove it her property." She then proceeded to establish her right of possession, as in A (a), — " so she produced her proof of ownership," and would have given the oath had a compromise not been effected; and rent would have been awarded her, as having been lawfully seised of the land, for the time during which she had been illegally deprived of its use and fruits.[2] So, in forcible dispossession, if the plaintiff would establish his right, he must substantiate his claim, as if he were not in actual possession.

The earliest law did not make any definite separation between possessory and petitory claims;[3] and it has been remarked how often we find the oldest forms persisting in the Anglo-Saxon law. Indeed, this separation seems sometimes

[1] Heusler, Gewere, pp. 76, 77.   [2] Vide Charter CCXX. (App. No. 10).
[3] V. Bethmann-Hollweg. Civil process, p. 53.

not to have been comprehended, in a sense that a previous decision must be reached on the question of possession. But it cannot be assumed, from the absence of a clear account of each step of the procedure, that such a distinction was unknown to Anglo-Saxon law; for the charters were often vague and general on legal points, and only aimed at presenting the results of litigation. In Charter CLXIV. (App. No. 5), Bynna seized lands belonging to the church of Worcester. In cases of forcible dispossession, the one displaced was nearer the proof; and the Bishop of Worcester therefore " confirmed these things with the witness of the charters which Æthelbald before granted to his predecessors." The dispossession gave him the *rôle* of defendant in the proof.

Another striking example of this procedure is found in Charter MCCLXXXVIII. (App. No. 21). The claimant, Leofsunu, on the ground that the land belonged to his wife from a grant to' her former husband, forcibly seized possession. As usual, he was not considered as having seisin ; but the claim to possession led to the establishment of his opponent's right of possession. The judgment awarded the proof to Archbishop Dunstan, who proceeded to show a testamentary right from the owner, Ælfeh. The Archbishop himself swore to his right to the land by will ; and he enforced this by use of a large number of community-witnesses, who also swore as to the assertion contained in their principal's oath. "And there were many more, a thousand men, who gave the oath." , Other examples of this procedure are found in Charters MXXXIV. (App. No. 12), CCXLV. (App. No. 13), and in the trial on Penenden Heath (App. No. 31).

In other cases where both parties claimed seisin, one might overcome the other's assertion by establishing an older possession ; but, if these claims were evenly balanced, one might claim a right of possession such as ownership. If, however, both could advance such a right, recourse would be had to the manner of acquisition of their right, and hereditary right overcame purchase. Real, uncontested possession gave the right to prove the title to possession ; and this must be settled first. That such questions could not always be safely decided by the one-sided means of proof is evident, since each party might bring the prescribed number of witnesses. Here is the opening through which later change arose in the kind and way of producing the evidence by witnesses. It was through the procedure for real estate[1] that a freer method of proof was introduced after the Norman Conquest, by an examination of the witnesses (*inquisitio per testes*), which exercised a most powerful influence in placing the procedure on a modern footing. The conquerors brought with them a better-developed polity, which they engrafted on the slower growth of Anglo-Saxon law. Therefore, from this position it is now possible to look back and see the influence of land on the legal development, and how prominent a factor it has been in accomplishing this result.

B. (*a.*) In cases where the defendant was acknowledged to be in possession, and had not obtained it by force, the plaintiff might yet win the possession. This procedure, based on contract for a fixed object, had the character of both a real and obligatory action. As shown before, *traditio* gave a real right and an action for investiture against the seller, that the buyer might acquire a full ownership; and the seller was bound to deliver possession. The existence of this procedure is pointed to in : —

.WILL. I. 23 : " Si voluerit quis *conventionem terrae tenendae* adversus dominum suum disrationare, per pares suos de eodem tenemento (par ses pers de la tenure meimes), quos in testimonium vocaverit, disrationabit, quia per extraneos id facere non poterit."

The establishment of a contract for land must be proved by the plaintiff with witnesses of the same circle of landtenure. The " de eodem tenemento " was evidently a Norman provision, and this law simply enforced this rule in regard to a procedure already existing. The plaintiff having sued for a fulfilment of the obligation, the defendant might simply deny any such bargain or sale by his oath; or present a relevant objection by facts from which it would appear he

[1] Brunner, Zeugen und Inq. p. 139 ff.

was under no obligation to deliver the land. For the sale might have been concluded under agreements which were not kept. If no such defence could be made, the plaintiff could compel the defendant to a surrender of the property according to the terms of the obligation.

This procedure is illustrated by a charter (App. No. 33) which concerns the dispute as to the plaintiff's right to services over lands held by the defendant. From the German conceptions of possession, as already shown, the seisin of the over-lord was often a seisin over revenue or profits ; and, in a contest between the over-lord and his inferior, the holder of the derived right had seisin and its procedural advantages. In such a case as this, the abbot would have the right of proof, if the plaintiff could not bring forward and substantiate a positive assertion, which, if proved, would destroy all rights of the defendant. But this case is good evidence that seisin did not invariably give the right of proof. The plaintiff resorted to community-witnesses to prove the long-standing existence of the obligation under which the holder of this land rested for the services in question. " The bishop then claimed legal witnesses who, in the time of King Edward, had seen these things, and had performed the aforesaid services for the bishop." To this positive claim the defendant could make no answer, for " the abbot said he had not witnesses against the bishop." After this claim and answer by the parties, which constituted the *litis contestatio*, came the judgment: " It was decided by the chief men that the bishop name his witnesses, and produce them on an appointed day ; and that they should prove by oath the allegations of the bishop." The plaintiff received the proof ; but, on the appointed day, the defendant resigned all objections, and did not require the oath of the bishop. For, as in Charter DCXCIII. (App. No. 22), " it would be better to omit the oath rather than give it, because, after the oath, there could be no amicable arrangement."

Inasmuch as the legal relations regarding land were more varied than for movables, the class of cases where land was granted only for the time being, under an obligation to return, as in the case of a mortgage for security of a loan, was naturally wider than the corresponding division of movables. It would include the case of a lessor or pledgeor, suing for return of land after the lapse of the lease or pledge; or of an owner suing on the death of a life-annuitant. But in all cases the procedure was the same, and depended largely on the same principles already known in similar cases for movables. Suit could be brought by the plaintiff or plaintiff's heir against the present possessor, and the former need not state his real right, but simply claim that he granted the land to the defendant under fixed and obligatory terms for return. But it usually appeared what right was claimed by the plaintiff. The defendant might raise a relevant objection by proving his ownership in the property; or claiming that, although he held the land as pledge, the time of return had not yet arrived. If no such defence could be made, the plaintiff, in case no documents existed, went to the proof of his assertion with the oath. Anglo-Saxon law gives a clear instance of this procedure in Charter CCCCXCIX (App. No. 18). Eadgifu brought suit against Goda for the return of lands which her father had pledged to him as security for a loan of thirty pounds. Upon claim and answer being made, it appeared that the plaintiff averred the payment of the thirty pounds by her father before his death, which Goda denied. Here, as in the procedure of movables, when the procedure hinged on an act of the claimant, a denial on the part of the defendant only forced the former to a proof of the asserted act.[1] Then the judgment was decreed by the Witan " that Eadgifu should cleanse her father's hand by [an oath of] as much value [namely, thirty pounds]." And this oath having been rendered, the property was restored to her.

This class includes those cases wherein lands which an individual held of the grantor, and not of the king,[2] were forfeited by the commission of a crime to the grantor, who had an action for their recovery against any holder. These

---

[1] Cf. *supra*, p. 201.

[2] Cn. II. 13 : " And whoever does a deed of outlawry, let the king have power of the frith. And if he have boc-land, let that be forfeited into the king's hands; be he man of whatever man he may." Cf. *supra*, the quotations in another essay, pp. 65, 66.

crimes by which land was forfeited were, usually, theft, adultery, rebellion, or cowardice in the service of his lord.

Such a right was claimed in Charter CCCXXVIII. (App. No. 17), by the writer of the document against Helmstan, who had committed theft. The legal rule of reversion to the grantor in such cases was undoubtedly true, as shown by : —

Cn. II. 78 : " Let him forfeit all that he owns, and his own life ; and let the lord seize his possessions and his land, which he previously gave him ; and if he have boc-land, let that pass into the hands of the king." [1]

This rule was the basis of the plaintiff's claim, which worked as a personal claim for the surrender of the land. The plaintiff cited the corresponding case of Ordlaf, in which the working of the rule seemed to have been unquestioned. " And Ordlaf took possession of his land *because it was his grant* that he occupied, and he [Helmstan] could not forfeit his [Ordlaf's land to the king]." And likewise " I took possession of my land." The procedure might take two directions, according to the character of the defence. If the defendant claimed ownership in the property, the assertion of fief-right by the plaintiff was but simple opposition to the existing conditions, and the possessor would have the right to the proof. But if it was admitted by the defendant that he had only such a right to the property as had been granted him by the plaintiff, then the crime and its consequences were the special aim of the procedure. The plaintiff then set forward most clearly and minutely the acts of the defendant by which he claimed restitution of the land, and a right to dispose of it to another : —

" Thereupon, after this, about a year and a half, or I know not whether two years after, he stole the untended oxen at Fonthill, by which he was altogether ruined, and drove to Cytlid, and there one surprised him, and his spereman followed up the fugitive's tracks. When he fled, then a bramble cut him over the face. When he wished to deny, then one said to him that, as a proof. Eanulf Peneard-ing then came upon him, who was sheriff, and seized all the property

1 *Vide* also Charter MCCLXXXVIII (App. No. 21) and *supra*, p. 111.

that he [Helmstan] owned at Tisbury. I asked him why he did so;
he said that he [Helmstan] was a thief, and his property was adjudged
to the king, because he was a king's man."

Stress was put upon every detail connected with the crime
as an evidence that such had been committed. And by this
claim he would establish his right to the land. In this con-
tingency, the defence was either negative or positive. 1. The
defendant might absolutely deny having committed the act;
and by the usual rules, as in criminal cases, he would go to
the clearing-oath and prove his innocence. 2. Or if the defendant raised positive assertions, from which his innocence
resulted, he had advanced a relevant objection, and accordingly went to the proof himself. In the present case, the
defendant evidently could not have made either defence, and
the plaintiff should have full right to his land.

This division includes all other cases which had no criminal character, but which arose from acts that caused a
reversion to the grantor. A disregard of the obligations
arising from contract, such as injury to the property, refusal
to perform services, or pay the revenues, created conditions
under which an action could be brought for a surrender of
the land. And the positive assertion of such a claim gave
the proof to the plaintiff, unless the defendant could oppose
to it some relevant objection.

B. (b.) The plaintiff might also force the possessor to
surrender by disputing the right of the defendant's auctor
to convey the land in question. The way taken by the
property could be followed back, as in the pursuit of stolen
movables, until the man was reached who by the alienation
injured the rights of the plaintiff; and by proof of this the
plaintiff destroyed all right of the defending possessor to
retain the land. To this rule the Charter of Ely (App.
No. 35) is directly opposed, and its forgery would therefore
be best proved by this fact. It is also in opposition to other
clear and well-authenticated charters, and to the known
principles of German procedure.

In Charter DCCCCXXIX. (App. No. 25) the Church of

Rochester held lands which, it seemed, could not be alienated from the church, — a condition probably in the conveyance
of the original charter from the giver.   On the accession of
Bishop Godwine, he found that lands at Snodland, of which
he had the original charters, had been alienated, and were
now in the possession of Leofwine.   The plaintiff then laid
claim to the land " that was formerly alienated from the
church," on the above grounds of a limitation and injury to
his rights by the unauthorized and illegal sale to Leofwine.
To this positive claim, the defendant could offer no relevant
defence.   Although he showed his *bona fide* possession by the
deeds of alienation from his auctor, yet this was no refutation
of the assertion of an illegal transfer by the auctor proved by
the production of the documents.   The bishop would have
received the land ; but in reconciliation Leofwine was granted
a life-occupancy.

Charter DCCCXCVIII. (App. No. 27) gives a clearer
example of the procedure, and at the same time a negative
proof of the non-existence in Anglo-Saxon law of any legal
usucapio.   No mention of the " praescriptio triginta annorum " of the continent is made in the cases where it would
have been most natural ; and the only reference to it is in
a charter[1] recording the decree of a church-council in regard
to a right of refection.   Moreover, Charter CCLVI. (App.
No. 14) gives an instance of contested real estate, in which
thirty-four years had passed since the previous attack by the
same plaintiff, without the slightest hint of any influence
arising from prescription.   There is certainly no evidence to
prove its existence in Anglo-Saxon law, but every reason to
believe the contrary.   Admittedly of Roman origin, it existed
in those German codes which had been exposed to Roman
influence ; yet, even though issue must be taken with historians of reputation on this point, it is certain that no effect
whatever of any Roman influence can be found in Anglo-
Saxon polity.

This charter (No. 27), first mentioned, declares that Leofric
sold and conveyed lands to Æthelstan under the king's leave,

[1] CLXXXiV. (App. No. 7).   .

and the witness of the whole Witan, with full and undisputed right; and that a charter was given to Æthelstan. Then the plaintiff, Wulfstan, claimed possession from Æthelstan, on the ground that the defendant's auctor was not capable of alienating the land. No period of time is mentioned as serving to protect the defendant in his position of *bona fide* purchaser, although the suit was brought " after many years." The court first passed judgment on the justice of the defendant's acquisition, and declared his right to be good. But this was no relevant defence to a claim asserting the inability of his auctor to alienate, however well the conveyance was made. The plaintiff advanced a positive assertion not met by the defence. Having shown his own right, the defendant withdrew from the procedure, and then had an action for indemnification against the auctor, Leofric. As in the procedure for movables, the case now stood between the plaintiff, Wulfstan, and the auctor, Leofric, as a new defendant. The substance of Wulfstan's right is not given, but seems to have been a claim such as would have resulted in his going to the proof, and gaining a decision against Leofric ; for a settlement was made by the friends of the parties satisfactory to the plaintiff. Wulfstan now granted a clear title of the land to Leofric, who then conveyed the land anew to Æthelstan " clear and uncontested." It would be difficult to find a clearer statement of the principles of this procedure than in this case, and one confirmed by the known principles of the Sachsenspiegel and other German laws. Possession, if from an unauthorized grantor, was not legal possession, and had no protection except that of indemnity against the grantor.

A similar case is to be found in Charter MXIX. (App. No. 6). King Offa, of Mercia, bequeathed lands to his heirs which had been taken from King Cenwulf of the West-Saxons. King Cenwulf had no title to the lands, and afterwards sent back the stolen charters of the lands which he held to the church at Dover, to which they belonged. After the death of Offa, the church of Dover laid claim to the lands and asked restitution from Offa's heirs, who held only by such right as their devisor could have had. The plaintiff presented a full substantiation of his claim by the presentation of his charters, and showed his right to the land, and the illegal possession of the defendants. Those from whom the defendants received had no title by which they could convey the land. The bequest had been made to them without right, and therefore the plaintiff received the lands; since no right could be shown by the defendants as a rebuttal of the positive claim and proof of the plaintiff.

In the suit of Godwine, and others of this division, it is seen how unnecessary it was to claim a real right to the land as a substantiation; while, on the other hand, the pivotal point of the suit lay in the question whether the sale or alienation was unauthorized or not, and whether the plaintiff suffered injury thereby. It was immaterial whether the plaintiff's claim was based on a real or obligatory right. In suits of this kind in the Sachsenspiegel, the expression in use, "*Gewere* brechen," explains that the defendant's *Gewere* was untenable. This class included cases where the seller was only a guardian, or annuitant, or a conditional holder, or holder by right of pledge, or was a debtor to the plaintiff. And such a class cannot be comprehended by the Roman designations of real or personal suits. In the Roman vindication the plaintiff must prove his ownership or acquisition; and, if this were established, it resulted as a consequence that another could not undertake a legal sale of the property, and so the defendant could not have a legal right of possession. But from the corresponding cases in the Sachsenspiegel we are assisted in understanding the elements in the suit, which are passed over by the Anglo-Saxon charters. From these it appears that the real right of the plaintiff was not taken into account and made the subject of proof and contradiction; but the suit was based on the question whether, from the relations of the auctor to the plaintiff, the former was authorized to make the sale to the defendant. Such a basis for the action must separate this division of the German procedure for land from the Roman *rei vindicatio*, which was founded on a real right. The Roman suit was based on positive, the German suit on negative, grounds: in the one, the plaintiff asserted *his* right of ownership; in the other, he asserted that the *defendant* could have no right, because his auctor had no authority to alienate.

If the defendant could show that he had not received of the auctor designated by the plaintiff, he offered a valid defence. But, from the methods of transfer of land, it could scarcely happen that the auctor could not be identified. No defence could be based on the way and manner of his acquisition; and, if he would contest the charge that his auctor made an unauthorized sale, the defendant must appeal to his auctor. If the auctor's defence failed, the defendant's right of possession disappeared. The case of Charter DCCCXCVIII. (App. No. 27) declares the principle, which is confirmed by the Saxon sources of the continent. The auctor obtained the possession, and the advantages, of seisin, by appearing in the action, and could in his turn vouch in his auctor, until the person was reached who made the unauthorized sale. The course was the same as in stolen movables, except that, according to the Sachsenspiegel, the *forum rei sitae* was *always* competent. This process of warranty shows well that the object of the suit was to determine on and examine the question whether the sale was unauthorized, or not. Then the action of the plaintiff against the auctor last vouched would be of the character described in the division just preceding B. (*a.*); and the proof would be assigned by the principles shown above. Here it can be seen how impossible it would be, through a desire to give a French-like finish and rotundity to a theory, to lay down a rule which would grant the proof always to the plaintiff, or always to defendant, with unvarying accuracy. Those who have argued the effectiveness of seisin, or, on the other hand, the so-called "stronger right," have fallen into the snare set in matters which do not admit of such an inflexible rule. The proof and the consequent decision of the case went to the assertion which was decided to be relevant from the concrete nature of each special case; and it was thus determined whether the plaintiff or the defendant went to the proof, and of what kind; and to him was the possession given.

B. (*c.*) This rule will be shown in suits based on inheritance, the last division in the procedure of land. But to this class are not to be referred those suits which, however they involve questions relating to inheritance, are not solely founded on a right of inheritance. If the devisor had rights to the payment of money, or to the surrender of property, the heir must conduct his claim in the same manner as the devisor would have done were he alive, since the heir entered into the same legal *persona* as his devisor. Yet this suit was not based on the right of inheritance, but on the personal obligation under which the defendant lay for the performance of the duty.

Charter CCLVI. (App. No. 14) cannot be a suit properly based on inheritance right, but belongs more properly to A. (*a.*) Æthelwulf laid claim to lands in the possession of the church of Dover, which held them from Oswulf by hereditary grant. The plaintiff had previously made an unsuccessful attempt against Oswulf's heirs, and the Witan had held that the heirs had a good right as devised by Oswulf.[1] The plaintiff claiming a right of purchase through his devisor, in whose place he stood, the defendant who was in acknowledged possession was simply forced by the plaintiff's claim to prove his right by oath. When the rights of the parties were thus opposed, seisin gave the power of establishing the right of the possessor by oath ; this was done, and enforced by many community-witnesses.

A similar case is given in Charter CCXVIII. (App. No. 9) of a suit concerning inheritance, but not based on a right of inheritance. In such a case, the plaintiff's assertion was opposed to the possession of the defendant, and worked, since the defendant had the seisin, only to force him to a proof of his right. This suit, therefore, would also properly belong to the class of suits for the maintenance of possession, A. (*a*), and not to this division, where possession was won by a right of inheritance. To this division are referred those

---

[1] This might have been decreed on the basis of Æthelr. III. 14 : "And he who remains, without attack and suit, in peace while he lives, let no one, then, after his death, lay claim against his heirs."

cases based on inheritance solely, with an assertion suitable to break the seisin of the opponent.

The German suit of inheritance bore a close resemblance to the Roman action of *hereditatis petitio*. But the *vindicatio* permitted to the Roman heir was based on the ownership of the devisor, whose acquisition was to be proved by the heir. The plaintiff having asserted that he was the heir, and having substantiated both claims, it followed that he was the owner of the property, and therefore surrender was demanded. The suit was based on ownership, and was a real action. The action of the German law, on the contrary, did not enter into the question whether the devisor was owner or not ; the procedure did not aim at the discussion and establishment of the devisor's means of acquisition. The action was founded simply on the assertion that the plaintiff had a better right to the inherited property than the defendant. The foundation of the suit was not a real right, but a right of inheritance. And this action was given alike for movables or immovables, with the same distribution of proof, except that some evident differences must be observed.

The charters are clearer on the questions of inheritance than on other subjects. Charter MCCLXXXVIII. (App. No. 21) declares how the plaintiff brought suit for lands in behalf of the church of St. Andrew, on the ground of a right of succession by will from Ælfeh. The defendant held forcible possession, based only on the ground that his wife's former husband was a nephew of Ælfeh. The basis of the suit is clearly shown. The defence was, of course, irrelevant to the claim of succession by will, and the positive assertion of the claimant went to the proof. The usual form of proof was employed ; and the plaintiff made an oath to his right, which was strengthened by community-witnesses.

Charter CCCXXVII. (App. No. 16) tells of a suit based on testamentary right, in which the plaintiff advanced a right arising from conditions connected with the bequest. The devisor granted it to Eanbald on this condition, — that the land should not pass to any layman ; and that, if no one in orders could be found among his kin, it should revert to the church of Worcester. The property passed from Eanbald to Eastmund; and, on the latter's death, it came into the hands of laymen. Against these, as defendants, the Bishop of Worcester brought suit to gain possession by the conditions of the original bequest. The assertion of a better right of inheritance by the plaintiff was supported by documents; but the defence gave up the case, and a compromise was effected, which conceded the right of the bishop.

A similar case is shown in Charter CLVI. (App. No. 4). Lands were bequeathed by Hemele and Duda to Worcester, after the death of their legal heirs. The action of the Bishop of Worcester as plaintiff was based on this right of reversion against one of the heirs, as defendant, who wished to set aside the will. The case did not go to a decision; but the plaintiff had witnesses to prove his assertions, and a reconciliation was effected, conceding the right of the plaintiff.[1]

The mere assertion of a right by the plaintiff was sufficient to set the procedure in motion, and cause the defendant to prove his right, and from the resulting situation of the case was it possible to decide the necessity of further and stronger claim by the plaintiff. In the case of Charter CXLIII. (App. No. 3), the mere assertion of an inheritance-right would have been sufficient; but, since the defendant could probably not offer a better inheritance-right, or even any such right, the plaintiff would go to the proof. But here again a compromise shuts us out from the actual course of the procedure.

It will be necessary to speak of the institution of German law by which property was given as *Morgengabe* in this connection, and to show its separation from right of inheritance. This distinction Laband has pointed out more clearly from the character of the actions raised to enforce or defend claims to *Morgengabe*. This institution was an integral part of the German law, by which the husband provided for the wife in case of widowhood. On the granting of the *Morgen-*

---

[1] This case might almost be classed with Charter CLXXXVI. *Vide supra,* p. 237.

gabe, the authorities on the Sachsenspiegel agree that the wife acquired ownership in the property, although the husband again acquired the gift by right of inheritance in case the wife died before him.   In other words, the widow stood precisely in the position of a third party who had acquired by gift or sale.   Her *Morgengabe* was not ruled by the conditions of other property belonging to her husband, which made up his inheritance and was divided among his heirs.   The widow, who, as plaintiff, demanded possession from the heirs, or who, as defendant, refused surrender of the *Morgengabe* to the heirs, did not rest her claim on inheritance.   Her property, by that institution, seemed as much separated from the inheritance of her husband as if she were a stranger, and held it by purchase.   Charter DCCIV. (App. No. 26) points out this distinction clearly.   Ætheric had been guilty of treason, and had never made his peace with the king before his death.   His widow, upon a threat that the king would revive the charge and appropriate his estates, offered, through the archbishop, to give her own *Morgengabe* to the church, if the king should " let the terrible charge fall, and Ætheric's will should stand, — that is, as before mentioned, the land at Boccing to Christ Church, and his other land to other holy places, as his will manifests."   Her morning-gift seems to have been safe from the danger of reversion to the crown, which befell all lands and property of a traitor, and was *her own* to offer as a recompense for pardon.   In a legal contest, the basis of the suit rested solely on the proof of right to possession by the widow, arising from a gift by her husband when living.

In conclusion, it is seen that the gap between the old executive procedure, as manifested in the actions for movables, and a contradictory procedure, based on an examination of material right, has been bridged by the legal development in the land-procedure.   The old means of proof by oath and witnesses found a successful rival in documents which aided the progress of the development.   The rule *Hand wahre Hand* of movables did not hold of land ; and *traditio*, or the contract of sale, gift, or other bargain, created a real right, which gave the buyer an action against any holder. *Investiture* (or its common form of *Auflassung*) was a formal resignation of possession, which in no wise affected ownership, but was necessary to that full possession with an enjoyment of the fruits which constituted *Gewere* or *seisin*. And this seisin was the legal possession of German law, the correlative, but not the synonyme, of the Roman *possessio;* for the legal conceptions of the Germans were widely separated from those of the Romans. The rules of the procedure, also, differed from the Roman. The simple claim of one party against another in possession balanced the situation, and seisin conferred an advantage in giving to the possessor the rôle of defendant and the oath to his right. But neither seisin nor a so-called stronger right always gave the right of proof. Laband has compared the decision on the proof to an auction. If one party asserted seisin, the other might outbid him by claiming older seisin ; but, if their claims to seisin were evenly balanced, the plaintiff did not have the proof unless he advanced a right of possession, such as ownership. Then, if these claims equalized each other, the plaintiff could only outbid the other by resorting to the manner of acquisition, where inheritance would be a better right than purchase. No rule can be laid down as to the proof, since the essence of the decision was in assigning *relevancy* to the counter-claim. The *relevant* objection of the defendant gave him the proof ; otherwise the plaintiff had the proof. And the preceding divisions have been based on the assignment of proof : —

A. Judicia retinendae vel recuperandae possessionis.

B. Judicia adipiscendae possessionis.

Division A. is subdivided into classes :

(1) Where the seisin of one party was admitted, and

(2) Where both parties claimed seisin. In the first subdivision, the defendant received the proof ; in the second, after one of the claimants was recognized as in possession, the case was the same as in the former section. And it was an established rule, that forcible dispossession did not deprive

the dispossessed party of the advantages of seisin. Division B. is subdivided into three sections; where the plaintiff acquired possession by an assertion either of (1) a right arising from such obligations as contract and mortgage, which included forfeiture of land to the grantor on commission of a crime; or (2) the fact that the defendant's auctor had no power to alienate, and thereby injured the plaintiff's right (the *bona fide* possessor not being protected in Anglo-Saxon law by any *praescriptio*); or (3) a better right of inheritance. Morning-gifts were not included in inheritance, since they occupied the same legal position as other gifts or sales.

VI.

In the most primitive period of German society, and when through the doctrine of self-help, the individual himself exercised active judicial powers, the punishment of crimes, as well, perhaps, as the civil procedure of distress, lay without the jurisdiction of courts, — which did not indeed exist. The German was himself judge and warrior; he levied execution and exacted blood for blood by the sovereign powers vested in himself by that most democratic of all constitutions. The archaic German procedure, as Siegel[1] has said, is essentially and radically characterized by the absolute independence (as opposed to the judicial power) by which the individual enforces his right. How far this is distinguished from the criminal jurisdiction of England to-day, is very apparent. "Every breach of the peace is a transgression against the king. . . . He alone can prosecute criminals; . . . and no one must presume of his own authority to exact vengeance from those who have wronged him."[2] Therefore it is one of the most instructive lessons in the history of English law to trace the growth of the power of government over the individual; the establishment of courts of justice; the gradual suppression of private warfare; the substitution of permanent kings for temporary leaders; and, in the course of time, the assump-

[1] Geschichte des deut. Gerichtsverf. p. 51.
[2] Allen, Inquiry into the Rise and Growth of the Royal Prerog., p. 88.

tion by the king of the "ideal attributes of absolute perfection, absolute immortality, and legal ubiquity." The king of to-day stands in bold contrast to the individual among the ancient Germans; and the prosecution instituted at the instance of the king, to the "prosecution by appeal" at the instance of a private party, which long existed in English law, — a remnant of the earliest polity of the Anglo-Saxons.

In the most archaic German society, before the organization of courts and a civil government, — a condition, perhaps, similar to that of the North American Indians, — it is fully accepted that each individual was the protector of his own rights by whatever power he possessed, and was in the same manner the avenger of his wrongs. Both in civil distress and vengeance for injuries, this was a period of summary action by the individual. Vengeance, arising from the doctrine of self-help,[1] was the manifestation of this summary execution in the sphere of criminal law, and can be defined as killing, or an assault with arms, resulting in death or wounds,[2] and presupposing a wrong for which retaliation was made. German society was organized on a basis of the peace,[3] or "frith," and every violation of the peace was a wrong. On the organization of the state, vengeance was a crude method of executing law, since it was not allowed unless clearly used by the individual as an instrument of law. For the folk-courts, as investigation has fully shown,[4] were

[1] *Vide* Schmid, p. 652.

[2] Cf. Wilda, p. 157, ff. In the sources of Northern law, vengeance was also used in the sense of an enmity which caused (1) the injured party to seize, bind, and bring his foe before the court; or (2) to pursue his suit unrelentingly until outlawry was imposed.

[3] Of the two words for peace in Anglo-Saxon law, *frið* and *grið*, the latter was introduced through the Danes, and first appears in Edw. and Guth. 1. As distinguished from frið, or the general peace, which was the synonym of mund, grið denoted the particular protection under which certain persons and places stood.

[4] Rogge holds that they were courts of mediation. But Wilda (pp. 197, ff. 209) disproves this position, and his view has been adopted by Köstlin (p. 62). Cf. Æthelr. III. 13, § 1: "Et ubi taynus habet duas optiones, amicitiae vel lagae, et amicitiam eligit, stet hoc ita firmum *sicut ipsum judicium* (dom)." To my mind there can be no doubt what the Germans would have *wished* their courts to be; but a great variance between law and fact was not rare. Tacitus

not mere courts of intercession. Where the Gragas and Northern law gave the individual power to kill,[1] the folk-laws gave the power to seize an offender, but only in case of resistance to slay him.[2] It was a fundamental rule of German law that vengeance must be authorized by previous permission of the court; or, if it preceded the judgment, it must afterwards be justified before the same tribunal.[3] Vengeance, therefore, could not legally be an act of pure free-will, since the avenger could always be brought to answer for his deed, and to show reason why he slew his foe.[4] The common example of this vengeance in the folk-laws was against the thief caught in the act (*handhabbende*);[5] but the kinsmen of the slain must swear an oath not to pursue the feud (*unfáh*). The idea of vengeance with the Germans was simply that of an angry man;[6] and he who inflicted on his foe a cold-blooded vengeance, by castration, poisoning, or other cruelties, committed an infamous deed. Moreover, secrecy was forbidden to the avenger,[7] even in the case of

---

assigns to the folk-community the authority for the public punishments and the fines. Compare, however, this passage from Sir Henry Maine: "There is much reason, in fact, for thinking that, in the earliest times and before the full development of that kingly authority which has lent so much vigor to the arm of the law in most Aryan communities, but which was virtually denied to the Irish, Courts of Justice existed less for the purpose of doing right universally, than for the purpose of supplying an alternative to the violent redress of wrong" (Ear. Hist. of Inst., p. 288).

[1] Even for assault, threats, or injuries to property. Wilda, p. 162.

[2] Edw. and Guth. 6, § 5: "And if he fight and wound any one, let him forfeit his wer." § 6: "If he kill any one, let him be an outlaw (utlaga), and he who loves the law pursue him with the hue and cry." § 7: "And if it results that he is slain, because he opposed the law of God and the king, if it can be proved, so let him lie uncompensated."

[3] Köstlin, p. 64, and n. 6; Wilda, pp. 160–166, 168, 305–313; Maurer, p. 28.

[4] Ine, 16: "Qui furem occiderit, debet inveritare cum juramento, quod illum culpabilem et de vita forisfactum occidisset, et non solvat." Ine, 21: "Si quis sic occisi weram exigat, licet inveritari, quod pro jure sit occisus, et non solvatur ipsius occisi congildonibus vel domino suo." Cf. also Ine, 35. *Vide* Wilda, p. 162.

[5] Withr. 25; Ine, 12, 16, 21, 28, 35 (Pr.); Æthelst. II. 11, IV. 6, VI. 8, § 3; Henr. 59, §§ 20, 23; 64, § 5; 74, § 3; 92, § 10. Ed. Conf. 36.

[6] Wilda, p. 158.

[7] Ine, 21, § 1: "Si celaverit, et fiat deinceps quandoque notum, tunc ampliabit mortuo ad juramentum, quod licet parentibus suis purgare eum."

an outlaw, who could be slain without compensation.[1] Publicity gave the avenger the power to prove his *bona fides* by co-swearers: —

HENR. 83, § 6: "If any one kill another in revenge, or self-defence, let him take to himself none of the goods of the dead, neither his horse, nor helmet, nor sword, nor any money; but in wonted manner let him arrange the body of the dead, — his head to the west, his feet to the east, upon his shield, if he it have; and let him drive deep his lance, and hang there his arms, and to it rein in his steed; and let him go to the nearest vill, and to him whom he shall first meet, as well as to him who has *socn*, let him declare it; that he may have proof and make defence against his [foe's] kinsmen and friends."[2]

But, generally, vengeance was allowed in those cases in which outlawry would have been the penalty, and was exercised somewhat after the manner of a punishment. The formula in Anglo-Saxon law ran thus: "Homini liceat pugnare."[3] Any conception of a *lex talionis*, as assumed by Kemble, was foreign to early German law, and was only a subsequent effect of the church.[4] The kinsmen of the slain could exact vengeance from the doer and his kinsmen[5] until the sum of the wergelds of the slain kinsmen equalled the wergeld of the person avenged.[6] The procedure of the Northern law in making a successful party in an accusation the executioner[7] was almost repeated in Cnut's day: —

[1] The Lex Rib. required that the slayer should publicly expose and guard the slain for a fixed number of days.

[2] Another procedure was sometimes adopted. Without waiting for a suit by the relatives of the slain, the avenger went before the court and established the legality of the act. Sachsp. I. 69, 64; II. 14, § 2. *Vide* Wilda, p. 163. Njal-Saga, c. 64, p. 99 ff. The suit was regularly brought against the dead, and judgment urged. Then, — a curious confirmation of the position of the heir in the legal *persona* of the devisor, shown before, — the heir conducted the suit for the dead.

[3] Alfr. 42, § 5.

[4] Alfr. (Einl.) 15; Maurer, Krit. Uebersch. III. 29; Kemble, Sax. in Engl, Vol. I. pp. 269–270; Wilda, p. 158, and n. 3.

[5] For the rights and obligations of the family in regard to the feud, *vide supra*, p. 140.

[6] Anh. VIII. 1.

[7] Wilda, p. 167.

Cn. II. 56: "Qui murdrum aperte perpetrabit, reddatur parentibus interfecti."

Alfred [1] also allowed immediate vengeance before a judgment in case a husband found another within closed doors or under a covering with his wife, daughter, sister, or mother. But the Anglo-Saxons did not permit vengeance for bodily injuries or mere threats as in the old Northern law. [2]

If A had slain B without cause, it was an unallowed breach of the peace; but if C, B's kinsman, slew A in revenge for B's death, it was a case of vengeance. It is now possible to draw a distinction between *vengeance* and *feud*. [3]

Feud does not presuppose a right of feud. The word *fœhð* has the simple meaning of *enmity*, but its equivalent, *feud*, was chiefly used in the sense of *vengeance* in the folk-laws. [4] In the above example, when C was seeking with his kinsmen to revenge B's death, if A and his kinsmen resisted, — as was usually the case, — and prepared to defend themselves, a private war arose, which could strictly be called "feud," or warfare in our sense. At this point the wild spirit of freedom among the Germans, and a pride, which forbade all submission, led naturally, in a rude system of government, to a resistance whose consequences were perilous to the state and destructive to life and peace. Even the offender who appeared at the court came prepared to gain by force a protection which might be denied him by a judgment of outlawry; and therefore the accuser must be attended by such numbers as insured a bloody conflict, if he hoped to prosecute his suit. [5]

---

[1] Alfr. 42, § 7.

[2] Wilda, pp. 160, 161.

[3] This is the equivalent of Maurer's distinction between *legal* and *illegal* feud. which is a little obscure. Krit. Uebersch. III. p. 28. Schmid also admits the same thing, p. 571.

[4] *Vide* Wilda, p. 189. Schmid (p. 571) says: "Fehderecht" was the right of one to treat his opponent as an enemy, and to exercise vengeance against him, —using feud in the sense of vengeance also. Curiously enough, the word "feud" was unknown to the Northern Law, vengeance alone being used.

Cf. Edm. II. 1 (Pr.): "If any one afterward kill a man, let him himself bear the enmity (fœhðe)." Also Ine 74.

[5] The guilds were required to attend a brother to the court if charged with a serious crime; and the decrees of the state were often made inoperative by such regulations. *Vide* Wilda, p. 186.

This conflict led to others, the loser always endeavoring to compensate himself, and the victor to humble and subdue his foe.[1] While vengeance was an appendage of the law, like private execution in the procedure of debt, feud, in the sense in which the word will be here used, was outside of the law, and in bold opposition to it ; it was the antagonistic element of the individual warring against the interests of society, and which society was naturally, and generally without success, striving to control.   For it must be kept in mind, more than has commonly been done, that law and fact were varying and different quantities in their relation to each other.   The high-spirited and democratic Germans were not quick in bending their wills and in imbibing objective law ; in fact, the feud which was chronicled by Tacitus[2] held its position even in England long after the Conquest.   This system of vengeance and feud occupied a large place in the Anglo-Saxon laws, as well as in other German codes ;[3] but many attempts were made to control it.

The great step toward the limitation of vengeance and the

---

[1] Cf. Allen, p. 101 : "Among the ancient Germans, if any one was wronged, it was the duty of his relations and friends to resent his injury, and take part in his quarrel.   His adversary was in the same predicament.   However questionable his conduct, he found kinsmen and associates to maintain his cause.   The redress which the one party demanded, the other thought it pusillanimous to grant.   Violence was resorted to ; retaliation followed ; and a civil, or rather domestic, war ensued."

[2] Germ. c. 22 : "Suscipere tam inimicitias seu patris seu propinqui quam amicitias necesse est.   Nec implacabiles durant ; luitur enim etiam homicidium certo armentorum ac pecorum numero, recipitque satisfactionem universa domus : utiliter in publicum ; quia periculosiores sunt inimicitiae iuxta libertatem."

[3] Its history and bearings were first definitely established by Wilda's great work (Das Strafrecht der Germanen, 1842) ; but Kemble (Saxons in England, Vol. I. Chap. X., 1848), afterwards wrote without acquainting himself with this, and afforded Konrad Maurer (Kritische Ueberschau, III., pp. 26–62, 1858) an opportunity to attack him with success, and at the same time to present a picture of the workings of feud in Anglo-Saxon law.   Wilda has based his conceptions of the German criminal system on the assumption that a system earlier than that of the folk-laws is to be found in the Gragas, Sagas, and other Northern sources. This, if true, furnishes an historical connection for the later period of the folk-laws, and has been accepted by Köstlin (p. 63), and Maurer (Krit. Uebersch.). Compare also, Sohm, Proced. de Lex Sal., pp. 122, 123.

consequent feuds was the extension of the system of compositions[1] over cases of killing.   In the case given above, if A offered B's wergeld to C, the state guaranteed the peace to A, and forbade C to exercise vengeance.   But if the wer were not paid, then C could fight his foe, as is expressed in the old proverb, " Bicge spere of síde óðer bere."   This step,[2] although probably not fully recognized in the earliest laws,[3] was surely reached in the time of Ine and Alfred.   The first case was only of an unfree Welshman who had slain an Englishman : —

Ine 74 : " Si servus Waliscus Anglicum hominem occiderit; debet ille, cujus est, reddere eum domino et parentibus, *aut LX sol. dare pro vita sua.*

§ 1. " Si dominus ejus nolit hoc capitale pro eo dare, liberum faciat eum, *et solvant parentes illius weram occisi,* si cognationem habeat liberam ; *si non habeat,* observent eum inimici sui."

If neither the lord nor his kinsman would make a settlement, then only might vengeance be taken.   And it is to be noticed that whatever duty was formerly imposed on the kin to aid in exacting vengeance seems to have been transferred under the composition system to a duty in paying the wer. But the familiar law of Alfred is more definite : —

Alfr. 42 (Pr.) : " Also, we decree that the man who knows his foe to be home-sitting *shall not fight him before he asks satisfaction.*"

The same chapter then goes on to illustrate by other provisions the principle that the injured party could only

---

[1] The system of compositions is mentioned here without further explanation, because it will be treated hereafter, and because it has seemed best to treat feud and vengeance without interruption, only introducing other subjects so far as they affect this.

[2] Christianity contributed essentially to the substitution of compositions for outlawry and vengeance, by its teaching mildness and forbearance (Wilda, p. 820).

[3] Since it is most probable that compositions were first fixed by private agreement, and later adopted by the courts, a trace of this arbitration, and therefore an evidence of the slender hold the composition system had as yet attained at that time, is to be found in Æthelbert, 65 : "If a thigh shall be broken, let him pay 12 sh. ; if he become lame, then must the friends arbitrate."

proceed to vengeance after he had given his foe every opportunity to make compensation, or if his foe resisted : —

§ 1 : " If he have power to surround and besiege his foe, let him
watch him during seven days, and not attack him, if he (foe) wish to
remain there. If he wish to surrender and give up his arms, let him
guard him unhurt thirty days, and announce it to his kinsman and
friends " [*i.e.* in order that they might make composition for him].

§ 3. " If he have not power to besiege him within, let him go to
the ealdorman and ask aid; if he be unwilling to aid him, *let him go
to the king before he attack his foe.*"

§ 4. " If any one comes on his foe unexpectedly, . . . if his foe be
willing to give up his arms, let him be held thirty days, and announce
it to his friends. *If he be unwilling to give up his arms, then may he
fight him.*"

The preliminary procedure in which negotiation was made
for the settlement is thus described : —

Edm. II. 7 : " First, according to folk-right, ought the slayer to
give pledge to his spokesman, and the spokesman of the slayer to the
kindred of the slain, that the slayer will make them full satisfaction.
Then should security be given to the spokesman, that the slayer may
draw nigh in peace, and himself give pledge for the wer. When he
has given his wed for this, let him further find a werborh, or security
for payment of the wer. After this shall have been done, let the peace
(mund) of the king be raised between them." [1]

Such was the aim of Anglo-Saxon law ; but that its decrees
were practically nugatory in regard to vengeance is shown by
the necessity of subsequent laws, as well as the influence of
other matters : —

Æthelr. IV. 4. § 1 : " If he fight before he demands his satisfaction, and live, let him pay the king's ' burhbrece ' of five pounds."

The state desired to see a weakening of the family bonds
as a means of diminishing the blood-vengeance, and decrees

---

[1] Cf. Anh.VII. 1, 4 : " When that is done then let the king's peace be established, that is, that they all of either kindred, with their hands in common upon
one weapon, engage to the mediator that the king's peace shall stand." *Vide*
Henr. 76, §§ 1, 5-7.

were passed with this aim;[1] but with little success.[2] The church employed its influence in the amelioration of vengeance and feud, and so far as the establishment of asylums in the churches[3] effected any thing, or protection in going to and coming from a church festival, she succeeded. But, notwithstanding the efforts of church and state, vengeance and private warfare continued throughout the whole Anglo-Saxon period. The government was only as strong as unruly ealdormen permitted ; the people were turbulent ; and it was reserved to William the Conqueror to strengthen the power of the state, and effect the practical suppression of feud. Yet it was not until the reign of Edward IV. that the last example of private warfare occurred.[4]

In the early legal history of the Germans, two different currents must be followed : one, that of vengeance and feud, out of real harmony with the state, and yet allowed to exist by the very power ready to destroy it ; and another of law, which sometimes mingled its current with the former. This last took place when the state legalized an act of private vengeance. When an offender broke the peace, he became *ipso facto* " peace-less " (*friedlos*) ; he was outside the pale of law and protection ; vengeance against him was not regarded as a crime, and his life was forfeit. By bringing the charge before the court, the permission of the community formed an enlarged right of vengeance, so to speak, in that by now engaging all members of the community to assume a state of warfare against the peace-breaker, he became an *outlaw*. In other words, vengeance was limited to such acts as, if brought to a legal decision, were followed by outlawry.[5] Finding the principles of summary action deeply imbedded in the early German mind, the state adapted that which they found in

---

[1] Alfr. 42, §§ 5, 6; Edm. II. 1.

[2] Æthelr. II. 6 ; VIII. 23 ; Cn. I. 5, § 2 ; cf. *supra*, pp. 71, 72, 139, 140.

[3] Alfr. 5, Pr. §§ 1-3 ; 42, § 2.

[4] Dugdale, Baronage, 1. 188, 362, 365. *Vide* Allen, p. 123, 124.

[5] The Gragas allowed killing in vengeance even for assaults, threats, and injuries to property ; but in all these cases the characteristic was, that if they came to a judgment outlawry would have been declared (Wilda, p. 162). In vengeance the individual became the judge, and acted on his own risk.

existence, and made outlawry a last resort, should the individual need the aid of the community. The old folk-community, as a confederacy bound to peace, was among the Anglo-Saxons held together by the king; and what was originally *folk-peace* became *king's* peace, without materially changing its meaning. The peace-breaker was " inimicus *regis* et omnium amicorum eius ; " [1] but yet he who held out against the law was declared " untrue to the folk " [2] (" tiht-bysig," and " folce ungetrȳwe ") and the old folk-peace. The excommunication from the folk-peace in its old meaning still existed, but with special emphasis on the relation to the king. The offender was put out of the pale of the peace (" fri-ð-leâsan " [3]); he was outside of all law (" utlah " [4]) until the king restored the peace to him (" friðian " [5]), or inlawed him again (" inlagie " [6]). But the outlaw was an enemy to the whole folk as well (" ûtlah wið eall folc " [7]), and his act was called *ûtlages weorc*.[8] And then because he was an enemy both of the king and folk, no one might harbor or support the outlaw ; this, if done, itself constituted a great crime.[9] His land was forfeited to him of whom it was held.[10] Rather is the outlaw to be hunted down and slain, and rightly termed a fugitive (" flȳma " [11]), on whose head a price was set.[12] He was a " lupinum caput," [13] a wolf, glad to escape the country, and spend his life as a wretch [14] (" wreccena ") ; and when excommunication from the church, as among the Anglo-Saxons, befell him, nothing more could be added to his dismal situation.

So among the ancient Germans it is clear that vengeance and outlawry contained no conception of a punishment as such ; but it was rather an *ex parte* proceeding based on the breach of the peace. The state put itself in an attitude of

---

[1] Æthelst. II. 20, § 7.
[2] Æthelr. I. 4 (Pr.).
[3] Cn. II. 15, (Pr.).
[4] Edw. and Guth. 6, § 6.
[5] Æthelst. II. 20, § 3.
[6] Cn. I. 2, § 4.
[7] Æthelr. I. 1, § 9.
[8] Cn. II. 13.
[9] Cf. Ine 30 ; and, for many corresponding passages, *vide* Schmid, p. 84.
[10] Cn. II. 13, 78. *Vide supra*, p. 250, ff.
[11] *Vide* Schmid, p. 575.
[12] Wihtr. 26.
[13] Ed. Conf. 6, § 2.
[14] Alfr. 4 (Pr.); Æthelr. VIII. 26.

war in regard to the offender, as it would have done against a foreign enemy.[1] In the earliest times outlawry was declared for killing and the more grave offences, which it will be well to term *causae majores*,[2] in opposition to lesser misdemeanors, or *causae minores*, which were settled by a composition from the remotest historical period.[3] *Causae majores* were premeditated, wilful, and not accidental[4] injuries to body and property, involving a breach of the folk-peace, in which the plaintiff could sue for outlawry; while in *causae minores* the suit could be brought only for a settled sum. This shows that the criminal system of the early Germans, however crude, aimed at the dispensation of justice; and Tacitus also states that the punishment was accommodated to the offence (*pro modo poena*). In the Northern sources, in which Wilda finds the oldest procedure, the *causae majores* included almost all offences, except slight injuries to property and body (which left no visible traces),[5] slander, &c.; while expiable offences, or *causae minores*, were few. If, then, Tacitus can be supplemented by the Northern law,[6] there were three stages of development; that is, three periods when one particular penalty preponderated over the others.

The first or earliest stage was when the *causae majores*, which were followed by outlawry, included, as just said, almost every offence. The Scandinavian sources are an example of this stage, with yet an apparent leaning toward the second. But the large number of the offences in this class diminished through several means. First, through the com-

---

[1] Maurer, Krit. Uebersch. III. p. 29.

[2] Cf. Wilda, p. 269. Wilda (p. 264 ff.) has termed these divisions "breaches of peace" (*causae majores*), and "breaches of law" (*causae minores*), — designations which must lead to much confusion in the lay mind. Therefore I have used other, but equivalent, terms.

[3] Wilda, p. 818; Maurer, Krit. Uebersch. III. p. 30. Expiation by payment seems to have been a common Aryan institution.

[4] For the German conceptions of *casus* and *culpa*, vide infra, pp. 295-7.

[5] Wilda, pp. 269, 270.

[6] The fact which makes this almost positively certain for Anglo-Saxon studies, is that Wilda makes many of his deductions from the Anglo-Saxon laws, and finds in them the same institutions as in Northern law (*vide* Wilda, p. 386).

position system (or the extension of the *causae minores* over those formerly *causae majores*), the prevalent class of penalties during the second stage. The *causae minores* now included by far the largest number of offences for which a fixed compensation was made; and, inasmuch as the peace was broken, as well as a damage done to the individual, a part of the sum went to the state as peace-money (*fredus*, from *frið*, and *wite* or *wette*), and another to the individual as damages (*bot*).[1] The development brought such of the *causae majores* as were least aggravated, like simple killing, under the head of *causae minores*, and permitted expiation by a payment.[2] Although this sum was at first the result of private agreement, later the state asserted the right to avert the vengeance from him who had paid, or offered to pay, the fixed sum. In the course of this second period, almost all the *causae majores*, which originally had been attended by outlawry, became expiable; except when the offender, or his kindred, refused to·make the settlement. These expiable *causae majores* differed from those offences always atoned for by a settlement in that, when the composition could not be, or was not paid, the offender laid himself open to the consequence of the old *causae majores*, — outlawry. These formed an intermediate class of *expiable causae majores*. This is the period of the folk-laws, which show an inclination to pass on to the third stage, or that of true punishments.

By the side of the *causae majores* and *minores*, or beside outlawry and compositions, there existed the third class of true punishments for particularly disgraceful crimes, to which neither outlawry nor compositions applied. While Tacitus speaks of the other offences, he mentions punishments of a different nature imposed for treason, desertion, cowardice, and adultery.[3] In these cases, the state appeared

---

[1] Tac. Germ. c. 12: "Sed et levioribus delictis pro modo poenarum equorum pecorumque numero convicti multantur. Pars multae regi vel civitati, pars ipsi qui vindicatur, vel propinquis suis exsolvitur."

[2] Apply to the question of vengeance and outlawry, *supra*, p. 268.

[3] Germ. c. 12: "Distinctio poenarum ex delicto. Proditores et transfugas arboribus suspendunt: ignavos et imbelles et corpore infames coeno ac palude, injecta insuper crate, mergunt." *Vide*, c. 21, 22.

18

not as a belligerent party against a member of society, but in a higher position, as that of castigator.[1] The number of these crimes for which originally a true punishment was inflicted gradually increased with the growth of legal conceptions. And in the few heavier *causae majores* for which no composition was allowed, the outlawry, from being a species of warfare in which the individual forces of the community were enlisted against the offender, gradually took on the character of a true punishment. The unlimited right to kill passed into a duty to catch and deliver the offender to the state. If he resisted capture, or escaped from custody, then he could as before be slain with impunity ; so that, although vengeance now began to be confined within narrow

---

[1] Tacitus, in his account of the German criminal system, has chronicled the existence of the means of *composition* as well as the public *punishments ;* but, strangely enough, made no mention of *outlawry* (cf. Wilda, p. 267, Köstlin, p. 72). This has led to the discussion of the question of the public punishments. Wilda is staggered by the omission of Tacitus, and does not boldly state whether he regards these cases as true punishments, or not; but inclines to the former (p. 267). Köstlin holds that they were not, and sums up his conclusions as follows: "Each crime is a breach of the peace, and by law is attended by outlawry. The consequence of this outlawry, in regard to offences which were committed directly against the community, is that which, in Tacitus, appears as public punishments ; in regard to other offences, the doer was given up to the vengeance of the injured kindred, in case the injured party or his legal representative did not prefer to sue for the compensation (busse). According to Tacitus, private crimes in general belong to this class, while the Northern laws made many of them inexpiable. In every case, private crimes only are expiable, not those committed against the community itself. If suit be brought for the compensation, the community decides; if the condemned refuse payment of the composition, then again outlawry befell him, so that he could be slain by any one without compensation ; and the same befell his companions bound to security in case they did not execute their obligation " (pp. 73, 74). Köstlin has tried to show that the above cases were a manifestation of the community, acting as an avenger (for which he can draw no support from his references to Wilda); and that the Germans had no conception of crime or delict in the modern sense. He argues that Tacitus saw in these cases the acts of the state as an " avenger ; " and, as a Roman, saw in them only true punishments (p. 72). But why is it not as fair on the other hand, admitting the existence of outlawry in his day, to suppose that Tacitus saw its exercise, and, as a Roman, could not see in it any thing but a true punishment, and, therefore, classed it with the actual cases of true punishment which he found ; finding, consequently, no reason to mention outlawry ? Maurer (p. 33) holds that the cases in question were true punishments, and finds support in so good an authority as Walter.

bounds, it was not yet extinct. The same progress, in order to better adapt the penalty to the crime, also converted the outlawry imposed for the less aggravated offences into perpetual or even temporary banishment; and the offender's life was forfeit only if he did not quit the country, or returned before his term expired. Then, at a time before this change in the outlawry was fully completed, the compositions assumed a position under the system of true punishments, and the violated peace was bought of the magistrate or king.

The Anglo-Saxon criminal system was still in the midst of the transition. Outlawry and vengeance appeared in Anglo-Saxon law, but in a limited form ; and the private composition still excluded public punishment. While true punishment had also obtained a foothold in the law. But while the ban of outlawry was originally the consequence of all great crimes, it now appeared among the Anglo-Saxons rather as an exceptional and last means of coercion. Maurer has clearly shown that outlawry was only allowed, as an external means of necessity, against the criminal who stubbornly opposed the usual course of the law.[1] And, therefore, vengeance was confined within the bounds set by outlawry ; for the state tried to enforce the rule that no one could proceed to self-help who had not first sought satisfaction in the regular way.[2] Even the thief caught in the act, whose life was always forfeit, could not be killed unless he opposed his production before the court.[3] He must be bound and taken to

[1] Alfr. 1; Edw. and Guth. 6; Æthelst. II. 20; Edg. III. 7; Æthelr. I. 1, 9, V. 31, VI. 38; Cn. II. 30, 33, 48; &c.

[2] *Vide supra*, p. 264.

[3] He had committed a crime by which he forfeited his life, or could, under the limitation of vengeance by compositions, pay the value of that life, or his wergeld : —

Ine, 12: " Si fur capiatur, mortem patiatur *vel vitam suam weregildo suo redimat.*"

And his slayer could be brought to account, if he did not give the thief an opportunity to buy off his life, and slew him before he attempted to fly : —

Ine, 28, § 1 : " Si repugnet vel aufugiat (*i.e.*, not before), *reus sit witae.*

Ine, 35 (Pr.) : " Qui furem occiderit, licet ei probare jurejurando, quod *eum fugientem* pro fure *occidit.*"

The laws show, therefore, that, if the slayer could not make oath that he

prison, and only if he tried to defend himself, or to escape, might he be slain : [1]—

ÆTHELST. II. 1, § 2: "Si velit se defendere, vel aufugare, tunc ei *postea* non parcatur." § 3: "Si fur ponatur in carcere, sit ibi XL noctibus, et inde redimatur foras per CXX sol., et eat cognatio eius in plegium, quod deinceps se abstineat."

Again, while a thief might thus be slain, and the act went unpunished, Anglo-Saxon law prescribed certain penalties against him who slew another in self-defence : —

HENR. 80, § 7: "Si quis in domo vel in curia regis fecerit homicidium vel hominiplagium, de membris componat. Et domum regis vel curiam hoc loco dicimus ubicunque in regione sua sit, cujuscunque feodum vel mansio sit. Si quis tamen legitimas coactionis testes habeat, vel Dei judicium offerat, quod *se defendendo* fecerit, Dei rectum ut *emendare* liceat.

It cannot be explained here that the compensation must be made because of a breach of a special peace, since the act *se defendendo* did not go without a fine in later English law.[2] For a solution of the difficulty, Von Bar[3] points to the fact

slew the thief trying to escape, he had no defence, and must pay the thief's wergeld. Cf. also Æthelst. VI. (Jud. Civ. Lond.) I, § 1: "Ut non parcatur alicui latroni supra XII annos et supra XII den., *de quo vere fuerit inquisitum, quod reus sit* et ad negationem aliquam non possit." — § 4: "Et fur, qui saepe forisfactus erit aperte, et ad ordalium vadat et reus appareat, occidatur, *nisi tribus sua vel dominus velit eum redimere secundum weram suam et pleno ceapgildo,* et plegiare, quod semper in reliquum cesset a malo."

Cf. Lex Angl. et. Wer. (Merkel) II. 5: "Homo in furto occisus nonsolvatur. Sed si proximus eius dixerit *innocentem occisum,* —— [let the slayer swear] 12 hominum sacramento furem credi *juste occisum.*"

[1] Cf. also the procedure of the Lex Salica: "At the same time that he uttered the hue and cry, the injured party seized him, and forthwith drew him, using force if necessary, before the court. If the court was not in session, the community immediately assembled, in order to judge the flagrant crime." (Sohm, p. 86, 87).

[2] Statut. Glocester, 6 Ed. I., 1278, c. 7: "Pourvu est ensement que nul brief ne issera desormais de la chancerie pour mort d'homme d'enquirer, si homme occist autre par misaventure ou *soi defendant* ou en autre maniere sans felony, mais celui soit *en prison* jusque à la venue des justices eyrans ou assigné à gaol deliverie, et se mit en pays devant eux de bien et de mal. Et si soi trouve par pays, qu'il le fist *soi defendant* ou par misaventure, donc fera les justices assavoir au Roi et le Roi lui en fera sa grace s'il lui plait."

[3] V. Bar. Beweisur. p. 72, ff.

that the German procedure awarded the proof according as the presumption, on *prima facie* evidence, leaned to one or the other party. If the slayer admitted the killing, and could assert that otherwise the slain would have committed a heavy crime, he went unpunished ; but if he admitted he had a dispute with the slain, and a combat thence arose, — this is *defensio* in the old laws, — it was probable that the killing, although not intentional, was culpable. It was possible that the slain might be innocent; but this could only be established by such an examination into the circumstances of the act as was unknown to the old procedure. Therefore German law assumed a *praesumptio juris et de jure* against the slayer, and presupposed a possible *culpa* of the slayer, in that he might have transgressed the bounds of strict self-defence. It is under such a principle as this, that, in English law, until a recent date,[1] while killing in order to prevent a great crime went unpunished, killing *se defendendo* was only in a measure excusable ; since the law presumed that whoever killed another in a contest was not wholly guiltless. So when Blackstone[2] recorded a punishment in this case to be the payment of an amount of property, in Anglo-Saxon law it was the payment of the wergeld.[3]

In Anglo-Saxon law, therefore, outlawry had given way partly to the system of compositions, and partly to the theory of true punishments. To the first corresponded expiable ("botwyrðe"), to the second inexpiable ("botleas") crimes, of which the former occurred most frequently in the earlier, the latter in the later, laws. As time passed, more civilized conceptions arose as to wrongs against society, and the energies of the state were directed more and more to the repression of crime and the punishment of the offenders. In

[1] *Vide* 9 Geo. IV. c. 31, § 10.   [2] IV. p. 184–188.
[3] The Sachsenspiegel (II. 14) gives a case, where if the slayer could not remain, as was required, with the dead body, nor bring the body before the court, he must pay the wette to the magistrate, and the wergeld to the relatives. In the Richtsteig Landrechts, if the slayer convicted the slain of a breach of peace, he need not pay the wergeld (V. Bar. p. 82). The above doctrine is evidently consistent with the killing of a thief caught in the act: if he was slain *as a thief*, the killing was justifiable ; otherwise not.

crimes of an especially serious nature, or those which had become too frequent, not even a compensation was allowed to be paid by the wrong-doer; and the state itself inflicted summary punishment. From the time of Alfred, the offences multiply for which no compensation could be received; and even crimes for which compensation could be received were also threatened with punishment, and thus became conditionally expiable at the will of the king.

Apart from the indemnification ("ceapgild") and the information-money ("meldfeoh"), in crimes expiated by compositions there was a double payment, one to the injured party, and another to the state. The first part of the "bot"[1] (from the root meaning to *better*) was intended to repair the wrong inflicted on an opponent, and, seeming to be an indemnification for honor, health, and such injuries as bore no market value,[2] implied a confession of the wrong done, and was, in fact, termed "satisfactio" by Tacitus; the second part was known as "wite,"[3] and was the purchase-money for the forfeited folk-peace in the old sense, the equivalent of "lahcop"[4] (law purchase). And since the king, under the Anglo-Saxon kingship, represented the old folk-peace, to him

---

[1] The comparative study of the German codes gives the following result in regard to fines:—

(1) The older the law, the more simple the system of payments. But in time they all became more complex; the sums paid instead of outlawry introduced a new series of amounts; and the old amounts were divided and multiplied in order to adapt them to the gravity of the offence.

(2) The amount of the wergeld formed a new basis of computation, and sometimes crowded out the older system.

(3) The payments gradually assumed more and more the character of punishments, often driving out all conception of a peace-money. .

(4) In some offences, as theft, the payment depended on the worth of the thing; and, therefore, always varied in amount (Wilda, p. 322, ff.).

[2] Wilda, pp. 314, 315.

[3] "Wite" meaning punishment, as Maurer points out (p. 45), was found in Norwegian, Icelandic, Swedish, and Danish, as well as Anglo-Saxon law. He has opened a question of derivation, whether "wite" originally meant "punishment," and afterward came to mean the fine inflicted as punishment; or whether it was originally the "peace money," and later took on the meaning of punishment, because the sum was so intended?

[4] Æthelr. III. 3. Cf. also (III. 8), "bicge lah," and (II. 1, Pr) "friŏ gebicgean."

usually went the *wite ;* but for some minor crimes to the hundred, or lord who had *sacu* and *socn.*

The basis of the *bot* made to the injured party in *causae minores* and expiable *causae majores,* was the "mund,"[1] or "mund byrd." The word meant the protection conferred by any one, and the peace he enjoyed ; and the "mund-bryce" was the sum to be paid for injury to this peace and protection. The amount of the "mund-bryce" varied with the rank of the person, and the gravity of the offence. In the Kentish laws the *bot* for the ceorl, eorl, and king were 6, 12, and 50 shillings respectively ;[2] but these were subsequently changed in amount and proportion.[3] Alfred[4] fixed the king's "borhbryce" or "mund-bryce" at five pounds (240 sh.), and the king's "burg bryce" (burgi infractura, invasio mansionis) at 120 shillings, and thus they remained from that time.[5] One of the expiable *causae majores* was simple killing, for which the *bot* to be paid was technically called *wergyld* (*leodgyld,* or *wer* and *leod* in short), varying according to the rank[6] of the slain, and including even the price of the king's life. The wergeld for the common freeman was 200 shillings in Wessex and Kent;[7] and in Mercia[8] and North-

---

[1] The equivalent in Northern law was "rettr" (Wilda, p. 854).

[2] Æthelbt. 5, 8, 13, 15; Withr. 2.

[3] The changes in the different ranks of society make it impossible to give an orderly statement of the various sums; while, in addition, each stem in England had a different system. But the duodecimal system (6, 12, &c.) continued to exist by the side of a decimal system (5, 10, 80, &c.) from Alfred's time.

[4] Alfr. 3, 40; *vide* Henr. 34, § 3, 76, § 4 (cf. Ine, 45). The pound contained 48 (or 50 in large payments, to cover worn coins) shillings, of five pennies each. The pound of 20 shillings of 12 pennies each was adopted after the Conquest.

[5] Æthelr. VIII. 11; Cn. II. 58.

[6] The primary division was into *Twy-, Six-,* and *Twelfhyndesmen,* whose wer was respectively 2, 6, and 12 hundred shillings. But the wer of the first or common freeman, was not 200 shillings throughout all England, as Wilda states (p. 408). To the time of Ine, the common freeman, *ceorl,* was simply opposed to the *eorl.* But the higher classes were known by either of the terms *eorl, gesith, thegen,* in opposition to ceorl, without positive distinctions. But *ealdorman* gained a higher station, and was a twelfhyndesman. In Cnut's time the ceorls had been depressed, and were termed *illiberales* (Cn. III. 21, &c.).

[7] *Vide* Maurer, p. 48, n. 1, who disproves Kemble's estimate of 180 shillings.

[8] *i.e.,* 200 Mercian shillings, or about 160 West-Saxon shillings.

umbria, 160 West Saxon shillings. For the king's thane, in Wessex and Northumbria 1,200, in Mercia 960,[1] West-Saxon shillings; for the eorl in Kent 600. For the ealdorman[2] in Northumbria[3] 4,800 West Saxon shillings. The king's wergeld in Wessex stood in relation to the common freeman, 60 : 1; in Mercia, 72 : 1; in Northumbria, 112 : 1; but in the Kentish codes there is no mention of the king's wergeld. One part of the king's wergeld was paid to his own kinsmen, and another part (*cynegeld*) to the people.[4] A constituent part of the wergeld was the "healsfang" paid to the nearest of kin.[5] "Faeðbot" and "maegbot" were equivalent[6] words, and only the synonyms of wergeld.

The peace-money, or payment for breach of the public peace, was termed "wite," and was in its narrowest sense the equivalent of the "lahslit" of the Danes in England. The offender thereby bought back his position in the broken folk-peace, so that he could now make *bot* for the wrong to the injured party (mid þam hine sylfne *inlagige tô bôte*[7]). The Kentish laws fixed this fine at 30 shillings,[8] but it was changed according to the rank of the injured person,[9] or the doer,[10] and according to the gravity of the crime. For in theft, the worth of the stolen goods influenced the "wite."[11]

---

[1] *i.e.* 1200 Mercia shillings.   [2] cf. Stubbs, I. p. 152 ff.

[3] Although of different sums, the Northumbrians retained the relative amounts of the twy-, six-, and twelfhyndesmen, in the wer of the ceorl (666 thrymsen), lesser thane (2,000 thry.), and king's thane (4,000 thry.). *Vide* Wilda, p. 412. Cf. Maurer, p. 48, ff. Schmid, Gloss. pp. 687, 675, seems to think that these were not Northumbrian but Norfolk wers.

[4] Anh. VII. 2, § 1.

[5] Cn. III. 14: . . . "et pro culpa solvat regi *decem solidos*, quos Dani vocant Halfehang, alias Halsehang." Cf. Will. I. 9. But it was usually 1-10 of the wer. *Vide* Schmid, p. 608, and Wilda, p. 415. The office of this amount, and the reason of its position first in the order of payments, making up the wer, was that, because given to the immediate kin, it precluded from vengeance those most ready to avenge. It prevented also an appearance at the court, and, like the Norwegian "skovkaup," must be paid before the remaining wer; and acted as a permission to make further expiation. Also *vide supra*, pp. 128, 144.

[6] Ine, 74, § 2; Æthelr. VIII. 23, 24. *Vide* also Wilda, p. 388.

[7] Æthelr. VIII. 2.

[8] Ine, 6, § 3. The *lahslit* was 86 shillings. Edw. & Guth. 3, 7; Cn. II. 15.

[9] Ine, 6.   [10] Æthelr. VI. 52.

[11] Alfr. 9, § 1, &c.

Another form of " wite " appeared in cases of slaying as the
" manbot " and " fyhtwîte."[1] These payments were always
required,[2] and were probably the divisions of the " mund-
bryce ; "[3] the " manbot " belonged to the lord[4] independent
of his rights of sacu ; while the " fyhtwîte " went to the
king, or to a lord by special grant of jurisdiction, and appears
as belonging to the king's right of reservation.[5] These payments varied with the wergeld, but were usually 30 shillings
for a twyhyndesman.[6] Another payment of 120 shillings
(the same as his " burgbryce ") was the " oferhyrnes," or
" oferseunesse," made for a breach of the king's personal
peace ; but, from its original meaning as a private fine of the
king, it came to be used in the sense of a punishment for
disregard of different state commands, such as disobedience
to a summons of the court. In practice, however, no rule can
be laid down as to the amount of the peace-money, since it
was usually settled by agreement with the accused. The
expiation by money was but gradually taking the place of
the old outlawry, and, under the growing theory of punishments, the state only as an act of grace allowed composition
to the accused.

While Anglo-Saxon law has clearly distinguished between
expiable and inexpiable crimes, it must be understood that
the king always possessed an unlimited power of pardon ;[7]
although the exercise of this power was to be understood as
exceptional. So that, in one sense, no crime was absolutely
inexpiable. In cases where a criminal forfeited his life as a
punishment, he was sometimes allowed to pay his own wergeld to the state that his life might not be taken,[8] just as

---

[1] Maurer (p. 50) holds that these were the component parts of the old
" drihtinbeâh " (Æthelb. 6), or lord-ring, the equivalent of the Norwegian
" lögbaugr."

[2] Edm. II. 8. [3] *Vide* Wilda, p. 454.

[4] Ine, 70, 76 ; Cn. I. 2 ; Henr. 48, § 6, &c.

[5] Cn. II. 15, cf. Schmid, p. 629. [6] Ine, 70 (Pr.).

[7] Cn. II. 13 : . . . " wealde se coninge þæs friðes." Ine, 86, § 1 : . . . " nisi ei
rex parcere velit." Alfred (Einl. 49, § 7) declared treachery to a lord to be
inexpiable, but pardon was reserved by Edgar (III. 7).

[8] Æthelr. VIII. 2 ; Cn. II. 62.

formerly payment was made to escape outlawry. Such punishments as death, and cutting off the hand,[1] could be paid
for by the offender's wer; slander, which forfeited the tongue,
by half the wer.[2] " And be it in the king's doom whether
he shall or shall not have life."[3] In this way, the many punishments to life, body, freedom, property and honor,[4] might
be forgiven by the king.

Outlawry and compositions did not apply to a slave, who
was made to suffer with his skin, castration, hanging, stoning,
branding,[5] and like penalties, for his crime.   No composition
could be exacted, since his lord would be effected thereby.

It is now easy to understand the summary of offences in : —

HENR. 12, § 1: " Ex his placitis quaedam emendantur C solidis
[*i.e.*, 240 old shillings, the equivalent of the borgbryce],[6] quaedam
wera, quaedam wita, quaedam non possunt emendari, quae sunt: hus-
breche,[7] et bernet, et openthifthe, et eberemorþ, et hlafordswike, et
infractio pacis ecclesiae vel manus regis per homicidium [also add
witchcraft [8] and counterfeiting [9]].

§ 2: " Haec emendantur C solidis: griþebreche, stretbreche, fore-
stel,[10] burchbreche,[11] hamsokna,[12] flymonfirma.[13]

§ 3: " Haec emendantur wera, si ad emendationem veniat: qui in
ecclesia fecerit homicidium: persolutio furti vel robariae ;[14] qui furem
plegiatum amiserit; qui ei obviaverit, et gratis sine vociferatione di-
miserit; qui ei consentiet in aliquo; homicidium wera solvatur, vel
weralada negetur ; si uxoratus homo fornicatur ;[15] qui viduam duxerit

---

[1] Alfr. 6.   [2] Cn. II. 36.   [3] Ine, 6 (Pr.).
[4] For the possible punishments *vide* Schmid, p. 656. Also cf. Charter No. 29,
Appendix.
[5] Ine, 3, § 1; Alfr. 25, § 1; Ine, 24 (Pr.) ; Æthelst. IV. 6, § 5; Cn. II. 32.
[6] Cf. Henr. 35, § 2.
[7] Cf. Cn. II. 64, for housebreaking, arson, open theft and killing, and dis-
loyalty to one's lord.
[8] Æthelst. II. 6 ; Cn. II. 4, Cod. Dip. DXCI (App. No. 20).
[9] Æthelr. III. 8.
[10] Æthelr. V. 31.   [11] *i.e.*, burhbryce, cf. Henr. 10, § 1.
[12] A less crime than housebreaking, of a similar kind.
[13] Harboring an outlaw, cf. Æthelst. II. 20, § 8; V. (Pr.) § 3; Edm. II. 1,
§ 2; Cod. Dip. DCCXIV, DCCXIX, MCCCIV.
[14] Henr. 83, § 4; Anh. XV.; Æthelr. VIII. 4; Cn. II. 47, &c. Cf. Henr. 59,
§ 21.
[15] Cf. Cn. II. 54.

ante unum annum; qui in hostico, vel familia regis pacem fregerit, si ad emendandum venire poterit; si praepositus pro firmae adjutorio witam exigat [1] [also add rape [2] and kidnapping [3]]."

Having stated the Anglo-Saxon system of fines and punishments, it is now necessary to unfold the actual course of the procedure in which these were employed. The hundred courts were competent to judge only of the minor offences; treason, cases of outlawry, theft punished by death, secret killing, counterfeiting, arson, hamsocn, resistance to law, harboring outlaws, premeditated assault, injury to the highway, &c., belonged to the jurisdiction of the higher courts.[4]

Unlike the action of movables, the criminal procedure was begun before the court,[5] and the *Anefang* of movables found no corresponding act in criminal law; but in both it was the individual who put the judicial machinery in motion, and himself summoned the defendant. The action was brought to compel the defendant either to make compensation or clear himself of the charge. If it were a case of homicide, the defendant must give pledge to pay the wer; but, if he refused, his contumacy was met by outlawry and the use of private vengeance. The plaintiff must summon the accused three times in the presence of good witnesses to appear before the court,[6] a formula corresponding to the *mannitio* of the Lex Salica (c. 49): —

HENR. 82, § 1: "In omni causa, si quis inimicum residentem habeat, non ante impugnet eum, *quam ipsum ter et per bonos testes de recto requirat.*"

WILL. I. 47: "Si quis malam habens famam et de infidelitate rectatus *tertio vocatus* non compareat."

HENR. 41, § 2: "Qui residens est ad domum suam, *submoniri debet de quolibet placito cum testibus*, et si domi est, eidem dicatur, vel dapifero, vel denique familiae suae liberae denunciatur."[7]

---

[1] It should be added that false imprisonment (Will. I. 4), wounding (Will. I. 10), and trespass (Cn. II. 80; Henr. 17), were expiable.

[2] Cn. II. 52.   [3] Ine, 11; Alfr. (Einl.) 15.

[4] Henr. 10, § 1.   [5] Cf. Sohm, Procéd. de L. Sal. p. 79.

[6] *Vide supra*, p. 192, for the usual form, which corresponds closely to the *solem collocare* of the Lex Salica.

[7] Henr. 42, § 2: — "Et idem coram testibus suscepit, ut negari non possit."

It was one of the fundamental personal rights accorded by German law[1] that the accused should have a term in which to reply and prepare his proof, and thereby the defendant was permitted at least seven days before the assembling of the court, as usual in the movables procedure and actions brought before the shire court : —

HENR. 7, § 4: "Debet autem scyresmot et burgemot bis, hundreta vel wapentagia duodocies in anno congregari, *et sex* [*septem*[2]] *diebus ante summoniri*, nisi publicum commodum vel dominica regis necessitas terminum praeveniat."

After this extrajudicial summons, the defendant was required to make his appearance, unless detained by a legal essoin.[3] The accused must answer because of the force residing in the formal summons made by the plaintiff, since a refusal given to the plaintiff's demand was punished the third time by the fine of the king's "overseunesse" (120 shillings). That is, the act of the individual who made the summons was regarded as a constituent part of the procedure, and disregard of it entailed a heavy fine : —

ÆTHELST. II. 20 (Pr.): Si quis gemotum, id est publicum comitum, *adire supersederit ter, emendet overhyrnessam*, id est subauditionem regis, si placitum ipsum VII diebus praenunciatum sit."

But the penalty against a delinquent might be turned against the claimant, who did not appear to substantiate his charge ; the rigor of the law, acting, as Sohm has said, like a two-edged sword. In a case where charges were made that a thief was wrongly slain is found this provision :[4] —

ÆTHELST. II. 11: . . . "and if the kindred of the dead are not willing to come again to the appointed term, *let each one who before made the charge pay* 120 *shillings* [*i.e.*, the 'overseunesse '].[5]"

In fact the provisions against unjust accusations in Anglo-Saxon law, were many and severe.[6]

---

[1] Siegel, Gesch. des Deutsch. Ger., p. 58.

[2] The correctness of the number "septem," of which there is no doubt, is shown by Henr. 41, § 2 ; 46, § 1; 51, § 2, and other passages.

[3] *Vide supra*, p. 196.

[4] Cf. Henr. 74, § 2.

[5] The remainder of the section is quoted infra, p. 287.

[6] Cf. Edw. I. 1, § 5, and similar passages.

It will be necessary here to note a peculiar case, arising from the use of vengeance. All German codes regarded theft as a heinous crime, and it has been the subject of many laws which provided that the thief caught in the act could be immediately seized and imprisoned; or, if he resisted, killed. As before said, the common requisite in the use of vengeance was publicity, and this, therefore, gave rise to the necessity of the hue and cry[1] (*clamor*) in pursuit of a thief:

WILL. I. 4: "Si quis latronem sive furem, *sine clamore* et insecutione eius, cui dampnum factum est, *ceperit, et captum ultra duxerit, dabit X solid. de henwite*, et ad primam divisam faciet de eo justitiam."[2]

Such offenders, if caught in the act, had no right to the usual term in which to answer, and could be imprisoned immediately.[3] This procedure is shown by the passage just quoted, where, too, a fine of 10 sol. was imposed for a wrong use of the *ligare* ("henwite"). Like the summons, the *ligare* was an extrajudicial means of bringing the offender before the court. If no resistance were made to the seizure, the accused necessarily made his appearance, and the procedure took its regular course. He might then go to the proof and make denial: —

INE, 28 (Pr.): "Qui furem ceperit, habeat inde X sol, et rex ipsum furem, et parentes ejus abjurent ei factionem." § 1: "Si repugnet vel aufugiat, reus sit witae." § 2: "*Si negare velit, abneget secundum modum pecuniae et witae.*"

Or, if he confessed, and was condemned, he must pay his wergeld, or forfeit his life: —

INE, 12: "Si fur capiatur, mortem patiatur vel vitam suam weregildo suo redimat."

WITHR. 26: "If any one seize a freeman in the very deed, then let the king have power over three things: whether he be slain, or sold over the sea, or free himself with his wergeld."[4]

---

[1] Sohm says that, "The cry in ancient France was called *hu, hus* (Grimm, Rechts Alt., p. 878).'

[2] Cf. Will. I. 50: "Qui clamore audito insequi supersederit, de sursisa erga regem emendet, nisi se juramento purgare potuerit."

[3] *Vide* Æthelst. II. 1, and Sohm, Procéd. de L. Sal. p. 86, ff.

[4] Cf. Henr. 59, § 23: "Si [servus] in mortificantibus handhabbenda sit, sicut liber moriatur."

But if the supposed thief fled, or offered resistance to the
ligare, as was usual from a hope of escape, he might be slain
on the spot. The aim of the subsequent procedure was to
save payment of the thief's wergeld by the slayer;[1] to justify
his use of summary vengeance: —

INE, 16: "Qui furem occiderit, *debet inveritare cum juramento, quod
illum culpabilem* et de vita forisfactum *occidisset*, et *non solvat.*"

INE, 21: "If any one claim the wergeld of a slain man, he (slayer)
may prove that he killed him as a thief;[2] the kindred or lord of the
slain are not admitted to the proof."[3]   § 1: "If he conceal the deed,
and afterward it become known, then the way to the oath is open to
the slain man, so that his kindred may purge him."[4]

The claim *ex delicto* had been already satisfied by the death
of the offender.[5]

It will be necessary now to continue the regular course of
the procedure before the court, with both parties present.
There was first the *litis contestatio*, consisting of the solemn
charge by the claimant and the confession or denial of the
accused, followed by the judgment. The judgment separated
the *litis contestatio* from the proof. The procedure at the
first assize was closed by the judgment; the proof was given
at a second assize: —

HLOTH. and EAD. 10: . . . "so let the man [defendant], if the matter was adjudged, do the other his right in seven days, *be it in property or through an oath.*"

This shows, then, that the proof went on at a term subsequent to that in which the judgment was given.[6]

---

[1] Sohm (p. 88) has well shown that the procedure did not aim at a pursuit of
the delict committed by the thief, but at disculpation by the slayer.

[2] In Ine 85, he swore that he killed him "fugientem."

[3] Cf. the Latin text: . . . "et non solvatur ipsius occisi congildonibus vel
domino suo."

[4] Æthelst. II. 11: "Dictum est de illo, qui culpam exigit pro fure occiso, ut
eat se tertio, et duo sint de cognatione vel tribu patris, tertius de cognatione
matris, et jurent, quod in cognato suo nullum furtum erat pro quo vitae suae
reus esset; et cant alii cum XII, et superjurent eum in contaminationem, sicut
ante dicebatur."

[5] Sohm, p. 89.

[6] Cf. Lex Alam. 86, § 3: "In *uno* enim *placito* mallet causam suam: in
secundo si vult jurare, *juret* secundum constitutam legem. Et in primo mallo

The procedure was begun by the fore-oath of the plaintiff, who thus declared his *bona fides* in solemn form;[1] but, like the fore-oath sworn in the *Anefang* of the movables procedure, it did not act as proof. It prevented malicious men from making false and baseless accusations, and required that the existence of a real offence should be shown as a base for further proceedings.[2] Employed not only in civil but criminal actions, in both the fore-oath must contain the chief facts of the allegation; this was the case in the action for debt[3] and stolen property,[4] and, on the other hand, where the kindred claim the wergeld of a slain man on the ground that he was not a thief : —

Æthelst. II. 11 : " Dictum est de illo, qui culpam exigit pro fure occiso, ut eat se tertio, et duo sint de cognatione vel tribu patris, tertius de cognatione matris, et *jurent* [in the fore-oath] *quod in cognato suo nullum furtum erat pro quo vitae suae reus esset.*"

The oath given as *proof* at the second term is then described by the remainder of the section, viz. : —

" Et eant alii cum XII, et superjurent eum in contaminationem, sicut ante dicebatur."

The fore-oath, which seems to have played the same part as the obsolete " tangano " of the Lex Salica,[5] was a regular part of the procedure, never to be omitted : —

spondeat sacramentales, et fideiussores praebeat, sicut lex habet, et wadium suum donet Misso Comitis vel illi Centenario qui praeest, ut in constituto die aut legitime juret, aut si culpabilis est, componat, ut per neglectum non evadat." *Vide* also K. Maurer, Krit. Uebers. V. p. 204.

[1] Cf. Lex Baiuv. Decr. Tass. (De Pop. Leg.) VI. : ... "dicat, qui quaerit debitum : Haec mihi iniuste abstulisti, quae reddere debes, et cum tot solidis componere. Reus vero contra dicat : Non hoc abstuli, nec componere debeo. Iterata voce requisitor debiti dicat : Extendamus dexteras nostras ad iustum iudicium Dei. Et tunc manus dexteras uterque ad coelum extendat."

[2] A clear example of its nature is shown by a provision that the material evidence of a wound shown to the court dispensed with the fore-oath. Henr. 94, § 5 : " Si vulnus fiat alicui, et accusatus neget, se [defendant] sexto juret *sine praejuramento, quia sanguis et vulnus ipsum foraĕe praevenerunt.*" .

[3] *Vide supra*, p. 193, and Arch. X. 10.

[4] *Vide supra*, p. 208, and Anh. X. 2.

[5] *Vide* Sohm, p. 95.

ÆTHELST. II. 23, § 2 : "Et persequatur *omnis homo* compellatio-
nem suam praejuramento."

CN. II. 22, § 2 : "And let no fore-oath ever be omitted."[1]

The fore-oath could be sworn singly,[2] or with oath-helpers,
and had the same forms as the subsequent oath in proof; it
corresponded to this last, and was simple or triple, fractum,
non-fractum, planum or observatum, accordingly : —

CN. II. 22, § 1 : . . . "et inducatur simplex lada, *i.e.*, *purgatio*, simplici *praejuramento*, triplex lada triplici praejuramento." § 2 : "Si
taynus habeat credibilem hominem ad antejuramentum pro eo, sit.
Si non habeat, ipse taynus causam suam praejuret."[8]

In answer to the fore-oath, the accused must either confess
or deny ; he could have no positive assertions to establish by
way of exceptions, as in the procedure of movables. Then
followed the judgment.

In Roman law the judgment decided the dispute between
the litigants on the ground whether the claim was rightly
founded or not, and *after* the hearing of evidence. The German judgment, on the contrary, did not close the judicial
procedure, but was given *before* the hearing of proof. "The
former decides that the claim of the plaintiff is, or is not,
materially founded ; the latter that the claim and counter-
claim are relevant or not, from the procedural point of view.
It condemns the accused who confesses to pay the fine, or the
accused who denies, to furnish proof."[4]   So that the judgment was as a rule pronounced against the defendant. Apart
from the presiding officer of the court, the judgment was
theoretically given by the whole assembly ; but, practically,
and from convenience, often by a chosen number of "judices : "[5] —

---

[1] *Vide* Will. I. 14; Henr. 64, § 9; 66, § 8; Anh. I. 6.

[2] It seems very doubtful whether the accused also could have given a fore-
oath when we think of its nature and aim. But *vide* Schmid, p. 579, for the
very scanty authorities.

[8] Cf. Anh. V. 8.

[4] Sohm, p. 90. Cf. L. Sal., 56 : "Rachine burgii judicaverunt, ut aut ad ineo
ambularet aut fidem de composicione faceret."

[5] *Vide* North American Review, July, 1874, p. 243.

HENR. 5, § 5: "Judices sane non debent esse, nisi quos impetitus (accused) elegerii;[1] *nec prius audiatur vel judicetur, quam ipsi eligantur;* et qui electis consentire distulerit, nullus ei communicet, donec obtemparet."

Nor could it be said that this was a provision only arising from the influence of Norman law, as is shown by the earlier Anglo-Saxon laws: —

ANH. I. 3: "Postea vel coactus rectum faciat, qui antea gratis noluit. *Duodecim lahmen, i.e.,* legis homines, *debent rectum discernere* Walis et Anglis, VI Walisci et VI Anglici; et perdant omne quod suum est, si injuste judicent, vel se adlegient, quod rectius nescierunt."

ÆTHELR. III. 13: "*Et judicium stet, ubi tayni consenserint;* si dissideant, stet quod ipsi VIII dicent; et qui supervicti erunt ex eis, reddat unusquisque VI dimidias marcas."[2]

The language of the sources has no reference to a presiding officer when speaking of the "judices" and the judgment. The provision of Æthelred III. 13, moreover, has reference to the same body mentioned in Henr. 5, § 5, above; for the latter is completed by a succeeding section, as follows: —

HENR. 5, § 6: "Quodsi in judicio inter partes oriatur dissensio, de quibus certamen emerserit, *vincat sententia plurimorum*."[3]

The "judices" were taken from the "best of the county," but probably acted under the direction and advice of the presiding officer, who was supposed to be conversant with all the old customs.[4] They were under obligations to render justice, and the many provisions for clearing themselves of an unjust judgment by an oath to their ignorance proves, as a rule, their unprofessional character.[5]   An example of their

---

[1] Cf. Henr. 33, § 5: "Judices sane non debent esse nisi quos impetitus elegerit."

[2] It seems hardly necessary to resort to the explanation which Brünner (Schwurg. pp. 403, 404) has given, in order to show that it did not refer to the existence of a jury.

[3] Cf. also Henr. 31, § 2.

[4] Anh. III. 4, § 4: "Videat qui scyram tenet, ut semper sciat, quae sit antiqua terrarum institutio vel populi consuetudo."

[5] Edg. III. 3: "Et judex, qui injustum judicium judicabit alicui, det regi CXX sol., nisi jurare audeat, quod rectius nescivit, et admanniat scyrae praesul emendam illam ad manum regis." Cf. Cn. II. 15, § 1; Will. I. 13, &c.

use, as representatives of the whole body of the judicial assembly, is to be found in a case given in the Appendix (No. 32); having made an unjust judgment, they were required to purge themselves, as above, but failed.

The judgment, therefore, condemned the accused who confessed, to pay the fine, or prove his innocence. In either case he must give pledge for the fulfilment of the judgment.

The plaintiff could demand security [vadium recti] for the defendant's answer at the appointed term, and for the payment of all assessments made by the judgment.[1] The general expression " vadium recti " therefore included both the meaning of a pledge[2] " de judicio sisti " and " judicatum solvi," and played the same part in Anglo-Saxon procedure as the " judicial fides facta " of Sohm[3] in the Lex Salica. The first mention, and the character of the mortgage security, a variety of the formal contract, has been already given.[4] Its office in the procedure is described by : —

INE, 8 : " *Si quis sibi rectum roget* coram aliquo scirmanno vel alio judice *et habere non possit, et accusatus ei vadium recti dare nolit,* emendet XXX sol. et infra VII noctes faciat ei recti dignum."

HENR. 34, § 4 : " Vadium affirmandi vel contradicendi *judicium* in redditione debet dari."[5]

---

[1] *Vide* Henr. 52, § 1 (as summarized by Allen): " 1. Whoever is impleaded, at the suit of the king, by one of his judges, must give *vadium recti, i.e.,* security that he will answer the charge, and make good the damage, that may be awarded against him. 2. If he were not summoned to appear, and came not on that account, he must give the above-mentioned security, and find bail, if required. 3. But if he were legally summoned, and the day of trial fixed, he must answer without delay, if required by the judge, or lose his cause. 4. If he refuse to give the security required, after it has been three times demanded, he is guilty of *overseunessae,* and may be detained in custody till he finds bail or gives satisfaction: 'maxime si judicatum sit de vadio, si de capitalibus agatur in eo.' "

[2] *Vide* Schmid, p. 644.

[3] Procéd. de L. Sal., p. 105, ff.

[4] Hloth. & Ead. 8. *Vide supra,* pp. 190, 191.

[5] Henr. 61, § 17: " Quando autem aliquis inplacitatur sine domino suo, nisi de illis sit, in quibus statim oporteat responderi, ut de furto, de incendio, de murdro, de hamsocna, et capitalibus, terminum quaerat ac *respectum* (postponement), donec dominum suum habeat secundum rectum; et *iterum,* si opus est, *vadium det,* et plegios (bail) mittat." Cf. Will. I. 3; Henr. 61, § 5; 57, §§ 6, 7; 62, § 8.

As a formal contract, the "vadium recti" could not only be employed in the form of mortgage, but also of bail (*fidejussio, Bürgschaft*); and although the relatives of the accused were not his legal securities, it was most natural that they should undertake the pledge [1] : —

INE, 62: "When [2] a man is charged with an offence, and he is compelled to give pledge, and has not himself aught to give for pledge, then goes another man and gives his pledge for him,[3] as he may be able to arrange, on condition that he pass under his hand,[4] until he [defendant] can free himself from the pledge; but, if afterward one accuse him [defendant] again, and he is compelled to give pledge, and he who before gave pledge will not be answerable for him, and he [second plaintiff] take possession of him, so let him lose the pledge which he before gave."

If the accused fled, the pledgeor must pay the indemnification and the offender's wergeld to the king, or, as the case might be, the "wite" to whom it belonged.[5] The Mercian law gave a respite to the pledgeor of one month in which to bring the defendant to court; if he could not do so, he could swear that he did not know the defendant was a thief at the time he made the pledge and establish his *bona fides*, but was not relieved from making compensation.[6] If the accused gave this pledge, the means of satisfaction was in the hands of the plaintiff; but the accused was often a delinquent. If from inability the defendant could not give security or bail, he must go to prison : —

[1] Edw. II. 8; Æthelst. II. 8; Henr. 8, § 4.

[2] Cf. the rubric and first sentences of the Latin text: "De accusato *pro delicto* et iterum fuit accusatus. 62. Quando aliquis. . . . nec habet aliquid ad dandum ante certamen."

[3] *Vide* Alfr. 1, § 8; Æthelr. I. 1, § 7.

[4] The terms under which the defendant passed into the control of the fidejussor are given in : —

Henr. 89, § 3: "Liber qui se vadii loco in alterius potestate commiserit, et ibi constitutus dampnum aliquod cuilibet fecerit, qui eum in locum vadii suscepit, aut dampnum solvat, aut hominem in mallo productum dimittat, perdens simul debitum, propter quod eum in vadio suscepit; et qui dampnum fecit, demissus, juxta qualitatem culpae, cogatur emendare."

[5] Æthelr. III. 6; Cn. II. 30, § 6.

[6] Will. I. 3.

EDW. II. 3, § 2: "Si neutrum habeat, nec *pecuniam* suam nec alium *plegium,* tunc servetur ad judicandum."

CN. II. 35 (Pr.): "Si quis amicis destitutus vel alienigena ad tantum laborem venerit, ut plegium non habeat, in prima tihle, *i.e.,* accusatione, ponatur in carcanno, et ibi sustineat, donec ad Dei judicium eat." [1]

If, however, the accused were contumacious, he brought upon himself graver penalties, finally crowned by outlawry. Refusal three times to obey the summons, as said, was punished by the fine of the "overseunesse," and then judgment was made by the tribunal condemning the accused. The law of Æthelstan (II. 20) quoted above,[2] which treats of this procedure, gives no hint of any judgment intervening between the defaults and the seizure. But in rehearsing the same procedure of default, it is said by : —

WILL. I. 47 : "Si quis malam habens famam et de infidelitate rectatus tertio vocatus non comparet, *quarto die ostendunt summonitores tres defaltas* et adhuc summonitionem habeat, ut plegios inveniat et juri pareat. Quodsi nec sic copiam sui fecerit, *judicetur* sive vivus sive mortuus." [8]

This then shows that the plaintiff with the witnesses of the summons must prove the three separate acts of summons, which had been disregarded ; and repeat the act once again. Then judgment was declared against the absentee : —

HENR. 50 : "*Si quis* a domino vel praelato suo de nominatis placitis secundum legem inplacitatus, ad diem condictum *non venerit, omnium placitorum, de quibus nominatim inplacitabatur, incurrit emendationes,* nisi competens aliquid respectaverit."

That is, judgment was made condemning the absent defendant to pay the fine. Although there is no express mention of the judgment in this last passage, it is made in another law bearing on this very point: —

---

[1] Edw. and Guth. 8 (Pr.): "Et si quis ordinatus vel furetur, vel praelietur, vel purjuret, vel fornicetur, emendet sicut factum erit, sic weram, sic witam, sic lahslit, et erga Deum saltem emendet juxta sanctorum canonum doctrinam; *et plegium faciat inde, vel mittatur in carcere.*" Cf. Edw. and Guth. 4, § 2; Cn. III. 13 ; Henr. 65, § 5.

[2] *Supra,* p. 284.   [8] *Vide* Cn. II. 25 (Pr.).

Henr. 53, § 1 : . . . "et si de nominatis et susceptis placitis pulsa-batur, nisi competens aliquid intervenerit, *reus omnium judicetur.*"

The delinquent who still held out, and would not give satisfaction, or pay the fine of the *overseunesse*, was pursued by seizure of his property.   At this point is to be found a striking comparison with the earlier law of the Salian Franks.

The criminal procedure of the Lex Salica proved inade-quate, in that, only if the accused were willing to make the promise to fulfil the judgment, could the accuser receive any compensation through the execution ; and, if the offender fell under the ban of outlawry, it was profitless to the claimant; that is, the accused had power to decide whether the claim-ant should have satisfaction or not.   The Salian criminal procedure aimed not at procuring so many solidi for the plain-tiff, but at bringing the offender under the control of law ; so that a refusal to give satisfaction was followed not by a procedure of *execution* but. of contumacy.[1]   The Anglo-Saxon law had reached a higher development.   Outlawry was, from the growth of the theory of punishments, a last and severe means of direct coercion, which befell the recalci-trant offender ; and the procedure, instead of aiming solely, in case of a refusal to give satisfaction, at bringing the offender under the control of law, also aimed at giving the claimant pecuniary compensation.   This is the clear expres-sion of every provision relating to contumacy : —

Æthelst. II. 20, § 1 : " Si tunc [*i.e.*, after judgment against the delinquent] etiam rectum facere nolit, nec overhyrnessam reddere, *eant seniores homines omnes*, qui ad eam curiam obediunt, et *capiant quicquid habet*, et eum mittant per plegium."

Cn. II. 25 (Pr.) : . . . " videatur qui quarto placito mittantur ad eum, et inveniat tunc plegios, si possit; si non possit, exsuperetur [seized] sicut alter utrum poterit, sive vivus sive mortuus, *et capiatur omne quod habebit.*"

---

[1] Sohm, Procéd. de L. Sal. p. 122.   Sohm also says, in regard to the previous discussions on outlawry : " That which, looking from the standpoint of the composition system, is to us the procedure of contumacy, would be, looking from the standpoint of the ancient criminal system, only the execution of the primitive procedure of delict.   The *fides facta* would be necessary, in order to replace the ancient and severe execution by a new and much milder form, which aimed at recovering the fine."

HENR. 53, § 1 : " Quod si [after judgment] overseunessam dare et rectum facere renuerit, mittantur *qui de suo capiant*, et eum, si opus est, per plegium ponant. Si neque sic satisfecerit, totum quod habet amiserit, et idem capiatur, nisi plegios inveniat."

Every effort was made by which property should be found in payment of the " overseunesse " and the plaintiff's claim. If the property did not suffice, he was forced to find bail for the amount. That this was the purpose of the procedure is shown by the section of Cnut succeeding to the one just quoted : —

CN. II. 25, § 1 : "Si *solvatur repetenti capitale suum ;* reliqui habeat dominus ejus dimidium, hundretus dimidium." [1]

That the procedure of contumacy in Anglo-Saxon law aimed also at rendering satisfaction to the accuser, there can be no doubt. Further contumacy and resistance to the law, as before laid down, could be met by summary punishment : —

ÆTHELST. II. 20, § 5 : " Si plegium non habeat, idem capiatur."
— § 6 : " Si repugnet, *occidatur*, nisi aufugiet."
HENR. 53, § 1 : " Si repugnet et cogatur, *occidatur*."

Flight, then, forfeited all right to protection, and he became *ipso facto* an outlaw : —

ÆTHELST. II. 20, § 8 : " Si aufugerit, et aliquis eum interim firmabit, werae suae reus sit, nisi se possit idoneare, secundum ipsius profugi weram, *quod eum nesciebat flyman*, id est fugitivum esse."
HENR. 53, § 1 : " Si evaserit et aufugerit, *pro utlago reputetur*."

Leaving the outlaw, the procedure of proof by the accused at the second term will be now treated.

It will be necessary, first, to determine to whom the proof was awarded ; and, next, to explain the system of proof itself.

(*a*) The judgment in criminal actions having, as a rule condemned the accused either to pay, or prove his innocence,

---

[1] Cf. Cn. 33 : " Si quis homo sit, qui omni populo sit incredibilis, adeat praepositus regis et ponat eum sub plegio, qui *ad rectum habeat eum omnibus accusantibus*." § 1 : " Si plegium non habeat, occidatur et cum dampnatis mittatur ; si quis eum defendere praesumat, sint ambo unius recti digni."

Vide, also, Ine, 74, for a case of vengeance when no satisfaction could be gained from lord or kin of a slave.

the proof, therefore, on natural principles of equity, was usually awarded to the defendant. But in certain cases the plaintiff went to the proof: —

When a criminal caught in the act was pursued with the hue and cry, and brought before the court with evident marks of crime about him, the proof was awarded not to the accused, but to the accuser, who must swear with oath-helpers as to the guilt of the accused. Von Bar[1] has explained this and other cases on a principle of presumptions (*praesumptiones juris et de jure*) of the defendant's guilt, which under the circumstances seemed most probable. To allow the defendant, under solemn forms, to explain his innocence, when he was presumably guilty, was mere nonsense; and, therefore, the proof went most naturally to the plaintiff, who asserted the defendant's guilt, and whose oath was strengthened by irreproachable men. But if, on the contrary, the accused had immediately given himself up, it was the presumption from this act that he was innocent, and so he went to the proof himself.[2] In the earlier law, the possibility of a false accusation in regard to a criminal caught in the act was never considered, and it was reserved to the later German law to permit to swear, *e.g.*, that the object claimed to be stolen had been placed on his person by force; but, even in that case, the accused must not have kept the object concealed, that his neighbors might have no reason to suspect his truth.

Against Köstlin and others, Von Bar has shown that German law did conceive of the Roman distinctions of *casus* and *culpa*.[3] That one should be held always answerable for injuries inflicted by what might be in itself a meritorious act, was a principle too barbarous even for the rude ideas of justice among the ancient Germans; but still the doer was in many cases forced to make compensation for such an act. Where was the line to be drawn? Had the doer exercised that due care which would be expected of an intelligent man, he was free from *culpa;* and this was decided according to the probabilities of *casus* or *culpa* in the act.

---

[1] Beweisurtheil des germ. Proc. pp. 58–92.
[2] The oath was then sworn as in Ine, 28, § 2.'   [3] p. 64, ff.

(1) If the injury happened from the disobedience of certain fixed police regulations, the doer was held responsible: —

INE, 40 : " Ceorles weorðig, *i.e.* rustici *curtillum, debet esse clausum* aestate simul et hyeme. *Si disclausum sit,* et introeat alicujus vicini sui capitale per suum apertum, *nihil inde recipiat,* sed educat et patiatur dampnum suum."

The owner of the cattle could not be held for damages, inasmuch as the cattle would have inflicted no injury had the close been properly protected, and no *culpa* could be shown. Likewise, if a meadow held in common had been left open by some of the parties, these must indemnify the others, if cattle came in and inflicted any damage.[1] But if the meadow had been properly protected, and cattle had broken through the hedge, the owner of the cattle must be held responsible for their dangerous habits: —

INE, 42, § 1 : " Si vero sit animal, quod sepes frangat, et quolibet introeat, et dominus, cujus animal est, nolit ipsum custodire, vel non possit, capiat hoc in cujus acra obviabit, et occidat, et recipiat agenfriga corium ejus et carnem, et patiatur de cetero." [2]

Also, if strange swine were found in another's mast, indemnification was immediately taken by seizure of the swine.[3]

(2) Acts not forbidden in themselves, but possibly dangerous, such as shooting a weapon or driving a wagon, must be accompanied with the necessary care, to be determined from the nature of each special case. Inasmuch as the procedure never allowed an examination of the objective truth, the judgment in each case was assigned upon the *prima facie* presumption for or against *culpa*. And, as before explained, if there were a presumption of the defendant's

---

[1] Ine, 42 (Pr.). For other regulations, compare Ine, 29, and Alfr. 36 (Pr.) : "Inventum est etiam, si quis habeat lanceam *super humerum* suum, et homo asnasetur vel inpungatur, *solvat weram ejus sine wita*." § 1 : "Si *ante oculos* asnaset, *reddat werame* jus, *et* si possibilitatis accusetur in eo facto, *purget se juxta modum witae*." § 2 : "Et ita *remaneat de wita*, si acutum lanceae sit altius tribus digitis quam cuspis ; si equaliter ferantur acies et cuspis, *sine culpa* reputetur."

[2] Cf. Alfr. 24. The Sachsenspiegel made the owner of a pond responsible for damages from its overflowing.

[3] Ine, 49.

culpa, the plaintiff went to the proof with oath-helpers, and simply swore to his conviction of the defendant's guilt; if not, the defendant swore[1] without oath-helpers. Where intention was charged against the defendant, the stronger guaranty of oath-helpers was required; for while, on the one hand, a neighbor would be slow to swear in regard to a fatal accident that the accused did not act with carelessness, on the other, he could easily swear that the chief-swearer, whose character was known to him, would not have intentionally struck a death blow.

(*b*) In regard to the means of proof, it has been said already that wager of battle was unknown to Anglo-Saxon law; therefore it remains to speak only of the oath and ordeal. Since the witness-oath, sworn as to what was seen with the eyes and heard with the ears, was only possible, under the peculiarities of the German procedure, within the narrowest limits, resort must be had to the oath with oath-helpers. The whole power of the oath-helpers, as seen from their designation as *conjuratores, consacramentales, compurgatores*, lay in the fact that they swore to the credibility of their chief and the purity of his oath, and that their numbers and standing strengthened his assertion.[2] This is seen from the declaration of the oath-helper, as given in: —

ANH. X. 6: " By the Lord, the oath is pure and not false, which N. swore."

Nor could any one as chief-swearer take the oath who was not of good repute, or had ever before sworn a false oath.[3] As to oath-helpers, all German codes required that they should be full-grown and irreproachable men (" getrŷwe men," " áð-wyrðe "); and from these the oath derived its strength:

HENR. 66, § 9: " xxx consacramentales habeat, quorum nullus in aliquo reculpandus sit." [4]

---

[1] *e.g.*, The owner of a house, built for him by another which had fallen upon and injured the plaintiff, went to the proof without oath-helpers.

[2] While the witnesses made oath as to the truth of the plaintiff's assertion.

[3] Edw. I. 3: "Item diximus de illis hominibus, qui perjuri fuerint, si manifestum sit, vel eis juramentum fregerit, vel overcythed fuerit, ut deinceps non sint digni juramento sed ordalio." Cf. Ine, 46; Æthelst. II. 25; Cn. II. 36.

[4] Cf. Wihtr. 23; Æthelr. III. 4; Cn. II. 30, § 7; Will. I. 14, 15; Anh. I. 1.

Rank, moreover, gave additional strength; for a thane could have the effect of six ceorls.[1]

That the oath-helpers were not necessarily taken from the kindred of the chief-swearer is proved from the use of words and numerous authorities, as well as the essence of the oath system.[2] Although the oath-helpers swore only to the purity of their chief's oath, it is known that a possibility of knowledge on the part of the co-swearer was also considered of importance.[3] Therefore, because they must also be in a position to judge of their chief's character, the oath-helpers were naturally taken from his neighbors,[4] peers,[5] or kinsmen.[6] The number[7] of oath-helpers varied according to the importance of the charge, the property in question, the nature of the crime, the amount of the *bot*, *wite*, and the *wergeld*, and the personal trust enjoyed by the swearer. In the earlier laws, the oath was reckoned on a scale of " hides," which remains quite obscure, since it afterwards totally disappeared.[8]

In Anglo-Saxon law, the chief-swearer could choose the oath-helpers;[9] but in certain cases they were " named " by the magistrate, and the swearer was allowed a choice from the whole number : —

Edw. I. § 4 : . . . "nominentur ei sex homines, . . . et adquirat ex illis sex unum pro animali,"[10] etc.

---

[1] *Vide supra*, pp. 216, 217; and Anh. VIII. 1, 2; Henr. 64, §§ 2, 3.

[2] The Anglo-Saxon expressions for oath-helpers are only *æwda*, *æwdaman*, or *midstandað*.

[3] *Vide* K. Maurer, Krit. Ueber. V. p. 204.

[4] Edw. I. 1, § 4: "Nominentur ei sex homines de eadem geburscipa, in qua ille residens est." Cf. Hloth. and Ead. 5; Æthelst. II. 9.

[5] *Vide* Wihtr. 19, 21; Alfr. and Guth. 3; Æthelr. VIII. 19, 20; Cn. I. 5 (Pr.), § 1; Anh. II. 52, 53; Henr. 64, § 2: . . . "jurabunt, congruo numero consacramentalium, et qualitate parium suorum retenta."

[6] Henr. 64, § 4: "Qui ex parte patris erunt, fracto juramento, qui ex materna cognatione erunt, plane se sacramento juratores advertant." *Vide*, also, Anh. II. 51.

[7] Anglo-Saxon laws give various numbers of oath-helpers, as : 1, 2, 3, 4, 5, 6, 12, 24, 36, 48.

[8] For a discussion of the question, *vide* Schmid, p. 564.

[9] Æthelr. I. 1, § 2; Cn. II. 30, § 7, 44.

[10] Cf. Æthelst. II. 9; Cn. II. 65; Will. I. 14, 15; Henr. 66, § 6.   The choice

The Anglo-Saxons distinguished between the " ungecoren âð," sworn with oath-helpers chosen by the swearer himself, and the " cyre-âð,"[1] sworn with oath-helpers chosen by the magistrate;[2] and Schmid has deduced the rule, that, whenever the oath must be sworn collectively, the chief-swearer had the entire selection; otherwise, the magistrate " named " them.

The force of such a medium of proof[3] is more apparent when we consider the simple and public lives of the ancient Germans, and the opportunity each enjoyed of forming a safe judgment of the character of another; that, moreover, a certain time elapsed between the assize in which judgment was rendered and the assize in which the proof must be given; and that the oath-helper might refuse to swear, if he were not satisfied of his chief's truth.   Therefore, while a witness swore to the objective truth, and must state the fact as he with his eyes saw and his ears heard, under an appeal to the Deity, whether this operated for or against his chief, the oath-helper never swore against his chief; nor could any one swear to his chief's want of truth.   Therefore, with Maurer, it is best to decide that the oath with oath-helpers was a means of proof of considerable power in that early society, and that its *raison d'être* need not be sought by Rogge,[4] Gemei-

by the magistrate and by the swearer are both combined in Anh. II. 51. But that the oath-helpers were designated by the court, *vide* Æthelr. III. 13: . . . . : "praepositus nominet ipsam ladam," and Henr. 66, § 9. Sometimes they were chosen by lot. Henr. 66, § 10.

[1] K. Maurer (Krit. Ueber. V. p. 199) holds that the "rimâð" was the equivalent of "cyre-âð;" but Schmid (p. 566) does not state clearly what the "rimâð" was.

[2] *Vide* Schmid, p. 566.

[3] Maurer, however, points out that the very reason why those· to whom the chief-swearer was best known were chosen, was an argument against the force of the proof, in that they might be led by personal motives to give a false oath in his favor. But, while we must not gauge the simple living in the early time by the distrustful measure of to-day, it must be admitted that the force of the proof varied with the standards of different times and places.

[4] The oath-helpers, as viewed by Rogge (Ueber das Gerichtswesen der Germanen), were not a means of proof, but came into existence from the right of vengeance and feud. The peace-breaker, who had the choice between paying the composition and bearing the feud, was allowed, if innocent, to present him-

ner,[1] Waitz,[2] and others, through ingenious speculations. From this point of view, it will now be easy to explain the position occupied by the ordeal in the Anglo-Saxon procedure, and the rules by which it was governed.

As the witness-proof was insufficient, and the procedure needed the oath with oath-helpers, so, when this last means of proof became inadequate, a last resort lay in the judgment of God, or the ordeal. Of heathen origin,[3] although later encrusted with ecclesiastical forms, the ordeal was held to be a means similar to an oracle, by which God, in cases which did not allow further decision, would miraculously

---

self with his comrades in the feud, and with them as oath-helpers deny the deed. The oath-helpers stood on the side of their friend, as they would have done in the feud. Against this, Maurer (1) cites Wilda to show that no such choice was allowed. That it was not a question in regard to oath-helpers as to which party could bring the greatest number of men into the field, but whether the charge was well founded or not. (2) That oath-help was found as far back as the sources go, in *civil* as well as in criminal cases; so that it could not have had such an origin there. Rogge here maintains that the criminal procedure was older, and that oath-helpers came into civil cases later; but Maurer (p. 209, ff.) shows this to be untenable, and opposed to the whole meaning of earlier law.

[1] Gemeiner (Ueber Eideshülfe und Eideshelfer des älteren deutschen Rechtes, 10 ff., 37-8) holds that the wager of battle was the original means of showing the purity of an oath. In those cases which were expiable, it had first been replaced by the oath-help; and excluded feud the more fittingly because in the wager of battle each party was originally accompanied by an attendant, who afterward became the nucleus of the oath-helpers. But feud, compositions, and oath-helpers are found side by side. L. Sax. 18 (Merkel). Moreover, there is no mention of wager of battle in Anglo-Saxon law.

[2] Waitz (Deutsche Verfass. I. 210-2, &c.) declares against Rogge, and, with better reason, asserts that oath-helpers were originally taken from the kinsmen; that, because the kin were obliged to make recompense for the offender's wrong, they had a corresponding right, in case the offender was innocent, to prove the charge was unfounded; and that the right of election, and the choice of those outside the kindred, were a later development. This origin caused the close connection which existed between the oath-helpers and the amount of the composition, as if payment were made with oaths instead of money. Maurer argues that this close connection, unfortunately for Waitz, existed in civil cases also; and therefore another explanation must be given. Moreover, there is no proof that oath-help originally coincided with kinship; while, on the contrary, although kinsmen are mentioned as oath-helpers in the Lex Salica and the earliest laws, so also are those outside the kindred. Therefore, because oath-helpers *sometimes* came from the kindred, it is not just to conclude that they could come *only* from that class.

[3] Maurer seems to have shown this fully against Wilda. Krit. Ueber. V. p. 215, ff.

assist the innocent and unveil the truth. And, when permitted, it was regarded by the person concerned as a favor; since it allowed a last, although desperate, possibility of gaining a suit already lost.[1] The three varieties of ordeal in Anglo-Saxon law were those of fire, water, and the morsel. The candidate must fast three days, and was then led by the priest to the church, where mass was celebrated.[2] Before the communion was given him, the priest urged the candidate to a confession, if he were guilty. If silent, the priest then administered the communion to him. Before the ordeal of fire or water, of which the accuser had the choice,[3] was recited the *adjuratio*.

In the ordeal of cold water, holy water was prepared by the priest before mass, and taken to the place of ordeal. Having given the holy water to the candidate to drink, the priest recited the *adjuratio*, which adjured the Deity to take the innocent within the waters, but to cast the guilty forth from them. The accused was then disrobed, kissed the Bible and crucifix, was sprinkled with holy water, and thrown into the water. If the person sank, he was innocent; if he floated, guilty.

For the ordeal of fire and hot water, the same number of men from each side shall be present in the church where the fire is lighted. These men, who must have fasted and have abstained from their wives that night, must stand on each side of the space. Into this the candidate steps, and, grasping the hot iron, carries it across the floor nine feet distant. The hand is then covered, and opened again in three days: if the wound had festered and showed bloody matter (*sanies crudescens*), the accused was guilty; if he was uninjured, his innocence was proven. For a single ordeal, the iron weighed one pound; for a three-fold ordeal, three pounds. In the ordeal of hot water, the hand was plunged into the water for a stone hanging by a rope; then the arm was covered and opened, as in the ordeal of hot iron. In a single

---

[1] Maurer, Krit. Uebersch. V. p. 215.
[2] The forms are given at great length in Anh. XVII.
[3] Æthelr. III. 6; Anh. XIII.

ordeal, the hand was only plunged in as far as the wrist; in a triple ordeal, to the elbow.[1]

The ordeal of the morsel, or "corsnæd," seems to have been most used with the clergy.[2] A morsel of bread or cheese weighing an ounce was prepared, and, after the usual forms, it was given to the candidate to swallow, if he could. The *adjuratio* exhorted the Deity to treat the guilty one as follows: —

ANH. XVII., III.: "Fac eum, domine, in visceribus angustari, ejusque guttur conclude, ut panem vel caseum istum, in tuo nomine sanctificatum, devorare non possit hic, qui injuste juravit."

If the candidate turned pale and trembled, he was held guilty.

The general rule for the use of the ordeal is contained in: —

CN. III. 11: "Sed purgatio ignis nullatenus admittatur, nisi ubi nuda veritas nequit aliter investigari."

The failure of the usual means of proof would be best illustrated by the case of a friendless stranger who had been charged with a crime. Under an accusation such that a single oath would have been impossible, having, of course, no friends who would swear to his credibility, his only escape from condemnation was through the desperate chance of an ordeal: —

CN. II. 35 (Pr.): "Si quis amicis destitutus vel alienigena ad tantum laborem venerit, ut plegium non habeat, in prima tihle, *i.e.*, accusatione, ponatur in carcanno, et ibi sustineat, donec ad Dei judicium eat."[3]

Or, in other cases, when for any reason oath-helpers failed the accused, the ordeal was his only resort: —

WILL. I. 14: "Quod si [juramentum] defecerit, et jurare cum eo noluerint, defendet se per judicium aquae vel ignis."

In fact, the ordeal was a means of strengthening an assertion when oath-helpers failed, and served the same office.[4] It

---

[1] Æthelst. II. 23, § 1.
[2] *Vide* Æthelr. VIII. 22, 24; Cn. I. 5, § 2.
[3] Cf. Cn. III. 18; Henr. 65, § 5.
[4] Schmid, p. 640.

was employed by perjured men, by those who were not " âð-
wyrðe," and those who had been " over-sworn ";[1] and if
any one had been charged with crimes of a peculiarly bad
character, as killing with burning, treason, or witchcraft.[2]
Whether a single or threefold ordeal was taken depended
on the gravity of the offence. Although forbidden by some
German codes, Anglo-Saxon law permitted the slave to go to
the ordeal.[8]

In conclusion, it is possible to find a connection between
English law and the primitive institutes of the early period
of summary execution. Vengeance existed, after the organization of society, as an instrument of the law, but in varying
forms ; since such an act must be justified, if necessary,
before a legal tribunal ; as, *e.g.*, the slaying of a thief caught
in the act. Also, such vengeance must be free from premedi-
tation and cruelty, and no concealment was allowed. But
while vengeance was justifiable killing, the opposition to its
exercise gave rise to private warfare, or feud, as here used.
The attempt was made to restrain this undue exercise of
power by the individual, by many decrees ; but they were
generally powerless during the Anglo-Saxon period. Yet
the most effectual and satisfactory result came through the
introduction of the composition system, as early as Ine and
Alfred. By the side of vengeance, and closely bound to it,
arose the institution of outlawry, founded on the fact that
German society was based on the " frið " or peace, and that
any peace-breaker became originally " peaceless," and liable
to be killed by any member of the community. In short, it
was an enlarged means of vengeance, acceptable to an arm-
bearing people like the Germans.

---

[1] *Vide* Edw. I. 3; Æthelst. II. 7; VI. 1, § 4; Æthelr. I. 1; III. 8; Cn. II.
22, § 1; 30 (Pr.); Will. I. 14; Henr. 65, § 3; 67, §§ 1, 2.

[2] Æthelst. II. 4, 5, 6, §§ 1, 2; 14, § 1; Æthelr. III. 8; IV. 5, &c. And between Englishmen and Welshmen, it was the regular means of proof (Anh. I.
2, 8). On Sundays and Feast Days it was forbidden (Edw. and G. 9; Æthelr.
V. 18; VI. 25; Cn. I. 17, &c.).

[8] Æthelst. II. 19; Æthelr. I. 2; Cn. II. 82. Women also proved their innocence by ordeal. *Vide* Ed. Conf. 19.

But these institutions were mere adaptations of private exertion, and contained no principle of punishment such as is known to the criminal system of to-day, which arose by slow development from the slightest germ. Wilda has made it probable that the earliest stage of the criminal system, as given in Northern law, was distinguished by the preponderance of outlawry: making the *causae majores*, which were attended by outlawry, the most numerous; and the *causae minores*, for which compensation only could be demanded, very few in number. The second stage, or the time of the folk-laws, showed a growth of the *causae minores*, and a consequent diminution of the *causae majores*, and was distinguished by the preponderating number of expiable offences. By the side of these two systems had existed a third, — that of true punishment, which later, in the third stage, absorbed those of the *causae majores* which had not become expiable. Outlawry and vengeance did not disappear from the criminal system; but became punishments of last resort, or only in exceptional cases. Eventually, the system of punishments extended over the composition system also.

Anglo-Saxon law was in the midst of the transition from the second to the third stage. Outlawry was the last penalty only of stubborn resistance to the law; and vengeance was possible, with a few exceptions, only after satisfaction had been asked in vain, or to prevent a crime, or when one caught in the act tried to escape; but not in *se defendendo*. The theory of compositions was fully acknowledged, and the punishments increased rapidly after Alfred's time.

Of the compositions, a part went to the injured person, and a part to the state. The special price awarded for unjust slaying to the injured persons was the wergeld, which varied in different parts of England, and for the different and complex ranks of society in each section; but the wergeld of the common freeman was equal to or somewhat less than 200 shillings.

The procedure was begun with an extrajudicial summons of the individual by the plaintiff, under solemn forms, at sunset; and the third refusal to heed this summons was punishable with the *overseunesse* of 120 shillings; and a similar penalty befell the accuser who would not continue the suit. As in the action for stolen movables, the judicial procedure began with a fore-oath, in order to prevent trivial accusations. This, with the confession or denial of the defendant, was the *litis contestatio*, and, with the judgment, completed the procedure in the first assize. A short interval elapsed in which the proof might be prepared for the second assize. But, if the condemned did not give pledge to fulfil the judgment and made default, he was followed by the procedure of contumacy; in which the one who would not find pledge, or who fled, suffered confiscation of property, and finally became an outlaw.

In the assize of proof, the defendant as a rule went to the oath with oath-helpers; but the proof was given to the plaintiff whenever the guilt of the defendant was presumably clear; as in case of a thief caught in the act, or whenever *culpa* was apparent. In *casus*, the defendant swore, and simply explained his innocence. The oath-helpers must be considered to be a real means of proof; because, although they swore to the purity of the chief-swearer's oath, they were selected from peers, neighbors, and kinsmen, in order that they might be able to judge of the character of their chief. Whenever the swearer was not oath-worthy, a perjurer, "oversworn," or friendless, or when he could not find oath-helpers, he must go to the ordeal either of fire or water; if of the clergy, to that of the morsel.

20

APPENDIX.

To Professor F. A. MARCH of Lafayette College, and to Professor F. J. CHILD of Harvard College, acknowledgment is due for essential assistance in the translation of the Anglo-Saxon Charters included in this collection.

SELECT CASES IN ANGLO-SAXON LAW.

———oo⟩⦿⟨oo———

No. 1.   NOTHHELM, 734–737.

Cod. Dip. LXXXII.

THIS is not a suit at law, but a case in which a church council regulates the right of possession to church property, and certifies to the nature of the title. Land had been granted to two women, Dunna and her daughter Bucga, for the construction of a monastery. Bucga seems to have died, leaving her mother Dunna sole proprietor. Dunna, on her own death, bequeathed all her land, including the monastery, to her grand-daughter, Hrotwar, entrusting the deeds to the possession of Hrotwar's mother, whose name is not mentioned. When Hrotwar came of age, and demanded possession of the deeds, her mother alleged that they had been stolen. Thereupon the daughter appealed to the church council, which caused a certified statement of the case to be made out and delivered to her for her protection.

———————

GLORIOSISSIMUS Mercensium rex Aethelred, cum comite suo, subregulo Huuicciorum Oshero, rogatus ab eo, terram xx cassatorum iuxta fluuium, cui uocabulum est Tillath, duabus sanctimonialibus, Dunnan uidelicet et eius filiae Bucgan, ad construendum in ea monasterium, in ius ecclesiasticum sub libera potestate, pro uenia facinorum suorum condonauit, propriaeque manus subscriptione hanc eorum donationem firmauit. Praefata autem Dei famula Dunne, constructum in prae-

———————

ÆTHELRED, most glorious king of the Mercians, with his ealdorman Oshere, under-king of the Hwicci, at his request, for the pardon of his own sins, granted twenty hides of land, near the river Tillath, to two holy women, — namely, Dunna and her daughter Bucga, — to hold in free possession, according to church right, for the purpose of constructing a monastery thereon; and he confirmed this donation by the subscription of his own hand. Now, the aforesaid servant of God,

dicto agello monasterium, cum agris suis nec non et cartulam descriptionis agri, cui tunc sola ipsa praeerat, filiae, nimirum filiae suae, in possessionem, ad dominum migratura largita est. Sed quia haec in paruula adhuc aetate erat posita, cartulam conscripti agri, necnon et omnem monasterii procurationem, quoad usque illa ad maturiorem peruenisset aetatem, matri illius maritatae conseruandam iniunxit. Quae cum cartulam reddi poposcisset, illa reddere nolens, furtu hanc sublatam respondit. Quo tandem omni negotio ad sanctam sacerdotalis concilii synodum perlato, decreuit omne uenerabile concilium, cum reuerentissimo archiepiscopo Nothelmo, hanc cartulam donationis, vel regum vel supradictae Dei famulae Dunnan, manifestissime describi, praefataeque Abbatissae Hrotuuari reddi, eiusque possessionem monasterii firmissimam esse ; damnato nimirum eo, atque anathematizato synodi sacratissimae decreto, qui cartam illam subscriptionis agri primitiuam vel per furta vel quolibet modo fraudulenter auferendo subripere praesumpserit. Atque hoc decernit sacra synodus, ut post obitum eius, sicut ante statutum fuit a senioribus eius, ad episcopalem sedem castrum Uueogernensis liber hic, cum terra, reddatur.

Dunna, being about to depart to the Lord, gave the monastery constructed on the aforesaid land, together with her own lands, and a charter descriptive of the territory over which she then had herself sole authority, to the daughter, namely, of her own daughter, as her possession. But, because she was then of immature age, Dunna entrusted to the married mother of the child the charter of the aforesaid land, and the charge of the whole monastery, until the child should come to maturer years. When she then demanded that the charter should be given up, her mother refused to surrender it, alleging that it had been stolen. All this affair having at last been brought to the holy synod of the sacerdotal council, the whole reverend council, with the most reverend Archbishop Nothelm, decreed that this deed of grant, both that of the kings and that of the aforesaid servant of God, Dunna, should be most clearly written down, and given to the aforesaid Abbess Hrotwar, and that her possession of the monastery should be the firmest possible ; at the same time declaring him who should have presumed to abstract the original charter, either by theft or by any kind of fraud, to be condemned and anathematized by the decree of the holy synod. And, further, the holy synod decreed, that, after her death, as had been formerly determined by her parents, this charter, together with the land, should be returned to the church at Worcester.

No. 2. CYNWULF, 759.

Cod. Dip. CIV.

COINRED gave land to Abbot Bectun. Bectun's successor, Catwal, sold the land to Abbot Wintran, giving him a new charter, but retaining the original charter with the signatures. Subsequently a dispute arose between the two monasteries, Wintran's being in possession of the land and the other holding the original charter. The Witan effected a compromise, and ordered a new charter to be drawn up.

. . . QUAPROPTER ego Coinredus, pro remedio animae meae et relaxacione piaculorum meorum, aliquam terrae particulam donare decreuerim uenerabili uiro Bectune abbati, id est xxx. manentes: . . . nam earumdem supradictarum cespites pro ampliori firmitate euangelium superposui, ita ut ab hac die tenendi, habendi, possidendi, in omnibus liberam et firmam habeat potestatem. . . . Successor abbatis praenominati Bectuni Catuuali nomine dedit terram supra designatam .xxx. manentium Uuintran abbati pro pecunia sua, et scripsit libellum alium donationis huius atque possessionis suprascriptae, subtraxit tamen et donationis primae litteras et subscriptiones regum, episcoporum, abbatum atque principum, quia inter caetera terrarum suarum testimonia haec eadem terrae particula conscripta non facile potuit eripi neque adhuc potest: et propterea, decedentibus primis testibus longa

---

. . . WHEREFORE, I, Coinred, for the relief of my soul and the remission of my sins, have decreed to give to the venerable Abbot Bectun a certain parcel of land, that is, thirty hides. . . . Now, for more ample confirmation, I have placed sods of the aforesaid lands upon the gospels, so that from this day he may have free and firm power in all things, of holding, having, and possessing. . . . Catwal, the successor of the aforesaid Abbot Bectun, gave the aforesaid land of thirty hides to Abbot Wintran for his money, and wrote another charter of this donation and of the aforesaid possession; but withheld the writings of the first donation, with the signatures of the kings, bishops, abbots, and chief men; because, from the other testimonies of his lands, the description of this parcel could not easily be detached, and yet cannot be. And, after the death of the first witnesses, a long

deceptatio inter familias duorum monasteriorum orta est et perseverat usque nunc: habebant autem hanc terram semper ex quo a praefato abbate primo data est Uuintran successores eius; et alterius familiae et successores primum libellum, qui manibus praedictorum testium roboratur. Iccirco ego nunc atque rex noster caeterique quorum testificatio et subscriptio infra notatur, reconciliauimus eos in pace, partim data pecunia, partim iuramento adhibito in testimonium; ut deinceps successores Uuintran abbatis, id est Eguuald et familia eius quae est in monasterio quod dicitur Tissebiri, cum licentia alterius familiae cui praeest Tidbald abbas, habeant possideantque perpetualiter terram de qua diu altercatio erat: et praesens libellum ego discripsi atque excerpsi ab illo primitus dato Bectuno abbati, concedente scilicet Tidbaldo abbate et familia eius, et dedi Eguualdo abbati, testibus infra notatis consentientibus atque confirmantibus hanc scripturam, reprobrantibus autem alia scriptura quae sunt edita de hac terra. Et haec acta sunt ab incarnatione domini nostri Ihesu Christi. DCCLVIIII. Indictione XII.

---

dispute arose between the families of the two monasteries, which has continued till now; for the successors of Wintran always retained possession of this land, from the time when it was first given to Wintran by the aforesaid abbot; and the family and successors of the other retained the first charter, which was confirmed by the hands of the aforesaid witnesses: — Therefore I, now, and our king and the others, whose witness and signature are herein contained, have reconciled them in peace; in part money being given, and in part an oath added in evidence; so that henceforth the successors of Abbot Wintran — that is, Egwald and his family, in the monastery which is called Tisbury — with the license of the other family, of which Tidbald is abbot, may have and possess in perpetuity the land so long disputed. And, with the consent of Abbot Tidbald and his family, I have drawn up and extracted the present charter from that originally given to Abbot Bectun, and have given it to Abbot Egwald; the witnesses herein named consenting to and confirming this writing, and annulling other writings which have been put forth concerning this land. And these things were done in the year 759 from the incarnation of Jesus Christ, indiction 12.

No. 3.   HEATHORED, 781.

Cod. Dip. CXLIII.

OFFA complained that the church at Worcester unjustly held land belonging to the inheritance of his kinsman, Æthelbald. A suit was brought before the Witan, ending in a compromise.

. . . QUARĖ ego Heaðoredus, deo dispensante supplex Huicciorum episcopus, insimul etiam cum consensu et consilio totius familiae meae quae est in Uuegerna ciuitate constituta, diligentissime scrutans cogitaui atque de pace uel statu aecclesiastica rimatus sum. Equidem de aliquibus agellis conflictationis quaerulam cum Offano, rege Merciorum, dominoque dilectissimo nostro habuimus. Aiebat enim nos, sine iure haereditario propinqui eius, Aeðelbaldi scilicet regis, haereditatem sub dominio iniusto habere; id est, in loco qui dicitur aet Beathum. XC. manentium, et in aliis multis locis ; hoc est, aet Stretforda XXX. cassatos ; aet Sture .XXXVIII. Simili etiam uocabulo aet Sture in Usmerum .XIIII. manentium, aet Breodune .XII. in Homtune XVII. cassatorum. Haec autem praefata contentionis causa in sinodali conciliabulo demissa in loco qui dicitur aet Bregentforda. Reddidimus quoque illo jam nominato regi Offan, monasterium illud celeberrimum aet Baþum, sine ullo contradictionis obstaculo, ad habendum, uel etiam, cui dignum duxisset, ad tribuendum ; semperque perfruendum,

---

. . . WHEREFORE I, Heathored, by the grace of God humble bishop of the Hwicci, with the advice and consent of all my family in Worcester, diligently inquiring, have meditated and pondered concerning the peace and state of the church. We have had a dispute about some lands with Offa, king of the Mercians, and our beloved lord ; for he said that we, without hereditary right, held in our unlawful possession the inheritance of his kinsman, King Æthelbald : that is, at Bath ninety hides, and in many other places ; that is, at Stratford thirty hides ; at Stour, thirty-eight hides ; also at Stour, of the same name, in Usmere, fourteen hides ; at Bredon, twelve hides ; and in Homton, seventeen hides. Now, the aforesaid cause of strife was laid before the synodal council in the place which is called Brentford. We restored to the aforesaid King Offa that well-known monastery at Bath, to have, or even to give to whomever he should think worthy, without

iustis eius haeredibus libentissime concessimus; et in australe parte
fluminis ibi iuxta quod dicitur Eafen .xxx. cassatos addidimus, quam
terram mercati sumus digno praetio a Cyneuulfo rege Uuestsaexna
Quapropter idem ille praefatus rex Offa, ad reconpensationis satisfactionem, et pro unanimitate firmissimae pacis, praefata loca aet Stretforda, aet Sture, aet Breodune, in Homtune, aet Sture in Usmerum,
extra omni controuersionis et ammonitionis causa, ea libertate, . . .
concessit . . .

dispute; and we most willingly granted it to be always'enjoyed by his
legal heirs. And on the south side of the river near by, which is called
Avon, we have added thirty hides, which we bought for a just price from
Cynwulf, king of the West Saxons. Wherefore the aforesaid King Offa,
for this consideration, and for the establishment of a firm peace, conceded the aforesaid places at Stratford, at Stour, at Bredon, in Homton, and at Stour in Usmere, free from all cause of counter-claim, to
our aforesaid church at Worcester, with this liberty.

——∘∘⊹⊕⊹∘∘——

No. 4.   HEATHORED AND WULFHEARD, 789.

Cod. Dip. CLVI.

HEMELE and Duda left their inheritance to their heirs, and, after
their death, to the church at Worcester. Wulfheard, one of the heirs,
tried to set aside this reversion, and the Bishop of Worcester brought
suit before the Witan to prevent his doing so. The Witan decided in
favor of the bishop.

———

. . . ANNO dominici incarnationis DCC°LXXX°VIIII°. indictione
vero XII⁑ qui est annus XXXi. regni offan strenuissimi Merč regis factum est pontificale conciliabulum in loco famosa qui dicitur celchyð
praesidentib: duob: arčepiš Iamberhto scilicet et Hygberhto mediante

———

. . . IN the year of our Lord's incarnation 789, indiction 12, —
which is the thirty-first year of the reign of Offa, most mighty king
of the Mercians, — an ecclesiastical council was held in the famous
place which is called Caelchyth; the two archbishops Iamberht and

quoq: offan rege cum uniuersis principibus suis; ibi inter alia plura aliqua contentio facta est inter heathoredum epiš et Wulfheardum filium Cussan de haeriditate hemeles et dudae quod post obitū suorū nominarent ad weogornacaestre, hoc est intanbeorgas et bradanlege uoluisset ergo uulfheardus illum agellulum auertere ab ecclesia praefata in weogornacaest cum ignorantiae et insipientiae si potuisset. Tunc ille episcopus illum refutabat cum his testibus qui eorum nomina infra scripta liquescunt coram synodali testimonio. Et aiebat quod ei rectum non fierat ulli alio post se tradere praeter et antedictā ciuitatem hoc est weogrinacaestor. Et propter eorum prece et amore qui illam terram adquisierunt et ad ecclesiam praefatam dedissent illi senatores familiae consentientes fuerunt ut illud custodiret et haberet diem suum. Tunc arc episc simul cum uniuersis prouincialibus episc ita finem composuerunt et reconciliauerunt. ut wulfheardus terram possideret tamdiu uiueret et postquam uiam patrum incederet sine aliqua contradictione illuc ad weogornense ecclesiae terras atq: libellus cum semetipso redderet ubi corpora requiescunt hemeles et dudae.

Hygberht presiding, King Offa also taking part with all his chief men. There, among several other disputes, was one between Heathored the bishop and Wulfheard, son of Cussa, about the inheritance of Hemele and Duda, which, after the death of their heirs, they assigned to Worcester: that is, Inkberrow and Bradley. Wulfheard wished to divert that land from the aforesaid church at Worcester, taking advantage of her ignorance, if he could. Then the bishop refuted him with these witnesses, who inscribe their names in this writing, with the witness of the synod; and said that it was not right for him to give it after himself to any other than to the aforesaid city, — that is, Worcester. And, on account of the prayer and love of those who had acquired this land, and had given it to the aforesaid church, they, the elders of that church, consented that he should keep it, and have it for his life. Then the archbishop, together with all the provincial bishops, made a composition, and reconciled them, so that Wulfheard should possess the land so long as he lived; and, after he had gone the way of his fathers, without any contradiction he should restore the land and the charter, with himself, to the church at Worcester, where rest the bodies of Hemele and Duda.

No. 5.　　　　　　Offa, 794.

Cod. Dip. CLXIV.

This is a suit brought by the Bishop of Worcester for lands, of which his church had been forcibly dispossessed. A charter of King Æthelbald was shown, and the land was adjudged to the bishop, and his rights confirmed.

. . . Contigit autem in diebus Offani regis Merciorum quod Bynna, comes regis, sustulit sine recto hanc terram aet Austan .v. manentes, quod Aeðelbald rex ante liberauit, et hoc recte pertinebat ad sedem episcopalem in Uuegrin ciuitate. Tunc fuit synodus in loco, qui dicitur Clofeshoas, anno ab incarnatione Christi .DCC.XC.IIII. regni Offani .XXXVII. anno. Tunc episcopus Heaðoredus, cum conscientia totius synodalis concilii referebat, et fiducialiter incunctanterque confirmauit cum testimonio scripturarum illarum quae Aeðelbald rex ante in aeternam libertatem suis processoribus praescripsit. Et tunc rex cum omni consilio sancti concilii consentiebat, quod episcopus praefatus salua manu accipiebat in contenditum suam propriam praenominatam terram, et hoc cum confirmatione sanctae crucis Christi omnes munierunt, ut firma et infracta permaneat in aeuum.

. . . Now, it happened in the days of Offa, king of the Mercians, that Bynna, king's ealdorman, took without right this land at Aston-magna of five hides, which King Æthelbald before freed; and this rightly belonged to the episcopal see of Worcester. There was then a synod in the place which is called Clovesho, in the year of Christ's incarnation 794, in the thirty-seventh year of the reign of Offa. Then Bishop Heathored, with the witness of the whole synod, laid the matter before them, and credibly and without delay confirmed these things with the witness of the charters [of those lands] which Æthelbald before granted to his predecessors to hold freely for ever. And then the king, with the advice of all the synod, consented that the aforesaid bishop should receive in security the aforesaid land as his own, without dispute. And this all have strengthened with the confirmation of the holy cross of Christ, that it may remain firm and unbroken for ever.

No. 6.   ARCHBISHOP ÆTHELHEARD, 798.

Cod. Dip. MXIX.

ÆTHELBALD, King of Mercia, gave the monastery at Cookham to
the church of Dover, and deposited the charters on the altar.
Dæiheah and Osbert stole the charters, and gave them to Cenwulf,
king of the West-Saxons, who appropriated the lands. Then Offa, king
of Mercia, among other conquests, took Cookham from Cenwulf. Afterwards Cenwulf repented, and sent the charters back to Dover. But Offa
kept the lands without the charters, and bequeathed them so to his heirs.
Then in a synod at Clovesho, in the second year of the reign of Offa's
successor, King Cenwulf of Mercia, the title to Cookham was brought up
by Bishop Æthelheard, and the lands were adjudged to belong to the
church at Dover. In settlement with the heirs of Offa, Dover received
Fleet, and gave Cookham with Pectanege to Cynethryth.

. . . EGO Aethelhardus larga omnipotentis dei gratia annuente
Dorobernensis aecclesiae metropolitanus, cum praestantissimo rege nostro Cenulfo, conuocans uniuersos prouinciales episcopos nostros, duces
et abbates et cuiuscunque dignitatis uiros, ad synodale concilium in
locum qui nominatur Clouesho, . . . prolatae sunt inscriptiones monasterii quod uocatur Coccham in medium, terrarumque sibi adiacentium;
quod uidelicet monasterium, cum omnibus ad illud pertinentibus terris,
rex inclytus Merciorum Aethelbaldus aecclesiae saluatoris quae sita est
in ciuitate Dorobernia dedit; utque illius donatio perseuerantior fieret,
ex eadem terra cespitem et cunctos libellos praememorati coenobii, per
uenerabilem uirum Cuthbertum archiepiscopum misit, et super altare
saluatoris pro perpetua sua salute, poni praecepit.   Sed post mortem

. . . I, ÆTHELHEARD, by the grace of omnipotent God archbishop
of the church of Dover, with our most illustrious King Cenwulf, con-
voking all our provincial bishops and ealdormen and abbots, and men
of every rank, to a synod at Clovesho, . . . the charters of the
monastery called Cookham, and of the adjacent lands, were produced.   This monastery, with all the lands belonging thereto,
Æthelbald, the renowned king of the Mercians, gave to the Church
of our Saviour at Dover; and, to confirm the donation, he sent by
that venerable man, Archbishop Cuthbert, a sod from the same land,
and all the charters of the aforesaid monastery, and ordered them to

praefati pontificis, easdem inscriptiones Daeiheah et Osbertus, quos
idem pontifex alumnos nutriuit, maligno acti spiritu furati sunt, et
Cenulfo regi Occidentalium-Saxonum detulerunt; at ille, accipiens
statim testimonia litterarum, praedictum coenobium cum omnibus ad
illud rite pertinentibus suis usibus coaptauit, neglectis praenominati
archiepiscopi Cuthberti dictis et factis. Item, Bregwinus et Ianbertus
archiepiscopi per singulas synodus suas, questi sunt de iniuria aecclesiae saluatoris illata; et apud Cenulfum regem Occidentalium-Saxonum, et apud Offam regem Merciorum qui uidelicet saepememoratum
coenobium Coccham et alias urbes quamplurimas Cenulfo rege abstulit, et imperio Merciorum subegit. Tandem Cenulfus rex sera ductus
poenitentia, telligraphia, id est, libellos quos a supradictis hominibus
Daeiheah et Osberto iniuste perceperat, cum magna pecunia, aecclesiae
Christi in Doroberniam remisit, humillime rogans ne sub tantae au-
thoritatis anathemate periclitaretur. Uerum rex Offa praememoratum
coenobium Coccham, sicut sine litteris accepit, ita quanto tempore
uixit, detinuit, et absque litterarum testimonio suis post se haeredibus
reliquit. Secundo autem anno regni Cenulfi facta est synodus sicut
supra est praelibatum apud Clouesho; at ego Aethelhardus . . . libel-

---

be placed on the altar of our Saviour, for his eternal salvation. But,
after the death of the aforesaid prelate, Dæiheah and Osbert, whom
he had nurtured as sons, led by an evil spirit, stole these charters, and
carried them to Cenwulf, king of the West Saxons. But he, at once
on receiving the testimony of the charters, appropriated to his own
use the aforesaid monastery, disregarding the acts and words of Cuthbert, the archbishop. Likewise Bregwin and Ianbert, in each of their
synods, complained of the injury to the church, both before Cenwulf,
king of the West Saxons, and before Offa, king of the Mercians, who
wrested the aforesaid monastery of Cookham, and very many other
cities, from Cenwulf, and placed them under the power of Mercia.
Then King Cenwulf, with late repentance, sent back the charters
which he wrongfully received from the aforesaid men, Dæiheah and
Osbert, with much money, to the church of Christ at Dover, humbly
asking that he be not placed under the anathema. But, as King Offa
without charters received the aforesaid monastery of Cookham, so he
retained it as long as he lived, and left it without charters to his heirs.
And, in the second year of the reign of King Cenwulf, a synod was
held, as has been above mentioned, at Clovesho; and I, Æthelheard,
. . . brought to the council the charters of the aforesaid monastery;
and, when they had been read before the synod, they unanimously de-

los praefati coenobii Coccham, in concilium detulimus; cumque coram synodo relicti fuissent, omnium uoce decretum est iustum esse ut metropolis aecclesia saepepraefatum coenobium Coccham, cuius inscriptiones in suo gremio habebat, perciperet, quo sub tanto tempore tam iniuste spoliata fuerat. Tunc autem placuit mihi Aethelhardo dei gratia archisacerdoti et Cynethrythae abbatissae quae eodem tempore saepedicto coenobio praefuit, ac senioribus ex utralibet parte, Cantia scilicet et Bedeforde, ad hoc ibidem congregatis, quatenus ipsa Cynethrytha in regione Cantia daret mihi pro commutatione saepepraefati coenobii, terram centum et decem manentium, sexaginta cassatorum uidelicet in loco qui dicitur Fleote, et triginta in loco qui dicitur Teneham, in tertio quoque loco ubi dicitur Creges aewylma, uiginti. Quas scilicet terras olim rex Offa sibi uiuenti conscribere fecit, suisque haeredibus post eum; et post eorum cursum uitae, aecclesiae quae sita est apud Beodeford consignari praecepit, . . . ut ipsa abbatissa a me percipiet saepe-nominatum coenobium cum suis inscriptionibus; et ego terras et libellos terrarum illarum quas mihi in Cantia reddit, ab ea acciperem, quatenus nulla imposterum inter nos haeredesque nostros et Offae regis surgat controuersia . . . Ego quoque Aethelhardus archiepiscopus concedo Cynithrithae abbatissae monasterium quod situm est in loco qui dicitur Pectanege ad habendum, quod mihi rex pius Egfridus haereditario iure possidendum donauit atque conscripsit.

---

creed that it was just that the metropolitan church should recover the aforesaid monastery, whose charters it held in its bosom, and of which it had been despoiled so unjustly and so long. Then I, Æthelheard, archbishop, and Cynethryth, abbess at that time of the aforesaid monastery, and the elders on both sides, namely in Kent and Bedford, assembled there for the purpose, decided that Cynethryth herself should give to me in Kent, in exchange for the aforesaid monastery, one hundred and ten hides of land, — sixty in the place called Fleet, thirty in Tenham, twenty in Cregesæwylma. These lands King Offa had caused to be conveyed to him when alive, and to his heirs after him; and, on their death, he commanded them to be conveyed to the church at Bedford. . . . And it was decided that the abbess should receive from me the aforesaid monastery, with its charters; and that I should receive the lands in Kent, and charters of the same, which she gave up to me, in order that no trouble should hereafter arise between our heirs and those of King Offa. . . . I, Æthelheard, archbishop, also grant to Cynethryth, abbess, the monastery of Pectanege, which the pious King Egfrith gave to me, to hold and to bequeath.

No. 7.　　DENEBERHT AND WULFHEARD, 803.

Cod. Dip. CLXXXIV.

THIS seems to be a case of arbitration between churches by a church council, rather than a suit at common law. Deneberht, Bishop of Worcester, claimed against Wulfheard, Bishop of Hereford, the right of refection in two monasteries belonging to the latter church. Wulfheard denied Deneberht's title, and also alleged thirty years' possession. Deneberht proved the exercise of the right by his predecessors, and the interruption of the possession. Finally, by the intervention of the archbishop, the suit was compromised.

- - -

. . . ANNO dominicae incarnationis DCCC°.III°. indict. XI⁹. uero qui est annus VII. regni Cenwulfi pii regis Merciorum, factum est sinodale conciliabulum aet Clofeshoum, praesidente Aethelheardo archiepiscopo ; . . . ibi etiam inter alia plura facta est contentio inter Deneberhtum, Uueogernensis aecclesiae antistitem, Uulfheardumque Herefordensem praesulem. Sunt autem monasteria in parochia Deneberhti Celtanhom, Beccanford, quae olim in antiquis diebus ad Herefordensem aecclesiam praestita fuerunt, in quibus postulabat suam pastum qui ei episcopali iure pertinebat, ipse Deneberht sibi reddi. Uulfheard autem e contra narrabat, ut ei nullam dare debuisset, neque umquam antecessores illius aliquam ibi haberent. Et si erat umquam, iam XXX. annis et eo amplius nemo illum, neque ante-

- - -

. . . IN the year of our Lord's incarnation 803, indiction 11, — that is, the seventh year of the reign of Cenwulf, pious king of the Mercians, — a synodal council was held at Clovesho, Archbishop Æthelheard presiding. . . . There, among several other matters, a dispute arose between Deneberht, bishop of the church at Worcester, and Wulfheard, Bishop of Hereford. Now, Cheltenham and Beckford are monasteries in the diocese of Deneberht, which formerly, in old times, were given to the church of Hereford. In these, Deneberht demanded that his right of refection, which belonged to him by episcopal right, should be restored to him. Wulfheard, on the other hand, said that he ought not to give him any refection, nor had his predecessors ever had any refection there ; and, if it was ever so, now

cessores eius, huiuscemodi pastu pulsaret neque tangeret. Deneberht autem cum testimonio narrabat, ut Uuermund episcopus pastum acciperet aet Beccanforda, Haðoredus similiter aet Celtanhomme, insuper et ipse Uuulfheard ei pecuniam daret pro pastu, haecque cum testimonio comprobauit. Cum uero huiuscemodi hinc et inde multa contenderunt, uentum est ad sermonem, ut archiepiscopus Deneberhtum rogabat dimidia sibi huius pastus praestare et altero anno semper aet Beccanforda suam refectionem acciperet, altero aet Celtanhomme. Ille autem respondebat se et uelle et debere in omnibus eius parere praeceptis; hoc modo tamen in testimonio totius sinodi in diem eius praestare et non amplius; idque litteris confirmare ut scient omnes qui eius sunt successores, quod ipse nunquam intermittit, quod Uueogernensi aecclesiae ad utilitatem recte pertinet. . . .

---

for thirty years and more no one had ever either demanded or received such refection from him or his predecessors. Then Deneberht narrated with witness how Bishop Wermund received refection at Beckford, and Hathored, in the same way, at Cheltenham; how, moreover, Wulfheard himself gave money to him, instead of the refection; and these things he proved with witness. When, in this way, they asserted many things on this side and on that, it came to speech that the archbishop asked Deneberht to give up, for his sake, half of this right of refection, so that he should receive his refection always, one year at Beckford, and the second at Cheltenham. Then he replied that he wished and ought in all things to obey his precepts, yet with this limitation, in the witness of the whole synod, to give it for his life only and no longer; and to confirm this in writing, that all his successors may know that he never neglects any thing which rightly pertains to the advantage of the church at Worcester. . . .

21

No. 8.　　　　　　ÆTHELRIC, 804.

Cod. Dip. CLXXXVI.

ÆTHELRIC apparently wished to dispose of his lands by will, and suit was brought to prevent his doing so (perhaps by his legal heirs). The Witan decided that Æthelric had the right.

. . . ANNO ab incarnatione Christi .DCCC.IIII. Indictione .XII. ego Aethelric, filius Aethelmundi, cum conscientia synodali inuitatus ad synodum, et in iudicio stare, in loco qui dicitur Clofeshoh, cum libris et ruris, id est, aet Uuestmynster, quod prius propinqui mei tradiderunt mihi et donauerunt, ibi Aethelhardus archiepiscopus mihi regebat atque iudicauerat, cum testimonio Coenuulfi regis, et optimatibus eius, coram omni synodo, quando scripturas meas perscrutarent, ut liber essem terram meam atque libellos dare quocunque uolui. . . .

. . . IN the year of Christ's incarnation 804, indiction 12, I, Æthelric, son of Æthelmund, with the knowledge of the synod, being summoned thereto, to stand in judgment in the place which is called Clovesho, with the charters of the land at Westminster, which formerly my kinsmen gave and delivered to me, there Archbishop Æthelheard presided and judged, with the witness of King Cenwulf, and all his chief men, in the presence of the whole synod, when they had examined my charter, that I was free to give my land and charters wherever I would. . . .

No. 9.   BEORNWULF OF MERCIA, 824.

Cod. Dip. CCXVIII.

THE monastery of Berkley brought suit against Bishop Heaberht for the monastery of Westbury, part of the inheritance of Æthelric. The oath was given to the bishop, who was in possession and held the charter. After thirty days, the bishop swore to his title.

. . . ANNO uero ab incarnatione domini nostri Ihesu Christi DCCC XXIIII. Indictione autem II. regnante Beornulfo, rege Merciorum, factum est pontificale et sinodale conciliabulum in loco qui dicitur Clofeshoas, praesidente ibi rege praefato, ac uenerando uiro Wulfredo archiepiscopo illo conuentu regente ac moderante. Illic omnes episcopi nostri, et abbates, et uniuersi Mercensium principes, et multi sapientissimi uiri congregati adessent, ubi, inter alia plura colloquia, aliqua contentio allata est inter Heaberhtum episcopum, et illam familiam aet Berclea, de haereditate Aethelrici filii Aethelmundi, hoc est, monasterium, quod nominatur Uuestburh. Habuit autem episcopus ante nominatus terram illam cum libris, sicut Aethelricus ante praecepit, ut ad Uueogernensem aecclesiam redderetur. Statuta est autem atque decreta ab archiepiscopo, et ab omni sancta sinodo illa consentienti, ut episcopus, qui monasterium et agellum cum libris haberet, cum iura-

. . . IN the year of the incarnation of our Lord Jesus Christ 824, indiction 2, in the reign of Beornwulf, king of the Mercians, a pontifical and synodal council was held in the place which is called Clovesho, the aforesaid king presiding, together with the venerable man, Archbishop Wulfred. There all our bishops and abbots, and all the chief men of the Mercians, and many of the wisest, were assembled, when, among several other suits, one was brought between Bishop Heaberht, and the chapter at Berkley, about the inheritance of Æthelric, son of Æthelmund, — that is, the monastery which is called Westbury. Now, the aforesaid bishop held this land, with the charter, according to Æthelric's command that it should revert to the church at Worcester. Then it was ordered and decreed by the archbishop, and by all the holy synod consenting, that the bishop, who had the monastery and the land, with the charter, on the oath of

mento dei servorum presbiterorum, diaconorum et plurimorum mona-
chorum, sibi in propriam possessionem terram illam cum adiuratione
adiurasset. Et ita finita est praescripta illa contentio coram episcopo :
post xxx. noctes illud iuramentum to Uuestmynstre deductum est. . . .

---

servants of God, priests, deacons, and very many monks, should swear
that land to himself, to his own possession, with an oath. And so the
aforesaid dispute was ended, in the presence of the bishop. After
thirty days, that oath was performed at Westminster. . . .

———∘∘⦂∘∘———

No. 10.   WULFRED, 825.

Cod. Dip. CCXX.

CENWULF of Mercia deprived Archbishop Wulfred, against his will, of
his dignity and lands. After the death of Cenwulf, the archbishop sued
his daughter and heir, Cwenthrytha, before the Witan; and obtained a
judgment against her for restitution, and compensation for damages.
This judgment seems not to have been carried into effect. King Beornwulf interposed to bring about a reconciliation ; and, after several efforts, a settlement was effected by the submission of Cwenthrytha.

ANNO vero Dominicae incarnationis DCCCXXV., indictione III.,
de diuersis Saxoniae partibus congregatum est synodale concilium in
loco praeclaro quae nominatur aet Clofeshoum. praesidente. . . .
Uulfredo archiepiscopo . . . seu etiam Beornuulfo regi Merciorum
. . . caeterisque episcopis et abbatibus necnon et ducibus, omniumque
dignitatum optimatibus . . . generositatem stabilitatemque regni
terrestris consiliantes ac quaerentes . . . Tantumdem uero inter alia-
rum allocutionum uerba patefactum est quod praefatus archiepiscopus
Uulfredus per inimicitiam et uiolentiam auaritiamque Coenwulfi regis

---

IN the year of the Lord's incarnation 825, indiction 3, a synodal council was assembled, from the different parts of Saxony, at
the famous place called Clovesho, Archbishop Wulfred presiding.
. . . as also Beornwulf, king of the Mercians, . . . and the other
bishops and abbots and ealdormen, and most eminent persons of all
ranks [being present], taking counsel and making inquiry in regard
to the excellence and stability of the earthly kingdom. . . . At
length, among other matters of discussion, it was made known that

. . . in testimonio totius populi omni dominatione propria priuatus est. . . . Postea etiam ille praedictus rex Coenwulf cum suis sapientibus ad regalem uillam Lundoniae perueniens ad hoc eodemque concilium illum archiepiscopum cum suo foedu foenoreque principum suorum inuitabat. Tuncque in eodem concilio cum maxima districtione illo episcopo mandauit quod omnibus rebus quae illius dominationis sunt dispoliatus debuisset fieri omnique de patria ista esse profugus et nunquam nec uerbis domne papae nec Caesaris seu alterius alicuius gradu huc in patriam iterum recipisse nisi hoc consentire uoluisset; hoc est quod illam terram aet Iogneshomme ccc. manentium reddidisset istamque pecuniam tradidisset cxx. librarum. Sed et ille episcopus hanc reconciliationem diu recussans . . . tamen tantundem . . . coactus, hac conditione hanc reconciliationem sic inuitus consensit: ut omni potestate oboedientiaque quae ad illius episcopalem sedem pertinebant iuxta auctoritatem gradus eius dignus fuisset, sicut praedecessores eius iuxta iustam ordinem in pristinis temporibus ante per omnia habuerant . . . Sed nihil huius condicte conditionis impletum est. . . . Postea uero contigit ut in temporibus praedicti Beornwulfi regis ad illamque praenominatam synodum aet Clofeshoum ille archiepiscopus Uulfred Cwoenthrytham abbatissam heredem Coenwulfi

---

the aforesaid Archbishop Wulfred, by the enmity, violence, and avarice of King Cenwulf, . . . in witness of the whole people, had been deprived of all his rightful authority. . . . Afterwards, also, the aforesaid King Cenwulf, coming with his Witan to the royal residence at London, invited that archbishop thereto under his own guaranty, and with the surety of his chief men. Then, in this same council, with the greatest severity, he ordered the bishop to be despoiled of every thing which belonged to his authority, and to be utterly exiled from this country, and never to return to it, either at the intercession of the Lord Pope or of the Emperor, or of any other person of whatsoever rank, until he had consented to this, — namely, to return the three hundred hides of land at Iogneshomme, and to give up the one hundred and twenty pounds of money. And the bishop, after long refusing this settlement, yet at last, . . . under compulsion, unwillingly consented, on this condition, — that he should enjoy all the power and obedience which belonged to that episcopal see, according to the authority of his rank, in all respects as his predecessors had held it in former times. . . . But nothing of all this stipulated condition was performed. . . . But it afterwards happened that, in the time of the aforesaid King Beornwulf, Archbishop Wulfred summoned to the aforesaid

cum eadem hereditate illius inuitabat, emendationemque sibi omnium
supradictarum molestiarum iniuriarumque postulauit, quas ille idem
rex Coenwulf sibi et ecclesiae Christi . . . perpetrasset. Tunc uero
omnis ille synodus ad aequitatem inuenerunt huncque iudicium unanimo consensu constituerunt: quod illi episcopo reddere omnia debuisset quod uiolentia abstulerat in omnibus rebus quibus cum aliqua
iniuria in omni spatio illa spoliata fuerat, et alteram similem partem
ad hoc ipsum adiecisse, et omnem usum emendasse qui in ipsa spatio
confracta fuerat.   Postea autem placuit Beornwulfo regi . . . reconciliationem et emendationem diligentissime facere. . . . In postremo
autem ille praenominatus episcopus . . . hanc . . . reconciliationem
. . . suscepisset ut illa abbatissa Cwoenthryth filia Coenwulfi he-
resque illius . . . terram . . . c. manentium illo archiepiscopo cum
propriis et antiquis telligraphis et cum eadem libertate quam ante
habuerat in perpetuam hereditatem ad habendam et possidendam
postque dies eius cuicumque ei placuerit dereliquendum tradiderat
. . . Sed statim ista praedictae reconciliatio confracta est . . . Ite-
rumque secundo anno postquam haec omnia ita peracta sunt, haec
eadem abbatissa illius episcopi colloquium flagitabat eumque in pro-
uincia Huicciorum expetiuit illo in loco quae nominatur Oslafeshlau,

---

synod at Clovesho the Abbess Cwenthrytha, Cenwulf's heir, together
with his inheritance, and demanded compensation for all the aforesaid
evil and injury which the same King Cenwulf . . . had inflicted on him
and the church of Christ.   And then all that synod equitably adopted
and unanimously affirmed this judgment, — that she ought to restore
to the bishop every thing which had been violently taken from him
during all that time, and make good all injury, and add as much more
over and above, and make compensation for the use during the same
period.   But afterwards it pleased King Beornwulf . . . to make
most earnestly a compromise and settlement. . . . At last, also, the
aforesaid bishop accepted . . . this . . . compromise, — that the Abbess Cwenthrytha, daughter and heir of King Cenwulf, should deliver
to the archbishop land to the amount of one hundred hides, . . . together with the ancient charters belonging to it, and with the same
freedom which he had before, to hold and possess in perpetual inheritance, and to bequeath to whomsoever he would. . . . But this treaty
of reconciliation was immediately broken. . . . And again, in the
second year after all these things so took place, this same abbess
asked an interview of the aforesaid bishop, and sought him out in the
province of the Hwicci in the place which is called Oslafeshlaw, and

eique suam insipientiam confessa est retardate reconciliationis . . .
Tum autem illa abbatissa cum omni humilitate promiserat ut omne
quod ei reddita non fuerat . . . emendare uoluisset . . . Tuncque
episcopus hoc idem consensit. . . .

confessed to him her folly in regard to the delay of the reconciliation.
. . . Then, too, the abbess, with all humility, promised to make
amends for all that had not been restored to him. . . . And then the
bishop gave his consent to the same. . . .

───oo°o°oo───

No. 11.   BEORNWULF OF MERCIA, 825.

Cod. Dip. CCXIX.

THIS was an action in the nature of an appeal, by the Bishop of
Worcester, from a decision of the bailiffs encroaching on old rights of
the chapter in the wood-pastures at Sutton. The bishop claimed, under
established custom of Æthelbald's day, two-thirds of the woods and mast.
The Witan allowed him the oath, and he established his claim.

. . . þy gere ðe wes from cristes gebyrde agæen eahta hund wintra
and xxv and sio aefterre indictio wæs in rime and wæs biornwulfes
rice mercna cyninges ða wæs sionoðlic gemot on ðære meran stowe
ðe mon hateð Clofeshoas and ðær se siolfa cyning biornwulf ond his
biscopas ond his aldormenn ond alle ða wioton ðisse ðiode ðær gesom-
nade wæron ða wæs tiolo micel sprec ymb wudu-leswe to suðtune
ongægum west on scyrhylte waldon ða swangerefan ða læswe forður
gedrifan ond ðone wudu geþiogan ðon hit aldgeryhto weron ðon
cuæð se biscop and ðara hina wiotan ðet hio him neren maran ondeta
ðon hit aræded wæs on Aethelbaldes dæge ðrim hunde swina mæst ond

. . . THE year that was from Christ's birth eight hundred and
twenty-five agone, and was the second indiction in number, and was
the reign of Beornwulf, king of the Mercians, there was a synodal
gemot at the famous place called Clovesho; and there the aforesaid
King Beornwulf, and his bishops and his ealdormen, and all the
witan of this people, were there assembled. Then was a very great
suit about the wood-pastures at Sutton, westwards, in Scirholt. The
bailiffs wished to extend the pasture, and feed out the wood further
than it was old right. Then said the bishop and the chapter's counsellors that they did not confess more to them [the bailiffs] than as it

se biscop [and ða higen*] ahten twæde ðæs wuda ond ðæs mæstes. ða geræhte Uulfred arcebiscop ond alle ða wiotan ðet se biscop ond ða higen mosten mid aðe gecyðan ðet hit sua wære aræden on Aeðelbaldes dæge ond him mare to ne sohte ond he ða sona se biscop beweddade eadwulfe ðæm aldormen ðæs aðæs biforan allum ðæm wiotum ond him mon ðone gelædde ymb xxx næhta to ðæm biscopstole et wiogoerna ceastre in ða tiid wæs hama suangerefa to suðtune ond he rad ðæt he wæs et ceastre and ðone aað gesæh ond gesceawade sua hine his aldormon heht Eadwulf ond he hine hweðre ne grette. . . .

* And ða higen. Conjectural for ða tugen, which gives no meaning.

---

was administered in Æthelbald's day, — mast for three hundred swine; and the bishop and the chapter had two-thirds of the wood and the mast. Then Archbishop Wulfred and all the Witan decreed that the bishop and the chapter might declare on oath that it was so administered in Æthelbald's day, and that he claimed no more. And the bishop at once pledged the oath to Eadwulf, the ealdorman, before all the Witan; and it was administered to him after thirty days, at the bishop's seat at Worcester. At that time, Hama was bailiff at Sutton, and he rode to Worcester, and saw and looked at the oath, as his ealdorman, Eadwulf, commanded him, and he yet did not greet him (the bishop). . . .

——⚬⚬❧⚬⚬——

No. 12.   ARCHBISHOP WULFRED, 825.

Cod. Dip. MXXXIV.

OFFA granted some land at Denton to Abbot Plegheard, who conveyed it to the church at Selsey. The church having been despoiled of this land, suit was brought before the Witan for recovery, and restitution ordered.

. . . ANNO ab incarnatione Christi. DCCC.XXV. indictione tertia, anno secundo regni Beornulfi regis Merciorum, synodus fuit ad Clobesham, praesidente archiepiscopo Wulfredo; post mortem uero Coenulfi regis Merciorum multae discordiae et innumerabiles dissonanciae

---

. . . IN the year of the incarnation of Christ 825, indiction 3, in the second year of the reign of Beornwulf, king of the Mercians, a synod, over which Archbishop Wulfred presided, was held at Clovesho. After the death of Cenwulf, king of the Mercians, many discords and

extollebantur contra unius cuiusque principalium personarum, regum et episcoporum, et pastorum aecclesiarum dei, erga plurima saecularia negotia; ita ut multum dispoliatae fuerant per loca diuersa aecclesiae Christi in rebus, in terris, in tributo, in omnibus causis. . . . Episcopus Australium-Saxonum Coenredus fuerat spoliatus de aliqua parte terrae illius .xxv. aecclesiae quae uocitatur Deanton, quod Plegheard abbas dudum tradidit ad sedem episcopalem quae est in Selesegh, cum corpore suo, quod ei rex Offa ante condonauerat et conscripserat de haereditate aecclesiae Bedingehommes, quam ipse sibi adquisierat in haereditatem propriam. Tunc in praefata synodo iudicatum est ut ille episcopus, cum consensu et unanimi consilio episcoporum et abbatum seu principum, in ius proprium aecclesiae haereditatem sine ullo obstaculo accipiat; sicut et ante prius at Caelchythe iudicatum est inter Coenulfum regem et Wehthunum de eiusdem terrae assumptione, coram archiepiscopo Aethelheardo, tertio anno Coenulfi regis. Et haec acta sunt coram omni concilio at Clobeshom, cum consensu et licentia regis et principum et archiepiscoporum, quorum nomina infra annotantur. . . .

---

countless disputes arose among kings, bishops, and priests of the church of God concerning secular matters, so that the churches of Christ in different places had been despoiled of their property, lands, and tribute. . . . Cœnred, bishop of the South Saxons, had been despoiled of a certain part of that twenty-five hides of church land called Denton, which, together with his body, Abbot Plegheard long since conveyed to the episcopal see at Selsey, [and] which King Offa had before given and booked to him out of the inheritance of the church at Beddingham, which he had acquired for himself as hereditary property. Then, in the aforesaid synod, it was decreed that this bishop, by the consent of the bishops and nobles, should receive the inheritance of the church, without hindrance, in full ownership as before it had been adjudged at Cælchyth between King Cenwulf and Wehthun concerning the seizure of the same land, before Archbishop Æthelheard, in the third year of the reign of King Cenwulf. And these things were done in the presence of the whole assembly at Clovesho, with the approval and permission of the king and his chief men and the archbishops, whose names are written below. . . .

No. 13.   BERHTWULF, MARCH 28, 840.

Cod. Dip. CCXLV.

BERHTWULF, king of the Mercians, despoiled the church at Worcester
of certain lands. Suit was brought by Bishop Heaberht, who presented
his charters before the Witan, and the lands were restored.

. . . ANNO autem ab incarnatione eiusdem dei et domini nostri
Ihesu Christi .DCCCXL°. Indictione III. Contigit autem quod Berh-
tuulf rex Merciorum, tollerat a nobis et tradidit terram nostram quod
recte ac iure sub proprio potestate ac libera possessione cum firma
donatione tradita est et concessa et firmata ad sedem episcopalem, id
est, ad Uueogernensem aecclesiam rex praefatus suobus propriis hominibus condonauit, sicut se inimici homines docuerunt, hoc est, Stoltun,
Uassanburna, Cyneburgingctun, Tateringctun, Codesuuelle. Tunc per-
rexit ille episcopus Heaberht, cum suis secum senioribus, in pascha, ad
Tomeworðie et suas libertates et cartulas ante nominatorum terrarum
secum habentes et ibi ante regem eiusque proceres fuerunt allecta et
ibi Merciorum optimates deiudicauerunt illi, ut male ac iniuste dispo-
liati essent in suo proprio. Tunc illis terra sua reddita est cum pace,
et simul etiam ille episcopus hanc donatiuum regem predonauit iterum
in Uuelesburnan, hoc est IIII. caballos bene electos, et unum anulum in
XXX. mancusis et discum fabrefactum in tribus pundis et duas albas

. . . IN the year of the incarnation of our Lord and Master Jesus
Christ 840, of the indiction 3, it happened that Berhtwulf, king of
the Mercians, led by wicked men, took from us, and gave away to his
own men, our land, — Stoulton, Washborne, Kingston, Tarrington,
and Codswell, — which had been given, granted, and confirmed,
rightfully and lawfully, with full power and free possession, to the
episcopal church at Worcester. Then Bishop Heaberht, with his
elders, at Easter, went to Tamworth, taking the liberties and charters
of the aforesaid lands ; and there, before the king and his nobles, they
were read, and the Mercian nobles decided that they had been wrongfully and unjustly despoiled of their property. Then their land was
returned to them in peace ; and the bishop besides presented this gift
to the king, at Wellsburne, namely : four chosen horses, a ring worth
thirty mancuses, a wrought dish of three pounds' weight, and two

cornas in IIII. libris, et ille regina dedit duos equos bonos et duas stea-
pas in twaem pundum, et unam cuppam deauratam in duobus pundis.
Et tunc rex cum testimonio has terras firmiter liberauit sibi in aeuum
coram suis archontis uniuscuiusque necessitatis et sustulionis. . . .

---

silver drinking-horns of four pounds; and he gave to the queen two
good horses, two stoups of two pounds, and one gilded cup of two
pounds. And then the king, with witnesses, freed the land for ever
from every burden, in the presence of his nobles. . . .

No. 14. ÆTHELUULF, 844.

Cod. Dip. CCLVI.

OSWULF, ealdorman of East Kent, devised his property to the church
after the death of his wife and children. A dispute having arisen concerning the will, a decision of the Witan was obtained confirming its
provisions. Thirty-four years after, Æthelwulf claimed that the land
devised by Oswulf had been sold to his father; but the Witan decided
the suit against him, and gave the oath to the churches.

. . . IDCIRCO etenim Osuulf dei gratia dux atque princeps prouinciae Orientalis Cantiae circa suae propriae hereditatis iura tractare
studuit. Et hoc coram beatae memoriae Uulfredo archiepiscopo co-
ramque abbatis Uuernotho atque Feolgeldo caeterisque fidelissimis et
religiosissimis Ceolstano, uiz; Aethelhuno atque Heremodo presbyte-
ris aecclesiae Christi, necnon saepe coram sociis suis et amicis fidissi-
mis, qualiter post discessionem suam circa haereditatem suam imposterum agere uoluisse, id est, ut post dies uxoris suae et filii eius Ear-
duulfi filiae quoque suae Ealfthrythae, ad aecclesiis dei omnia dare deo

---

. . . THEREFORE Oswulf, by the grace of God ealdorman of East
Kent, desired to execute a testament; and in the presence of Wulfred, of blessed memory, and Wernoth, and Feolgeld, and other most
trusted and Christian men, — namely, Ceolstan, Æthelhun, and Here-
mod, priests, — and of his most faithful friends, he showed what disposition he wished to be made of his property after his death. He
commanded that, after the death of his wife and of her son Eardwulf,
and his daughter Ealfthryth, all his property should be given to God and
His holy church, under their testimony, as is clearly and plainly shown

et sanctis eius sibi in sempiternam hereditatem sub eorum testimonia
dare praecepit, a sicut in altera kartula manifeste et lucide comproba-
tur.   Sed tamen post obitum Osuulfi ducis surrexit excitata a quibusdam quaestio et contentio magno circa hereditatem Osuulfi contra
uxorem eius Beornthrythae; . . . sed utrique partes ad synodale concilium aduocari et inuitari iubebantur: et cum ad synodum deuenis-
sent et diligenti inuestigatione ueritatis sententia utrarumque partium
a sancto synodo, quae facta est in loco praeclaro aet Aeclea, quaerendo
examinaretur, inuentum est nihil iustius nec rectius esse posse constare,
quam sic perseuerare haereditatem Osuulfi sicut ipse Osuulf prius proprio arbitrio per omnia donare coram praedictis testibus decreuerat:
atque ita hoc etiam ab illo sancto synodo perpetuae perdurare deiudicatum est. . . . Sed . . . ille antiquus uenenatissimus serpens . . . post cur-
ricula quantorum annorum, id est, XXXIIII, iterum . . . haereditatem
sanctorum eius adgrauere . . . conatus est. . . . Quamobrem congre-
gata multitudine spiritalium saeculariumque personum in Dorouernia
ciuitate, anno dominicae incarnationis DCCC.XLIIII. indict. Aetheluulfo regi presente atque Aethelstano filio eius, Ceolnotho quoque
archimetropolitano archiepiscopo, necnon Tatnoth presbitero electo
ad episcopalem sedem Dorobreui, id est, ciuitatis Hrofi, cum principibus, ducibus, abbatibus, et cunctis generalis dignitatis optimatibus, inter quas etiam ille uenenatissimus anguis cognomento Aetheluulf, . . . deueniens, . . . dicens haereditatem Osuulfi ducis cum auro et

---

in the other charter.   But after the death of ealdorman Oswulf, a great
dispute arose concerning the inheritance of Oswulf against his wife. . . .
But both parties were summoned to the synod; and when they came,
and the claims of each had been carefully examined by the synod convoked at Aclea, it was found that nothing more just or right could be
determined than to maintain the testament of Oswulf as he had himself
first executed it, in the presence of the aforesaid witnesses; and this decree was to continue for ever.   But that most deadly serpent, after the
lapse of thirty-four years, made another attack upon the inheritance of
the holy ones of Christ.   Wherefore, in the year of the incarnation
of our Lord 844, an assembly of spiritual and temporal lords having
been convened in the city of Dover, in the presence of King Æthelwulf and his son Æthelstan, and the metropolitan Archbishop Ceolnoth, and Tatnoth, chosen priest of the episcopal church of Rochester,
with the lords, ealdormen, abbots, and all the nobles, that most poison-
ous reptile, Æthelwulf by name, . . . said that the property devised
by Oswulf had been purchased by his father, Æthelheah, with gold

argento patris sui Aethelheah esse comparatum, et per hoc spoliare aecclesiam dei, . . . ad quas haereditas illa pertinebat, . . . nisus est. Tunc ille archiepiscopus Ceolnoth et familia eius, id est aecclesiae Christi illa, per ordinem replicauit qualiter in illo sancto synodo de illo reconciliatum et deiudicatum est. At ille nolens adquiescere, neque iudicio synodis et probabilium patrum sanctionibus, neque adsertione et ueredicà uoce episcopi uel alicuius personis, tunc etenim a sapientibus et prudentibus trutinatum ac diiudicatum est, familiam aecclesiae Christi, et familiam aet Folcanstane, familiam quoque at Dobrum, necnon et familiam aet Liminge ad quos haereditas illa pertinebat, iusto iuramenta haereditatem illam sibi ipsis contra haereditatem Aethelheahes castigare; nam et ita fecerunt. Iurauerunt xxx. homines de familiis praedictis, xii. presbeteri, caeteri communi gradus; et sic etiam illa altercatio utrarumque partium perenniter sedari decretum est. . . .

---

and silver, and thereby strove to despoil the church of God. Then Archbishop Ceolnoth and his chapter duly unfolded what had been decreed in that holy synod. But, he refusing to submit to the decision of the synod, or to the voice of the bishop, or of any person, then it was decreed by the Witan that the chapter of Christ's Church, and the family at Folkstone, and at Dover, and at Lyminge, to whom this inheritance belonged, should by just oath claim that inheritance for themselves against the inheritance of Æthelheah; and this they did. Then thirty men of the aforesaid families swore, — twelve priests, the others common monks; and so that dispute was decreed to be for ever settled. . . .

No. 15.   DUKE ÆTHELUULF, 897.

Cod. Dip. CCCXXIII.

KING CENULF left certain property to the church of Winchcombe, with the injunction that no one should convey it away for a longer term than one life. A part of the inheritance was found in the possession of Wullaf, who held it by a grant from Cynethryth to his father for three lives, whereupon the Witan adjudged the gift to be void; but the land was granted to Wullaf to hold during his life, on condition that it should go to the church at Worcester after his death.

ANNO dominicae incarnationis .DCCC.XCVII. indictione uero. xv. eo anno contigit quod Aetheluulf uenerabilis dux recitauit et inuestigauit haereditarios libros Cenuulfi regis, et in priuilegiis illius scriptum inueniebat, quod nullus haeres post eum licentiam haberet haereditatem Cenuulfi quae pertinet ad Wincelcumbe alicui hominum longius donandam uel conscribendam quam dies unius hominis ; . . . Accidit autem tunc inter alias locutiones, quod Aetheluulf loquebatur de illa terra quae appellatur Inuptune. V. manentium, ad Uullafum qui tunc eam possidebat, quoniam de haereditate ipsius Cenuulfi fuit. Tunc ille dicebat quod Cynethryth patri suo illam terram dies trium hominum donasset, et Aelflaed sibi postea trium addidisset ; sed Aethelred et illi omnes adiudicabant, quod illa donatio aliter stare non posset, nisi sicuti in diebus Cenuulfi constitutum erat. Tunc ille praedictus Wullaf red-

---

IN the year of the Incarnation of our Lord 897, indiction 15, it happened that the revered Duke Æthelwulf read and examined the charters conveying the inheritance of King Cenwulf, and found it written in his privileges that, after him, no heir should have the power to give or convey the inheritance, which belongs to Winchcombe, to any man for a longer term than one life. . . . But, then, it happened that, among other discourse, Æthelwulf spoke to Wullaf, who then possessed them, about the five hides of land called Upton, because they were a part of the inheritance of Cenwulf himself. Then Wullaf said that Cynethryth had given that land to his father for three lives, and Ælflæd had added three more. But Æthelred and they all adjudged that this donation could not stand in any other way than it had been appointed in the days of Cenwulf. Then the aforesaid

didit Aetheluulfo pristinos libellos a Cynethrytha et Aelflaeda con-
scriptos, et Aedeluulfus ei istum postea scribere praecipiebat : ea
namque dictione, ut habeat et perfruatur per tempora uitae suae, et
postea sine contradictione reddatur ad sedem episcopalem quae est in
Uneogernensi ciuitate, antistiti, qualiscumque rector et gubernator
illius tunc existerit, pro redemptione animae Cenuulfi regis et omnium
haeredum ipsius, necnon quoque et pro renouatione et reconciliatione
pacis inter illam familiam quae est in Uueogernensi ciuitate et illam
quae est in Uuincelcumbe. . . .

Wullaf gave up to Æthelwulf the original charters written by Cynethryth and Ælflæd; and Æthelwulf ordered this charter to be given
him, granting that he should have and enjoy the land during his life,
on the condition that, afterwards, it should go to the Episcopal Church
at Worcester, to the abbot, or whatever rector, or governor, should
then exist, for the redemption of the soul of King Cenwulf, and all
his heirs, and also for the renewal of peace between the families of
Worcester and Winchcombe.

———∞◦⦂◦∞———

No. 16.   WERFRITH, ABOUT 900.

Cod. Dip. CCCXXVII.

SUIT brought by the Bishop of Worcester before the Mercian Witan to
recover lands which had been granted out on special conditions, these
conditions not having been observed. The Witan sustained the claim,
and thereupon the land was regranted on new conditions.

IN usses dryhtnes naman haelendes Cristes ! Ic Werferð bisceop cyðe swa me Alchun bisceop saegde and eac mine gewrytu
wisodon ðaet Mired bisceop gesealde Eanbalde ðaet land aet Soppanbyrg mid ðis bebode. and seoððan Eanbald hit sealde Eastmunde and

---

IN the name of our Lord Christ the Saviour ! I, Bishop Werfrith,
make known (as Bishop Alchun told me, and also my charters
showed) that Bishop Mired granted to Eanbald the land at Sodbury,
with this injunction — and, afterwards, Eanbald gave it to Eastmund —

him bebead Mired bisceop bebod on Godes ealmihtiges noman and on
ðane halgan ðrinesse ðaet ða hwile ðe aenig man waere on hire
maegðe ðe godcundes hades beon walde and ðaes wyrðe waere ðaet
he ðonne fenge to ðam lande aet Soppanbyrg. gif hit ðonne hwaet
elles geselde ðaet hit naefre on laedu hand ne wende. Ac hit
seoððan eode to ðam bisceopstole to Weogornaceastre for heora ealra
saule. Ond he ða Eastmund aer his ende bebead on ðaes lifgendan
Godes noman ðam men ðe to ðam lande fenge ðaet he ðone on ða
ilcan wisan tofenge ðe Mired bisceop bebead. gif he ðonne to ðan
gedyrstig waere ðaet he ðaet abraece ðaet he wiste hine scyldigne
beforan Godes heahsetle aet ðam miclan dome. ða aefter Eastmundes
forðsiðe bereafode seo maegð ðaes ilcan londes ge ða gastas ðara
forðgewitenra manna ge ðone bisceop and ða ciricean aet Weogorna-
ceastre. and Heahberht bisceop oft ðaes myngode oððe ðaes landes
baed and seoððan Alchun bisceop for oft ða hwile ðe he waes. and
eac ic Werferð bisceop oft his baed and we ne mihton to nanum
rihte becuman aer Aeðelred waes Myrcna hlaford. ða gesamnode he
Mercna weotan to Saltwic ymbe maenigfealde ðearfe ge Godes daeles
ge worolde daeles. ða spraec ic on ða magas mid ðy erfegewrite and
wilnade me rihtes. ða beweddode me Eadnoð me and Aelfred and

and Bishop Mired enjoined him, in the name of Almighty God, and
that of the Holy Trinity, that while there were any man among their
kin who desired to be in holy orders, and should be worthy of it, that
he should succeed to the land at Sodbury ; if it happened otherwise,
that it should never come into a layman's hand ; but it should afterwards go to the bishop's see at Worcester for all their souls' sake.
And then he, Eastmund, before his end, enjoined in the name of the
living God the man who should take the land, that he should take
it in the same wise as bishop Mired commanded. If he, however,
should be presumptuous enough to break this [command] that he
should know that he would be guilty before God's throne at the
last judgment. Then, after Eastmund's death, his kinsfolk deprived
both the souls of the departed men, and the bishop, and the church
at Worcester, of this same land. And Bishop Heahberht often ad-
monished them of this, or asked for the land ; and afterwards Bishop
Alchun very often while he was [living], and also I, Bishop Werfrith,
often asked for it, and we could not obtain any justice till Æthelred
became lord of the Mercians. Then he assembled the Witan of the
Mercians at Saltwick about manifold needs both spiritual and temporal. Then I brought suit against the kinsfolk with the testament

Aelfstan ðaet hio oðer ðara dydon oððe hit me ageafon oððe on hira maegðe ðone man funden ðe to ðam hade fenge and to lande and me waere gehearsum for Gode and for worolde. ða Eadnoð ðe ðaet land haefde gebead hit ealre ðaere maegðe hwaeðer hit aenig swa gegan wolde ða waes aelc ðaes wordes ðaet him leofre waere ðaet he land foreode ðonne he ðaene had underfenge. ða gesohte he Aeðelred and Aeðelflaede and eac Aeðelnoð urne ealra freond and heo ealle to me wilnodon ðaet ic hine laete aet me ðaet land begeotan him to agenre aehte swelcum erfewæardum to syllenne swelce he wolde and ic ða swa dyde ealles swyðost for hiora bene and he eac me gesealde feowertig mancesa. and ic ða mid miru higna leafe aet Weogorna-ceastre him sealde ðaet lond on ece erfe and ða bec and ðaet East-mundes erðegewrit and eac ure agen raedengewrit ðaet waere him to ðam gerade ðaet land tolaeten ðe mon aelce gere gesylle fiftene scillingas claenes feos to Tettanbyrg ðam bisceope and him eac ðone nescrift healde.

[of Eastmund] and claimed justice for me. Then Eadnoth and Alfred and Ælfstan pledged themselves to me that they would do one of these [two things]; either they would give up [the land] to me, or would find among their kinsmen the man who would accept the order [of priesthood] and the land, and would be obedient to me in spiritual and in worldly matters. Then Eadnoth, who had the land, offered it to all their kinsmen [to see] whether any one would so acquire it. Then every one said that he would rather forego the land than take orders. Then he went to Æthelred and Æthel-flæd and also Æthelnoth, friend of us all, and they all desired me to let him acquire the land of me for his own property, to bestow on such heirs as he liked; and I then did so, most of all for their prayer, and he also gave me forty mancuses. And I then with the leave of my chapter at Worcester gave him the land in inheritance for ever, and the charters, and Eastmund's testament, and also our own certificate that the land was relinquished to him, on the condition that fifteen shillings of pure money be paid every year to the bishop at Tetbury, and he should also make his shrift to him. (?)

No. 17. ———, AFTER 900.

Cod. Dip. CCCXXVIII.[1]

THIS letter, written apparently to King Edward the Elder, explains a disputed title to five hides of land at Fonthill. In the reign of Alfred, a certain Helmstan committed a theft. Thereupon Æthelm claimed Helmstan's land at Fonthill, on grounds not stated. Helmstan obtained the intercession of the writer with the king to remove his outlawry. Æthelm's suit was then tried before arbitrators, who adjudged the oath to Helmstan, who appears then to have pledged himself to convey the land to the writer, in consideration of receiving his assistance in giving the oath. The oath was successfully given, and the writer received the land according to the pledge. He then allowed Helmstan a life occupancy. Helmstan soon afterwards drove off the oxen at Fonthill, was outlawed, and the land, coming again into the writer's possession, was exchanged for other land. Æthelm, in Edward's reign, attempted to recover the land, but seems to have desisted before trial.

+ LEOF ic ðe cyðe hu hit waes ymb ðaet lond aet Funtial að fif hida ðe Aeðelm Higa ymb spycð ða Helmstan ða undaede gedyde ðaet he Aeðeredes belt forstael. ða ongon Higa him specan sona on mid oðran onspecendan and wolde him oðflitan ðaet lond ða sohte he me and baed me ðaet ic him waere forespeca forðon ic his haefde aer onfongen aet biscopes honda aer he ða undaede gedyde. ða spaec ic him fore and ðingade him to Aelfrede cinge ða God forgelde his saule ða lyfde he ðaet he moste beon ryhtes wyrðe for mire forspaece and ryht race wið Aeðelm ymb ðaet lond ða het he hie seman ða waes ic ðara

---

BELOVED : I make known to you how it was about the land at Fonthill, the five hides that Æthelm Higa lays claim to. When Helmstan committed the crime of stealing Æthered's belt, Higa at once began to bring charges against him, among other accusers, and wanted to litigate the land from him. Then he sought me and prayed me to be his intercessor, because I had received him formerly from the bishop's hand before he committed the crime. Then I spoke in his behalf, and interceded for him with King Alfred, whose soul may God reward ; so he allowed him to be law-worthy at

---

[1] The original of this charter has also been consulted, and a few slight variations from Mr. Kemble's text have been adopted.

monna sum ðe ðaer to genemmed waeran and Wihtbord and Aelfric
was ða hraelðen and Byrhthelm and Wulfhun ðes blaca aet Sumor-
tune and Strica and Ubba and ma monna ðonne ic nu genemnan maege
ða reahte heora aegðer his spell ða ðuhte us eallan ðaet Helmstan
moste gan forð mid ðon bocon and geagnigean him ðaet lond ðaet he
hit haefde swa Aeðelðrið hit Osulfe on aeht gesealde wið gemedan feo
and heo cwaeð to Osulfe ðaet heo hit ahte him wel to syllane for ðon
hit waes hire morgen-gifu ða heo aest to Aðulfe com and Helmstan
ðis eal on ðon aðe befeng and Aelfred cing ða Osulfe his hondsetene
sealde ða he ðaet lond aet Aeðelðriðe bohte ðaet hit swa stondan
moste and Eadward his and Aeðelnað his and Deormod his and aelces
ðara monna ðe mon ða habban wolde ða we hie aet Weardoran nu
semdan ða baer mon ða boc forð and raedde hie ða stod seo hondseten
eal ðaeron ða ðuhte us eallan ðe aet ðaere some waeran ðet Helmstan
waere aðe ðaes ðe naer ða naes Aeðelm na fullice geðafa aer we
eodan into cinge and raedan eal hu we hit reahtan and bo hwy we hit
reahtan and Aeðelm stod self ðaer inne mid and cing stod ðwoh his
honda aet Weardoran innan ðon bure ða he ðaet gedon haefde ða
ascade he Aeðelm hwy hit him ryht ne ðuhte ðaet we him gereaht
haefdan cwaeð ðaet he nan ryhtre geðencan ne meahte ðonne he

my intercession and plead against Æthelm about the land. Then he
[Alfred] ordered an arbitration. I was one of the men who were
named for the purpose, and Wihtbord and Ælfric, who then was robe-
keeper, and Byrhthelm and Wulfhun the black, of Somerton, and
Strica, and Ubba, and more men than I can now name. Then each of
them told his tale. Then it was the opinion of all of us that Helmstan might go forth with the charters and prove his right to the land,
that he held it as Æthelthrith gave it to Oswulf in full property for
a fair price; and she told Oswulf that she was fully entitled to sell
it to him, because it was her morning-gift when she first came to
Athulf. And Helmstan included all this in the oath. And King
Alfred, when Oswulf bought the land of Æthelthrith, gave his signature to Oswulf that [the purchase] might so stand, and Eadward his,
and Æthelnath his, and Deormod his, and each of the men whom
they wished to have. While we were now engaged in reconciling
them at Wardour, the charter was brought forth and read. There
stood the signatures, all of them, thereon. Then it was the opinion
of us all who were at the arbitration, that Helmstan was so much
nearer to the oath; but Æthelm was not fully satisfied before we
went to the king; and reported in full how we judged it, and why

ðone að agifan moste gif he meahte ða cwveð ic ðaet he wolde
cunnigan and baed ðone cing ðaet he hit andagade and he ða swa dyde
and he gelaedde ða to ðon andagan ðone að be fullan and baed
me ðaet ic him fultemade and cwaeð ðaet him waere leofre ðaet he
. . . alde ðonne se að forburste oððe hit aef . . . aede ða cwaeð ic
ðaet ic him wolde fylstan to ryhte and naefre to nanan wo on ða
gerada ðet he his me uðe and he me ðaet on wedde gesealde and we
ridan ða to ðon andagan ic and Wihtbord rad mid me and Byrhthelm
rad ðider mid Aeðelme and we gehyrdan ealle ðaet he ðone að be
fulan ageaf ða we cwaedan ealle ðaet hit waere geendodu spaec
ða se dom waes gefylled and leof hwonne bið engu spaec geendedu
gif mon ne maeg nowðer ne mid feo ne mid aðá geendigan
oððe gif mon aelcne dom wile onwendan ðe Aelfred cing gesette
hwonne habbe we ðonne gemotad and he me ða boc ða ageaf swa
he me on ðon wedde aer geseald haefde sona swa se að agifen
was and ic him gehet ðaet he moste ðes londes brucan ðe hwile ðe he
lifde gif he hine wolde butan bysmore gehealdan ða on ufan ðaet
ymban oðer healf gear nat ic hweðer ðe ymb twa ða forstael he ða
unlaedan oxan at Funtial ðe he mid ealle fore forwearð and draf to
Cytlid and hine mon ðaeraet aparade and his speremon ahredde ða

---

we judged it; and Æthelm himself stood there present with us,
and the king stood, washed his hands within the chamber at Wardour; when he had done this, he asked Æthelm why our judgment
seemed to him not right, he said that he could not think any
thing more just than that he [Helmstan] should give the oath, if he
could. Then said I that he [Helmstan] wished to attempt it, and
prayed the king to appoint a day for it, and he did so; and he
[Helmstan] then took the oath in full on the day fixed, and asked me
that I should assist him, and said that he would rather that he [should
give me the land?] than the oath should break down or . . . . . .
Then I said that I would help him to right, and never to any wrong,
on condition that he granted me his [land], and he gave me that in
pledge. And we rode then at the appointed day, I, and Wihtbord
rode with me, and Byrhthelm rode thither with Æthelm, and we all
heard that he gave the full oath. Then we all said that it was a
finished suit, since the [king's] decision was complied with. And,
beloved, when will any suit be ended, if one may neither end with
money nor with oath, or if one will overthrow every judgment which
King Alfred has decided? When shall we then have finished a suit?
And he then gave me the charter as he had formerly pledged himself

spor wreclas ða he fleah ða torypte hine an hreber ofer ðaet nebb ða
he aetsacan wolde ða saede him mon ðaet to tacne ða swaf Eanulf
Penearding on waes gerefa ða genom eal ðaet yrfe him on ðaet he
ahte to Tyssebyrig ða ascade ic hine hwy he swa dyde ða cwaeð he
ðaet he waere ðeof and mon gerehte ðaet yrfe cinge forðon he waes
cinges mon and Ordlaf feng to his londe forðon hit waes his laen ðaet
he on saet he ne meahte na his forwy'rcan and tu hine hete ða flyman
ða gesahte he ðines faeder lic and brohte insigle to me and ic waes
aet Cippanhomme mitte ða ageaf ic ðaet insigle ðe and ðu him
forgeafe his eard and ða are ðe he get on gebogen haefð and ic feng
to minan londe and sealde hit ðon biscope ða on ðine gewitnesse and
ðinra weotena ða fif hida wið ðon londe aet Lidgeard wið fif hidan
and biscop and eal hiwan forgeafan me ða feower and an waes teoðing
lond ðonne leof is me micel neodðearf ðaet hit mote stondan swa hit
nu gedon is and gefyrn waes gif hit elleshwaet bið ðonne sceal ic and
wylle beon gehealden on ðon ðe ðe to aelmessan ryht ðincð.

----

to do, so soon as the oath was given; and I promised him that he
might enjoy the land so long as he lived, if he would keep himself
without reproach. Thereupon, after this, about a year and a half,
or I know not whether two years after, he stole the untended oxen at
Fonthill, by which he was altogether ruined, and drove to Cytlid, and
there one surprised him, and his spereman followed up the fugitive's
tracks. When he fled, then a bramble cut him over the face. When
he wished to deny, then one said to him that as a proof. Eanulf·
Penearding then came upon him, who was sheriff, and seized all the
property that he [Helmstan] owned at Tisbury. I asked him why
he did so; he said that he [Helmstan] was a thief, and his property
was adjudged to the king, because he was a king's man. And
Ordlaf took possession of his land because it was his grant that
he occupied, [and] he [Helmstan] could not forfeit his [Ordlaf's
land to the king]. And thou, then, didst give order to proclaim
him outlaw. Then he sought thy father's body, and brought a seal
to me, and I was at Chippenham with thee. Thereupon I gave the
seal to thee, and thou didst remit to him his citizenship and the property which he yet occupies. And I took possession of my land, and
gave it to the bishop, with thy witness and that of thy Witan, the five
hides for the land at Liddiard, in exchange for five hides; the bishop
and all the family gave me four, and one was tithing land. Then,
beloved, it is very necessary for me that it may stand as it is now ar-
ranged, and long has been. But if it shall be otherwise, then I shall
and will be holden to whatever in thy bounty seems right to thee.

In dorso. + and Aeðelm Higa eode of ðam geflite ða cing waes aet Worgemynster on Ordlafes gewitnesse and on Osferðes and on Oddan and on Wihtbordes and on Aelfstanes ðys blerian and on Aeðelnoðes.

Indorsed. + And Æthelm Higa desisted from the suit when the king was at Warminster, with witness of Ordlaf and Osferth and Odda and Wihtbord and Ælfstan the blear, and Æthelnoth.

—oo⟩⊙⟨oo—

No. 18.   EADGIFU, 961.

Cod. Dip. CCCCXCIX., MCCXXXVII.

SIGELM pledged land to Goda for thirty pounds. He having died in war, his daughter, Eadgifu, averred that he had, just before his death, redeemed the land, and bequeathed it to her. Goda denied the redemption, and refused to surrender the land. Eadgifu sued Goda, and the Witan gave her the oath to prove the redemption. Goda still refused to surrender till the king, Edward the Elder, threatened him with confiscation, when, as is averred, he did surrender. Still he did not escape a judgment for some offence not stated, which put his life and property in the queen's hands. In Edwy's reign, the sons of Goda again took possession of the land; but, in Edgar's reign, a new suit restored it to Eadgifu, who gave it to Christ's Church.

ANNO dominicae incarnationis DCCCCLXI., ego Eadgiva regina et mater Eadmundi et Eadredi regum, pro salute animae meae, concedo aecclesiae Christi in Dorobernia monachis ibidem deo servientibus has terras, Meapeham, Culinges, Leanham, Peccham, Fernlege, Munccetun, Ealdintun, liberas ab omni saeculari gravitate

EADGIFU cyð ðam arcebiscope and Cristes cyrcean hyrede hu hire land com at Culingon; ðaet is ðaet hire laefde hire faeder land and boc swa he mid rihte beget, and him his yldran lefdon.   Hit gelamp ðaet hire

EADGIFU makes known to the archbishop and the community of Christ's church how her land at Cooling came [to her]; that is, that her father left her land and charter as he rightfully got, and his

exceptis tribus, pontis et arcis con-. structione, expeditione. Qualiter autem istae terrae michi venerunt, operae praetium duxi intimare omnibus, scilicet Odoni archisacerdoti tociusque Britanniae primati, et familiae Christi, id est monachis in Dorobernia civitate. Contigit aliquando patrem meum Sigelmum habere necessitatem .xxx. librarum quas a quodam principe nomine Goda mutuo accepit, et pro vadimonio eidem dedit terram quae nominatur Culinges, qui tenuit eam septem annis. Septimo itaque anno expeditio praeparabatur per omnem Cantiam, cum qua Sigelmum patrem meum ire oportuit; cum vero se pararet venerunt illi in mente .xxx. librae quas Godae debebat, quas statim ei reddere fecit. Et quia nec filium nec filiam nisi me habuit, haeredem me fecit illius terrae et omnium terrarum suarum et libros michi dedit. Forte tunc evenit patrem meum in bello cecidisse; postquam autem idem Goda audivit defunc-

faeder aborgude xxx punda aet Godan, and betaeht him ðaet land ðaes feos to anwedde, and he hit haefde vii winter. Ða gelamp emb ða tid ðaet man beonn ealle Cantware to wigge to Holme. Ða nolde Sighelm hire faeder to wigge faran mid nanes mannes scette unagifnum, and agef ða Godan xxx punda, and becwaeð Eadgife his dehter land and boc sealde. Ða he on wigge afeallen waes, ða aetsoc Goda ðaes feos aegiftes and ðaes landes wyrnde oð ðaes on syxtan geare. Ða spraec hit faestlice Byrhsige Dyrincg swa lange oð ða witan ðe ða waeron gerehton Eadgife ðaet heo sceolde hire faeder hand ge-

---

parents left them to him. It happened that her father borrowed thirty pounds of Goda, and assigned him the land in pledge for the money, and he held it seven years. Then it happened about that time that all Kentishmen were summoned to Holme on military service; so Sighelm, her father, was unwilling to go to the war with any man's money unpaid, and gave thirty pounds to Goda, and bequeathed his land to Eadgifu, his daughter, and gave her the charter. When he had fallen in war, then Goda denied the return of the money, and refused to give up the land till some time in the sixth year. Then [her kinsman] Byrhsige Dyrincg firmly pressed her claim, until the Witan, who then were, adjudged to Eadgifu that she should cleanse her father's hand by

tum in bello esse, negavit sibi xxx libras persolutas fuisse, terramque quam pro vadimonio a patre meo accepit detinuit fere per sex annos. Sexto vero anno quidam propinquus meus nomine Byrhsige Dyring coepit instanter aperte conqueri apud optimates et principes et sapientes regni de injuria propinquae suae a Godone facta. Optimates autem et sapientes pro justicia invenerunt, et justo judicio decreverunt quod ego quae filia et haeres ejus sum, patrem meum purgare deberem, videlicet sacramento.xxx.librarum, easdemque .xxx. libras patrem meum persolvisse; quod, teste toto regno, apud Agelesford peregi; sed non tunc quidem potui terram meam habere, quoadusque amici mei regem Eduuardum adierunt, et illum pro eadem terra requisierunt. Qui videlicet rex eidem Godoni, super omnem honorem quem de rege tenuit, praedictam terram interdixit, sicque terram dimisit. Non multo autem post tempore conti-

claensian be swa miclan feo, and heo ðaes að laedde on ealre ðeode gewitnesse to Aeglesforda, and ðaer geclaensude hire faeder ðaes agiftes be xxx punda aðe. Ða gyt heo ne moste landes brucan aer hire frynd fundon aet Eadwarde cyncge ðaet he him ðaet land forbead swa he aeniges brucan wolde, and he hit swa alet. Ða gelamp on fyrste ðaet se cynincg Godan oncuðe swa swyðe swa him man aetrehte bec and land ealle ða ðe he ahte, and se cynincg hine ða and ealle his are mid bocum and landum forgeaf Eadgife to ateonne swa swa heo wolde. Ða cwaeð heo ðaet heo ne dorste for gode him swa

---

[an oath of] as much value [namely, thirty pounds]. And she took oath to this effect at Aylesford, on the witness of all the people, and there cleansed her father in regard to the return of the money, with an oath of thirty pounds. Even then she was not allowed to enjoy the land until her friends obtained of King Edward that he forbade him [Goda] the land, if he wished to enjoy any [that he held from the king] ; and he so let it go. Then it happened, in course of time, that the king brought so serious charges against Goda, that he was adjudged to lose charters and land, all that he held [from the king, and his life to be in the king's hands]. The king then gave him and all his property, charters, and lands to Eadgifu, to dispose of as she would. Then

git eundem Godonem coram rege
ita inculpari, quod per judicium judicatus sit perdere omnia
quae de rege tenuit, vitamque ejus
esse in judicio regis. Rex autem
dedit eundem michi et omnia sua
cum libris omnium terrarum suarum ut de eo facerem secundum
quod promeruit. Ego autem pro
timore dei non ausa fui reddere ei
secundum quod contra me promeruit, sed reddidi ei omnes terras
suas excepta terra duorum aratro-
rum apud Osterland; libros autem terrarum non reddidi ei, probare enim volui quam fidem de
beneficio contra tot injurias michi
ab eo illatas tenere vellet. Defuncto autem domino meo rege
Edwardo, Æthelstanus filius suscepit regnum, quem videlicet regem requisivit idem Godo ut pro
eo me rogaret quatinus ei redde-
rem libros terrarum suarum. Ego
autem libenter, devicta amore videlicet regis Æthelstani, ei omnes
libros terrarum suarum reddidi,
excepto libro de Osterlande, quem

leanian swa he hire to geearnud
haefde, and agef him ealle his
land butan twam sulungum aet
Osterlande, and nolde ða bec agifan aer heo wyste hu getriwlice
he hi aet landum healdan wolde.
Ða gewat Eadward cyncg and
fencg Aeðelstan to rice. Ða Godan sael ðuhte, ða gesohte he ðone
kynincg Aeðelstan and baed ðaet
he him geðingude wið Eadgife
his boca edgift, and se cyncg ða
swa dyde and heo him ealle agef
butan Osterlandes bec, and he ða
boc unnendre handa hire tolet,
and ðara oðerra mid eaðmettum
geðancude ; and uferran ðaet
twelfa sum hire að sealde for ge-
borenne and ungeborenne ðaet

---

said she that she durst not, for [fear of] God, make such a return to him
as he had merited from her, and gave up to him all his lands except two
hides at Osterland, but would not give up the charters before she
knew how truly he would hold them in regard to the lands. Then
King Edward died, and Æthelstan took the throne. When it seemed
to Goda seasonable, he went to King Æthelstan, and prayed him to
intercede with Eadgifu for the return of his charters; and the king
then did so, and she returned him all except the charter of Osterland;
and he relinquished the charter voluntarily to her, and thanked her with
humility for the others. And, further, he, with eleven others, gave an
oath to her, for born and unborn, that the matter in dispute was for

scilicet humiliter bona voluntate dimisit. Insuper pro se et omnibus parentibus suis, natis et nondum natis, nunquam quaerimoniam facturos de praedicta terra, secum acceptis undecim comparibus suis, michi sacramentum fecit. Hoc autem factum est in loco qui nominatur Hamme juxta Laewes. Ego autem Eadgiva habui terram cum libro de Osterlande diebus duorum regum Æthelstani et Eadmundi filiorum meorum; Eadredo quoque rege filio meo defuncto, despoliata sum omnibus terris meis et rebus. Duo quoque filii jam saepenominati Godonis, Leofstanus et Leofricus, abstulerunt michi duas superius nominatas terras Culinges et Osterlande, veneruntque ad puerum Eadwium, qui tunc noviter levatus est in regem, et dixerunt se majorem justiciam in illis terris habere quam ego. Remansi ergo illis terris et omnibus aliis privata usque ad tempora Eadgari regis. Qui cum audisset me ita dehones-

ðis aefre gesett spraec waere, and ðis waes gedon on Aeðelstanes kynincges gewitnesse and his wytena aet Hamme wið Laewe, and Eadgifu haefde land mid bocum ðara twegra cyninga dagas hire suna. Ða Eadred geendude and man Eadgife berypte aelcere are, ða naman Godan twegen suna, Leofstan and Leofric, on Eadgife ðas twa foresprecenan land aet Culingon and aet Osterland, and saedon ðam cilde Eadwige ðe ða gecoren waes ðaet hy rihtur hiora waeron ðonne hire; ðaet ða swa waes oð Eadgar astiðude, and he and his wytan gerehton ðaet hy manfull reaflac gedon haefden, and hi hire hire are gerehton

---

ever settled; and this was done in the witness of King Æthelstan and his Witan, at Hamme, near Lewes. And Eadgifu held the land, with the charters, during the days of the two kings, her sons [Æthelstan and Eadmund]. Then Eadred died, and Eadgifu was deprived of all her property; and two sons of Goda (Leofstan and Leofric) took from Eadgifu the two before-mentioned lands at Cooling and Osterland, and said to the child Edwy, who was then chosen king, that they were more rightly theirs than hers. This then remained so, till Edgar obtained power; and he and his Witan adjudged that they had been guilty of wicked spoliation, and they adjudged and restored to her her property. Then, by the king's

tatam et despoliatam, congregatis principibus et sapientibus Angliae, intellexit enim me cum magna injusticia rebus et terris meis despoliatam, idem rex Eadgarus restituit mihi terras meas et omnia mea. Ego autem licentia et consensu illius testimonioque omnium episcoporum et optimatum suorum, omnes terras meas et libros terrarum propria manu mea posui super altare Christi quae sita est in Dorobernia. . . .

and agefon. Ða nam Eadgifu be ðaes cynincges leafe and gewitnesse, and ealra his bisceopa ða bec and land betaehte into Cristescyrcean mid hire agenum handum up on ðone altare lede ðan hyrede on ecnesse to are. . . .

---

leave and witness, and that of all his bishops [and chief men], Eadgiva took the charters, and made a gift of the land to Christ's Church, [and] with her own hands laid them upon the altar, as the property of the community for ever. . . .

No. 19.   EADGAR, 966.

Cod. Dip. MCCLVIII.

FORFEITURE of Bromley and Fawkham, by the widow of Ælfric, to the king, for the theft of the charter of Snodland. The Bishop of Rochester bought them of the king, and allowed the widow a life-occupancy. She thereupon assumed property in them, and was supported by the shire gemot.

✝ Ðus waeron ða land aet Bromleage and aet Fealcnaham ðam cinge Eadgare gereht on Lundenbyrig, þurh Snodinglandes landbec, ða ða preostas forstaelon ðam biscope on Hrofesceastre, and gesealdan heo Aelfrice Aescwynne sunu wið feo dearnunga. And heo Aescwyn

---

THUS were the lands at Bromley and at Fawkham assigned to King Eadgar, at London, through the charters of Snodland, which the priests stole from the Bishop of Rochester, and sold to Ælfric, the son of Æscwyn, secretly, for money. And Æscwyn, Ælfric's mother, formerly gave them to the church. When the bishop had

Aelfrices modor sealde heo aer ðiderin; ða geacsode se biscop ðaet ða bec forstolene waeron, baed ðara boca ða geornlice. Under ðam ða gewatt Aelfric, and he baed ða lafe syððan oð man gerehte on cinges þeningmanna gemote ðaere stowe and ðam biscope ða forstolenan becc Snodiglandes and bote aet ðaere þyfðe; ðaet waes on Lundene, ðaer waes se cing Eadgar, and se arcebiscop Dunstan, and Aethelwold biscop, and Aelfstan biscop, and oðer Aelfstan, and Aelfere ealdorman, and fela cynges witena. And man agaef ða into ðaere stowe ðam biscope ða becc; ða stod ðara wyderan are on ðaes cinges handa; ða wolde Wulfstan se gerefa niman ða are to ðaes cinges handa, Bromleah and Fealcnaham; ða gesohte seo wydewe ða halgan stowe and ðane biscop, and agaef ðam cinge Bromleages boc and Fealcnahames; and se byscop gebohte ða becc and ða land aet ðam cinge on Godeshylle, mid fiftegan mancesan goldes and hundteontigan and þrittegam pundum, þurh forespraece and costnunge into sancte Andrea; siððan ða lefde se biscop ðare wydewan ðara lande bryces. Under ðam ða gewatt se cing: ongan ða syððan Byrhtric ðare wydewan maeg, and heo to ðam genedde ðet hy brucan ðara landa on reaflace; gesohtan ða ðane ealdorman Eadwine and ðaet folc,

---

learned that the charters were stolen, he earnestly asked for the charters. Meanwhile Ælfric died, and he [the bishop] after this sued his widow until they adjudged the stolen charters of Snodland to the church and the bishop, at a gemot of the king's officers, and the indemnity for the theft. This was in London, where was King Eadgar and Archbishop Dunstan and Bishop Æthelwold and Bishop Ælfstan, and the other Ælfstan, and Alderman Ælfere, and many of the king's Witan. And the charters were then deposited in the church, [in charge of] the bishop. Then the widow's property stood in the king's hands. Reeve Wulfstan wanted to take the property into the king's hands, — Bromley and Fawkham; but the widow came to the holy church and the bishop, and gave up to the king the charter of Bromley and of Fawkham. And the bishop bought the charters and the land of the king at Godshill, for fifty mancuses of gold, and a hundred and thirty pounds, by intercession and urgency, for Saint Andrew's. Then, afterwards, the bishop allowed the widow the enjoyment of these estates. Meanwhile the king died: then, afterwards, began Byrhtric, the widow's kinsman, and constrained her that they should occupy the lands by force. Then they sought the ealdorman, Eadwine, and the people, who were God's adversaries,

ðe waes Godes anspreca, and geneddan ðane biscop be ealre his are agiftes ðara boca; ne moste he beon ðara ðreora nanes wyrðe ðe be eallum leodscipe geseald waes on wedde, tale, ne teames, ne ahnunga.

and forced the bishop, by [penalty of] all his possessions, to the return of the charters; nor was he allowed to make use of any one of those three [modes of proof] which was granted by every people on [giving] pledge, neither tale, nor team, nor ownership.

———ꝏꙮꙮꝏ———

No. 20.   ÆTHELWOLD, 963–975.

Cod. Dip. DXCI.

THIS charter witnesses an exchange of lands. In tracing the title of one of the parcels of land, the following case of murder by witchcraft is set forth.

. . . AND ðaet land aet Aegeleswyrðe headde an wyduwe and hire sunu aer forwyrt, forðan ðe hi drifon [i]serne stacan on Aelsie Wulfstanes faeder, and ðaet werð aereafe and man teh ðaet morð forð of hire inclifan. Ða nam man ðaet wif and aðrencte hie aet Lundenebrygce, and hire sune aetberst and werð utlah, and ðaet land eode ðam kynge to handa, and se kyng hit forgeaf ða Aelfsie, and Wulfstan Uccea his sunu hit sealde eft Aeðelwolde bisceope. . . .

. . . AND a widow and her son had formerly forfeited the land at Aylesworth, because they drove iron pins into [an image of] Ælsie, Wulfstan's father, and this was law-breaking; and the [image on which they had practised] murder was taken out of her closet. They took the woman, and drowned her at Londonbridge; and her son escaped and became an outlaw, and the land went into the king's hands; and the king then granted it to Ælfsie; and Wulfstan Uccea, his son, gave it afterwards to Bishop Æthelwold. . . .

No. 21. ÆTHELRED, 965–993.

Hickes. Diss. Epist. 59.   Cod. Lip. MCCLXXXVIII.

Ælfeh bequeathed Wouldham to the Church of Saint Andrew, in Rochester, leaving Cray to his nephew's widow as her morning-gift. She married Leofsun, and they entered by force upon Wouldham, as hers through her first husband. The bishop recovered the land by suit in the shire gemot.

_____

Rex Aethelberhtus primum hereditaverat de Wuldaham apostolum S. Andream et ecclesiam suam in Hrofecestra aeterno jure, et commisit illud manerium Eardulfo episcopo Hrofensi ad custodiendum, et ejus successoribus. Igitur in manibus successorum ablatum est iterum apostolo, et ecclesiae suae in manibus regum, ita quod plures reges unus post alterum habuerunt illud postea usque ad tempus regis Eadmundi. Tunc quidam probus homo nomine Aelfstanus Heahstaninc emit illud a rege Eadmundo, et dedit illi pro eo centum duodecim mancas auri et xxx libras denariorum. Hujus pecuniae majorem partem dedit postea ipsi regi Aelfegus filius ipsius Aelfstani. Postea mortuo rege Eadmundo, Eadredus rex he-

+ Ðus waeron ða seox sulung aet Wuldaham sancte Andrea geseald into Hrofesceastre. Aethelbryht cinc hit gebocode ðam apostole on ece yrfe and betaehte hit ðam biscope Eardulfe to bewitenne and his aeftergaencan ; ða betweonan ðam wearð hit ute, and haefdon hit cynegas oð Eadmund cinc ; ða gebohte hit Aelfstan Heahstaninc aet ðaem cince mid hundtwelftigan mancesan goldes and þrittigan pundan, and

THUS were the six hydes at Wouldham given to Saint Andrew at Rochester. King Æthelbert deeded it by charter to the apostle in perpetuity and delivered it to Bishop Eardulf and his successors to administer. Then among them it was alienated, and the kings had it down to king Eadmund. Then Ælfstan Heahstaninc bought it of the king for a hundred and twenty mancuses of gold and thirty pounds, and his son Ælfeh gave him almost all this. After King Edmund, King

reditavit inde predictum Aelfstanum in aeternam hereditatem. Itaque post mortem hujus Aelfstani, praefatus Aelfegus, qui regi Eadmundo dederat majorem partem pecuniae pro patre suo propter Wuldeham, successit huic Aelfstano in hereditatem. Qui statim conclusit et omnino confirmavit totum quod pater suus in vita sua fecerat. Hic autem fratri suo Aelfrico et terras atque pecunias patris sui ita plene subtraxit quod ipse Aelfricus nichil omnino inde poterat habere nisi servitio illud ab eo promeruisset, quemadmodum quilibet extraneus. Tamen praecogitatus tandem Aelfegus propter consanguinitatis fraternitatem concessit illi Earhetham et Craeiam et Aeinesfordam et Wuldeham in diebus vitae suae tantum, in praestito solummodo. Itaque mortuo Aelfrico, Aelfegus statim accepit omnia praestita sua quae fratri suo viventi praestiterat. Aelfricus autem habuit filium nomine Eadricum. Aelfegus vero non habuit. Et ideo Aelfegus concessit illi Eadrico Earhetham et Craeiam et Wuldeham, et re-

ðaet him sealde maest eal Aelfeh his sunu: aefter Eadmunde cincge ða gebocode hit Eadred cinc Aelfstane on ece yrfe: ða aefter Aelfstanes daege waes Aelfeh his sunu his yrfeweard, and ðaet he leac on halre tungon, and ofteah Aelfrice his breðer landes and aehta butan he hwaet aet him geearnode; ða for ðaere broðorsibbe geuðe he him Earhiðes and Craegan and Aenesfordes and Wuldahames his daeg; ða oferbad Aelfeh ðaene broðor and feng to his laene; ða haefde Aelfric sunu Eadric hatte, and Aelfeh nanne: ða geuðe Aelfeh ðam Eadrice Earhiðes and Craegan and Wul-

---

Eadred deeded it to Ælfstan in perpetuity. Then, after Ælfstan's day, Ælfeh, his son, was his heir; and [all] this he established in due form and deprived his brother Ælfric of land and property, unless he earned it of him by service. Then, because of his brotherlove, he granted him Erith, and Cray, and Ænesford, and Wouldham for life. Ælfeh then outlived his brother, and, resumed possession of his grant. Ælfric had a son called Eadric, and Ælfeh had none; so Ælfeh granted Eadric Erith, and Cray, and Wouldham, and held Ænesford

tinuit in manu sua Aeinesford. Mortuus est autem ipse Eadricus absque commendatione vel distributione rerum suarum; tunc iterum Aelfegus accepit praestita sua omnia. Habebat etiam ipse Eadricus uxorem et non liberos. Hac de causa concessit Aelfegus illi viduae donum dotis suae tantum quod ei dederat Eadricus, quando eam primum accepit uxorem, in Craeia. Et tunc remansit Litelbroc et Wuldeham in praestito suo. Postea quando ei visum ac placitum fuit, accepit firmam suam in Wuldehame, et in aliis volebat similiter facere, sed iterum infirmatus est, et quia infirmatus est valde, misit illico ad archiepiscopum Dunstanum ut veniret ad eum. Qui absque mora venit ad eum et locutus est illi in loco illo qui vocatur Scelfa. Ibi coram archiepiscopo fecit Aelfegus commendationem sive distributionem omnium rerum suarum, et constituit unam partem ecclesiae Christi Cantuariae, et alteram partem ecclesiae S. Andreae, et tertiam partem uxori suae. Postea fuit quidam Leofsunu, qui uxorem

dahames and haefde himsylf Aenesford; ða gewat Eadric aer Aelfeh cwideleas, and Aelfeh feng to his laene; ða haefde Eadric lafe and nan bearn; ða geuðe Aelfeh hire hire morgengife aet Craegan, and stod Earhið and Wuldaham and Lytlanbroc on his laene; ða him eft geðuhte, ða nam he his feorme on Wuldaham, and on ðam oðran wolde, ac hine geyflade; and he ða sende to ðam arcebiscope Dunstane, and he com to Scylfe to him and he cwaeð his cwide beforan him, and he saette aenne cwide to Cristes cyrican and oðerne to Sancte Andrea and ðane þriddan sealde his lafe. Ða braec

---

himself. Then Eadric died, intestate, before Ælfeh, and Ælfeh resumed possession of his grant. Eadric had a widow and no child; then Ælfeh granted her her morning-gift at Cray; and Erith, and Wouldham, and Littlebrook stood at his disposal. When it seemed good to him, he took his [rights of] farm at Wouldham, and intended to do so in the other places. But he became ill; and he then sent to Archbishop Dunstan, and he came to Scylf to him, and he declared his testament before him, and he deposited one [copy of his] testament in

Eadrici nepotis Aelfegi relictam accepit sibi in uxorem, et per ipsam mulierem incepit frangere constitutiones Aelfegi, quas fecerat coram archiepiscopo, et vituperare archiepiscopum, et testimonium ejus irritum facere. Tandem multa stimulatus cupidine cum illa muliere sua, quasi quadam securitate illius uxoris suae inductus intravit in terras illas absque concilio et judicio sapientum virorum. Quod ubi archiepiscopus audivit, sine omni mora induxit statim calumniam proprietatis in omnem distributionem Aelfegi, cui ipsemet affuit, et quae per eum facta fuerat. Diem ergo placiti hujus rei constituit archiepiscopus apud Erhetham per testimonium Aelfstani episcopi Lundoniae, et Aelfstani episcopi Hrofescestre, et totius conventus canonicorum Lundoniae, totius conventus ecclesiae Christi Cantuariae, et omnium orientalium et occidentalium Cantiae, et Wulfsii presbiteri qui tum vocatus est scirman, id est judex comitatus, et Brihtwaldi de Maerewurtha. Ad ultimum ita notificatum est in Suthseaxa,

syððan Leofsunu, þurh ðaet wif ðe he nam Eadrices lafe, ðaene cwide, and herewade ðaes arcebiscopes gewitnesse ; rad ða innon ða land mid ðam wife butan witena dome. Ða man ðaet ðam biscope ciðde, ða gelaedde se biscop ahnunga ealles Aelfehes cwides to Earhiðe on gewitnesse Aelfstanes biscopes on Lundena, and ealles ðaes hiredes, and ðaes aet Cristes cyrican, and ðaes biscopes Aelfstanes an Hrofesceastre, and Wulfsies preostes ðaes scirigmannes, and Bryhtwaldes on Maereweorðe, and ealra East-Cantwarena and West-Cantwarena, and hit waes gecnaewe on Suð Seaxan and on

---

Christ's Church, and another at Saint Andrew's, and gave the third to his widow. Then, afterwards, Leofsunu, through the wife that he took, Eadric's widow, broke the will and rejected the archbishop's witness, and rode in upon the land with his wife without a decree of the Witan. When this was made known to the bishop, the bishop proved ownership of all Ælfeh's bequest, at Erith, by witness of Ælfstan, bishop of London, and all the family, and of that at Christ's Church, and of Bishop Ælfstan of Rochester, and of Wulfsie the

23

et in Westseaxa, et in Middelse-
axa, et in Eastseaxa, quod archiepiscopus Dunstanus cum libris
ecclesiastici juris, et signo crucis
Christi, quam suis manibus tenebat, sui solis juramento adquisivit
in. aeternam hereditatem deo ac
S. Andreae apostolo omnes terras
illas quas Leofsunu sibi usurpa-
bat. Ipsum vero juramentum
archiepiscopi accepit Wulfsi scirman, id est judex provinciae, ad
opus regis, quandoquidem ipse
Leofsunu illud suscipere nolebat.
Insuper ad hoc perficiendum fuit
hoc quoque maximum adjumen-
tum temporibusque futuris maximum securitatis probamentum,
quod decies centum viri electissimi
ex omnibus illis supradictis comi-
tatibus juraverunt post archiepiscopum in ipsa cruce Christi, ratum
et aeternae memoriae stabile fore
sacramentum quod archiepiscopus
juraverat.

West Seaxan and on Middel-
Seaxan and on East-Seaxan, ðaet
se arcebiscop mid hisselfes aðe
geahnode Gode and Sancte Andrea mid ðam bocan on Cristes
hrode ða land ðe Leofsunu him
toteah. And ðaene að nam Wulfsige se scirigman, ða he nolde to
ðaes cinges handa; and ðaer waes
god eaca ten hundan mannan ðe
ðane að sealdan.

---

priest, who was shire-man, and of Bryhtwald of Mæreworth, of all the
East-Kentishmen and West-Kentishmen; and it was known in Sus-
sex, and in Wessex, and in Middlesex, and in Essex, that the archbishop with his own oath, with the books and on Christ's rood, proved
that the land which Leofsunu appropriated to himself belonged to
God and Saint Andrew. And Wulfsie, the shire-man, received the
oath for the king, since he [Leofsunu] refused to receive it. And
there were many more, a thousand men, who gave the oath.

No. 22.   WYNFLÆD, 990–994.

Cod. Dip. DCXCIII.

ÆLFRIC exchanged lands with Wynflæd. By some means, left perhaps
intentionally unexplained, Wynflæd had money of Ælfric's in her possession. Ælfric's son (?) Leofwine entered by force upon the land as
his property. Wynflæd appealed to the king, who sustained her, and noti-
fied Leofwine to that effect. Leofwine insisted upon a legal decision in
the shire-gemot; and the king sent the case by writ to the shire, who
gave the oath to Wynflæd, but stopped the suit by a compromise.

      ✠ HER cyð on ðysum gewrite hu Wynflaed gelaedde hyre ge-
witnesse aet Wulfamere beforan Aeðelrede cyninge. ðaet waes ðone
Sigeric arcebiscop and Ordbyrht biscop, and Aelfric ealderman, and
Aelfðrið ðaes cyninges modor. ðaet hi waeron ealle to gewitnesse
ðaet Aelfric sealde Wynflaede ðaet land aet Hacceburnan and aet
Bradanfelda ongean ðaet land aet Deccet. ða sende se cyning ðaer
rihte be ðam arcebiscope and be ðam ðe ðaer mid him to gewitnesse
waeron to Leofwine and cyðdon him ðis. ða nolde he butan hit man
sceote to scir gemote. ða dyde man swa. ða sende se cyning be
Aelvere abbude his insegel to ðam gemote at Cwicelmes-hlaewe and
grette ealle ða witan ðe ðaer gesomnode waeron. ðaet waes Aethelsige biscop, and Aescwig biscop, and Aelfric abbud, and eal sio scir,
and baed and het ðaet hi scioldan Wynflaede and Leofwine swa riht-
lice geseman swa him aefre rihtlicost þuhte. and Sigeric arcebiscop

      HERE is made known in this writing how Wynflæd brought
her witnesses before King Æthelred at Wolfmere, namely, Archbishop Sigeric, and Bishop Ordbyrht, and Ealdorman Ælfric, and
Ælfthrith, the king's mother; that they were all witness that Ælfric
gave to Wynflæd the land at Hagborn, and at Bradfield, in exchange
for the land at Datchet. Then sent the king forthwith by the Archbishop, and by those who were with him there as witnesses, to Leofwine,
and made this known to him. Then would he not [consent] without
it were referred to the shire-moot. So was it done. The king sent by
Abbot Ælfhere his seal to the gemot at Cuckamslow, and greeted all
the Witan that were there assembled, namely, Bishop Æthelsig, and
Bishop Æscwig, and Abbot Ælfric, and all the shire, and requested
and ordered that they should reconcile Wynflæd and Leofwine on
such terms as seemed most just to them; and Archbishop Sigeric sent

sende his swutelunga ðaerto, and Ordbyrht biscop his. ða getaehte
man Wynflaede ðaet hio moste hit hyre geahnian. ða gelaedde hio
ða ahnunga mid Aelfðryðe fultume ðaes cyninges modor. ðaet is
ðone aerest Wulfgar abbud, and Wulfstan priost, and Aefic ðara
aeðelinga discsten, and Eadwine . . . and menig god ðegen and god
wif ðe we ealle atellan ne magon. ða [waere] forðcomen eal se
fulla [að] ge on werum ge on wifum. ða cwaedon ða witan ðe ðaer
waeron ðaet betere waere ðaet man ðene að aweg lete ðone hine
man sealde, forðan ðaer syððan nan freondscype naere, and man
wolde biddan ðaes reaflaces ðaet he hit sciolde agyfan and forgyldan,
and ðam cyninge his wer. ða let he ðone að aweg and sealde
Aeðelsige biscope unbesacen land on hand ðaet he ðanon forð syððan
ðaeron ne spraece. ða taehte man hyre ðaet hio sciolde bringan his
faeder gold and siolfor eal ðaet hio haefde. ða dyde hio swa hio
dorste hyre aðe gebiorgan. ða naes he ða gyt on ðam gehealden butan
hio sciolde swerian ðaet his aehta ðaer ealle waeron. ða cwaeð hio
ðaet hio ne mihte hyre daeles ne he his. and ðyses waes Aelfgar ðaes
cyninges gerefa to gewitnesse and Byrhtric and Leofric aet
Hwitecyrcan and menig god man to eacan him.

---

his evidence thereto, and Bishop Ordbyrht his. Then Wynflæd was
instructed that she must prove it her property; so she produced her
proof of ownership, with the assistance of Ælfthrith, the king's
mother; namely, first Abbot Wulfgar and the priest Wulfstan, and
Æfic, the æthelings' steward, and Eadwine . . . and many a good
thane and good woman, all of whom we cannot name. Then would
have followed the whole full oath both of men and women; but the
Witan who were there said it would be better to omit the oath rather
than give it, because after the oath there could be no amicable arrangement, and they [Wynflæd and her friends] would ask for the property which had been taken from her, that he [Leofwine] should return
it and pay its value, and forfeit his wer to the king. So he [Leof-
wine] let the oath pass, and gave the land uncontested into Bishop
Æthelsig's hand, so as that he would make no future claim thereto.
Then she was instructed to bring all his father's gold and silver
that she had; then did she so, as she durst maintain by her
oath. Then was he not yet [willing to be] held to that [compro-
mise] unless she would swear that his property was all there. Then
said she that she might not [swear] on her part, nor he on his. And
to this was Ælfgar, the king's reeve, witness, and Byrhtric and
Leofric of Whitechurch, and many a good man besides them.

No. 23.   ÆTHELRED, 995.

Cod. Dip. DCXCII.

KING ÆTHELRED grants to his thane, Wulfric, certain lands which had belonged to Æthelsie, and been forfeited, by decision of the Witan, to the king, on account of the felony of Æthelsie.

. . . QUAPROPTER ego Aethelredus . . . cuidam . . . ministro . . . Wlfric . . . quandam ruris particulam, . . . ubi solicolae Dumbeltun appellant . . . concedo . . . Praedictum rus . . . in communi terra situm est . . . Praefatum rus per cuiusdam uiri infandae praesumptionis culpam qua audacter furtiue se obligare non abhorruit, cui nomen Aethelsige parentes indidere licet foedo nomen dehonestauerit flagitio ad mei iuris deuenit arbitrium, atque per me reuerendo ut iam praefatus sum ante conlatum est ministro. . . .

Đus waes ðaet land forworht aet Dumaltun ðaet Aeðelsige forwohrte Aeðelrede cyninge to handa. Đaet waes ðaenne ðaet he forstael Aeðelwines swin Aeðelmares suna ealdermannes : ða ridon his men to and tugon ut ðaet spic of Aeðelsiges huse : and he oðbaerst to wuda and man hine aflymde ða, and man gerehte Aeðelrede cyninge ðaet land and aehta : ða forgef he ðaet land Hawase his men on ece yrfe : and Wulfric Wulfrune sunu hit siððan aet him gewhyrfde mid ðam ðe him gecwemre waes, be ðaes cynges leafe and his witena gewitnesse. . . .

. . . WHEREFORE I, Æthelred, grant . . . to one of my thanes, . . . Wulfric, . . . a certain parcel of land . . . in the place called, by the inhabitants, Dumbleton. . . . The aforesaid land lies in the common land. . . . The aforesaid land came under my control by the criminal presumption of a certain man who dishonored the name Æthelsige, given him by his parents, by a foul crime ; and by me was granted to my honored thane, as before said.

Thus was the land at Dumaltun forfeited, which Æthelsie forfeited into the hands of King Æthelred. This was because he stole the swine of Æthelwine, son of Æthelmar, the ealdorman. His men then rode there, and took the bacon from Æthelsie's house ; and he escaped to the wood, and was then outlawed, and the land and property were adjudged to King Æthelred. He then gave the land in perpetual inheritance to his man Hawas ; and Wulfric (Wulfrun's son) afterwards exchanged with him, because it was more convenient for him, by the king's leave, and with witness of his Witan. . . .

No. 24.   ÆTHELRED, ABOUT 1000.

Cod. Dip. MCCCXII.

EADGAR, king of England, having given certain lands to the church at Abingdon, the gift was revoked, after his death, by the Witan, and the land adjudged to belong to Æthelred, his son. When Æthelred came to the throne, he restored other lands to the church as an equivalent for those it had lost through him. He proceeds, in the charter, to explain his title to these estates, which had belonged to a certain widow, Eadfled, and had been taken from her by Child Ælfric. Ælfric having been convicted of treason by the Witan, his property was forfeited to the king, who allowed Eadfled a life-occupancy in her lands. She, on her death, bequeathed them back to Æthelred, who grants them to Abingdon.

. . . EGO Aethelred ipsius opitulante gratia rex Anglorum inter uarias huius labentis saeculi uicissitudines ad memoriam reduxi qualiter in tempore pueritiae meae erga me gestum fuerit, dum pater meus rex Eadgar, uniuersae terrae uiam ingrediens, senex et plenus dierum migrauit ad dominum ; quod uidelicet omnes utriusque ordinis optimates ad regni gubernacula moderanda fratrem meum Eaduuardum unanimiter elegerunt, mihique terras ad regios pertinentes filios in meos usus tradiderunt. Ex quibus scilicet terris quasdam pater meus dum regnaret . . . ad monasterium quod Abbandun nuncupatur pro redemptione animae suae concessit, hoc est Bedeuuinde, . . . Hisseburna, . . . Burhbec. . . . Quae statim terrae iuxta decretum et praeceptionem cunctorum optimatum de praefato sancto coenobio uiolenter

---

. . . I, ÆTHELRED, by the aiding grace of Christ king of England, among the changing vicissitudes of this fleeting life, remembered how it fared with me in the time of my boyhood, when my father, King Eadgar, going the way of all the world, old and full of days, went to his Lord : inasmuch as all the nobles of both orders unanimously chose my brother Edward to govern the kingdom, and gave to me, for my use, the lands belonging to the sons of the king. Of these lands, my father, when king, for the redemption of his soul, granted certain ones to the monastery called Abingdon ; . . . namely, Bedwin, . . . Hussebourn, . . . Burbage. . . . According to the decree and command of all the nobles, these lands were immediately and forcibly taken from the aforesaid holy monastery, and, by the commands of

abstractae, meaeque ditioni hisdem praecipientibus sunt subactae; quam rem si iuste aut iniuste fecerint ipsi sciant. Deinde cum frater meus hoc aerumpnosum deseruit saeculum, . . . ego . . . et regalium simul et ad regios filios pertinentium terrarum suscepi dominium. Nunc autem quia mihi uidetur esse ualde molestum patris mei incurrere et portare maledictum, retinendo hoc quod ipse pro suae animae redemptione deo contulit donarium, et quia gratia dei me ad intelligibilem perducere dignata est aetatem, mihique per meorum optimatum decreta affluentem et copiosam terrarum largita est portionem, iccerco et ego ex mea propria haereditate praefatum sanctum coenobium munere congruo honorare et oportuna possessionum largitione ditare dispono. . . . Nomina uero terrarum quas ad praefatum libenti animo concedo monasterium haec sunt. Unum scilicet apud Feornebeorh, alterum apud Wilmaleahtun, tertium apud Cyrne. Has terrarum portiones Aelfric cognomento Puer a quadam uidua Eadfled appellata uiolenter abstraxit, ac deinde cum in ducatu suo contra me et contra omnem gentem meam reus existeret, et hae quas praenominaui portiones et uniuersae quas possederat terrarum possessiones meae subactae sunt ditioni, quando ad synodale concilium ad Cyrneceastre uniuersi optimates mei simul in unum conuenerunt et eundem Aelfricum maies-

---

the same, were placed under my power. Whether they did this justly or unjustly, may they themselves know! Then, when my brother died, . . . I, . . . received the crown, and also possession of the royal lands belonging to the sons of the king. But now, because it seems very hard to incur and bear the curse of my father for retaining that which he gave to God for the redemption of his soul, and because the grace of God has permitted me to live to the age of reason, and, through the decrees of my nobles, has conferred large and abundant quantities of land upon me, therefore I am disposed, from my own inheritance, to honor the aforesaid holy monastery with a fitting gift. But the names of the lands, which I grant to the aforesaid monastery with willing mind, are these: one at Feornebeorh, another at Wilmaleahtun, and the third at Charney. These lands Ælfric, surnamed the Child, forcibly took from a certain widow called Eadfled; and, when he criminally rebelled in his duchy against me and all my people, both the aforesaid lands and all he possessed were transferred to my control at the time when all my nobles assembled together in a synod at Charney, and expelled the same Ælfric from the country as guilty of treason; and all decreed, with one accord, that all his possessions were to become mine by law. Then, for the love of my nobles who advocated **her**

tatis reum de hac patria profugum expulerunt, et uniuersa ab illo possessa michi iure possidenda omnes unanimo consensu decreuerunt. Deinde praefatam uiduam, pro amore optimatum meorum qui eius apud me extiterant aduocati, suam haereditatem possidere clementi benignitate permisi, et ipsa tandem in extrema suae migrationis sententia mihi rursus earumdem terrarum possessionem benigno et libenti animo in perhennem dereliquit haereditatem. . . .

---

cause, with merciful kindness I permitted the aforesaid widow to possess her inheritance; and she, in her last moments, left to me again possession of these same lands as a perpetual inheritance. . . .'

———oo°o°oo———

No. 25.   GODWINE AND LEOFWINE, ABOUT 1000.

Cod. Dip. DCCCCXXIX.

SUIT of Godwine, Bishop of Rochester, against Leofwine, regarding land at Snodland, and compromise mediated.

✝ HER cyð on ðysum gewrite hu Godwine biscop on Hrofeceastre and Leofwine Aelfeages sunu wurdon gesybsumode ymbe ðaet land aet Snoddinglande on Cantwarabyrig. Ða ða se biscop Godwine com to ðam biscopstole þurh haese his cynehlafordes Aeðelredes cinges, aefter Aelfstanes biscopes forðsiðe, ða gemetae he on ðam mynstre ða ilcan swutelunga ðe his foregenga haefde and ðaermid on ðaet land spaec. Ongan ða to specenne on ðaet land — and elles for Godes ege ne dorste — oð ðaet seo spraec wearth ðam cynge cuð. Ða ða him seo talu cuð waes, ða sende he gewrit and his insegl to

---

✝ HERE is made known in this writing how Godwine, Bishop of Rochester, and Leofwine, Ælfeah's son, were reconciled in regard to the land at Snodland, in Canterbury. When Bishop Godwine came to the bishop's chair by command of his lord, King Æthelred, after the death of Bishop Ælfstan, he found in the minster the same deeds [of church property] that his predecessor had, and therewith claimed the land. He proceeded then to lay claim to the land, — and durst not do otherwise for fear of God, — until [at last] the suit became known to the king. When the charge was known to him, he

ðam Arcebisceope Aelfrice and bead him ðaet he and hys þegenas on
East Cent and on West Cent hy on riht gesemdon, be ontale and be
oftale ; ða ðaet waes ðaet se bisceop Godwine com to Cantwarabyrig
to ðam arcebiscope, ða com ðider se scyresman Leofric and mid him
Aelfun abbod and þegenas aegðer ge of East Cent ge of West Cent,
eal seo duguð ; and hy ðaer ða spaece swa lange handledon, syððon se
bisceop his swutelunge geeowod haefde, oð hy ealle baedon ðone biscop eaðmodlice, ðaet he geunnan scolde ðaet he moste mid bletsunga
ðaes landes brucan aet Snoddinglande his daeg ; and se biscop ða ðaes
getiðode on ealra ðaera witena ðanc ðe ðaer gesomnode waeran, and
he behet ðaes truwan, ðaet land aefter his daege unbesacen eode eft
into ðaere stowe ðe hit utalaened waes, and ageaf ða swutelunga ðe
he to ðam lande haefde ðe aer of ðaere stowe geutod waes, and ða
hagan ealle ðe he be westan ðaere cyrcan haefde into ðaere halgan
stowe. . . .

---

sent a writ and his seal to the Archbishop Ælfric, and bade him that
he and his thanes in East Kent and in West Kent should bring them
to a just composition by complaint and answer. Thereupon Bishop
Godwine came to Canterbury to the archbishop ; then came thither
the shireman Leofric, and with him Abbot Ælfun, and [the] thanes
both of East and West Kent, all the chief men. And they there
handled the claim, after the bishop had shown his deed, until they
all requested the bishop humbly to grant that he (Leofwine) might,
with his blessing, enjoy for his life the land at Snoddingland ; and
the bishop then granted this, to the gratification of all the Witan
there assembled. And he (Leofwine) promised covenant of this, —
that the land, after his day, should go uncontested back to the church
which had granted it out ; and he gave up the deeds which he had to
the land that had formerly been alienated from the church, and all
the inclosures that he had westward of the church, up to the church
bounds. . . .

No. 26.   ÆTHELRED, AFTER 1000.

Cod. Dip. DCCIV.

ÆTHERIC had traitorously advised the submission of Essex to Sweyn, but died without having had a trial. His widow brought his will to the king for approval ; but the king revived the old charge of treason before the Witan, and compelled the widow to surrender her morning-gift as consideration.

+ HER swutelað on ðison gewrite hu Aeðelred kyning geuðe ðaet Aeðerices cwyde aet Boccinge standan moste. Hit waes manegoñ earon aer Aeðeric forðferde ðaet ðam kincge waes gesaed ðaet hé waere on ðam unraede ðaet man sceolde on East-Sexon Swegeñ underfon ða he aerest þyder mid flotan com; and se cincg hit on mycele gewitnysse Sigerice arcebisceope cyðde ðe his forespeca ða waes for ðaes landes þingon aet Boccinge ðe he into Cristes cyrceah becweden haefde. Ða waes he ðisse spaece aegðer ge on life ge aefter ungeladod ge ungebett, oð his laf his hergeatu ðam cincge to Cocham brohte, ðaer he his witan widan gesomnod haefde. Ða wolde se cing ða spaece beforan eallon his witan uphebban and cwaeð ðaet Leofsige ealdorman and maenige men ðaere spaece gecnaewe waeroñ. Ða baed seo wuduwe Aelfric arcebisceop ðe hire forespeca waes, and Aeðelmaer ðaet hig ðone cincg baedon ðaet heo moste gesyllañ hire morgengyfe into Christes cyrcean for ðone cincg and ealne his

---

+ HERE is made known in this writing how King Æthelred granted that the will of Ætheric of Boccing might stand. It was many years before Ætheric died that it was said to the king that he was participant in the evil advice that Sweyn should be received in Essex, when he first came there with his fleet. And the king made it known with many witnesses to Archbishop Sigeric, who was his intercessor in the matter of the land at Boccing, that he had bequeathed to Christ's church. Then was he both in his lifetime and afterwards without either vindication or atonement on this charge, until his widow brought his heriot to the king at Cookham, where he had assembled his Witan from wide about. Then the king wanted to bring up the charge before all his Witan, and said that ealdorman Leofric and many men were cognizant of the charge. Then the widow prayed Archbishop Ælfric, who was her intercessor, and Æthelmere, that they should pray the king that she might give her morning-gift

leodscipe, wið ðam ðe se cing ða egeslican onspaece alete, and his cwyde stande moste, ðaet is swa hit her beforan cwyð, ðaet land aet Boccinge into Christes cyrcean, and his oðre landare into oðran halgan stowan swa his cwyde swutelað . . . Ðeos swutelung waes þærihte gewriten and beforan ðam cincge and ðam witon geraedd. . . .

---

to Christ's church for the king and all his people, on condition that the king should let the terrible charge fall, and that Ætheric's will should stand, that is, as before mentioned, the land at Boccing to Christ's church and his other property in land to other holy places, as his will manifests. . . . This certificate was at once written and read before the king and the Witan. . . .

———•o:o:••———

No. 27.   ÆTHELSTAN, AFTER 1000.

Cod. Dip. DCCCXCVIII.

SUIT of Wulfstan against Bishop Æthelstan, in the shire gemot, regarding land at Inkberrow. The bishop vouched in Leofric of Blackwell to warranty, and the case between Leofric and Wulfstan was then compromised by the influence of Leofric's and Wulfstan's friends.

+ HER swutelað on ðissum gewrite ðaet Eðelstan bisceop gebohte aet Leofrice aet Blacewellon fif hide landes aet Intebyrgan be Aeðelredes cinges leafe and be Aelfeges arcebisceopes gewitnesse, and be Wulfstanes arcebisceopes, and be ealra ðaera witena ðe ða on Englalande lifes waeron, mid ten pundan reodes goldes and hwites seolfres, unforboden and unbesacen, to geofene and to syllane, aer daege and aefter daege, sibban oððe fremdam ðaer him leofost were. And se cing het ðone arcebisceop Wulfstan ðaerto boc settan, and

---

+ HERE is made known in this writing that Bishop Æthelstan bought of Leofric, of Blackwell, five hides of land at Inkberrow, by King Æthelred's leave, and by witness of Archbishop Ælfeh and Archbishop Wulfstan, and of all the Witan that were then living in England, with ten pounds of red gold and white silver, unforbidden and undisputed, to give and to sell, during life and after, to kinsman or stranger, wherever best pleased him. And the king ordered Archbishop Wulfstan to prepare à charter therefor, and to deliver charter

Aeðelstane bisceope boc and land betecan unnandere heortan. Ða aefter ðisan manegum gearum soc Wulfstan and his sunu Wulfric on sum ðaet land. Ða ferde se bisceop to Sciregemote to Wigeranceastre and draf ðaer his spraece. Ða sealde Leofwine ealdorman and Hacc and Leofric and eal seo Scir his land claene ða he hit unforbodan and unbesacan behaet and settan daeg to ðaet man to ðam lande scolde faran; and ða ilcan ðe him aer landgemaere laeddon hit E[ðelst]an and cwaedan, gif ða landgemaere ealswa waeron swa man heo on fruman laedde, ðaet se bisceop ðaet lande ful rihte ahte. Ða com se bisceop ðaerto and se ðe him land sealde, and ða he him to [wit]nesse waeron, and com Wulfstan and his sunu and ða ðe hyra geferan waeron, and heo ealle ða ða landgemaere geridan ealswa heo man on fruman ðam bisceope laedde, and heo ealle cwaedon ðe [ðaer] waeron ðaet se bisceop ful riht ðaet lande ahte. Ða se ðaer geanwyrde waes ðe him lande sealde. Spaecon ða Leofrices freond and Wulfstanes freond ðaet hit betere waere ðaet heora seht togaed[dre wur]de ðonne hy aenige sace hym betweonan heoldan; sohtan ða hyra seht; ðaet waes ðaet Leofric sealde Wulfstane and his suna an pund and twegra ðegna að, and waere hymsylf ðridde, ðaet he ðam ilcan wolde beon gehealdan gif

---

and land to Bishop Æthelstan in all good will. Then, after these many years, Wulfstan and his son Wulfric laid suit to some part of that land. Then the bishop went to the shire-gemot at Worcester, and there urged his claim. Then Alderman Leofwine, and Hacc, and Leofric, and all the shire, gave his land clear, as he [the seller] promised it, unforbidden and undisputed, and set a day in order that men should go to the land, and the same men who formerly marked the bounds for him should do it [again] for Æthelstan, and they [the shire] said, if the bounds were so as they were marked at first, that the bishop rightfully owned the land. Then came the bishop thither, and he who granted him the land, and they who were his witnesses; and Wulfstan and his son came, and they who were his companions; and they all then rode the boundaries as they had been formerly marked for the bishop, and all who were there said that the bishop rightfully owned the land. Then he who granted him the land became the respondent. Then Leofric's friends and Wulfstan's friends said that it were better that they were reconciled together than that they had any suit between them: then they sought a settlement; this was that Leofric gave to Wulfstan and his son one pound and the oath of two thanes and himself the third, so that he [Wulfstan] would

seo spaec to Leofrice eode swa swa heo ða waes to Wulfstane gegan.
Ðis waes ure ealra seht : Wulfstan and his suna sealdon ða ðaet
land claene Leofric, and Leofric and Wulfstan and Wulfric ðam
bisceope claene lande and unbesacen, aer daege and aefter, to gyfanne
ðaer him leofost waere. . . .

be holden to the same if he, Leofric, should be involved in a suit as
Wulfstan had been. This was the settlement of us all. Wulfstan
and his son gave then the land to Leofric clear of dispute, and Leofric and Wulfstan and Wulfric conveyed it to the bishop, clear and uncontested, during life and after, to give where best pleased him. . . .

———∘∘⟨∘⟩∘∘———

No. 28.　　　　EANWENE, BEFORE 1038.

Cod. Dip. DCCLV.

Suit of Eadwine against his mother, Eanwene, regarding lands at
Wellington and Cradley. Nuncupative will of Eanwene, disinheriting
Eadwine.

 + Her swutelað on ðissum gewrite ðaet an scirgemot saet aet
Aegelnoðes stane be Cnutes daege cinges. Ðaer saeton Aeðelstan
biscop, and Ranig ealdorman, and Eadwine ðaes ealdormannes [sunu],
and Leofwine Wulfsiges sunu, and Ðurcil Hwita, and Tofig Pruda
com ðaer on ðaes cinges aerende ; and ðaer waes Bryning scirgerefa,
and Aegelweard aet Frome, and Leofwine aet Frome, and Godric
aet Stoce, and ealle ða ðegnas on Herefordscire. Ða com ðaer
farende to ðam gemote Eadwine Eanwene sunu, and spaec ðaer on
his agene modor aefter sumon daele landes, ðaet waes Weolintun and

---

 + Here is made known in this writing that a shire-gemot sat at
Aylton in King Cnut's day. There sat Bishop Æthelstan, and Ealdorman Ranig, and Eadwine, [son] of the ealdorman, and Leofwine, son
of Wulfsig, and Thurkil White; and Tofig Proud came there on the
king's errand ; and there was sheriff Bryning, and Ægelweard of
Frome, and Leofwine of Frome, and Godric of Stoke, and all the
thanes in Herefordshire. Then came there Eadwine, son of Eanwene,
faring to the gemot, and made claim against his own mother for a
piece of land; namely, Wellington and Cradley. Then asked the

Cyrdes leah. Ða acsode ðe bisceop hwa sceolde andswerian for
his modor; ða andsweorode Ðurcil Hwita and saede ðaet he sceolde
gif he ða talu cuðe. Ða he ða talu na ne cuðe, ða sceawode man
ðreo ðegnas of ðam gemote [ða sceoldon ridan] ðaer ðaer heo
waes, and ðaet waes aet Faeliglaeh, ðaet waes Leofwine aet Frome,
and Aegelsig ðe reada, and Winsig scaegðman. And ða ða heo
to hire comon, ða acsodon heo hwylce talu heo haefðe ymbe ða land
ðe hire sunu aefter spaec. Ða saede heo ðaet heo nan land haefde
ðe him aht to gebyrede, and gebealh heo swiðe eorlice wið hire suna
and gecleopade ða Leoflaede hire magan to hire, Ðurcilles wif, and
beforan heom to hire ðus cwaeð: Her sit Leoflaed min maege, ðe
ic geann aegðer ge mines landes, ge mines goldes, ge hraeglaes, ge
reafes, ge ealles ðe ic ah, aefter minon daege. And heo syððan
to ðam ðegnon cwaeð: Doð ðegnlice and wel! Abeodað mine
aerende to ðam gemote beforan eallum ðam godan mannum, and
cyðað heom hwaem ic mines landes geunnen haebbe, and ealre minre
aehte; and minan agenan suna naefre nan ðing; and biddað heom
beon ðisses to gewitnesse. And heo ða swae dydon; ridon to ðam
gemote and cyððon eallon ðam godan mannum hwaet heo on heom
geled haefde. Ða astod Ðurcil Hwita up on ðam gemote and baed

---

bishop who was to answer for his mother; then answered Thurkil
White and said that it was his part [to do so], if he knew the case.
As he did not know the case, they appointed three thanes from the
gemot, who should ride where she was; namely, at Fawley: these
were Leofwine of Frome, and Ægelsie the Red, and Winsie Shipman.
And when they came to her, then asked they what tale she had about
the lands which her son sued for. Then said she that she had no land
that belonged to him in any way, and she was vehemently angry with
her son, and called her kinswoman Leofled, Thurkil's wife, to her, and
said to her before them thus: Here sits Leofled, my kinswoman, whom
I grant both my land and my gold, both raiment and garment, and all
that I own, after my day. And she afterwards said to the thanes: Do
thanelike and well! Declare my errand to the gemot before all the
good men, and make known to them whom I have granted my land
to, and all my property; and to my own son nothing whatever; and
ask them to be witness to this. And they then did so, rode to the
gemot, and made known to all the good men what she had laid on them.
Then Thurkil White stood up in the gemot and asked all the thanes
to give his wife clear the lands that her kinswoman granted her, and
they did so. And Thurkil rode then to Saint Æthelbert's minster,

ealle ða ðaegnas syllan his wife ða landes claene ðe hire maege hire geuðe, and heo swa dydon ; and Ðurcil rad ða to sancte Aeðelberhtes mynstre, be ealles ðaes folces leafe and gewitnesse, and let settan on ane Cristes boc.

---

by leave and witness of the whole people, and caused [this] to be recorded in a church book.

———oo⚬ø⚬oo———

No. 29.   HARTHACNUT, 1040.

Florence of Worcester, sub anno.

CRIMINAL prosecution of Earl Godwine by the Archbishop of York and others, for causing the death of the Ætheling Alfred, in 1036. God-wine purged himself by oath, not denying the charge, but pleading the command of his lord.

. . . PRO nece sui fratris Aelfredi, adversus Godwinum comitem et Wigornensem episcopum Livingum, accusantibus illos Aelfrico Eboracensi archiepiscopo et quibusdam aliis, exarsit ira magna. Idcirco episcopatum Wigornensem Livingo abstulit et Aelfrico dedit ; sed sequenti anno ablatum Aelfrico, Livingo secum pacificato benigne reddidit. Godwinus autem regi pro sua amicitia dedit trierem fabre-factam, caput deauratum habentem, armamentis optimis instructam, decoris armis electisque .LXXX. militibus decoratam, quorum unusquis-que habebat duas in suis brachiis aureas armillas, sedecim uncias pen-dentes, loricam trilicem indutam, in capite cassidem ex parte deaura-

---

. . . HE [Harthacnut] was greatly incensed against Earl Godwine and Living, Bishop of Worcester, for the death of his brother Alfred, Ælfric, Archbishop of York, and some others being their accusers. For this reason he took the bishopric of Worcester from Living and gave it to Ælfric, but the following year he took it back from Ælfric and graciously restored it to Living, who had made his peace with him. Godwine, however, to obtain the king's favor, gave to him an admir-ably constructed ship which had a gilded prow, and was perfectly fitted out, and manned with eighty chosen men suitably armed, each of whom had two golden armlets weighing sixteen ounces on his

tam, gladium deauratis capulis renibus accinctum, Danicam securim auro argentoque redimitam in sinistro humero pendentem, in manu sinistra clypeum, cujus umbo clavique erant deaurati, in dextra lanceam, quae lingua Anglorum *ategar* appellatur. Insuper etiam, non sui consilii nec suae voluntatis fuisse, quod frater ejus cœcatus fuisset, sed dominum suum regem Haroldum illum facere quod fecit jussisse, cum totius fere Angliae principibus et ministris dignioribus regi juravit.

arms, and wore a triple coat of mail, a helmet, partly gilded, on his head, a sword with gilded hilt girt to his side, a Danish battle-axe adorned with gold and silver hanging from his left shoulder, in his left hand a shield with gilded boss and studs, in the right hand a lance, which is called, in English, *ategar*. Moreover, he made oath to the king, with nearly all the chief men and nobler thanes of England, that it was not by his advice, nor by his will, that the king's brother had been blinded, but that his lord King Harold had commanded him to do what he had done.

———∘∘⦂⊛⦂∘∘———

No. 30.   EALDRED, 1046–1060.

Cod. Dip. DCCCV.

TOKI, a king's thane, bequeathed land to the Bishop of Worcester. His son Aki laid claim to the land by right of inheritance. The case appears to have been brought before the shire court, and settled by compromise.

. . . HANC terram Toki, praepotens et diues minister regis, iure haereditariae successionis, liberam ab omni seruitio humano, praeter regale, quod dumtaxat toti patriae commune est, quamdiu uixerit tenens, mihi, ob amicitiam inter nos confirmatam, et pro animae suae remedio moriens testamento donauit. Sed cum filius suus Aki nomine,

. . . TOKI, a wealthy and powerful king's thane, on account of the friendship existing between us, and for the salvation of his soul, on his death-bed gave to me by testament this land, which he held, as long as he lived, by right of hereditary succession, free of all human service, except such as is royal and common to the whole country.

potens et ipse minister regis, patris testamentum irritum facere uolens, eam parentum successione ad suum ius reclamasset, fauente et consentiente ipso domino meo rege, et Leofrico comite, et caeteris optimatibus huius prouinciae attestantibus, datis sibi VIII marcis auri purissimi, liberam a sua et ab omni parentelae suae haereditaria proclamatione, eam mihi reddidit, et scripto coram testibus firmato reconsignauit, ut libere eam possem dare seu uendere cuicumque uellem absque ullius contradictione. . . .

But when his son, Aki by name, also a powerful king's thane, wishing to make void his father's testament, laid claim to this land as his own by succession to his father, by the favor and consent of the king himself, my lord, and by witness of Earl Leofric and the other chief men of this province, in consideration of the sum of eight marks of pure gold, he gave the land up to me, free from his own and from every hereditary claim of his kin ; and, by a writing confirmed in the presence of witnesses, he restored it to me, to give or sell freely to whom I pleased, without objection from any one. . . .

——∞⊙⋮⊙⋮∞——

No. 31. ARCHBISHOP LANFRANC AND ODO, BISHOP OF BAYEUX, 1072.

Wilk. Conc. v. 1, p. 323. Eadmer, Selden, p. 197.

ARCHBISHOP LANFRANC complained to the king that his church had been unjustly disseized of many lands and customs by Odo, Bishop of Bayeux, and his men. The king ordered the shire gemot to assemble. Geoffrey, Bishop of Coutances, presided as the king's justiciary. The archbishop recovered all the lands and customs. His customs on the king's lands and on those of Odo were also proved and adjudged to him by the court; and his own lands were declared free from all royal customs except three, which were defined.

TEMPORE magni regis Willelmi, qui Anglicum regnum armis conquisivit et suis ditionibus subjugavit, contigit Odonem, Bajocensem episcopum, et ejusdem regis fratrem, multo citius quam Lanfrancum

---

IN the time of the great King William, who conquered the English kingdom and subjected it to his rule, it happened that Odo, Bishop of Bayeux and the king's brother, came into England much earlier than

24

archiepiscopum in Angliam venire, atque in comitatu de Cantuar. cum
magna potentia residere, ibique potestatem non modicam exercere. Et
quia illis diebus in comitatu illo quisquam non erat, qui tantae fortitu-
dinis viro resistere posset, propter magnam, quam habuit, potestatem,
terras complures de archiepiscopatu Cantuarberiae, et consuetudines
nonnullas sibi arripuit, atque usurpans suae dominationi ascripsit.
Postea vero non multo tempore contigit praefatum Lanfrancum, Cado-
mensis ecclesiae abbatem, jussu regis in Angliam quoque venire, atque
in archiepiscopatu Cantuarberiae, Domino disponente, totius Angliae
regni primatem sublimatum esse. Ubi dum aliquandiu resideret, et
antiquas ecclesiae suae terras multas sibi deesse inveniret, et suorum
negligentia antecessorum illas distributas atque distractas fuisse re-
perisset, diligenter inquisita et bene cognita veritate, regem quam
citius potuit et impigre inde requisivit. Praecepit ergo rex comitatum totum absque mora considere, et homines comitatus omnes Fran-
cigenas, et praecipue Anglos, in antiquis legibus et consuetudinibus
peritos in unum convenire. Qui cum convenerunt apud " Pinende-
nam," omnes pariter consederunt. Et quum multa placita de dira-
tiocinationibus terrarum, et verba de consuetudinibus legum inter
archiepiscopum et praedictum Bajocensem episcopum ibi surrexerunt,

---

Archbishop Lanfranc, and resided in the county of Kent, where he
possessed great influence, and exercised no little power. And, because
in those days there was no one in that county who could resist a man
of such strength, by reason of the great power which he had, he
seized many lands belonging to the Archbishopric of Canterbury, and
some customs, and by usurpation added them to his rule. But it happened, not long after this, that the aforesaid Lanfranc, Abbot of Caen,
also came into England, by the king's command, and, by the grace of
God, was raised to the Archbishopric of Canterbury, and made pri-
mate of all the realm of England. When he had resided there
for some little time, and found that many lands anciently belonging
to his see were not in his possession, and discovered that, by the neg-
ligence of his predecessors, these had been seized and distributed,
after diligent inquiry being well assured of the truth, as speedily as
possible, and without delay, he made suit to the king on that account. Therefore the king commanded all the county to sit without
delay, and all the men of the county — Frenchmen, and especially
Englishmen, learned in the old laws and customs — to assemble.
When these were assembled on Penenden Heath, all together delib-
erated. And when many suits were brought there for the recovery

o

et etiam inter consuetudines regales et archiepiscopales, quae prima die expediri non potuerunt, ea causa totus comitatus per tres dies fuit ibi detentus. In illis tribus diebus diratiocinavit ibi Lanfrancus archiepiscopus plures terras, quas tunc tenuerunt homines ipsius episcopi; viz., Herbertus, filius Ivonis, Turoldus de Hrovecestra, Radulphus de Curva-spina, et alii plures de hominibus suis, cum omnibus consuetudinibus et rebus, quae ad easdem terras pertinebant, super ipsum Bajocensem episcopum, et super ipsos praedictos homines illius et alios; sc. Detlinges, Estokes, Prestetuna, Damtuna, et multas alias minutas terras. Et super Hugonem de Monteforti diratiocinavit Hrocinges et Broc; et super Radulfum de Curva-spina LX solidatas de pastura Ingrean [insula]. Et omnes illas terras et alias diratiocinavit ita liberas et quietas, quod in illa die, qua ipsum placitum finitum fuit, non remansit homo in toto regno Angliae, qui aliquid inde calumniaretur, neque super ipsas terras etiam parvum quicquam clamaret. Et in eodem placito, non solum istas praenominatas et alias terras, sed et omnes libertates ecclesiae suae, et omnes consuetudines suas renovavit, et renovatas ibi diratiocinavit: Soca, Saca, Toll, Team, Flymena, Frymthe, Grithbrece, Foresteal, Haimfare, Infangentheof, cum omnibus aliis consuetudinibus paribus istis, vel minoribus istis, in terris,

---

of lands, and disputes about the legal customs were raised between the archbishop and the aforesaid Bishop of Bayeux, and also about the royal customs and those of the archbishop, because these could not be ended on the first day, the whole county was detained there for three days. In those three days, Archbishop Lanfranc recovered many lands which were held by the bishop's men — namely, Herbert, son of Ivo, Turold of Rochester, Ralph de Courbe-Espine, and many others, with all the customs, and every thing which pertained to those lands — from the Bishop of Bayeux, and from his men above mentioned, and from others; namely, Detling, Stoke, Preston, Denton, and many other small lands. And from Hugh of Montfort he recovered Rucking and Brook; and from Ralph de Courbe-Espine, pasturage of the value of sixty shillings in Grean [Island]. And all those lands and others he recovered so free and unquestioned, that, on that day on which the suit was ended, not a man remained in the whole realm of England who could make any complaint thereof, or bring any claim, however small, to those lands. And, in the same suit, he recovered not only those lands aforesaid and others, but he also revived all the liberties of his church and all his customs, and established his right in them when revived, — soc, sac, toll, team, flymena-fyrmthe,

et in aquis, in sylvis, in viis, et in pratis, et in omnibus aliis rebus, infra civitatem et extra, infra burgum et extra, et in omnibus aliis locis. Et ab omnibus illis probis et sapientibus hominibus, qui affuerunt, fuit ibi diratiocinatum, et etiam a toto comitatu concordatum atque judicatum, quod sicut ipse rex tenet suas terras liberas et quietas in suo dominico, ita archiepiscopus Cantuarberiae suas terras omnino liberas et quietas in suo dominico. Huic placito interfuerunt Goisfridus, episcopus Constantiensis, qui in loco regis fuit, et justitiam tenuit; Lanfrancus archiepiscopus, qui, ut dictum est, placitavit, et totum diratiocinavit; Comes Cantiae, videlicet praedictus Odo, Bajocensis episcopus; Ernostus, episcopus de Hrovecestra; Agelricus, episcopus de Cicestra, vir antiquissimus et legum terrae sapientissimus, qui ex praecepto regis advectus fuit ad ipsas antiquas legum consuetudines discutiendas et edocendas in una quadriga; Richardus de Tunebrigge; Hugo de Monteforti; Willelmus de Arces; Haimo vicecomes; et alii multi barones regis, et ipsius archiepiscopi; atque illorum episcoporum homines multi, et alii aliorum comitatuum homines; etiam cum toto isto comitatu multae et magnae auctoritatis viri, Francigenae sc. et Angli. In horum omnium praesentia multis et apertissimis rationibus demonstratum fuit, quod rex Anglorum nullas consuetudines

---

grithbrece, foresteal, haimfare, infangentheof, with all other customs, equal to these or smaller, on land and on water, in wood, on road, and in meadow, and in all other things, within the city and without, within the burg and without, and in all other places. And it was proved by all those upright and wise men who were there present, and also agreed and judged by the whole county, that, as the king himself holds his lands free and quiet in his domain, the Archbishop of Canterbury holds his lands in all things free and quiet in his domain. At this suit were present Geoffrey, Bishop of Coutances, who represented the king, and held that court; Archbishop Lanfranc, who, as has been said, pleaded and recovered all; also the Earl of Kent, namely the aforesaid Odo, Bishop of Bayeux; Ernost, Bishop of Rochester; Æthelric, Bishop of Chichester, a very old man and most learned in the laws of the land, who was brought there in a wagon, by the king's command, to discuss and explain the ancient legal customs; Richard of Tunbridge; Hugh of Montfort; William of Arques; Haimo the Sheriff; and many other barons of the king and of the archbishop; and many men of those bishops; and other men of other counties; also men, both French and English, of much and great authority with all that county. In the presence of all these, it was shown, by many

habet in omnibus terris Cantuariensis ecclesiae, nisi solummodo tres. Et illae tres, quas habet, consuetudines hae sunt: Una, si quis homo archiepiscopi effodit illam regalem viam, quae vadit de civitate in civitatem; altera, si quis arborem incidit juxta regalem viam, et eam super ipsam viam dejecerit. De istis duabus consuetudinibus, qui culpabiles inventi fuerint atque detenti, dum talia faciunt, sive vadimonium ab eis acceptum fuerit, sive non, tamen insecutione ministri regis, et per vadimonium emendabunt, quae juste emendanda sunt. Tertia consuetudo talis est. Si quis in ipsa regali via sanguinem fuderit, aut homicidium, vel aliud aliquid fecerit, quod nullatenus fieri licet, si dum hoc facit deprehensus atque detentus fuerit, regi emendabit. Si vero deprehensus ibi non fuerit, et inde absque vade dato semel abierit, rex ab eo nihil juste exigere poterit. Similiter fuit ostensum in eodem placito, quod archiepiscopus Cant. ecclesiae in omnibus terris regis et comitis debet multas consuetudines juste habere. Etenim ab illo die, quo clauditur Alleluia, usque ad octav. Pasch. si quis sanguinem fuderit, archiepiscopo emendabit. Et in omni tempore, tam extra Quadragesimam, quam infra, quicunque illam culpam fecerit quae CILDWITE vocatur, archiepiscopus aut totam aut dimidiam emendationis partem habebit; infra Quadragesimam quidem totam, et extra aut totam aut

---

most evident proofs, that the King of England has no customs in all the lands of the church of Canterbury, except three only; and the three which he has are these: First, if any man of the archbishop digs into the king's highway which runs from city to city; second, if any one cuts down a tree near the king's highway, and lets it fall across the road, — concerning these two customs, those who are taken in the act while so doing, whether pledge may have been received from them or not, yet, at the prosecution of the king's officer and with pledge, shall pay what ought justly to be paid. The third custom is of this kind: If any one on the king's highway sheds blood, or commits homicide, or does any other unlawful thing, if he is seized in the act and detained, he shall pay the fine to the king; but, if he be not seized there, and shall once depart thence without giving pledge, the king can justly exact nothing from him. In like way, it was shown in the same suit, that the Archbishop of Canterbury ought to have many customs on all the lands of the king and of the earl; for, from that day on which Alleluia is ended to the octave of Easter, if any one sheds blood, he shall pay fine to the archbishop. And at any time, as well in Lent as at any other time, whoever commits that offence which is called cildwite, the archbishop shall have either the

dimidiam emendationem. Habet etiam in iisdem terris omnibus quae-cunque ad curam et salutem animarum videntur pertinere.

---

whole or half of the fine, — in Lent, the whole, and, at any other time, either the whole or half of the fine. He has also, in all the same lands, whatever seems to pertain to the care and safety of souls.

———oo⫯o꜀oo———

No. 32. GUNDULF, BISHOP OF ROCHESTER, AGAINST PICHOT, SHERIFF OF CAMBRIDGE, 1072–1082.

Hickes, "Dissertatio Epistolaris," 33.

THE Sheriff of Cambridge granted out land claimed by the Bishop of Rochester. Both parties appealed to the king, who sent the case by writ to the shire-court. The shire-court decided, under intimidation, as alleged, in favor of the sheriff. Odo of Bayeux, who presided, then com-manded the shire to elect twelve men who should swear to the truth of the decision. This was done, and the bishop accordingly lost the land. He afterwards, however, brought before Odo of Bayeux a charge of per-jury against the twelve men, and, on their failure to make defence, he recovered the land.

TEMPORE Willelmi regis Anglorum magni, patris Willelmi regis ejusdem gentis, fuit quaedam contentio inter Gundulfum Hrofensem episcopum et Pichot vice-comitem de Grondeburge pro quadam terra quae erat de Frachenham et jacebat in Giselham, quam quidam regis serviens Olchete nomine, vice-comite dante, praesumpserat occupare. Hanc enim vice-comes regis terram esse dicebat, sed episcopus eandem beati Andreae potius esse affirmabat. Quare ante regem venerunt. Rex vero praecepit ut omnes illius comitatus homines congregarentur

---

IN the time of William, the great king of England, father of King William of the same family, there was a dispute between Gundulf, Bishop of Rochester, and Pichot, Sheriff of Cambridge, in regard to a certain piece of land belonging to Frachenham, and lying in Gisel-ham, which one of the king's servants, named Olchete, had presumed to occupy by grant of the sheriff; for the sheriff said that this land belonged to the king, but the bishop affirmed that it rather belonged to St. Andrew. Therefore they came before the king; and the king

et eorum judicio cujus terra deberet rectius esse probaretur. Illi autem congregati terram illam regis esse potius quam beati Andreae timore vice-comitis affirmaverunt. Sed cum eis Bajocensis episcopus qui placito illi praeerat, non bene crederet, praecepit ut si verum esse, quod dicebant, scirent, ex seipsis duodecim eligerent, qui quod omnes dixerant jurejurando confirmarent. Illi autem cum ad consilium secessissent, et inibi a vice-comite conterriti fuissent, revertentes, verum esse quod dixerant, juraverunt.. Hi autem fuerunt: Eadwardus de Cipenham; Heraldus et Leofwine Exninge; Eadric de Giselham; Wlfwine de Landwade; Ordmer de Berlingeham, et alii sex de melioribus comitatus. Quo facto terra in manu regis remansit. Eodem vero anno monachus quidam Grim nomine, quasi a Domino missus episcopum venit. Qui cum audiret hoc, quod illi juraverunt, nimium admirans, et eos detestans, omnes esse perjuros affirmavit. Ipse enim monachus diu praepositus de Frachenham extiterat, et ex eadem terra servitia et costumas ut de aliis terris de Frachenham susceperat, et unus ex eisdem qui juraverunt in eodem manerio sub se habuerat. Quod postquam episcopus Hrofencis audivit ad episcopum Baiocensem venit et monachi verba per ordinem narravit. Quae ut episcopus audivit, monachum ad se venire fecit et ab ipso illa eadem didicit. Post

---

commanded that all the men of that county should be assembled, and by their judgment it should be decided to whom the land rightfully belonged. When they were met, they affirmed, through fear of the sheriff, that the land belonged rather to the king than to St. Andrew. But, because the Bishop of Bayeux, who presided over that county-court, did not altogether believe them, he commanded that, if they knew that which they affirmed to be true, they should elect twelve from their own number, who should confirm by an oath what all had said. But these, when they had gone out to consult, and had been there intimidated by the sheriff, on returning swore that what they had said was true. These men were Edward of Chippenham, Harold and Leofwine of Exning, Eadric of Giselham, Wulfwine of Landwade, Ordmer of Berlingham, and six others of the best of the county. Thereupon the land remained in the king's hand. But, in the same year, a certain monk, Grim by name, as though sent by God, came to the bishop. When he heard this which these men had sworn, filled with wonder and hatred for them, he affirmed that they were all perjured; for the monk himself had, for a long time, been Steward of Frachenham, and had received services and customs from that land, as from the other lands belonging to Frachenham, and had had

haec vero unum ex illis qui juraverant ad se fecit venire, qui statim ad ejus pedes procidens, confessus est se perjurum esse. Hinc autem cum illum qui prius juraverat ad se venire fecisset, requisitus se perjurum esse similiter confessus est. Denique mandavit vicecomiti ut reliquos obviam sibi Lundoniam mitteret, et alios duodecim de melioribus ejusdem comitatus, qui quod illi juraverunt, verum esse confirmaverant. Illuc quoque fecit venire multos ex melioribus totius Angliae baronibus quibus omnibus Londoniae congregatis judicatum est, tam a Francis quam ab Anglis, illos omnes perjuros esse, quandoquidem ille, postquam alii juraverant, se perjurum esse fatebatur. Quibus tali judicio condemnatis, episcopus Hrofensis terram suam, ut justum erat, habuit. Alii autem duodecim cum vellent affirmare iis qui juraverant se non consensisse, Baiocensis episcopus dixit ut hoc ipsum judicio ferri probarent. Quod quia se facturos promiserunt et facere non potuerunt, cum alii sui comitatus hominibus trecentas libras regi dederunt.

---

under himself one of those same men who had taken the oath. After the Bishop of Rochester heard this, he went to the Bishop of Bayeux, and narrated the monk's tale as he told it. When the bishop heard this, he caused the monk to come to him, and learned these same facts from himself. Thereupon he caused one of those who had taken the oath to come to him, who at once threw himself at the bishop's feet, and confessed that he had perjured himself. Then, when he had caused the one who led the oath to come to him, he too, on inquiry, confessed that he had perjured himself. And finally the bishop ordered the sheriff to send the others to him at London, and twelve more of the best men of the county, who had confirmed the truth of that which the others had sworn. He caused also many of the best barons of all England to come thither. And, when all these had assembled at London, it was adjudged, as well by French as by English, that these men were all perjured, inasmuch as he whom they had sworn after confessed that he had perjured himself. These men having been thus condemned by such judgment, the Bishop of Rochester had his land, as was just. But, since the other twelve wished to affirm that they had not been party in the fraud practised by those who had taken the oath, the Bishop of Bayeux said that they should prove this by the ordeal of hot iron; and because they promised to do this, and were unable to do it, they, with the other men of their county, paid three hundred pounds to the king.

No. 33. Bishop Wulstan against Abbot Walter of
Evesham, about 1077.

Heming Chart., tom. 1, p. 80. Dugd. Monast., i. 602.

The plaintiff in this suit claimed services for certain lands held by defendants. The case was sent by the king's writ before the county court at Worcester. Defendant was unable to produce witnesses. The court, therefore, allowed the bishop to offer proof by oath, and the abbot to bring his relics. On the appointed day, the parties appeared; and the defendant, having only his relics to swear on, hastened to abandon his case, and ask a reconciliation.

Haec commemoratio Placiti quod fuit inter W. Episcopum et Walterum abbatem de Eovesham, hoc est, quod ipse Episcopus declamabat super ipsum abbatem sacam et socam et sepulturam, et ciricsceat, et requisitiones et omnes consuetudines faciendas ecclesiae Wigornensi in hundredo de Oswaldes lawe, et geldum regis, et servitium, et expeditiones in terra et in mari de xv hidis in Hantona, et de iiii^or. hidis de Benningewrde, quas debebat abbas tenere de episcopo, sicut alii feudati ecclesiae ad omne debitum servitium regis et episcopi libere tenent. De hac re fuit magna contentio inter episcopum et abbatem, qui abbas diu resistens injuste hoc defendebat. Ad ultimum tamen haec causa ventilata et discussa fuit per justitiam et breve et praeceptum regis Willelmi senioris, quod misit de Normannia, in praesentia Gosfridi Constantiensis episcopi, cui rex mandaverat, ut in-

This is the report of the suit between Bishop Wulstan and Abbot Walter of Evesham, — that is, that the bishop claimed over the abbot sac and soc, and burial, and church-tax, and requisitions, and all customs owed to the church of Worcester, in the hundred of Oswald's law, and king's money, and service, and expeditions on land and sea, for fifteen hides at Hampton, and for four hides at Benningworth, which the abbot ought to hold of the bishop, as other feudatories of the church hold freely for every service due the king and bishop. In this affair was great contention between the bishop and the abbot, the latter resisting and unjustly defending a long time. At last, nevertheless, the cause was brought out and argued by the justice and writ and precept of King William the Elder, which he sent from Normandy, in the presence of Bishop Geoffrey, of Coutances, whom he

teresset praedicto Placito et faceret decernere veritatem inter episcopum et abbatem et fieri plenam rectitudinem.   Ventum est in causam.
Conventus magnus factus est in Wirecestra vicinorum comitatuum
et baronum ante Gosfridum episcopum.   Discussa est res.   Facta est
supradicta reclamatio W. episcopi super abbatem.   Abbas hanc de-
fendit.   Episcopus legitimos testes inde reclamavit, qui tempore regis
Eduuardi haec viderant, et praedicta servitia ad opus episcopi suscepe-
rant.   Tandem ex praecepto justitiae regis et decreto baronum itum
est ad judicium.   Et quia abbas dixit se testes contra episcopum non
habere, judicatum est ab optimatibus, quod episcopus testes suos no-
minaret et die constituta adduceret, et per sacramentum dicta episcopi
probarent, et abbas quascumque vellet relliquias afferret.   Concessum
est ab utraque parte.   Venit dies statuta.   Venit episcopus W. et
abbas Walterus, et ex praecepto Gosfridi episcopi, affuerunt barones,
qui interfuerant priori Placito et judicio.   Attulit abbas relliquias,
scilicet corpus sancti Ecguuini.   Ibi affuerunt ex parte episcopi pro-
babiles personae, paratae facere praedictum sacramentum : quarum
unus fuit Edricus qui fuit tempore regis Eduuardi stermannus navis
episcopi, et ductor exercitus ejusdem episcopi ad servitium regis ; et
hic erat homo Rodberti Herefordensis episcopi, ea die, qua sacramen-

---

commanded to be present at the aforesaid suit, and cause the truth to
be adjudged between bishop and abbot, and full right to be done.
Then the suit came on.   A great council was held at Worcester of
the neighboring counties and barons, before Bishop Geoffrey.   The
case was argued.   The aforesaid claim of Bishop Wulstan was made
against the abbot.   The abbot made defence.   The bishop then
claimed legal witnesses who, in the time of King Edward, had seen
these things, and had performed the aforesaid services for the bishop.
At length, by the precept of the king's justice and by the decree of
the barons, they came to judgment.   And, since the abbot said he had
not witnesses against the bishop, it was decided by the chief men that
the bishop name his witnesses, and produce them on an appointed day ;
and that they should prove by oath the allegations of the bishop ; and
that the abbot might bring what relics he wished.   It was agreed to
by both parties.   The appointed day came.   Bishop Wulstan came
and Abbot Walter, and by the precept of Bishop Geoffrey, the barons
were present who had been present at the former suit and judgment.
The abbot brought his relics, — to wit, the body of St. Ecgwin.   There
were present, on the part of the bishop, fit persons ready to take the
aforesaid oath ; one of whom was Edric, steersman of the bishop's

tum optulit, et nichil de episcopo W. tenebat. Affuit etiam Kinewardus qui fuit vicecomes Wirecestrescire, qui haec vidit et hoc testabatur. Affuit etiam Siwardus dives homo, &c. . . . Abbas autem videns sacramentum et probationem totam paratam esse, et nullo modo remanere si vellet recipere, accepto ab amicis consilio, episcopo demisit sacramentum, et totam querelam recognovit et omnem rem sicut episcopus reclamaverat, et inde, concordiam se facturum cum episcopo, conventionem fecit. Et inde sunt legitimi testes apud nos, milites homines Sanctae Mariae et episcopi qui hoc viderunt et audierunt, parati hoc probare per sacramentum et bellum, contra Rannulfum fratrem ejusdem Walteri abbatis, quem ibi viderunt, qui cum fratre suo tenebat illud Placitum contra episcopum, si hanc conventionem negare voluerit inter episcopum et abbatem. . . .

---

ship in the time of King Edward, and leader likewise of the bishop's army for the king's service; and, on that day when he took the oath, he was man to Robert, Bishop of Hereford, and held nothing of Bishop Wulstan. Kineward was present, Sheriff of Worcestershire, who saw these things, and witnessed this. There was present also Siward, a rich man, &c. . . . But the abbot, seeing the oath and all the proof ready, and no resource if he consented to receive it, by the advice of his friends gave up the oath to the bishop, and admitted the whole complaint and affair as the bishop had claimed; and thereupon he agreed to make a reconciliation with the bishop. And of this the legal witnesses for us are soldiers, men of St. Mary, and the bishops, who saw this and heard it, ready to prove it by oath and battle against Ranulf, brother of this same Abbot Walter, whom they saw there, who, with his brother, brought that suit against the bishop, if he should wish to deny this agreement between the bishop and abbot. . . .

No. 34.   THE SONS OF BOGE AGAINST ABBOT BRIGHT-NOTH.[1]

Hist. Eli., lib. i., xxxv.   Gale, xv. Scriptores.

BLUNTISHAM appears to have been forfeited to the crown, in consequence of the treason of Earl Toli. Having come into the hands of Wulnoth, it was sold by him to the Abbot of Ely. The sons of one Boge then sued to recover possession as heirs of their uncle, Tope ; alleging that the grandmother of Tope had taken part with the king at the time of Toli's rebellion, and was therefore entitled to the land. The case was tried at a court of six hundreds, and the court decided for the defendant, on two grounds, — first, that the allegations of the plaintiffs were false in regard to the claim of their uncle and his grandmother; second, that the possession of the charter was *prima facie* proof of ownership.

_____

. . . DICENTES quod avunculus eorum, Tope vocabulo dictus, illam terram jure haereditario possidere deberet ; hac ratione videlicet, quod avia ejusdem Tope existens in flore virginitatis suae de Bluntisham transierat, et requisierat Ædwardum Regem in territorio, quod dicitur Grantebrucge, tempore quo Toli comes provinciam de Huntedune contra Regem vi obtinuerat, ac ea de causa debuit illa suam terram jure habere. Quod totum sapientes illius provinciae et senes qui bene recordabantur tempestatis, qua Toli comes occisus fuerat apud

_____

. . . SAYING that their uncle, by name Tope, ought to possess that land by hereditary right ; for this reason, namely, that the grandmother of the said Tope, while still a maiden, had gone from Bluntisham, and sought King Edward, in the territory of Cambridge, at the time when Earl Toli held by force the county of Huntingdon against the king, and therefore she ought by right to have that land as her own ; all which the wise men and elders of that county, who well remembered the war in which Earl Toli perished at the river Thames, pronounced

_____

[1] The " Historia Ramesiensis " and the " Historia Eliensis " contain a considerable number of narratives which purport to be true records of suits at law. A careful examination of these narratives can leave little doubt that, whatever foundation of truth they may have, they are quite worthless as examples of Anglo-Saxon law. All have, therefore, been excluded from this collection, with two exceptions. These are inserted rather as the least improbable than as valuable in themselves. The supposed date of both is about the middle of the tenth century. Both are probably monkish inventions of the twelfth century.

Tamensem fluvium, dixere frivolum. Dixerunt etiam, quod Rex Ædwardus antea Huntedunensem provinciam adquisierat, suaeque ditioni subjugaverat, quam comitatum Grantebrucge habuisset; perhibuerunt quoque quod in toto vicecomitatu de Huntedune non erat terra tam libera, quae per forisfacturam non posset iri perditum, praeter duas Hydas juxta Spaldwic. Statuerint itaque ut Wlnothus Ædelwoldo Episcopo terram quietam de Bluntisham faceret, aut pecuniam acceptam sibi redderet; post haec convocatus totus comitatus Hunteduniae a Beorhtnotho Alderman, et ab Alfwoldo, et ab Ædrico. Nec mora, fit maxima concio, summonetur Wlnothus, adduxit secum illuc perplures viros fideles, scilicet, omnes meliores de VI Hundretis, et Lefsius modo de Ely detulit illuc cyrographum de Bluntesham. Quibus congregatis᾽ calumniam explicuerunt et causam ventilaverunt ac discusserunt, cognitaque rei veritate, per judicium abstulerunt Bluntesham a filiis Bogan pro duabus causis, quarum prima haec est, quia mentiti fuerant quicquid dixerant de Topa et de avia sua; altera vero haec est, quia proprior erat ille ut terram haberet qui cyrographum habebat quam qui non habebat. Tunc Wlnothus adduxit fideles viros plus quam mille, ut per juramentum illorum sibi vendicaret eandem terram, sed filii Bogan noluerunt suscipere jusjurandum, statuerunt

---

frivolous. They also declared that King Edward acquired Huntingdonshire, and had subjugated it to his sway before he had Cambridge. They also asserted that, in all the county of Huntingdon, there was no land so free as not to be lost by forfeiture, except two hides at Spaldwic. They also determined that Wulnoth should make over peaceably the land of Bluntisham to Bishop Æthelwold, or should return the money received therefor. Afterwards, the whole county of Huntingdon was convoked by Beorhtnoth, ealdorman, and by Alfwold, and by Ædric. Without delay, was held a great council; Wulnoth was summoned, and brought with him there many faithful men, — all the best, indeed, of six Hundreds; and Leofsius, too, brought then from Ely the charter of Bluntisham. When they were met, they explained the claim, declared the cause, and argued it; and, the truth being known, they took Bluntisham by judgment from the sons of Boga, for two reasons, — the first being that they had lied as to whatever they had alleged of Topa and his ancestress; the second, that it was more fitting that he who held the charter, than he who did not, should have the land. Then Wulnoth brought up faithful men, more than a thousand in number, to vindicate the said land to himself by their oath; but the sons of Boga refused the oath. So all decreed

itaque omnes ut Wlnothus Bluntesham haberet, et in fide promiserunt
se ei super hac re auxiliaturos et testificaturos idem, quod ibi fecerant,
si unquam alio tempore ille vel aliquis haeredum suorum opus haberet.

that Wulnoth should have Bluntisham, and they pledged themselves
that they would aid him in this matter, and would testify to what
they had done there, if ever, at another time, he or any of his heirs
should have need.

———oo⧫oo———

No. 35. Wensius against Bishop Æthelwold and Abbot Brightnoth.

Hist. Eli., lib. i., xlv.

Suit to recover lands of which plaintiff alleged that he had been
unjustly disseized. It appeared in evidence that the plaintiff had sold
the lands, and received the purchase-money, in witness of the Hun-
dred-court. The court held that no action would lie against the defendants, the land being already in the fourth hand ; that the same rule would
hold even if the land were in the third or second hand ; and that the
action must be brought against the heirs of the original purchaser.

... Contigit igitur quodam tempore, quod magna concio erat
statuta apud Witlesford & convenerunt illuc Ægelwinus alderman &
fratres sui Alfwoldus & Aegelsius & Episcopus Eswi & Wlflaed relicta
Wlstani & omnes meliores concionatores de comitatu Grantebrycge.
Assidentibus itaque cunctis surrexit Wensius Wlfrici cognatus &
fecit calumniam super terram de Suafham dixitque se & cognatos
suos injuste carere illa terra quando quidem pro ea nil habuissent videlicet nec terram nec terrae pretium. Audita igitur hac calumnia,

... It happened, therefore, at a certain time, that a great council was
appointed at Wittlesford; and Ealdorman Ægelwin and his brothers
Alfwold and Ægelsi, and Bishop Eswi, and Wulflæd, the widow of
Wulfstan, and all the best counsellors of the county of Cambridge
met there. When all were seated, Wensius, a kinsman of Wulfric,
arose and made claim to the land at Suafham, and said that he and
his kin were unjustly deprived of that land, since they had nothing
for it, neither land nor the price of land. When this claim had been

interrogavit Ægelwinus Alderman si aliquis esset ibi in populo qui sciret quomodo Wlstanus illam terram adeptus esset? Respondens ad haec Alfricus de Wickam dixit quod Wlstanus emerat eandem terram scilicet duas Hydas in Suafham a praedicto Wensio pro VIII libris. Et ut credibile quod dixerat haberetur, VIII hundreta quae sunt in australi parte Grantebrycge traxit in testimonium. Dixit etiam quod Wlstanus dederat Wensio illas VIII libras per duas vices, extremam tamen partem pecuniae & extremum denarium misit ei per Leofwinum Ædulfi filium qui dedit illi pecuniam in una cyrotheca involutam coram VIII Hundretis in quibus praedicta terra forte jacuerat. His ergo auditis statuerunt ut episcopus & abbas duas Hydas in Suafham sine omni calumnia haberent & pro libitu potirentur. Si autem Wensius aut cognati sui pecuniam aut aliud pretium pro illa terra amplius exigere voluissent, ab haeredibus Wlstani & non ab alio illud exigissent. Terra enim illa fuit modo in quarta manu & quamvis esset in tertia vel in secunda manu, similiter facere debuissent. . . .

---

heard, Ealdorman Ægelwin demanded if any one in the people knew how Wulfstan had acquired that land. Alfric of Wickham, in answer, said that Wulfstan had bought the said land — to wit, two hides at Suafham — of the aforesaid Wensius, for eight pounds; and, that what he said might be held credible, he called, in witness, eight hundreds of the southern portion of Cambridge. He further said that Wulfstan had given the said eight pounds in two payments to Wensius, and had sent the last part of the price and the last denarius to him by Leofwin, the son of Ædulf, who gave him the money wrapped up in a glove, before eight hundreds, in which the aforesaid land happened to lie. This, therefore, being heard, they decreed that the bishop and the abbot should have the two hides at Suafham free of claim, and possess them at pleasure. But, if Wensius or his relations wished further to demand money or another price for the land, they should demand it from the heirs of Wulfstan, and not from the others, for it was then in the fourth hand; and, even had it been in the third or second hand, yet ought they to do likewise. . . ..

INDEX.

Actions. No distinction between Roman real and personal, 184. For
Debt, 189. For Loan, 199. For stolen Movables, 202. For Land,
227. In Criminal Law, 262.

Adoption, 126, 155.

Æthelred. First general tax levied by Witan under him, 68. His reign,
38. Increase of wills during his reign, 107.

Alfred the Great. His laws, 10. His reforms in the Anglo-Saxon constitution, 20, 22. His judicial powers, 25. His revival of archaic
principles, 72. His will as to boc-land, 80, 81. His fleet, 119, note.

Anefang. An argument for real action, 197. Begins action for movables, 199, 203, 206. Not in criminal procedure, 283.

Arbitration. The habitual mode of settling disputes, 26, 53.

Army constitution. Condition of, at Norman Conquest, 118.

Arrha. Concluded the contract, 170, 189, 190.

Assize. Of proof separate from that of judgment, 188, 286.

Bail, or fidejussor, 190, 191, 291. See *Contract*.

Betrothal. Contract of, included warranty, 164, note 2, 196. As a real
contract of sale, 168. As a fictitious contract of sale, 170. As a
formal contract, 170–172. Kentish, 171.

Boc-land. How created, 100. Church influence, 101. A mode of transfer, 101. Characteristics of, 109. Reversion of, 111. History of,
112, 113.

Books. Division of, 102. Construction of, 102, 103. How declared and
recorded, 110. As evidence, 111, 112. As contract, 236. See *Documents*.

Borh-bryce. Disobedience to testare, 192. Amount of, 279.

Bot. Nature of, 273, 278, 279.

Burg-gemot, 22.

Casus and culpa. Existed in German law, 295.

Causæ cognitio. Not in earliest procedure, 184.

Chattels. Tripartite division of, 134, 136.

Clergy. Secular, belonged to the maegth, 140.

Cnut. His tendencies as a law-giver, 39, 44, 45. Grants by writ under,
44, 99, 100.

Common land. Why so called, 81. Division of, 82. Distinguished from
folkland, 82, 83. Village communities in England, 83. Destruction of communal system, 83, 84. Development of large estates, 84,

Oferhyrnes. Nature of, 281. Use of, 284. Of cold water, 301.
Ordeal. Proof of last resort, 188, 300. Similar to oracle, 188, 300. Of cold water, 301. Of fire and hot water, 301. Of morsel, 302. Office of, 302–303.

Parentelen-ordnung, 129–132.
Paternal authority. Extent of, 153. Over boys, how ended, 154–162. Over girls, how ended, 163. Comparison of views of Kraut and of Stobbe in regard to, 157–160.
Paternal kin, 125. Rights of, 138. Right of guardianship belonged to the, 180.
Personalty. No difference in the rules of succession to, and realty, 136.
Pignoris Capio. Originally extrajudicial, 183, note.
Pledge. See *Contract*.
Præscriptio. Not in movables, 199, 225, 226. Nor land, 253.
Procedure, Anglo-Saxon Legal, 183. Divisions of, 189. In actions for Debt, 189–202. In actions for Movables, 202–227. In Real Actions, 227–262. Criminal Procedure, 262–305.
Proof. Strictly formal, 186. Of three kinds, 186. Extended into domain of judgment, 188. Given in second assize, 286. To whom awarded in action of Debt, 194. Loan, 200. Stolen Movables, 211, 213. Land, 240. In Criminal Actions, 294–297.

Real action. Definition of, according to Roman law, 197. In English law, 197, note 3, 241, note 1.
Regio. Synonym of pagus, 15, 16. Used as equivalent for provincia, pagus, and shire, 16. The hundred of the seventh and eight centuries, 18.
Remainders, 105.
Representation. Right of, 132.

Sacu and socn. Origin and meaning of the terms, 40–42. No jurisdiction implied in the word " socn," 43, 44.
Seisin. Of movables, 204. Connected with the right to the movable, 184. Of immovables, as differing from that of movables, 233. Comparison between *possessio* and seisin, 233, 234. Of land, defined, 235. Effect on the assignment of proof, 238–240, 247.
Self-help. Judicial, in comparison with political institutions, 183. Manifest in private execution, 193. And vengeance, 266.
Sessio Triduana, 199, note 2, 210, note 1.
Ship-money, 119, note.
Shire. Origin of the modern shire in the primitive state, 19, 20. The primitive shire became the modern hundred, 18. This change took place in the ninth century, 18, 19.
Shire-court. Its origin in the primitive assembly of the state, 21. Its dignity, 21. Its survival in England contrasted with its suppression by the Franks, 21.